THE DEMON
ORORON

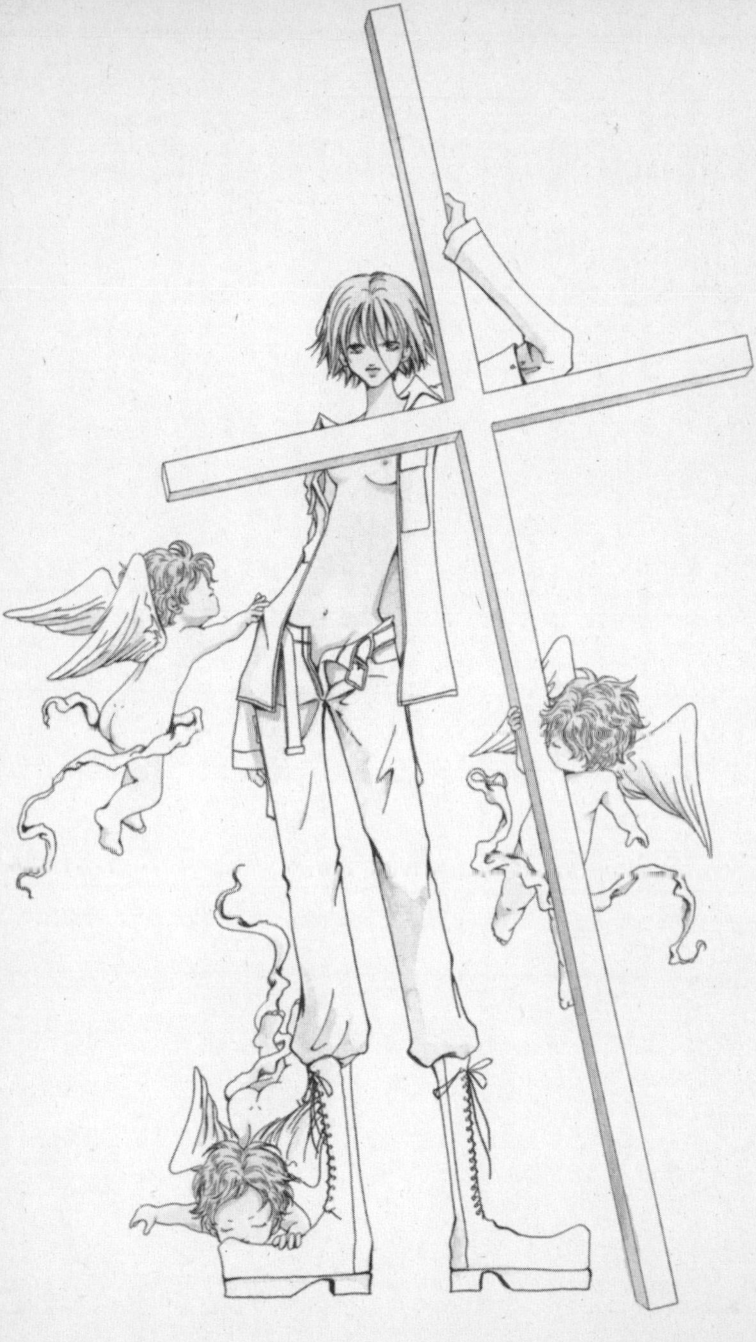

THE DEMON

ORORON

Volume 3

By Hakase Mizuki

HAMBURG // LONDON // LOS ANGELES // TOKYO

The Demon Ororon Vol. 3

By Hakase Mizuki

Translation - Tomoko Kamimoto
English Adaptation - Josh Dysart
Associate Editor - Troy Lewter
Retouch and Lettering - Keiko Okabe
Cover Design - Ray Makowski

Editor - Luis Reyes
Digital Imaging Manager - Chris Buford
Pre-Press Manager - Antonio DePietro
Production Managers - Jennifer Miller and Mutsumi Miyazaki
Art Director - Matt Alford
Managing Editor - Jill Freshney
VP of Production - Ron Klamert
President and C.O.O. - John Parker
Publisher and C.E.O. - Stuart Levy

A  Manga

TOKYOPOP Inc.
5900 Wilshire Blvd. Suite 2000
Los Angeles, CA 90036

E-mail: info@TOKYOPOP.com
Come visit us online at www.TOKYOPOP.com

ISBN: 1-59182-727-2

First TOKYOPOP printing: August 2004
10 9 8 7 6 5 4 3 2 1

Printed in the USA

The Demon Ororon

The Story Thus Far

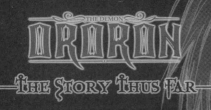

Chiaki, half mortal half angel, lived a strange but happy life in a quiet suburb on earth with Ororon, the king of Hell.

But nothing's ever easy when you're in love with the Devil. It wasn't long before assassins, spurred by a bounty placed on Ororon's head, came to destroy their peaceful life. The bounty hunters left Ororon no recourse but violence, and his brutal nature emerged, shocking the pacifist Chiaki with its murderous proficiency. Consumed by sorrow, overcome with confusion, Chiaki unconsciously, at the height of battle, triggered her own dormant, uncontrollable power.

Riding on the wave of an anguished scream, from inside her emerged a violent force that leveled the city, killing thousands.

In the wake of her psychic blast, Chiaki fell comatose and has yet to recover. Now Ororon; her best friend, Lika; Lucy, Ororon's vassal; and the monster brothers Shiro and Kuro watch over her while desperately on the run, trying to stay one step ahead of Hell's hunters.

That'll be enough to dive in, so let's go!

CONTENTS

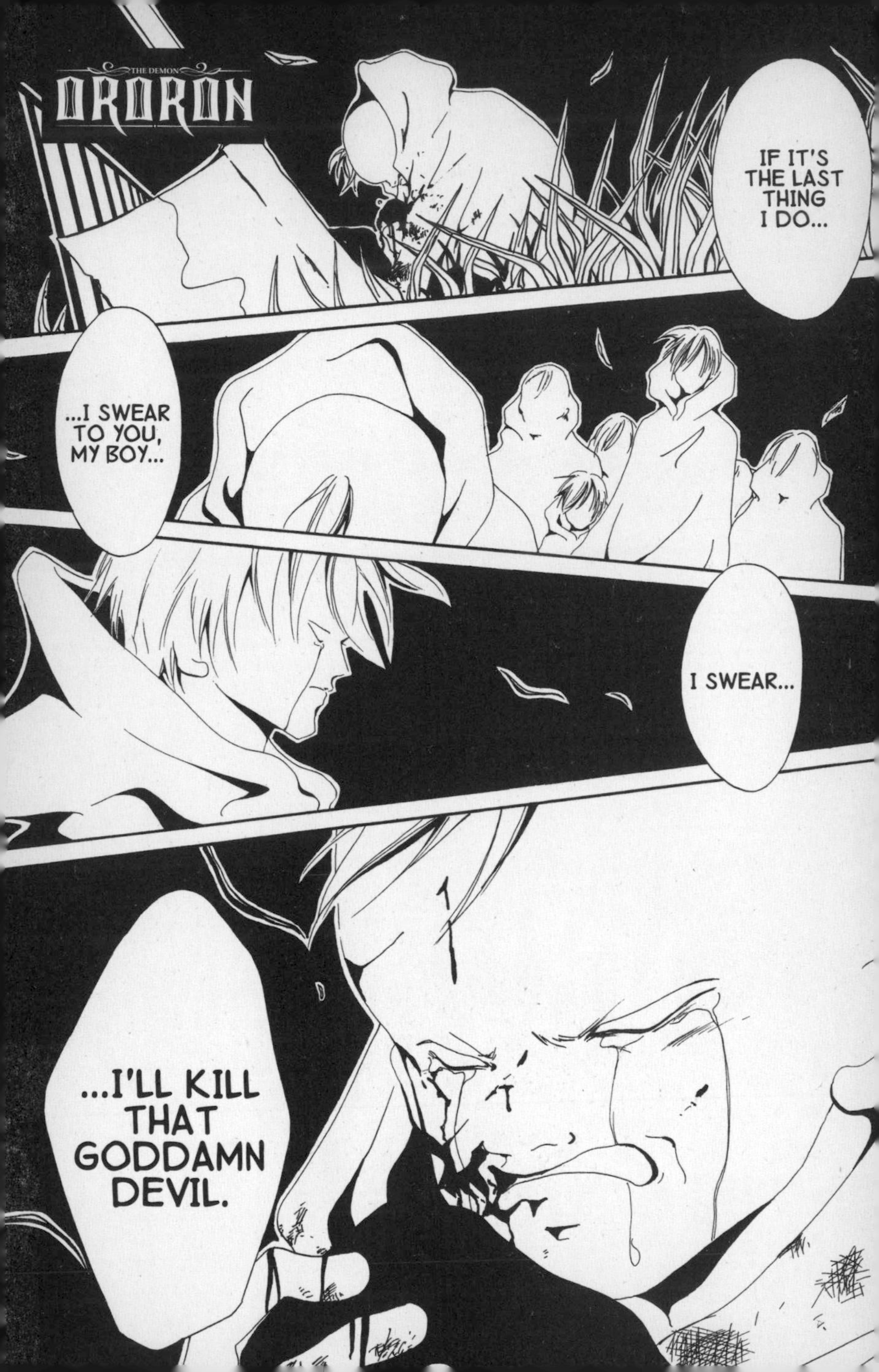
THE DEMON ORORON
IF IT'S THE LAST THING I DO...
...I SWEAR TO YOU, MY BOY...
I SWEAR...
...I'LL KILL THAT GODDAMN DEVIL.

THE DEMON
ORORON

悪魔のオロロン

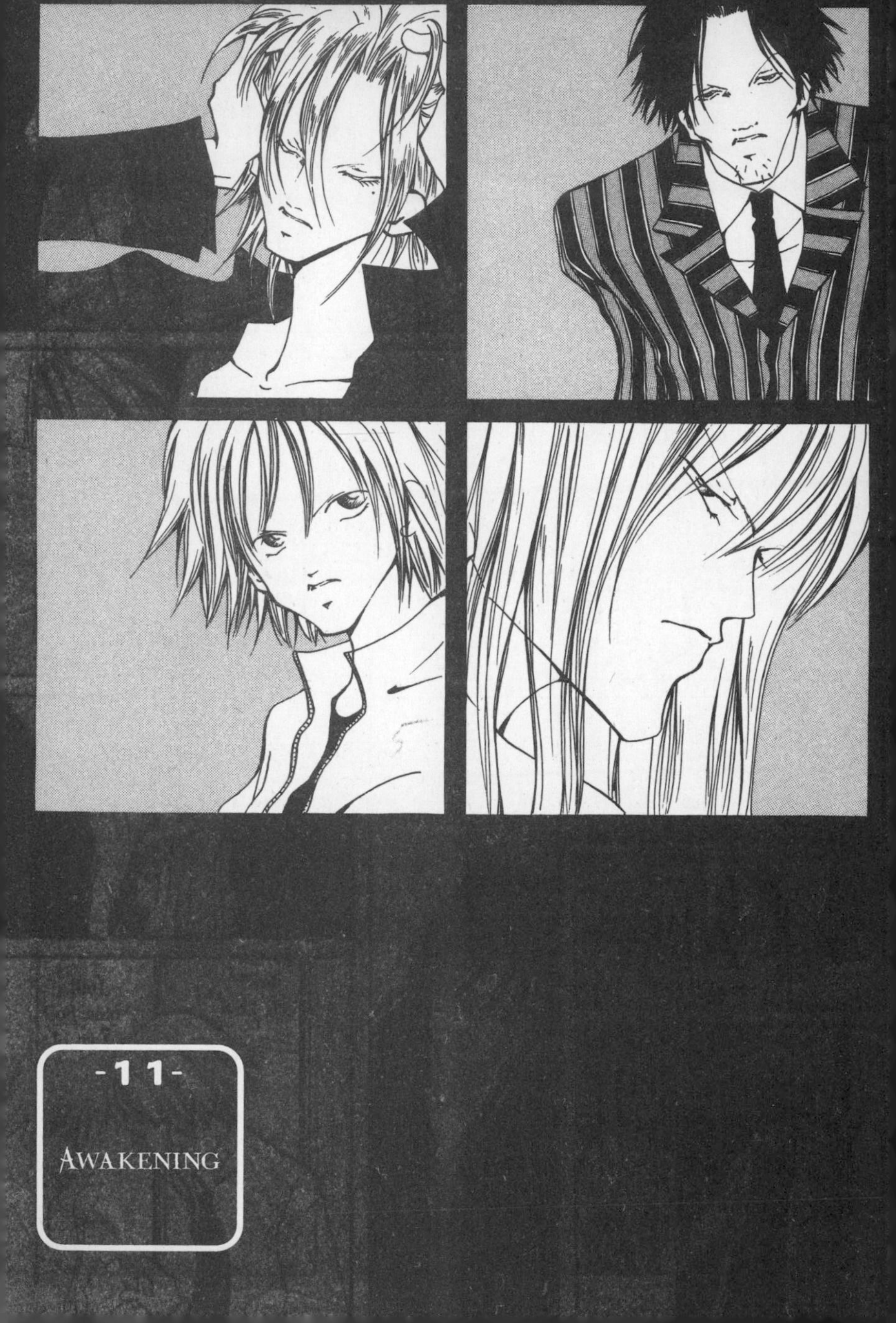

-11-

AWAKENING

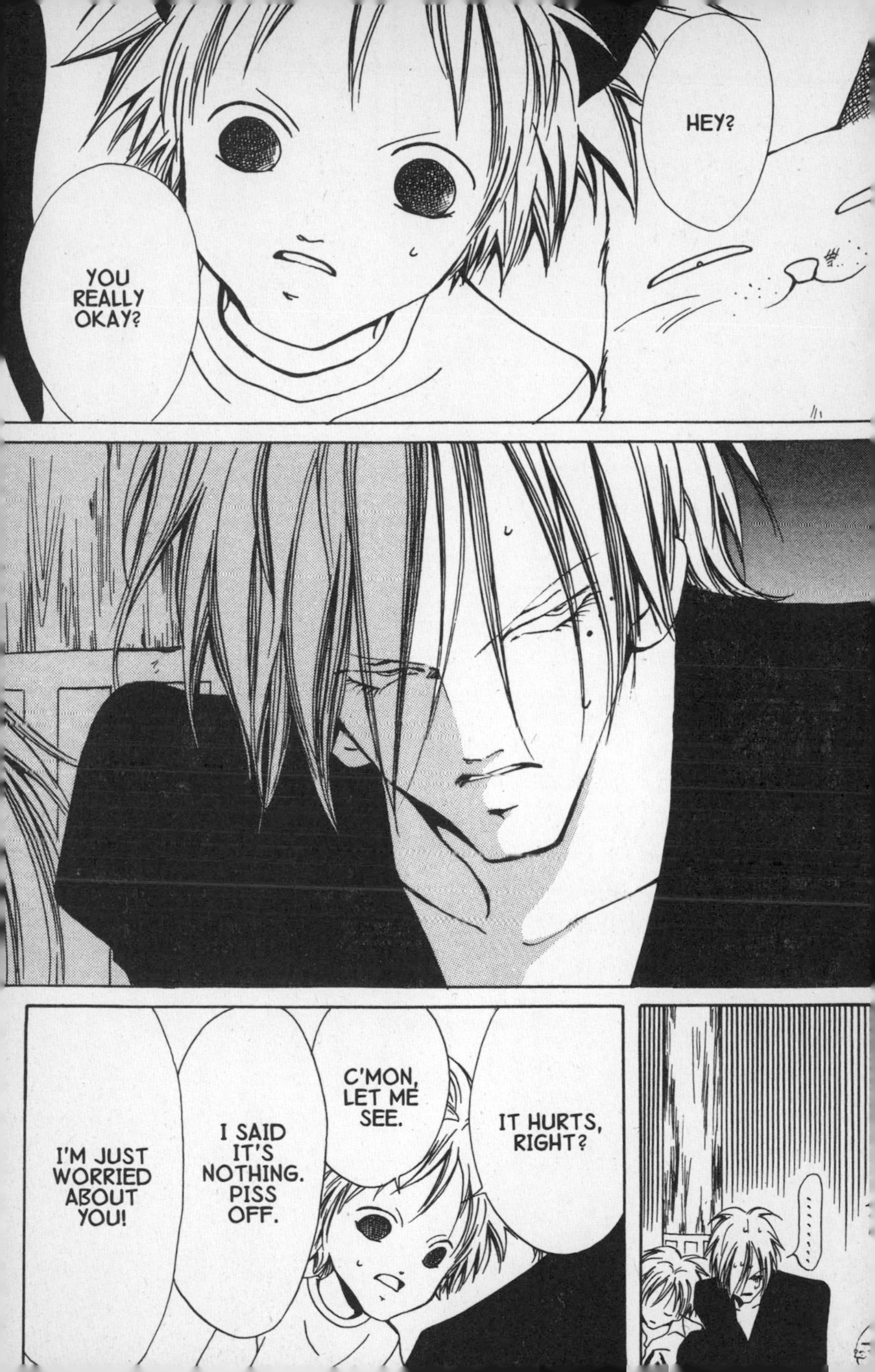
HEY?
YOU REALLY OKAY?
......
IT HURTS, RIGHT?
C'MON, LET ME SEE.
I SAID IT'S NOTHING. PISS OFF.
I'M JUST WORRIED ABOUT YOU!

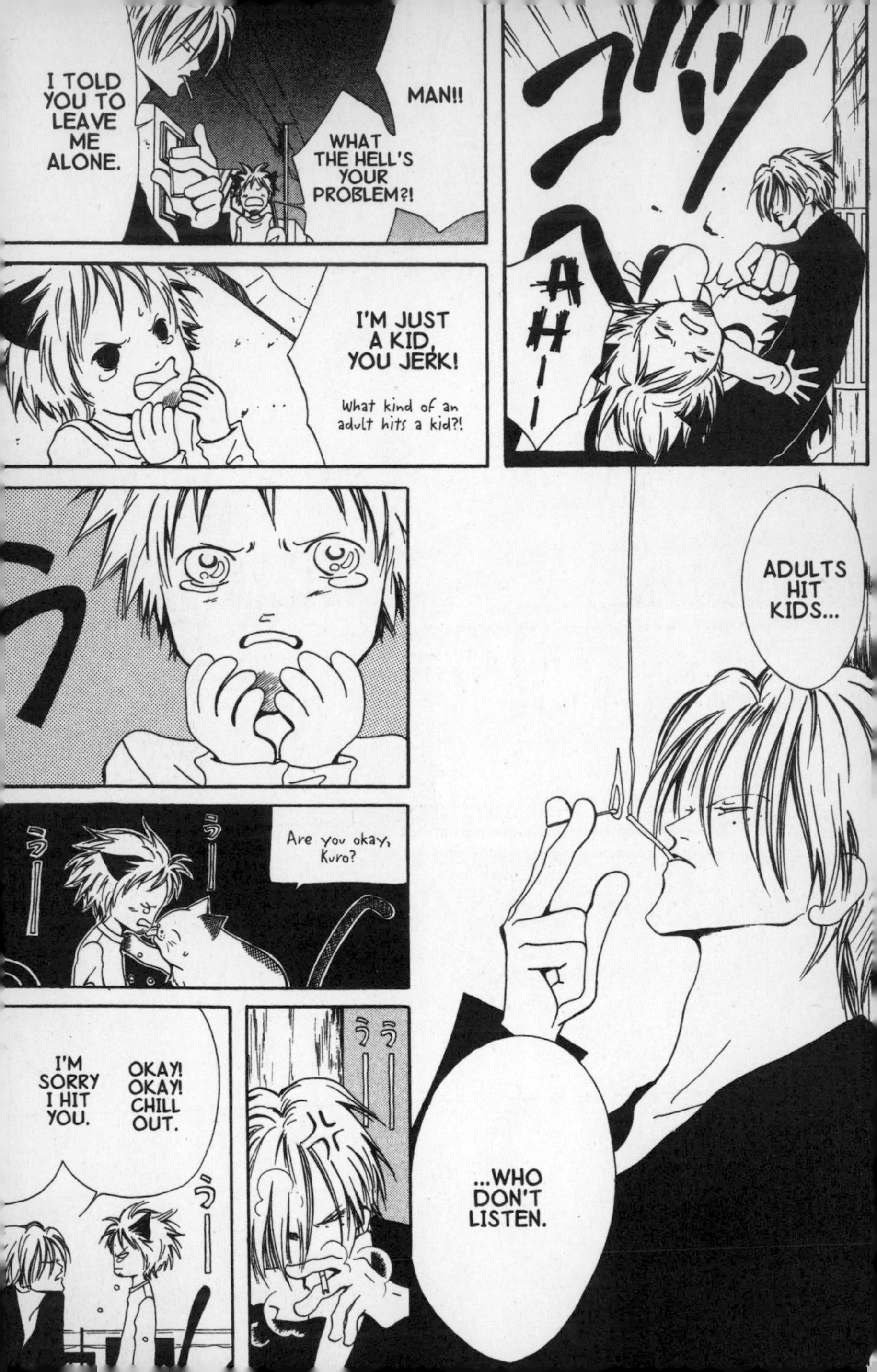
ゴッ
AH--
MAN!!
WHAT THE HELL'S YOUR PROBLEM?!
I TOLD YOU TO LEAVE ME ALONE.
I'M JUST A KID, YOU JERK!
What kind of an adult hits a kid?!
ADULTS HIT KIDS...
...WHO DON'T LISTEN.
う
うー
Are you okay, Kuro?
うう
うー
OKAY! OKAY! CHILL OUT.
I'M SORRY I HIT YOU.

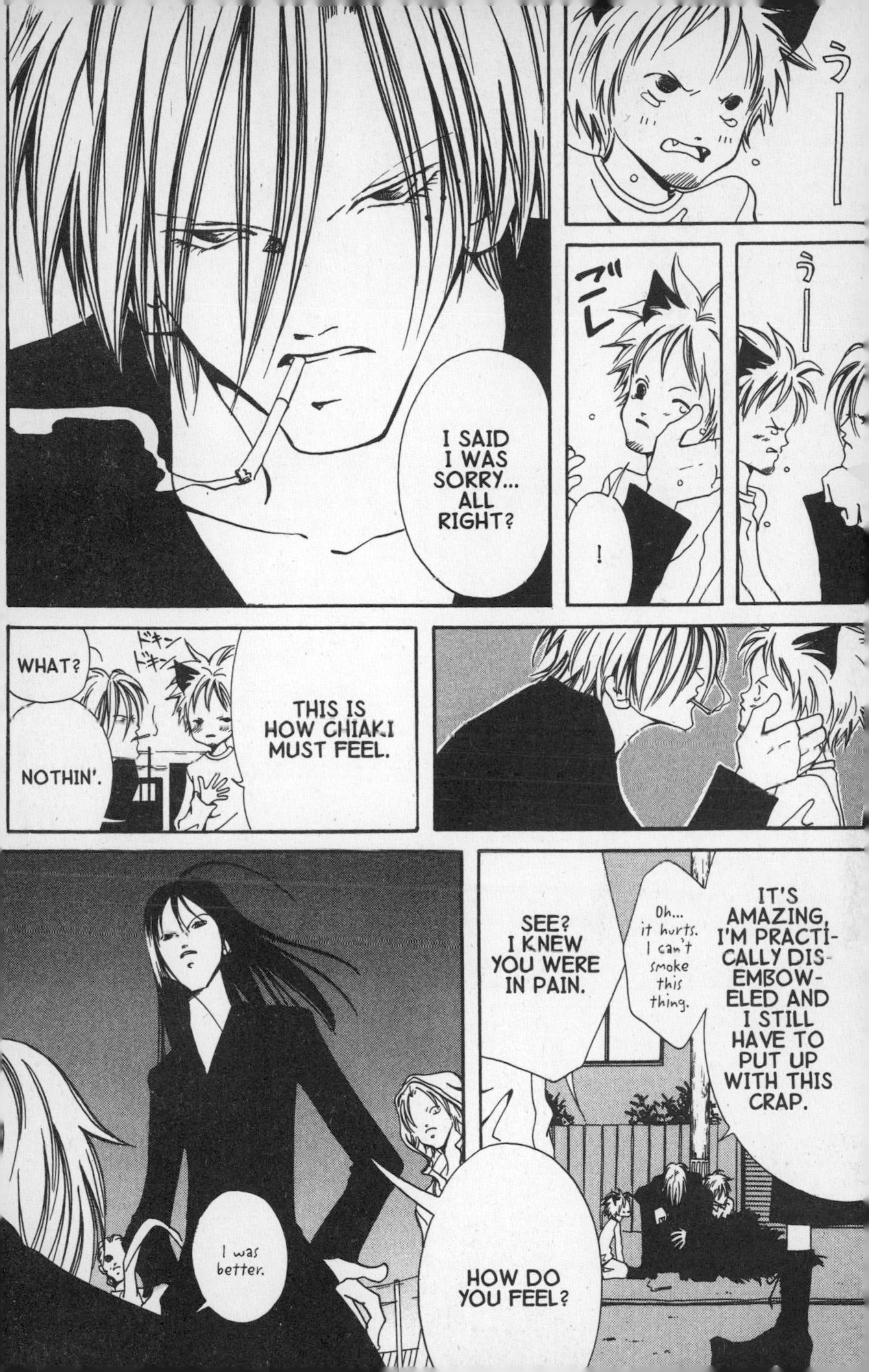
うー
うー
!
I SAID I WAS SORRY... ALL RIGHT?
THIS IS HOW CHIAKI MUST FEEL.
ドキン ドキン
WHAT?
NOTHIN'.
IT'S AMAZING, I'M PRACTI-CALLY DIS-EMBOW-ELED AND I STILL HAVE TO PUT UP WITH THIS CRAP.
Oh... it hurts. I can't smoke this thing.
SEE? I KNEW YOU WERE IN PAIN.
HOW DO YOU FEEL?
I was better.

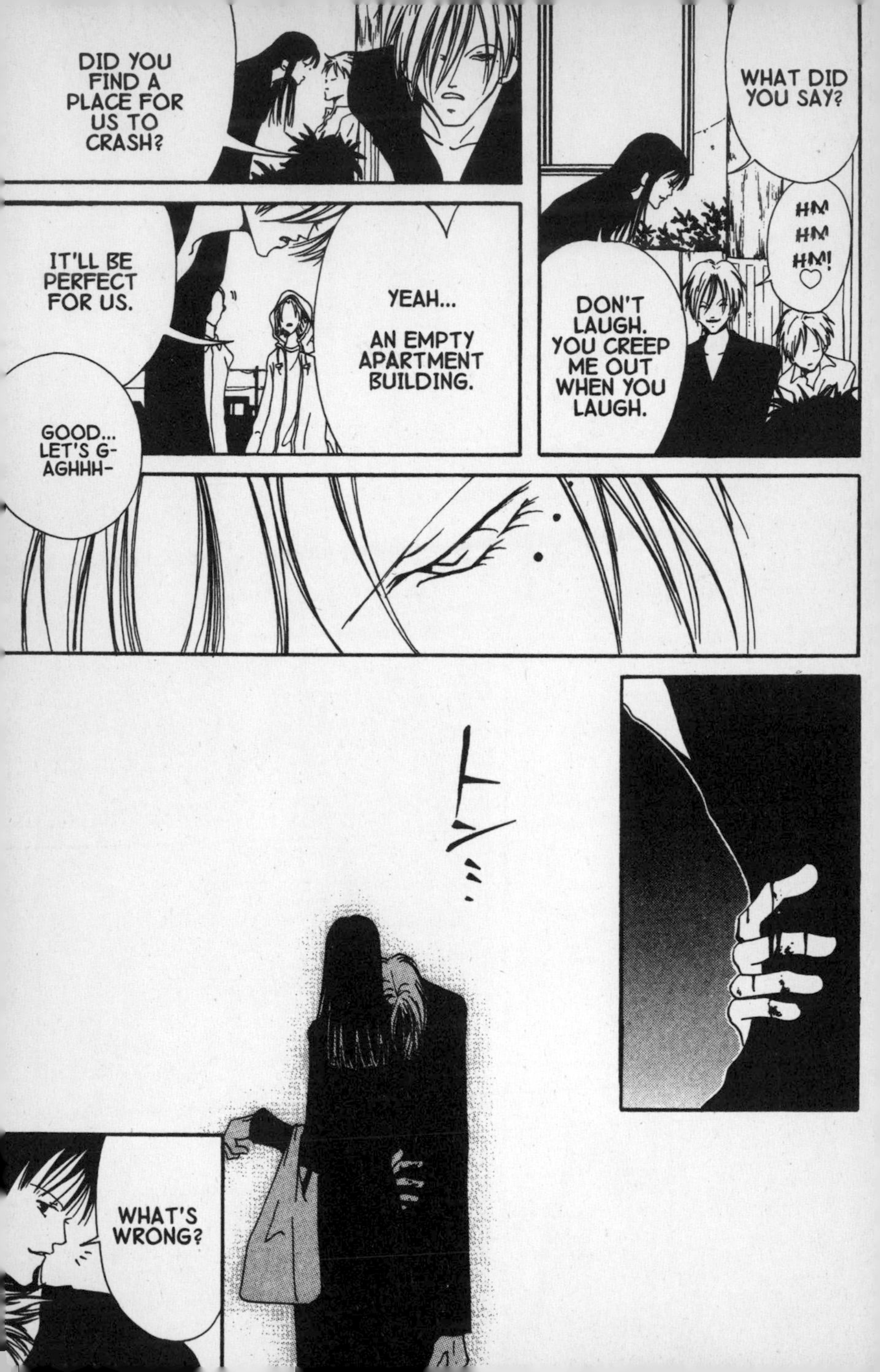
WHAT DID YOU SAY?
HM HM HM! ♡
DON'T LAUGH. YOU CREEP ME OUT WHEN YOU LAUGH.
DID YOU FIND A PLACE FOR US TO CRASH?
YEAH... AN EMPTY APARTMENT BUILDING.
IT'LL BE PERFECT FOR US.
GOOD... LET'S G-AGHHH-
WHAT'S WRONG?

NOTHING.

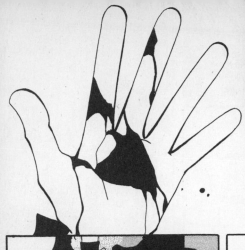

YOU'RE
ALL WET.

Let me help.

?

HMM.

And killing
the boy
in the park...
it's making
the wound
worse.

Damn.

All this
moving
around, and
keeping
the magic
barrier up...

ORORON?

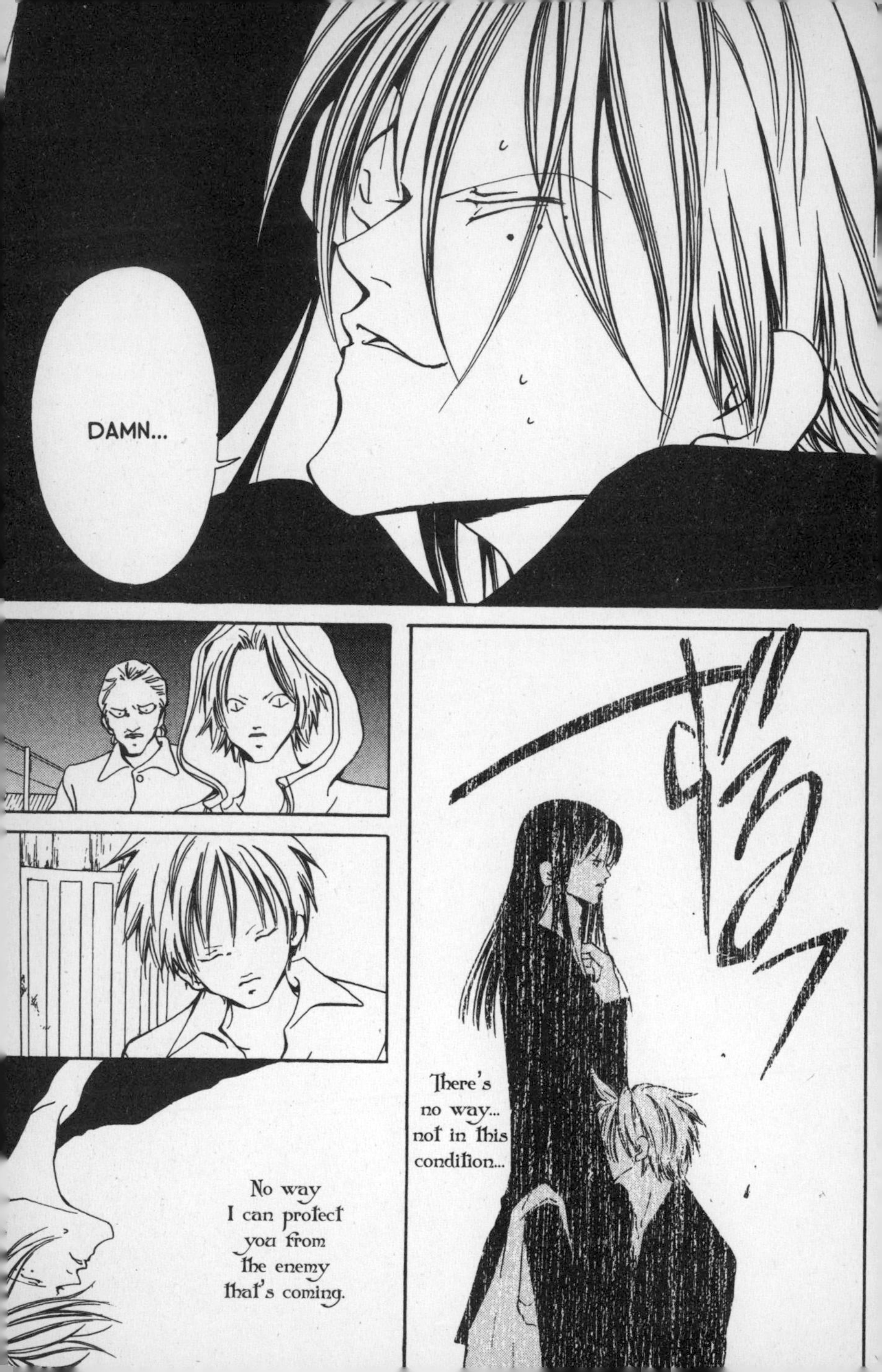
DAMN...
There's no way... not in this condition...
No way I can protect you from the enemy that's coming.

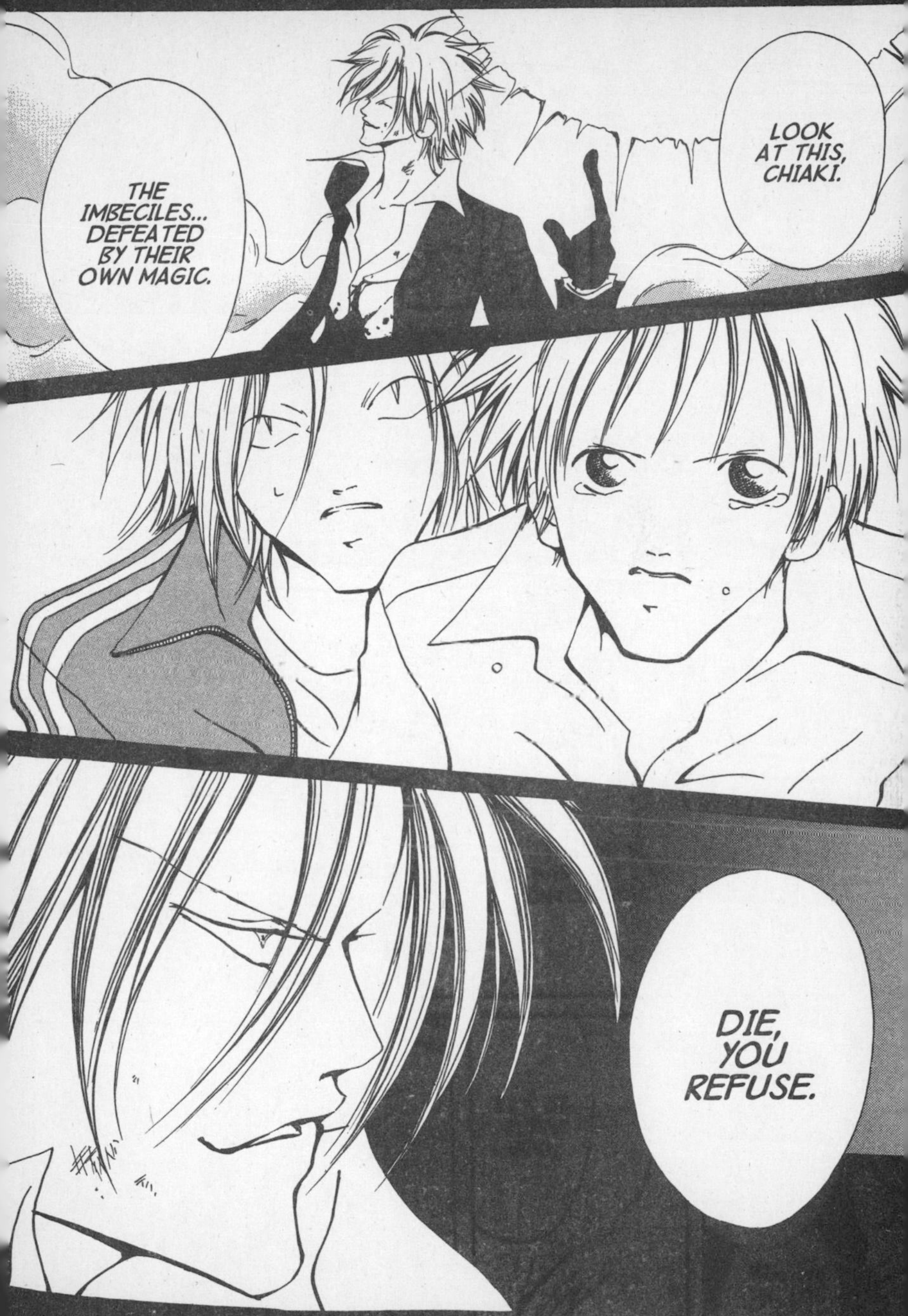
LOOK AT THIS, CHIAKI.
THE IMBECILES... DEFEATED BY THEIR OWN MAGIC.
DIE, YOU REFUSE.

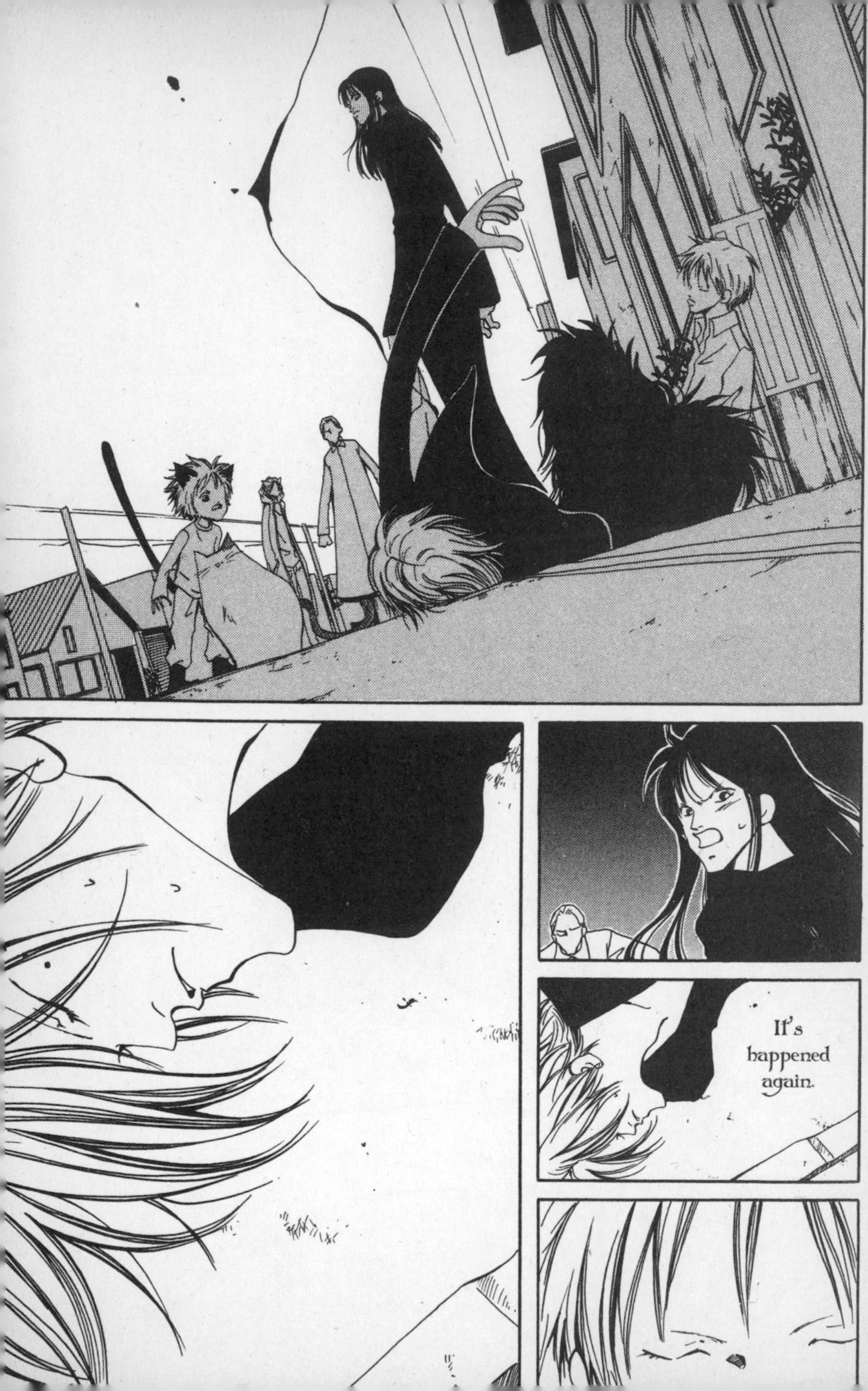
It's happened again.

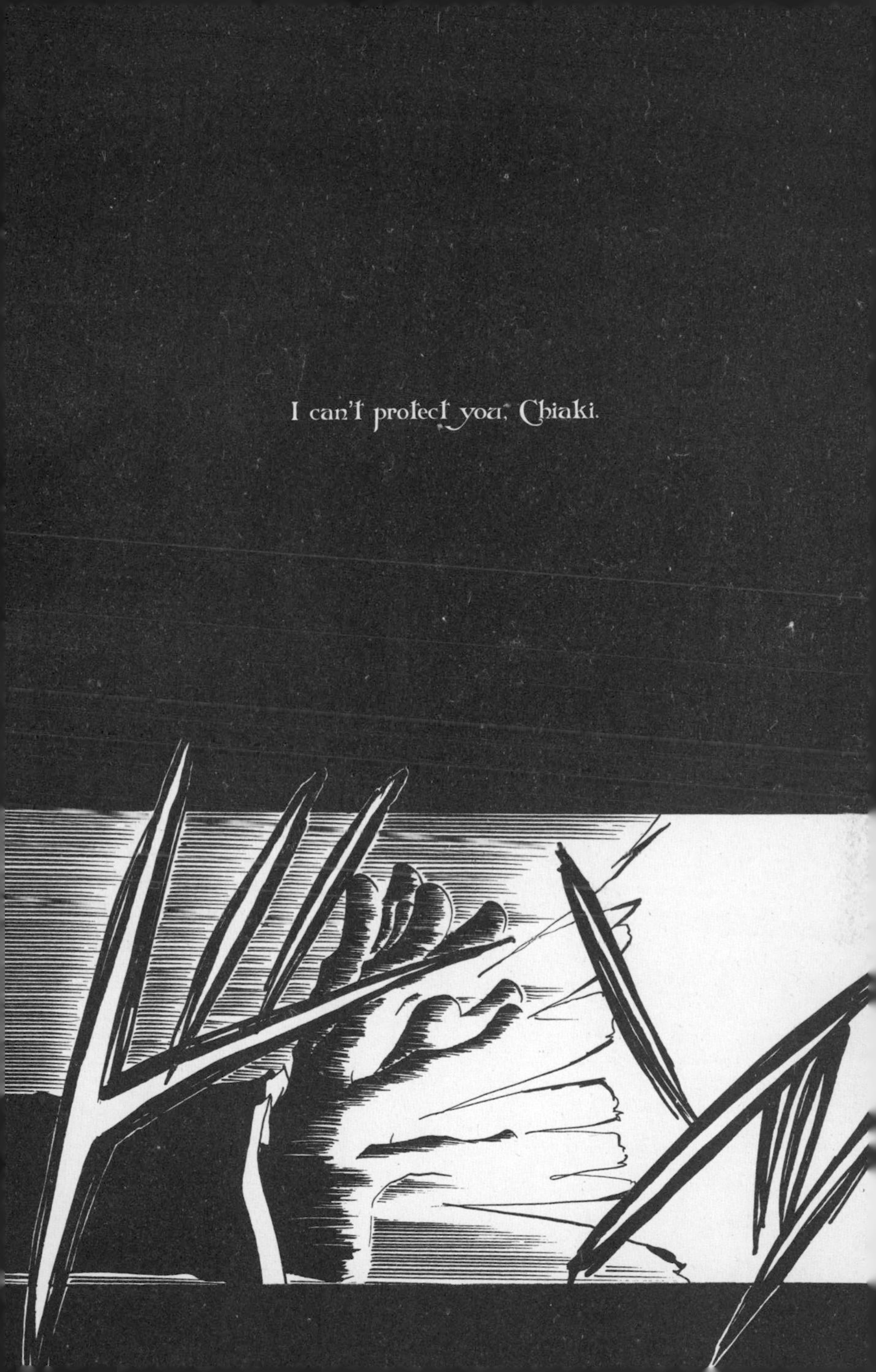
I can't protect you, Chiaki.

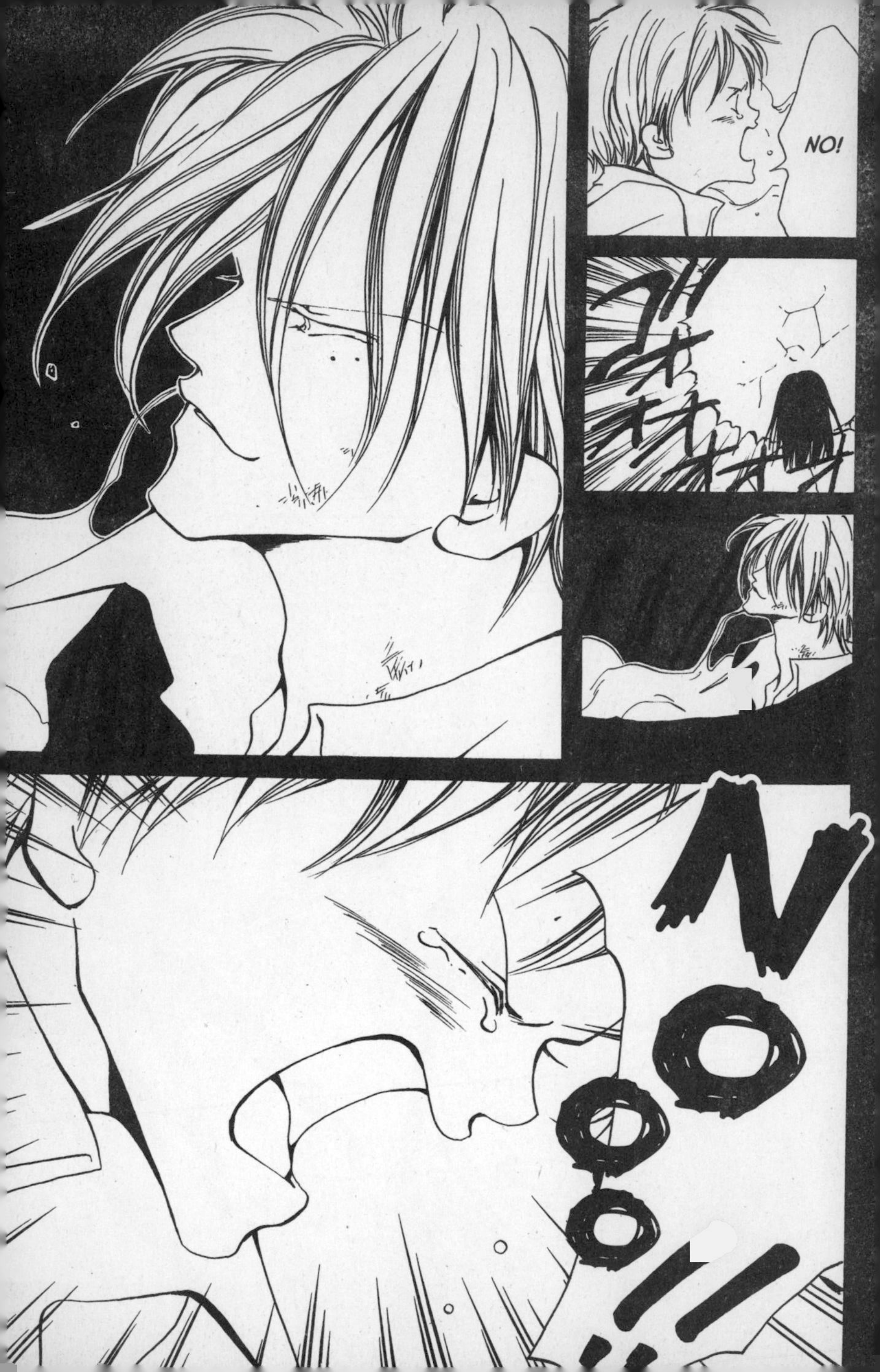
NO!
NOOO!!

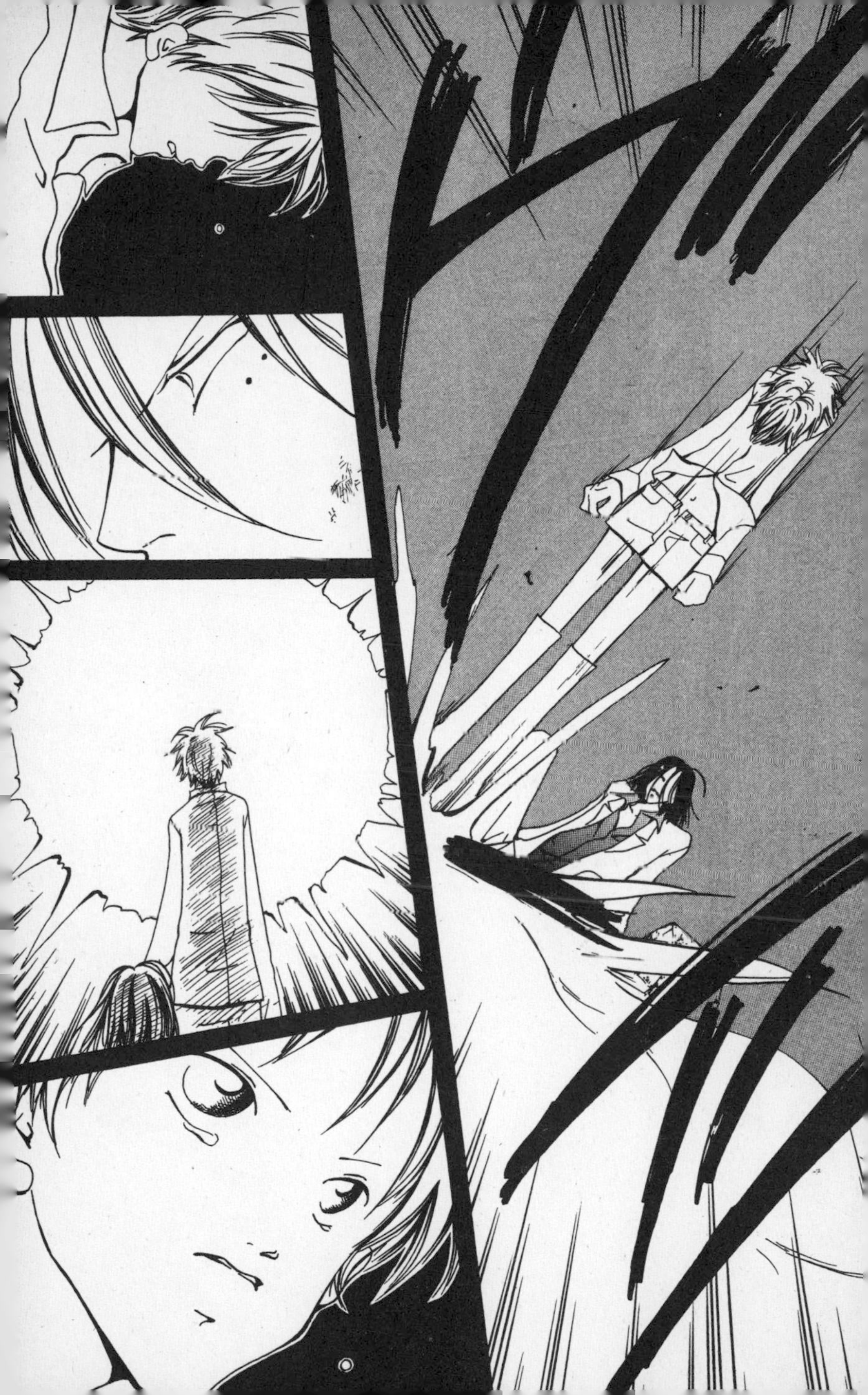

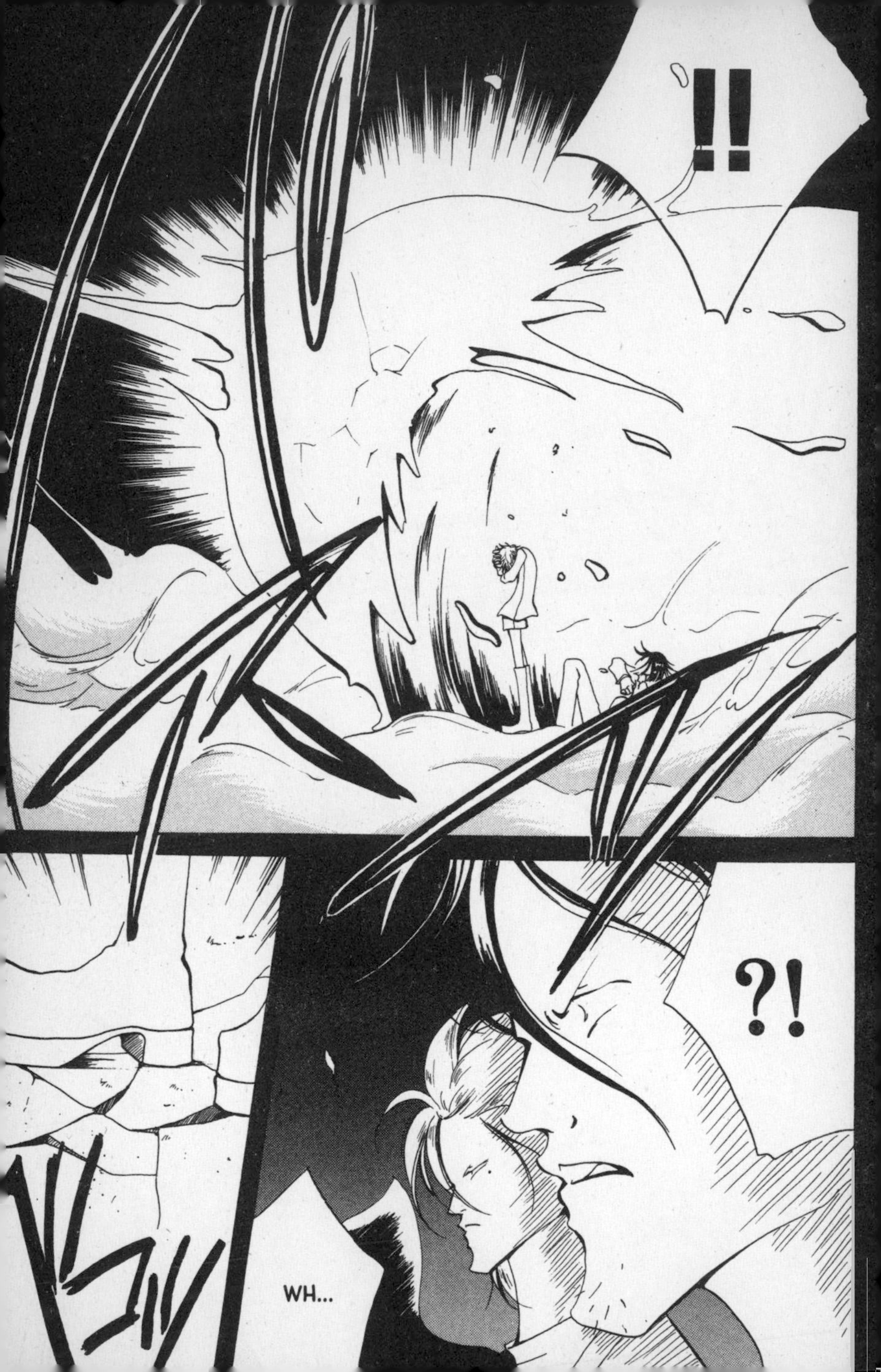
!!
?!
WH...

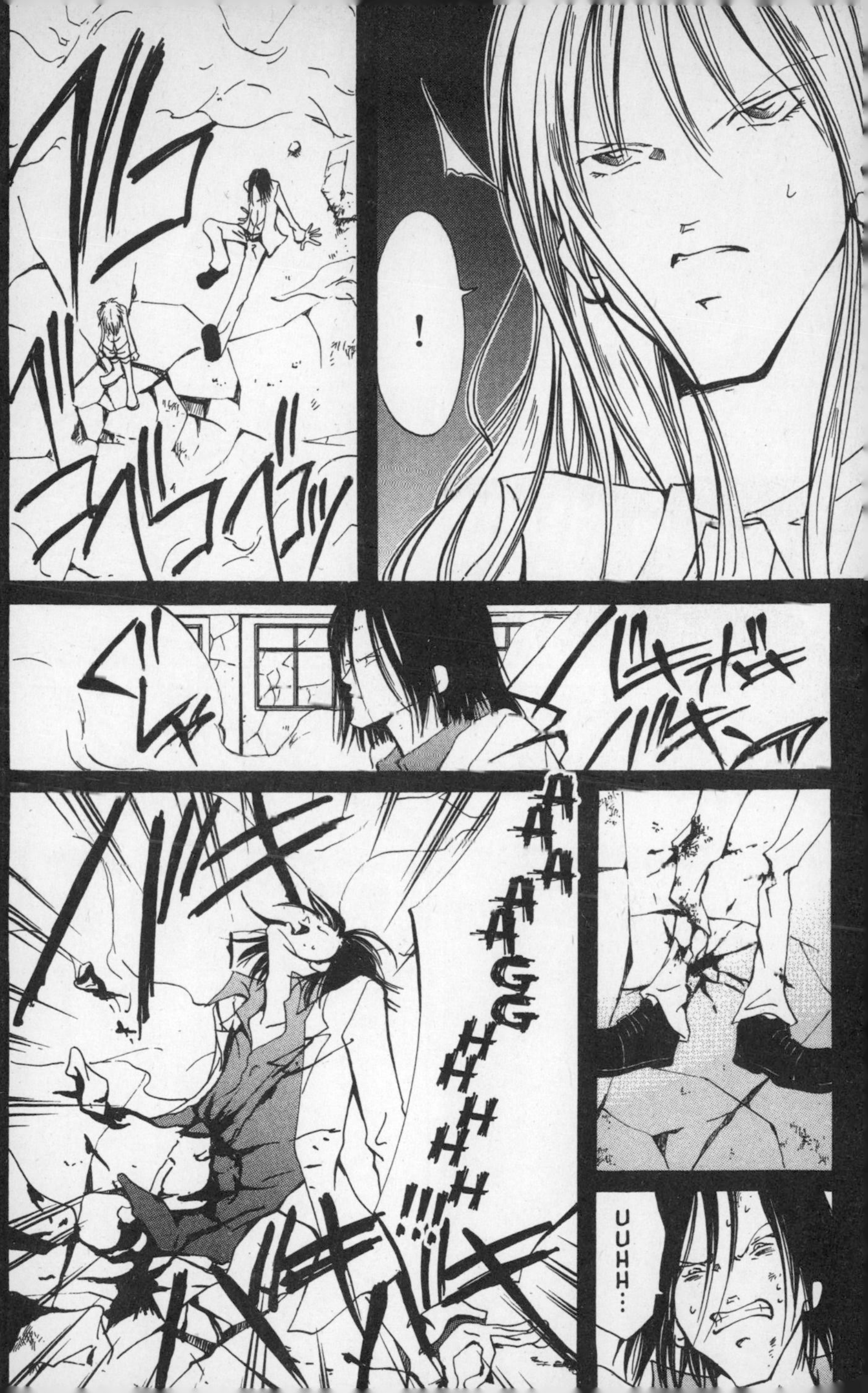
!
UUHH...
AAAAAGGHHHHHH!!!!

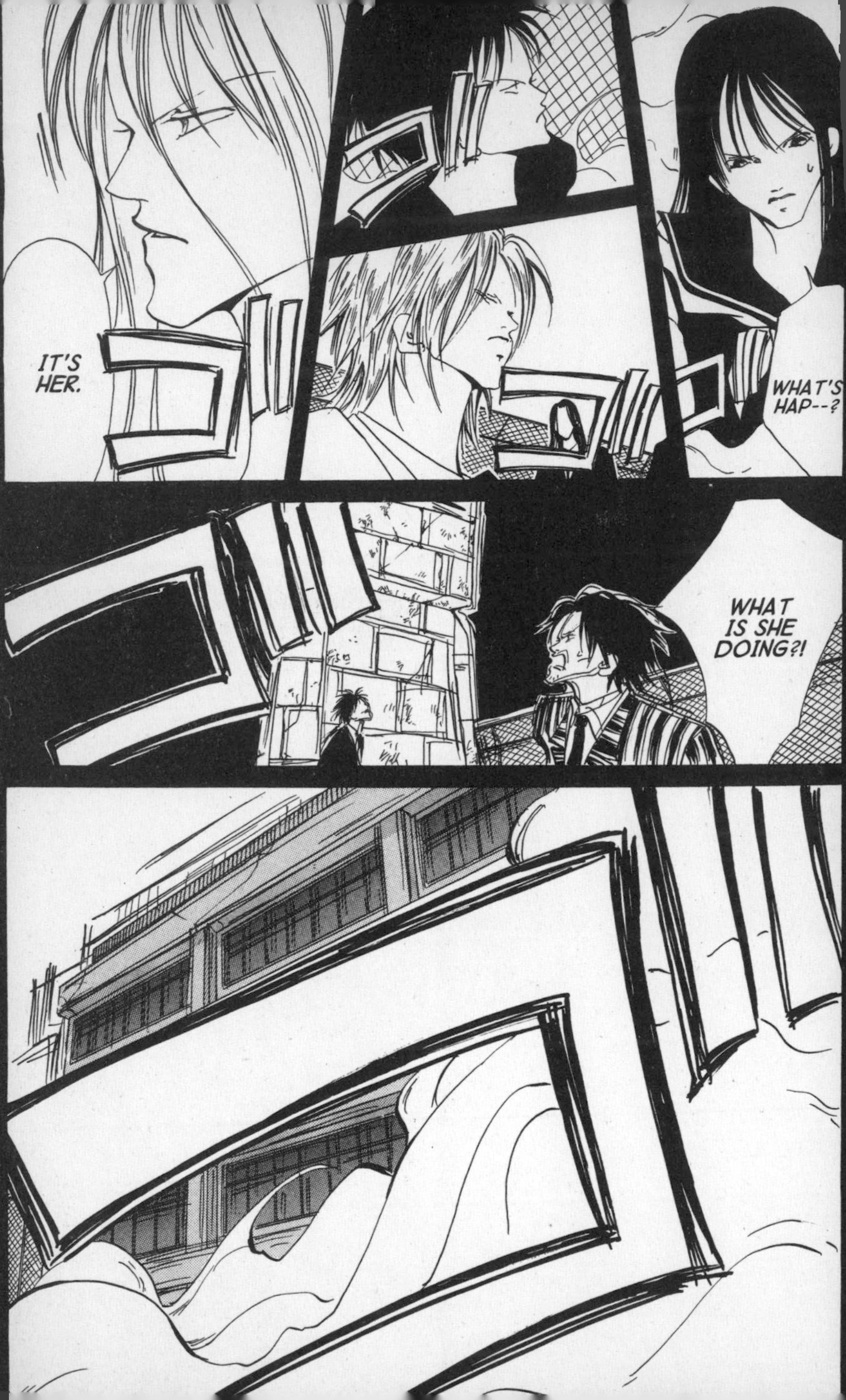
WHAT'S HAP--?
IT'S HER.
WHAT IS SHE DOING?!

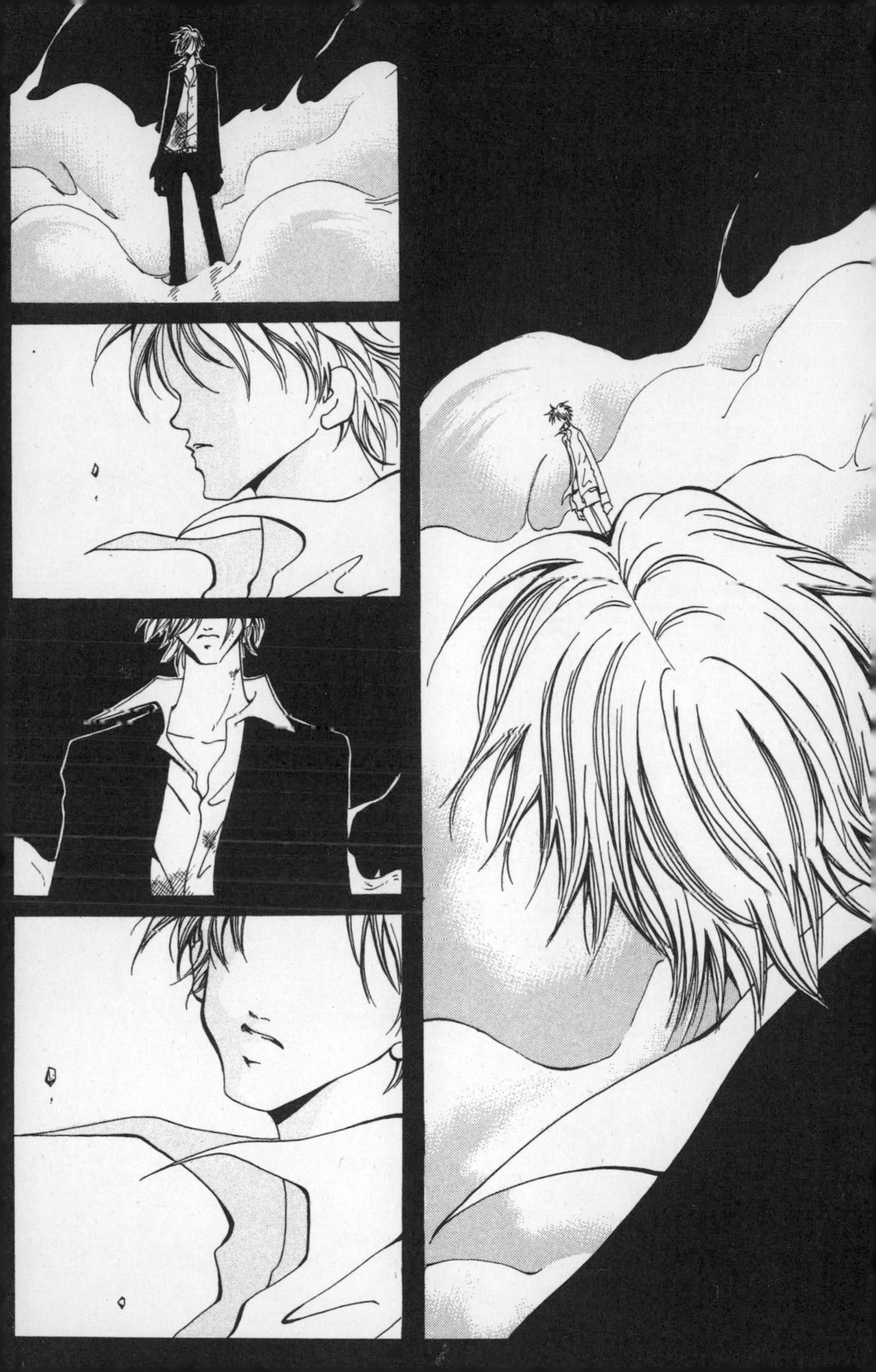

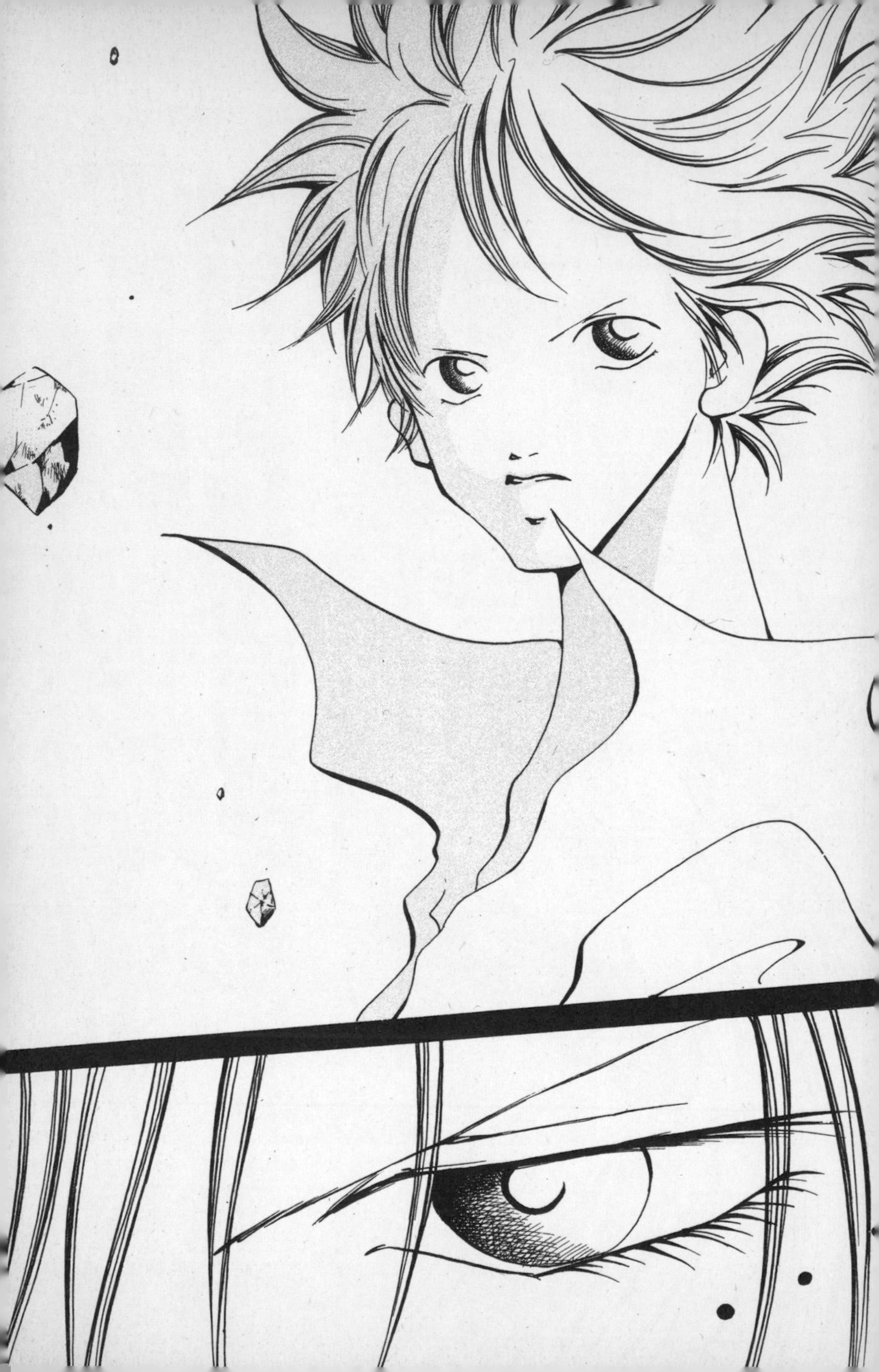

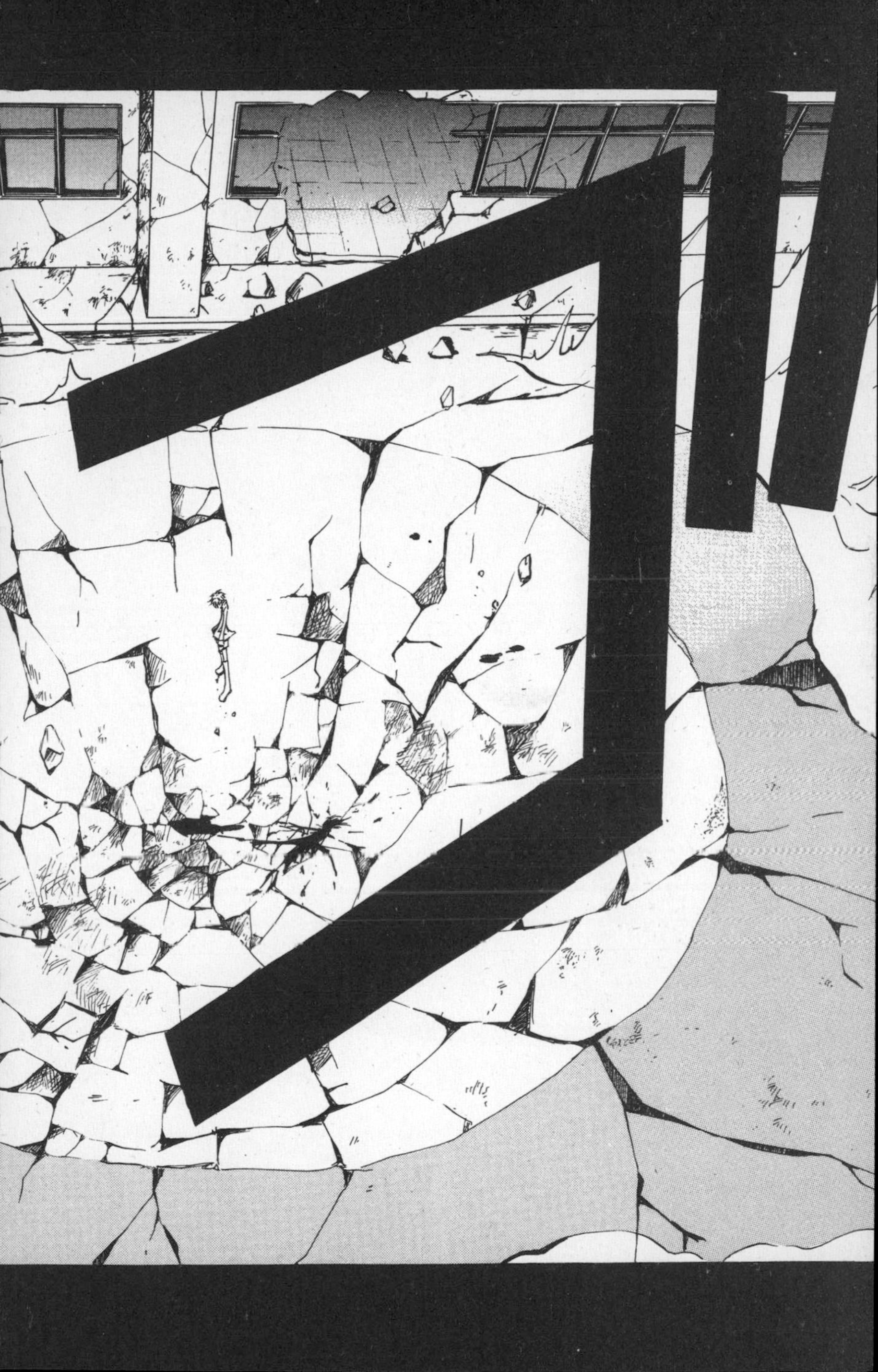

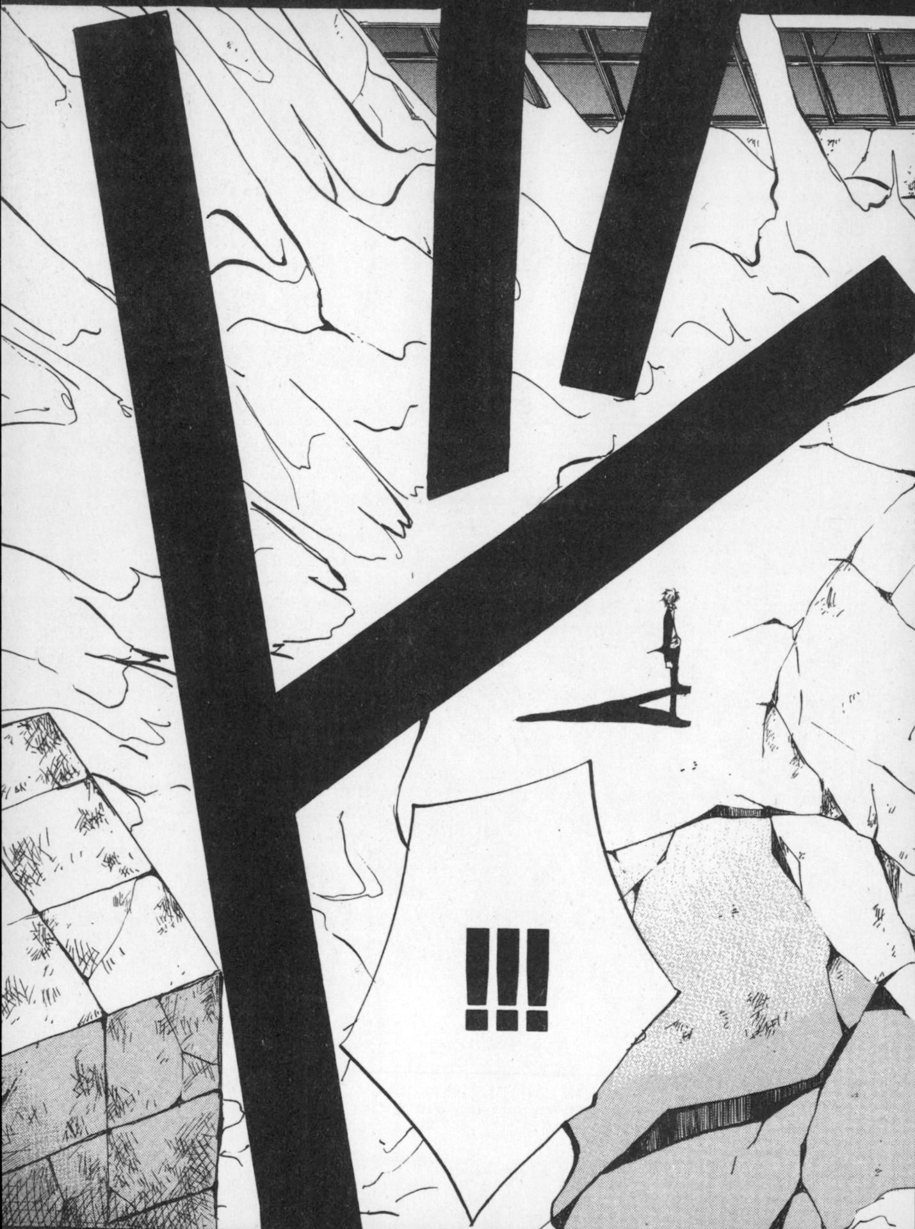
ド
!!!

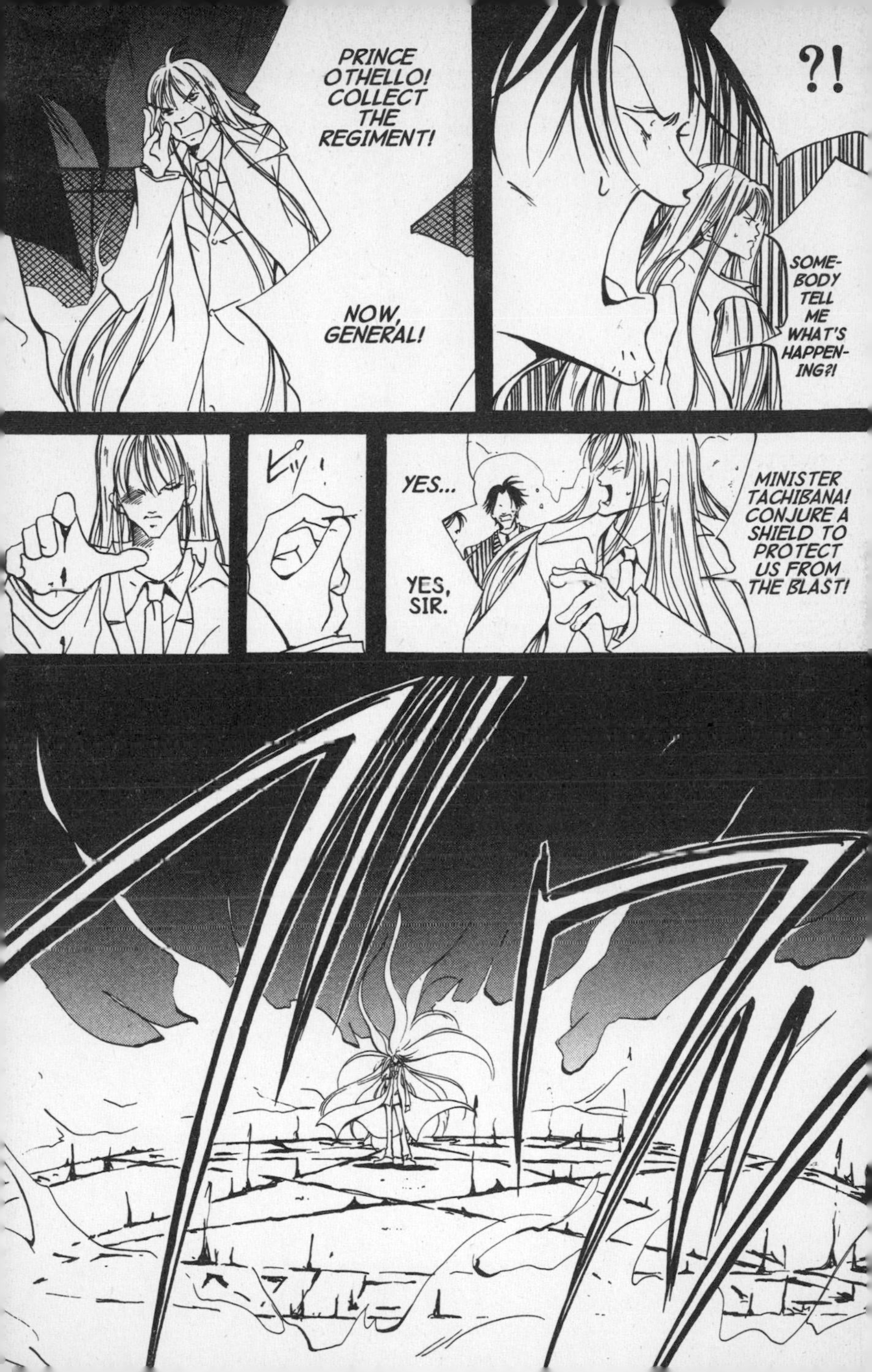
?!
SOMEBODY TELL ME WHAT'S HAPPENING?!
PRINCE OTHELLO! COLLECT THE REGIMENT!
NOW, GENERAL!
MINISTER TACHIBANA! CONJURE A SHIELD TO PROTECT US FROM THE BLAST!
YES...
YES, SIR.
ピッ

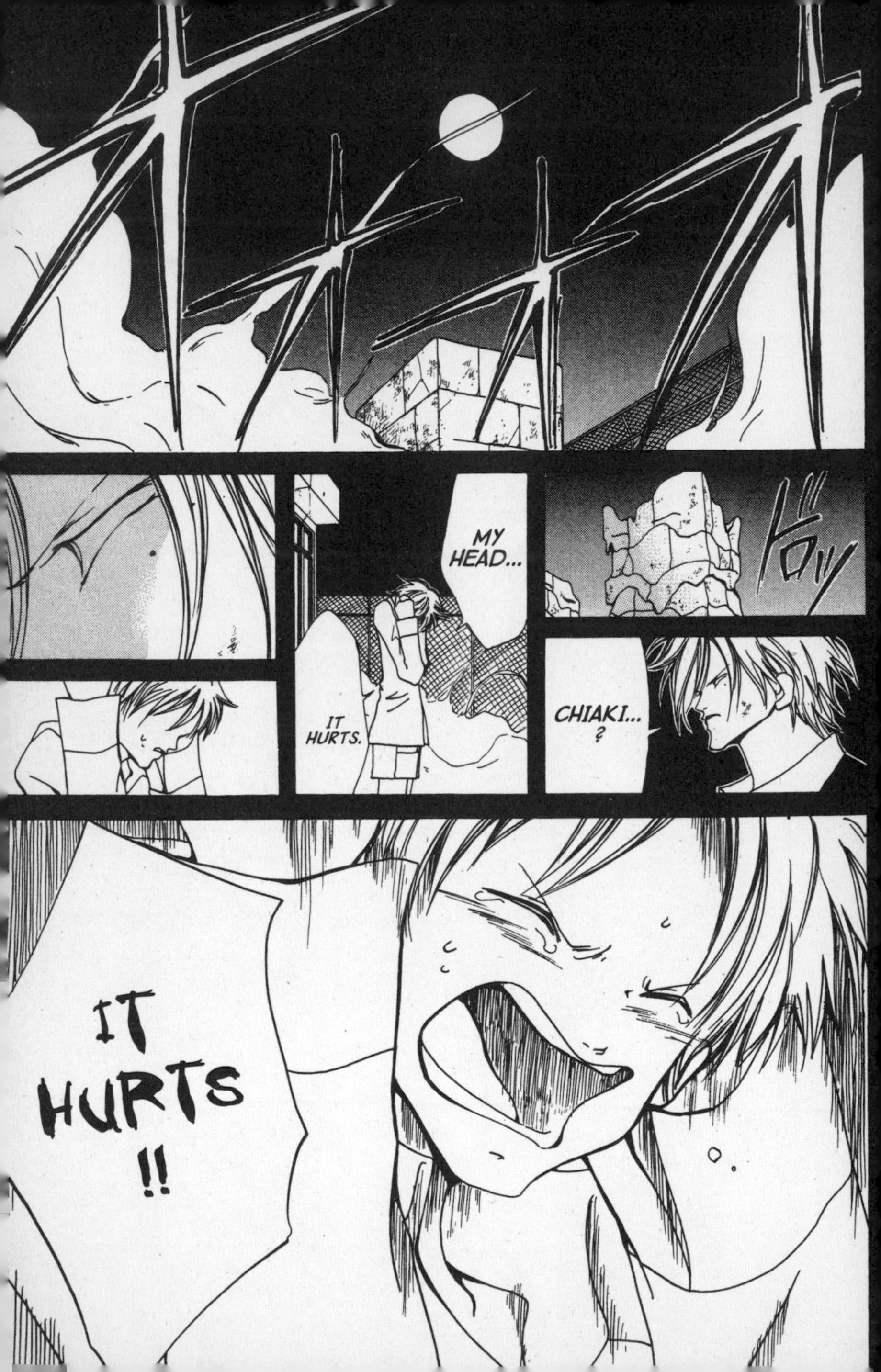
ドロッ
CHIAKI...?
MY HEAD...
IT HURTS.
IT HURTS!!

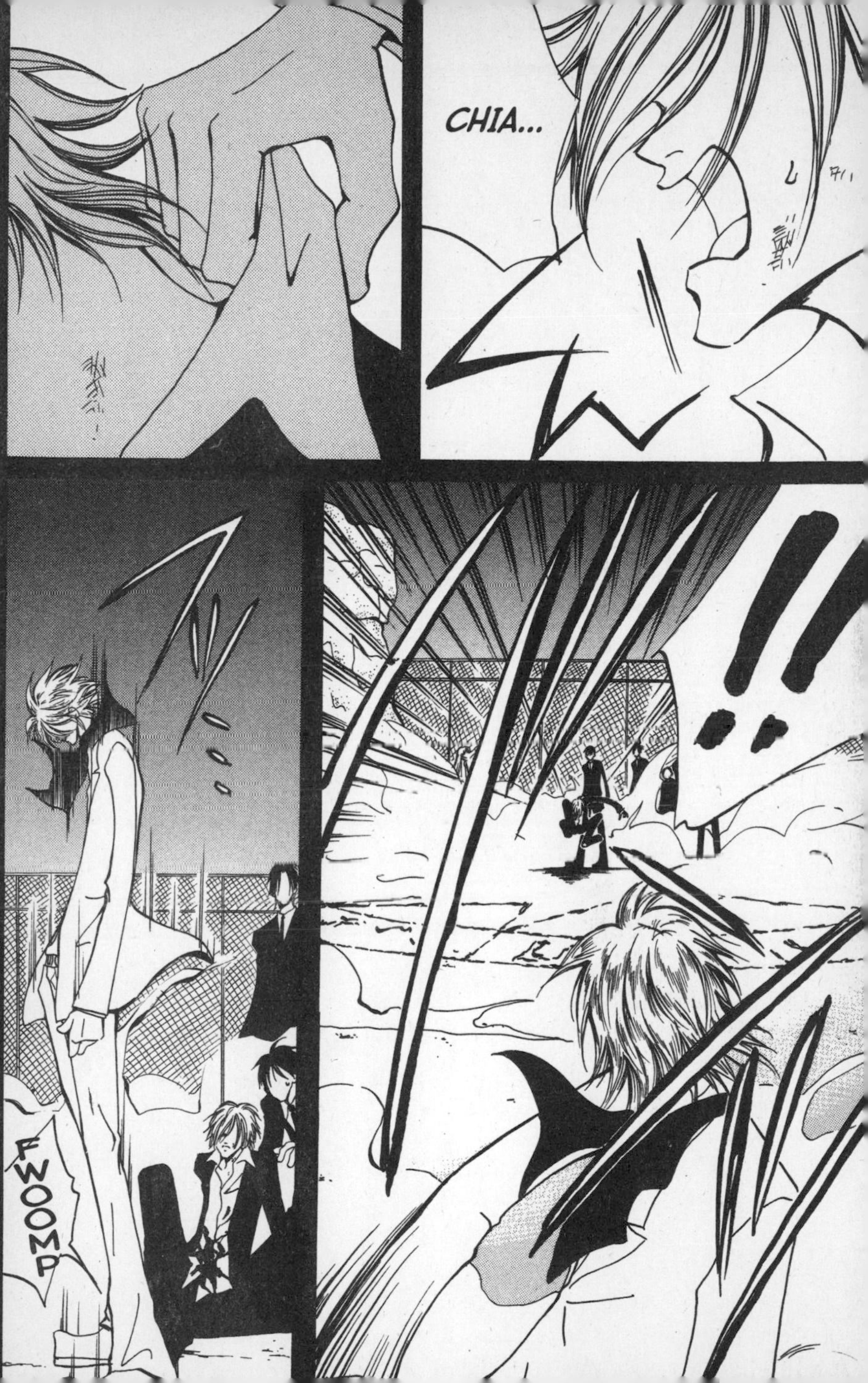
CHIA...
!!
FWOOMP

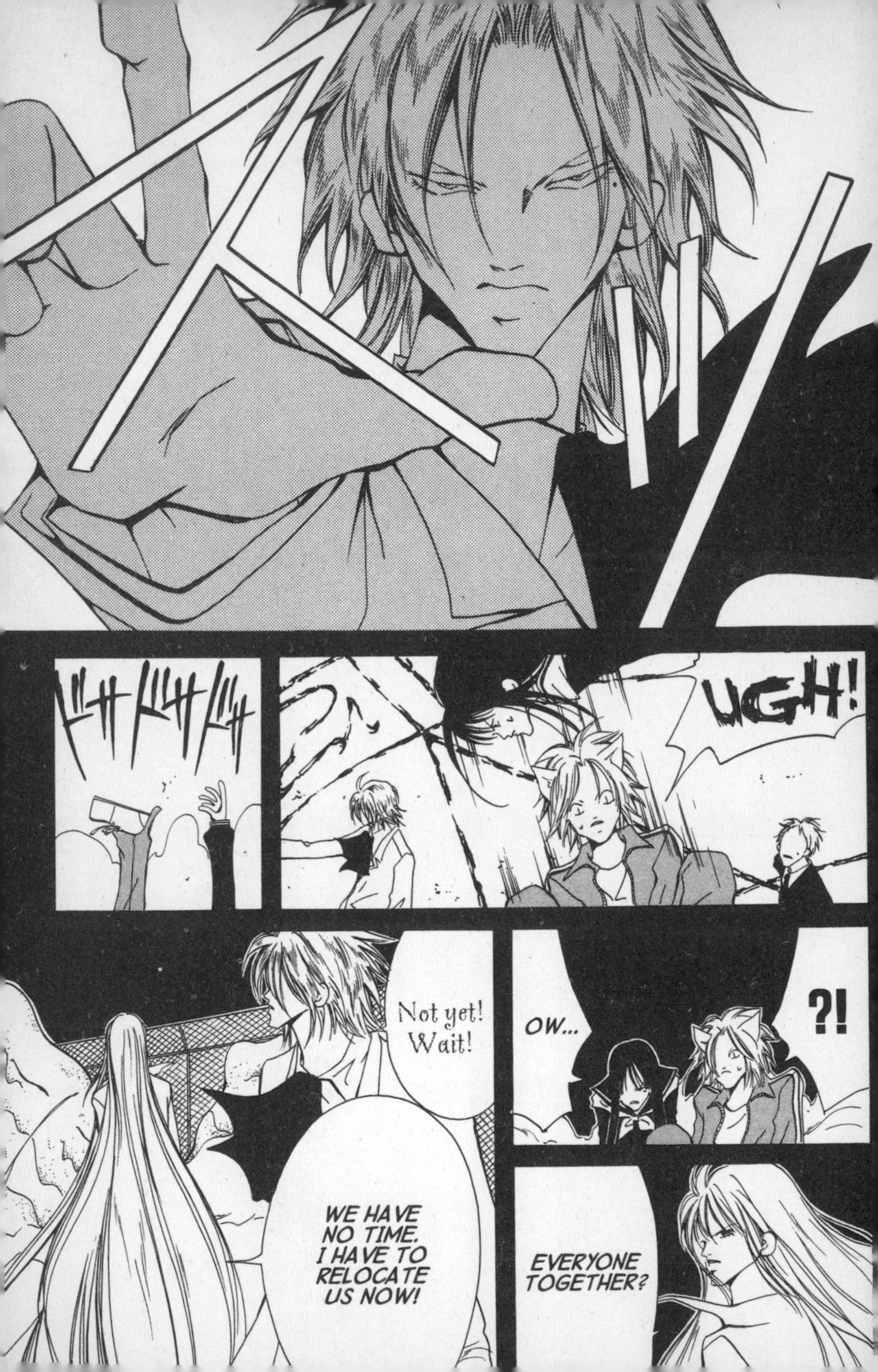
UGH!
ドサ ドサ ドサ
?!
OW...
EVERYONE TOGETHER?
Not yet! Wait!
WE HAVE NO TIME. I HAVE TO RELOCATE US NOW!

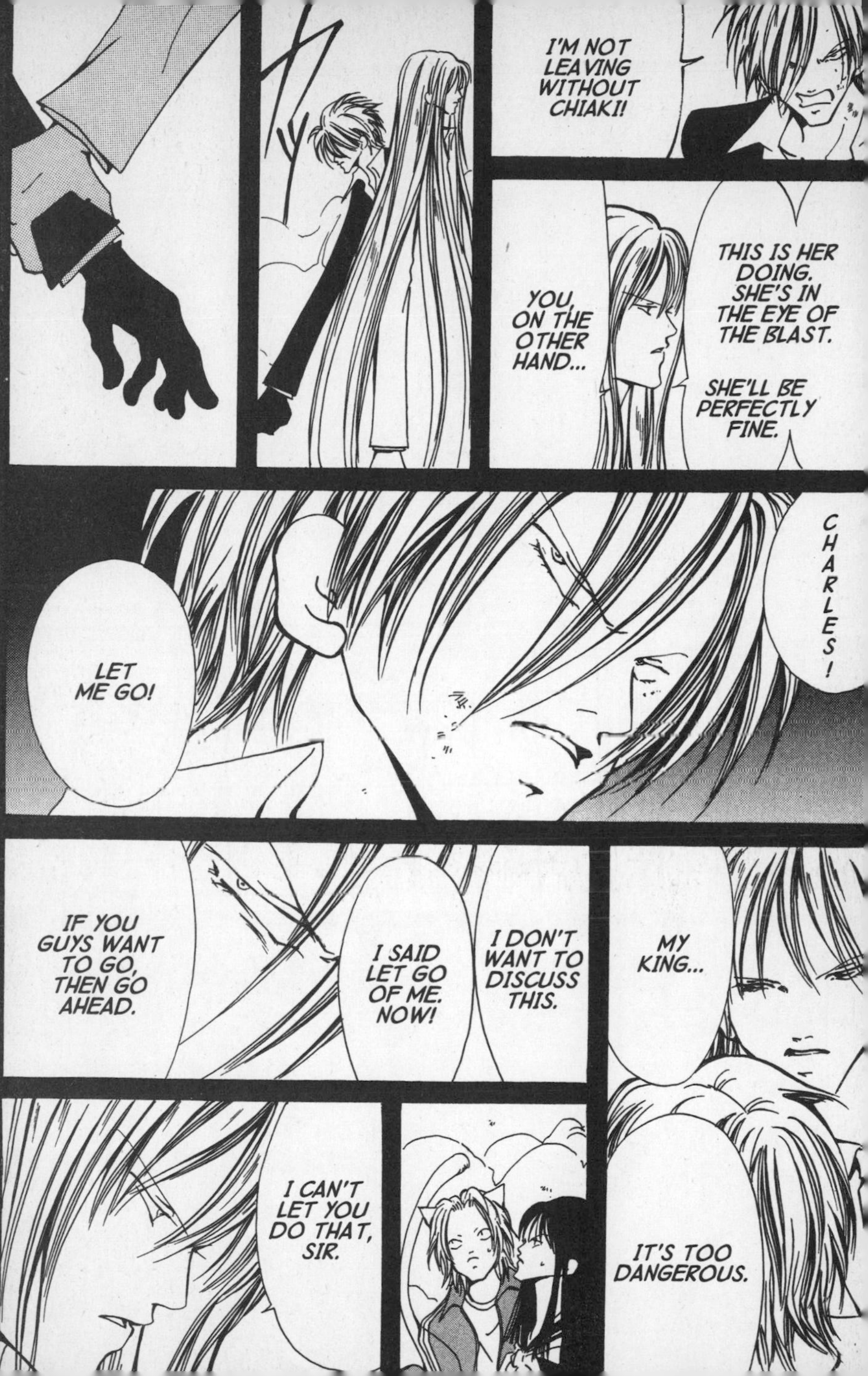
I'M NOT LEAVING WITHOUT CHIAKI!
THIS IS HER DOING. SHE'S IN THE EYE OF THE BLAST.
SHE'LL BE PERFECTLY FINE.
YOU, ON THE OTHER HAND...
CHARLES!
LET ME GO!
MY KING...
IT'S TOO DANGEROUS.
I DON'T WANT TO DISCUSS THIS.
I SAID LET GO OF ME. NOW!
IF YOU GUYS WANT TO GO, THEN GO AHEAD.
I CAN'T LET YOU DO THAT, SIR.

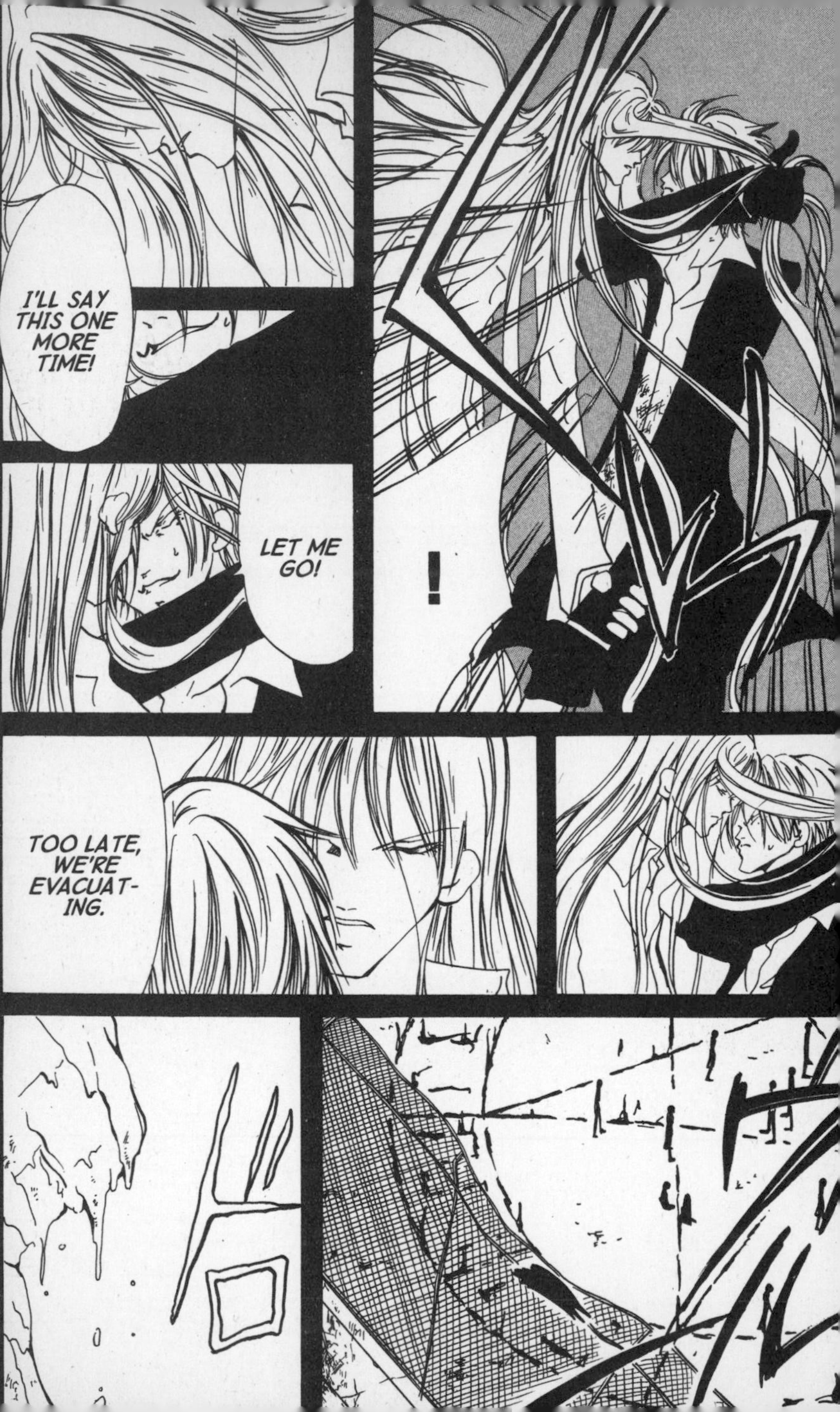
!
I'LL SAY THIS ONE MORE TIME!
LET ME GO!
TOO LATE, WE'RE EVACUAT-ING.

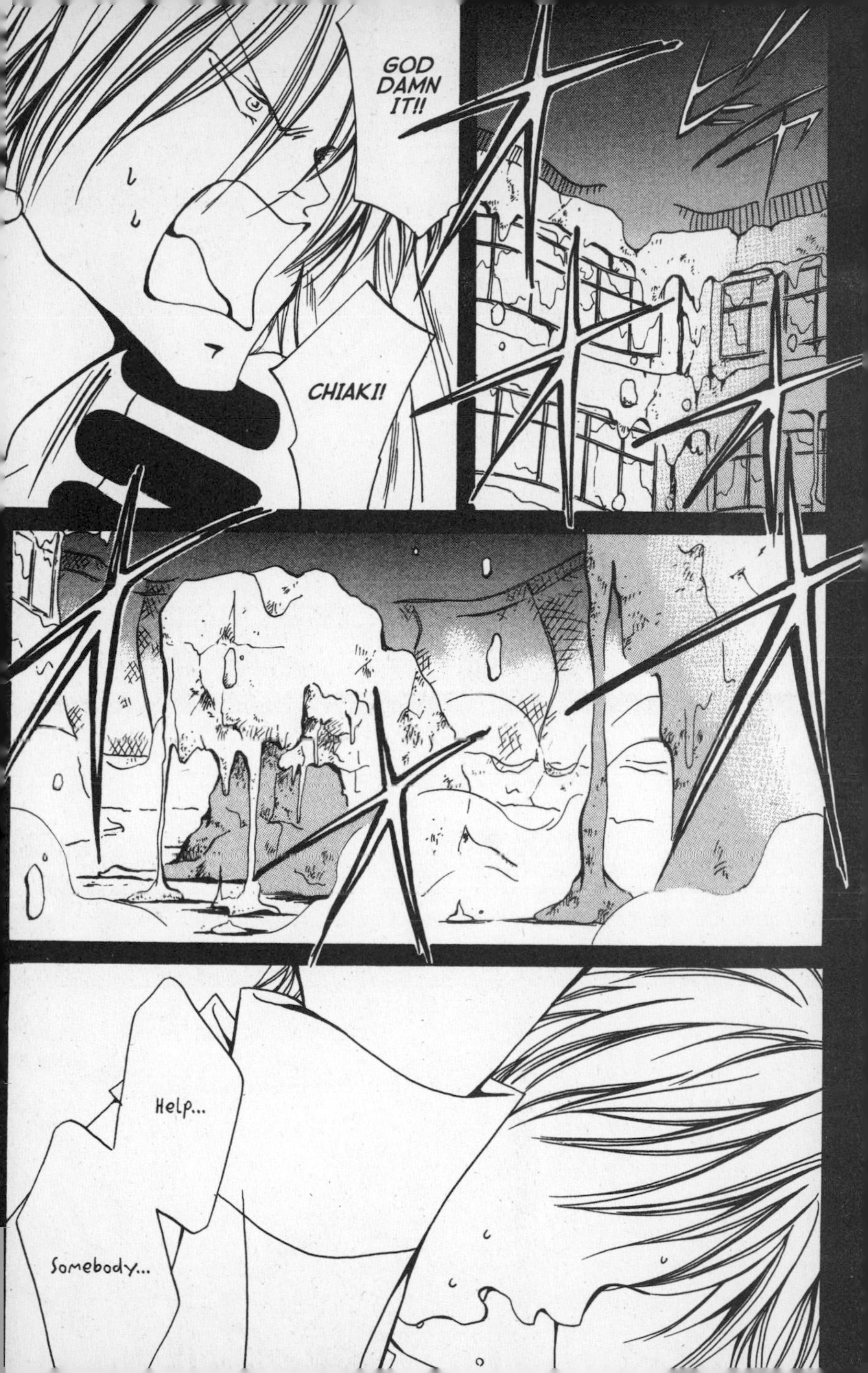
GOD DAMN IT!!
CHIAKI!
Help...
Somebody...

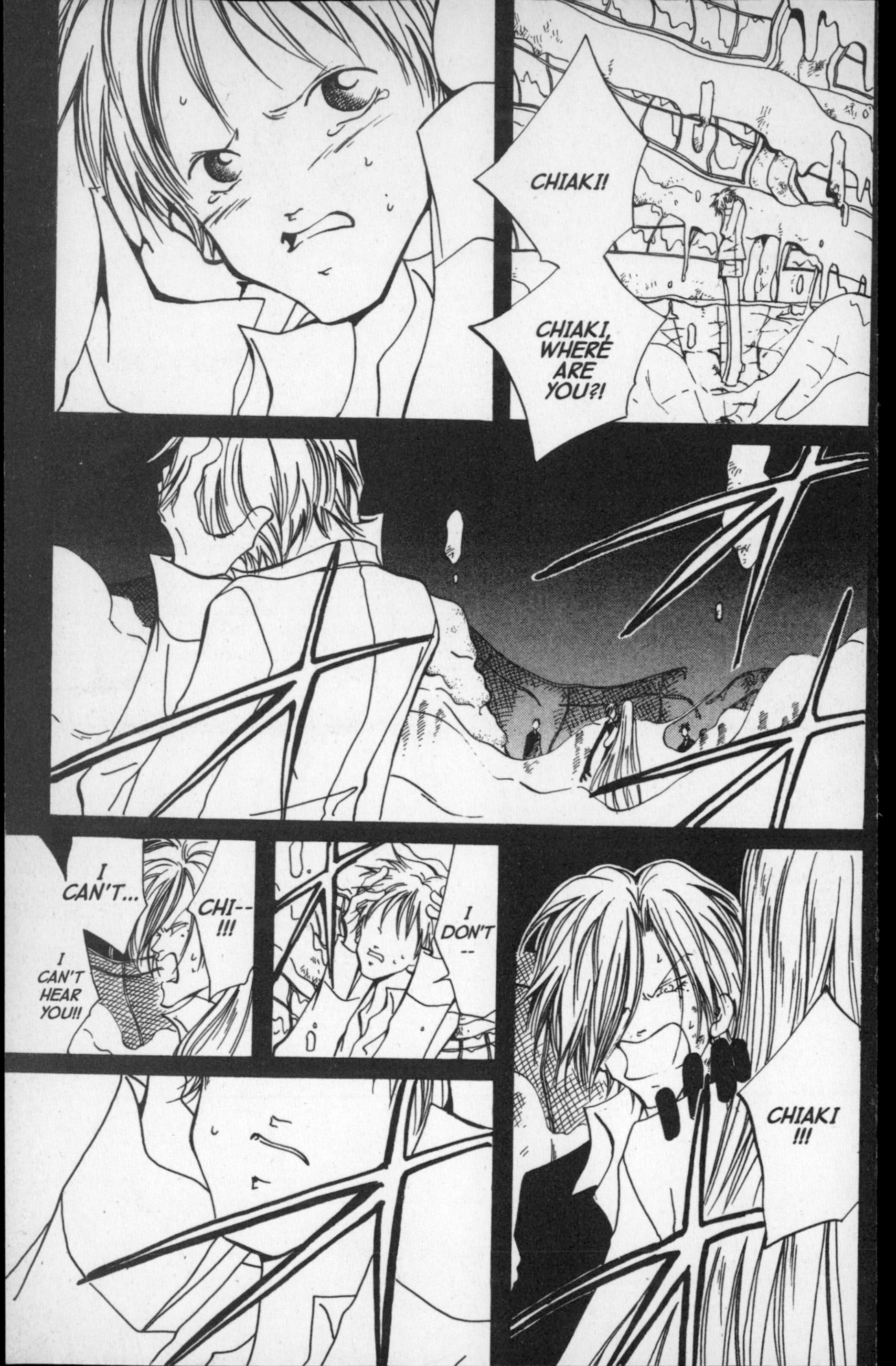
CHIAKI!
CHIAKI, WHERE ARE YOU?!
CHIAKI !!!
I DON'T --
I CAN'T...
CHI-- !!!
I CAN'T HEAR YOU!!

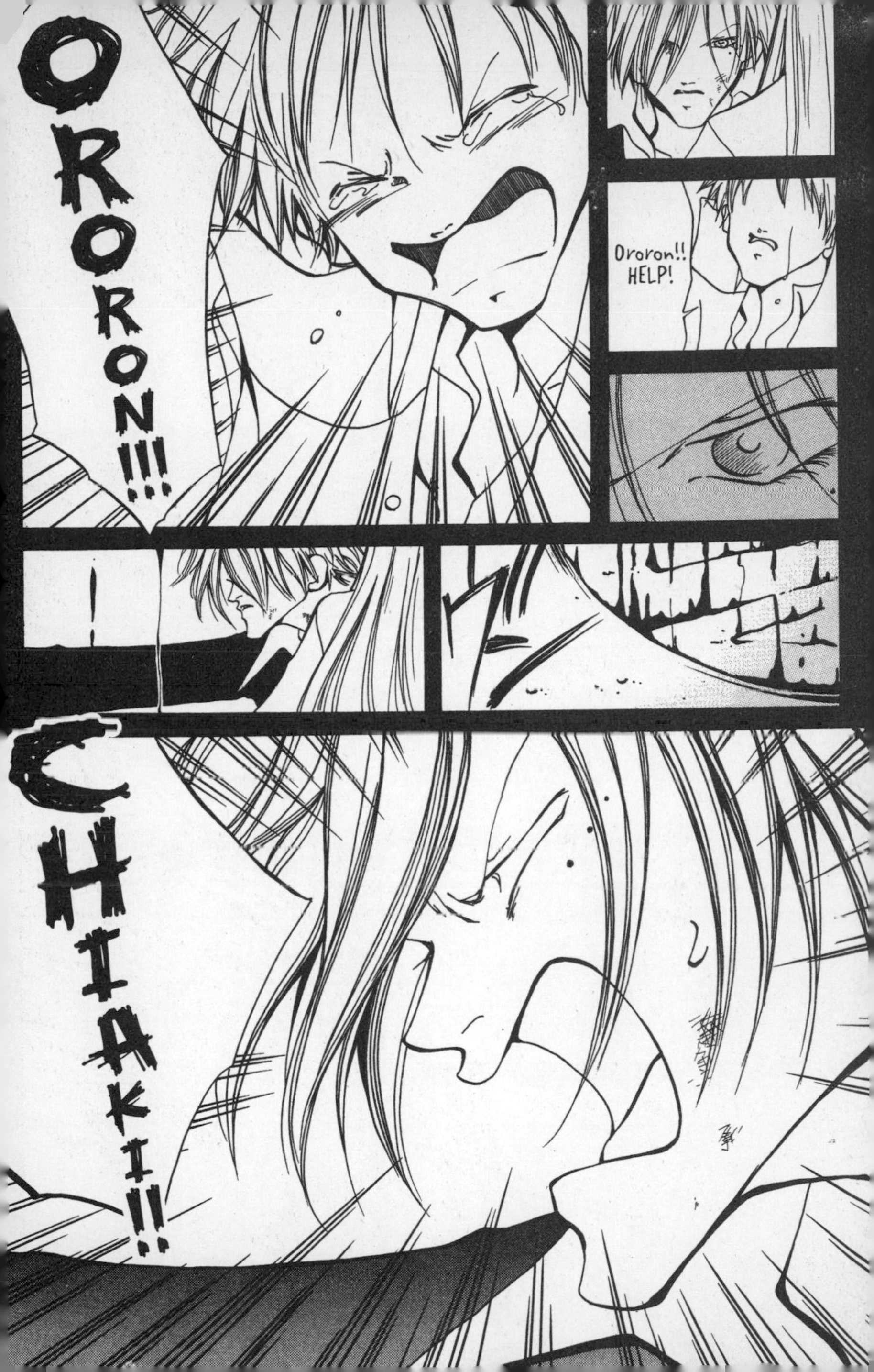
Ororon!!
HELP!
ORORON!!!
!
CHIAKI!!

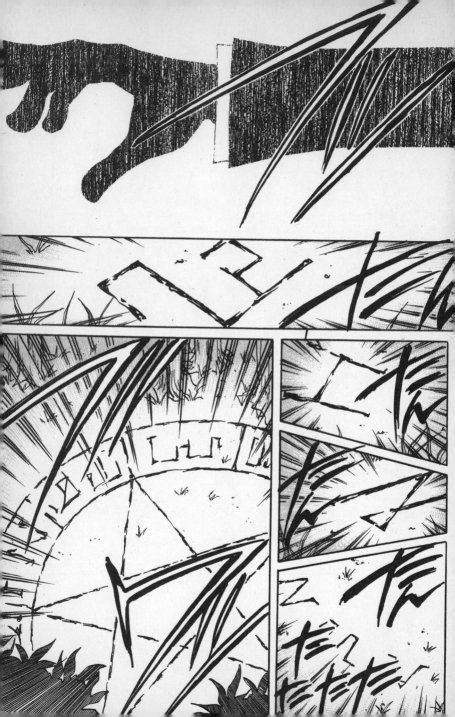

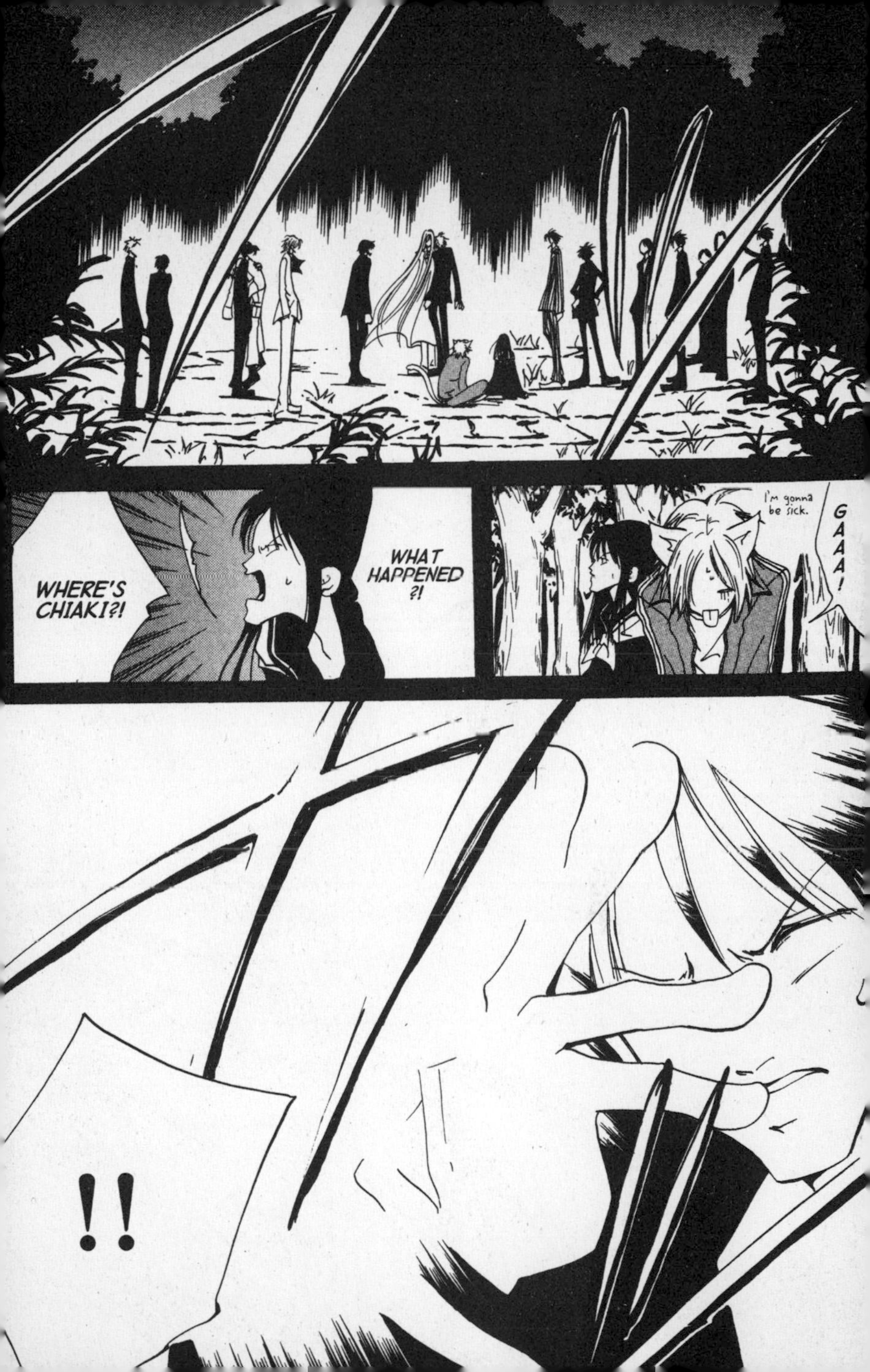
GAAA!
I'm gonna be sick.
WHAT HAPPENED?!
WHERE'S CHIAKI?!
!!

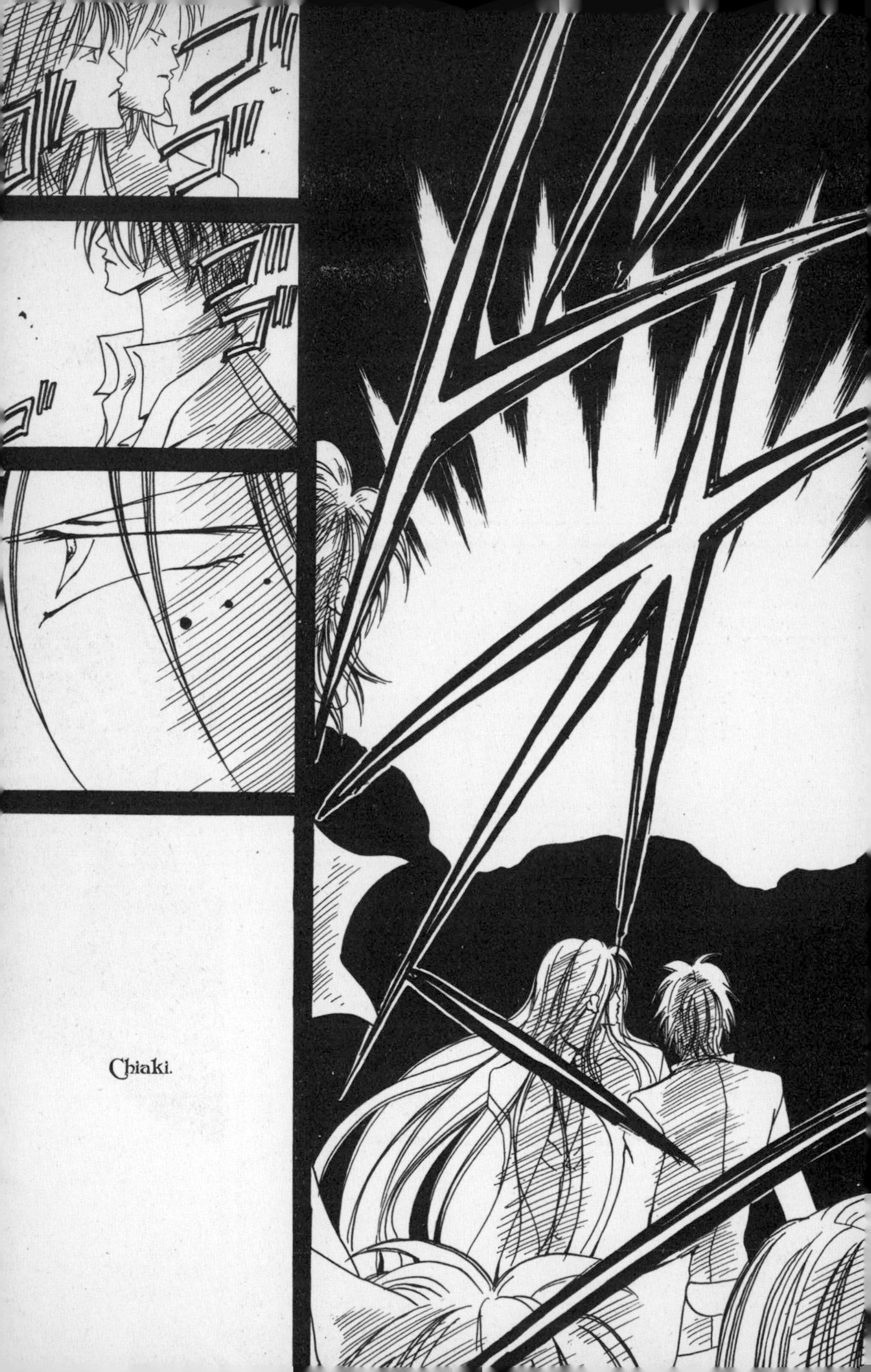
Chiaki.

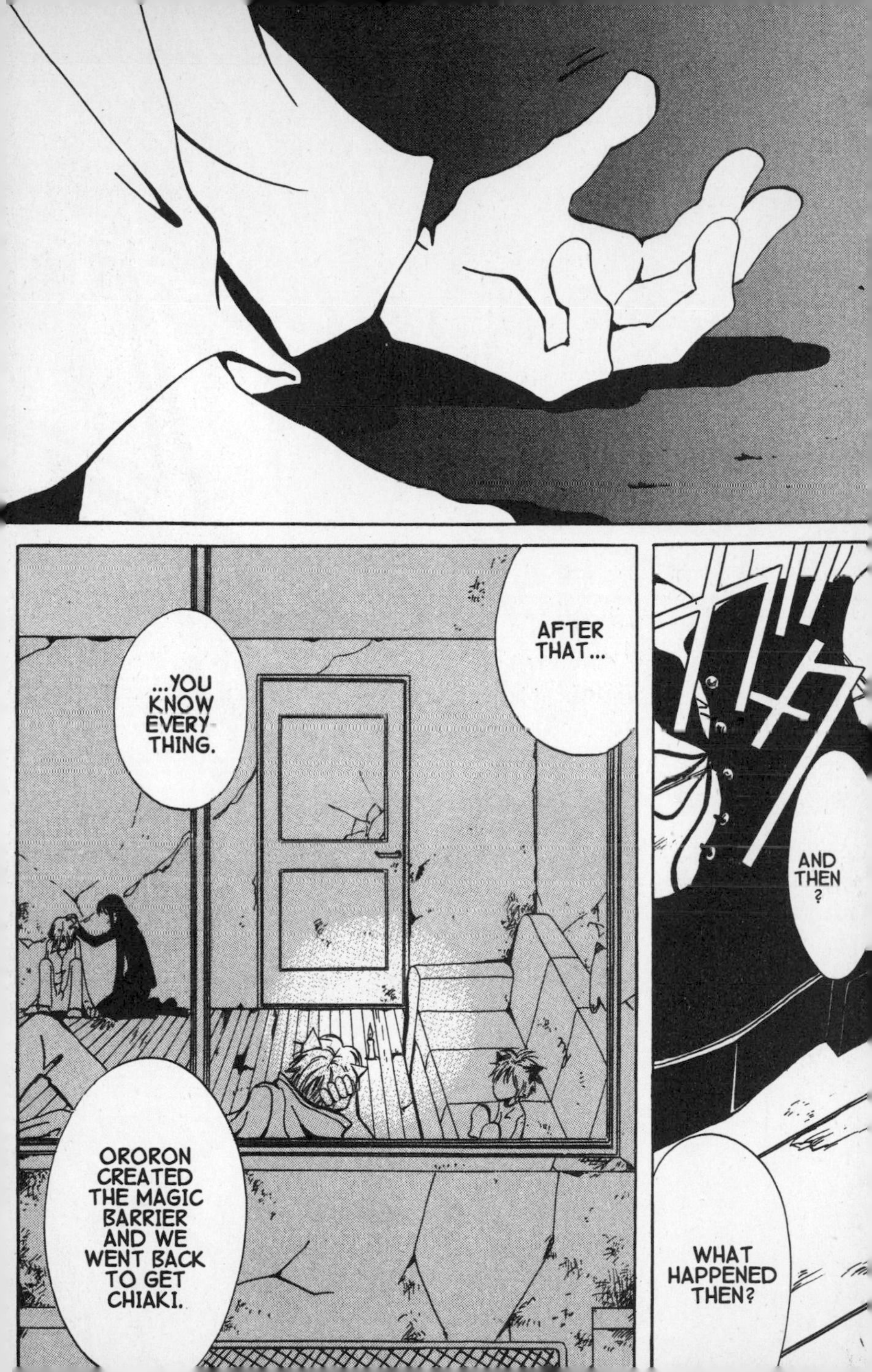
ガタ
AND THEN?
WHAT HAPPENED THEN?
AFTER THAT...
...YOU KNOW EVERYTHING.
ORORON CREATED THE MAGIC BARRIER AND WE WENT BACK TO GET CHIAKI.

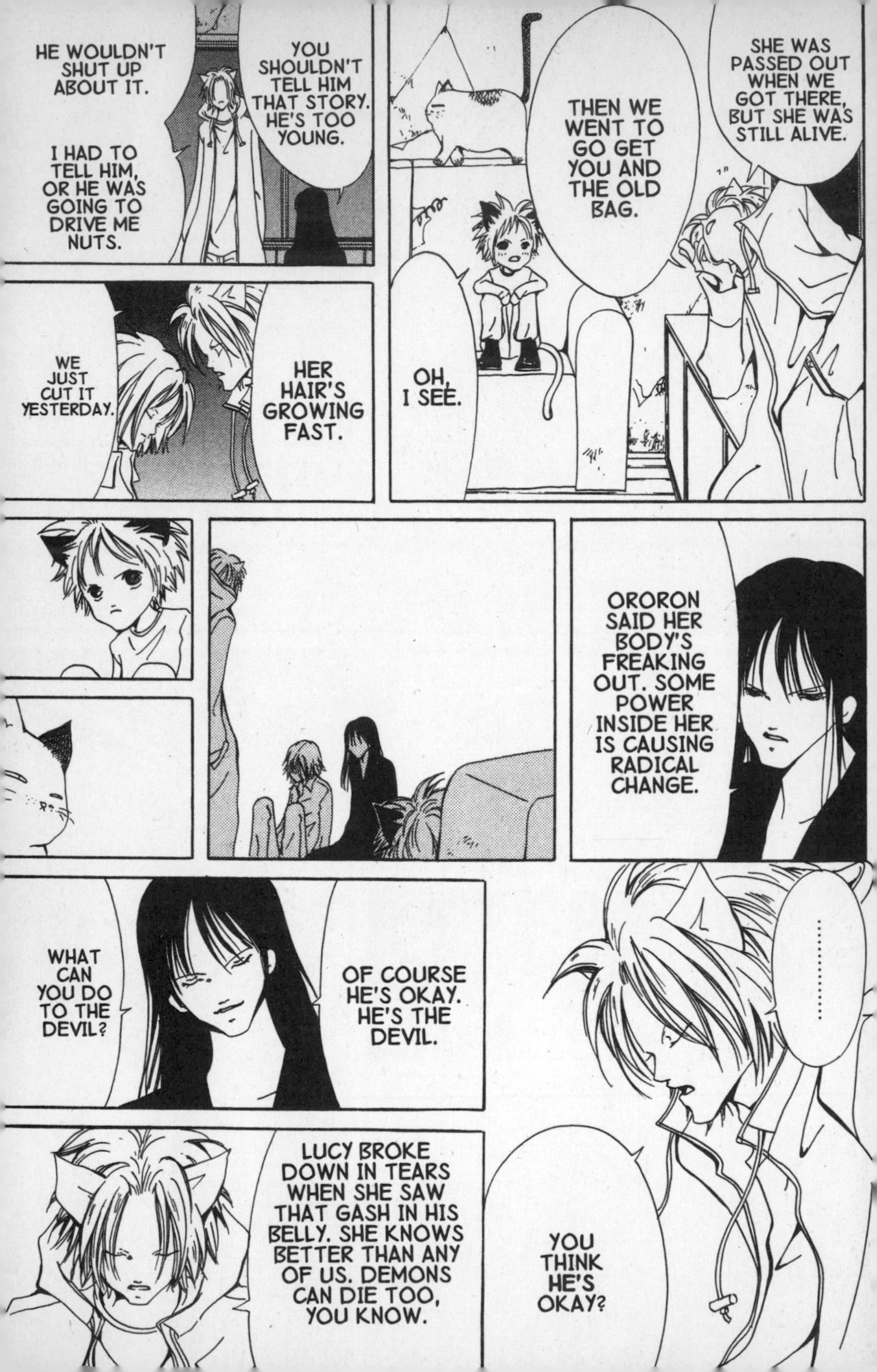
SHE WAS PASSED OUT WHEN WE GOT THERE, BUT SHE WAS STILL ALIVE.
THEN WE WENT TO GO GET YOU AND THE OLD BAG.
OH, I SEE.
YOU SHOULDN'T TELL HIM THAT STORY. HE'S TOO YOUNG.
HE WOULDN'T SHUT UP ABOUT IT.
I HAD TO TELL HIM, OR HE WAS GOING TO DRIVE ME NUTS.
HER HAIR'S GROWING FAST.
WE JUST CUT IT YESTERDAY.
ORORON SAID HER BODY'S FREAKING OUT. SOME POWER INSIDE HER IS CAUSING RADICAL CHANGE.
......
YOU THINK HE'S OKAY?
OF COURSE HE'S OKAY. HE'S THE DEVIL.
WHAT CAN YOU DO TO THE DEVIL?
LUCY BROKE DOWN IN TEARS WHEN SHE SAW THAT GASH IN HIS BELLY. SHE KNOWS BETTER THAN ANY OF US. DEMONS CAN DIE TOO, YOU KNOW.

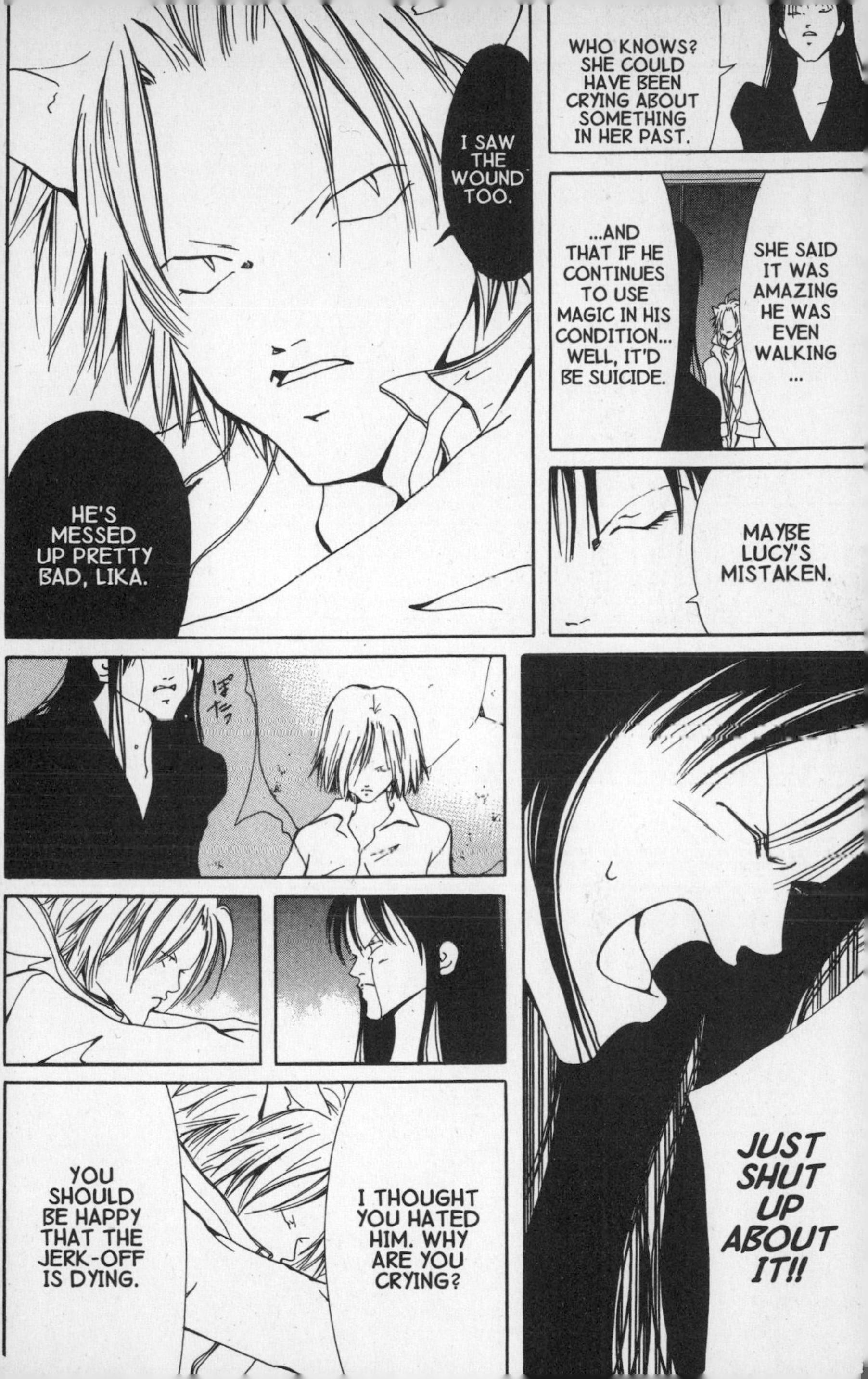
WHO KNOWS? SHE COULD HAVE BEEN CRYING ABOUT SOMETHING IN HER PAST.
SHE SAID IT WAS AMAZING HE WAS EVEN WALKING ...
...AND THAT IF HE CONTINUES TO USE MAGIC IN HIS CONDITION... WELL, IT'D BE SUICIDE.
MAYBE LUCY'S MISTAKEN.
I SAW THE WOUND TOO.
HE'S MESSED UP PRETTY BAD, LIKA.
JUST SHUT UP ABOUT IT!!
ぽた
I THOUGHT YOU HATED HIM. WHY ARE YOU CRYING?
YOU SHOULD BE HAPPY THAT THE JERK-OFF IS DYING.

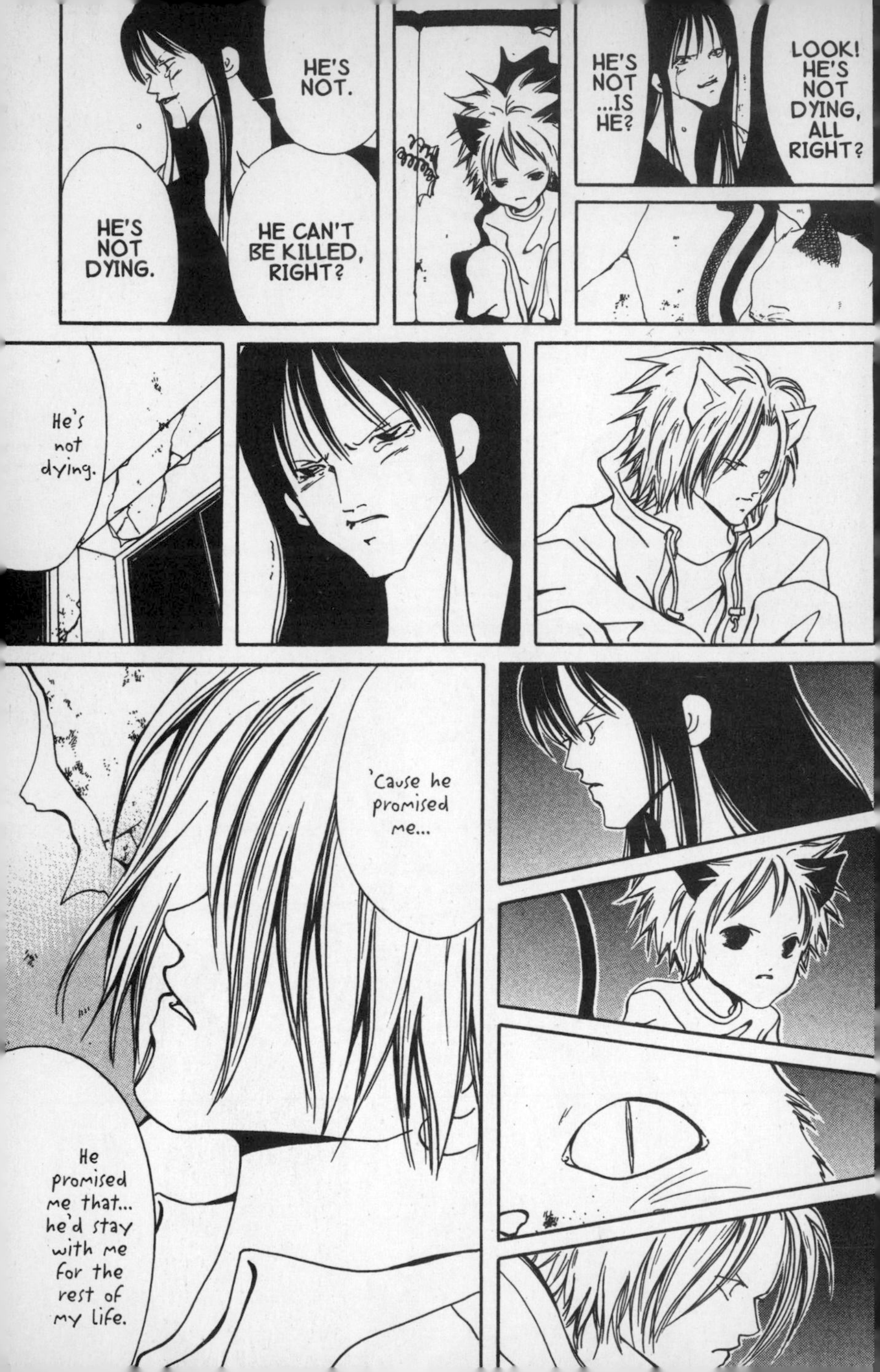
LOOK! HE'S NOT DYING, ALL RIGHT?
HE'S NOT ...IS HE?
HE'S NOT.
HE CAN'T BE KILLED, RIGHT?
HE'S NOT DYING.
He's not dying.
'Cause he promised me...
He promised me that... he'd stay with me for the rest of my life.

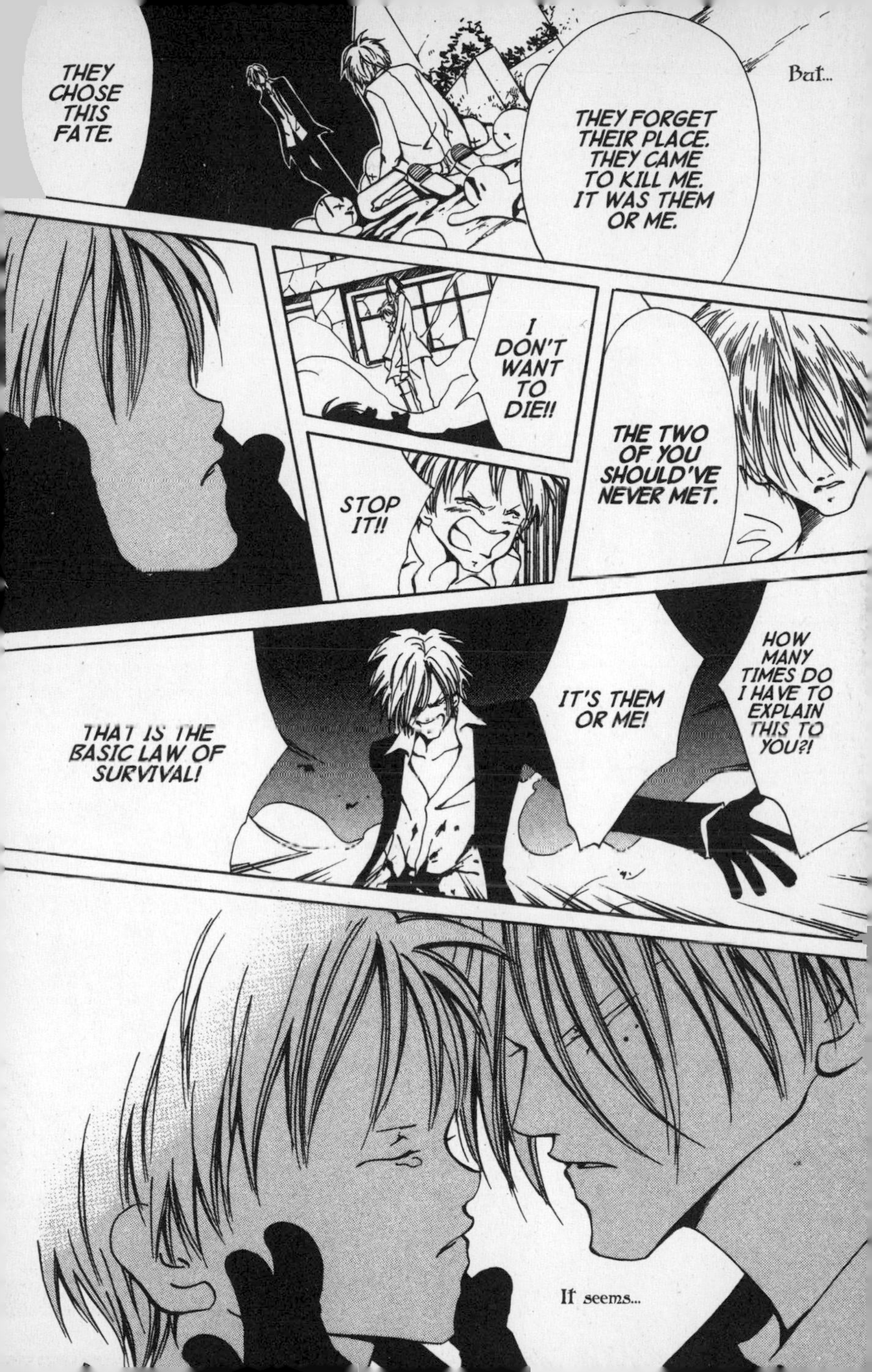

But...
THEY FORGET THEIR PLACE. THEY CAME TO KILL ME. IT WAS THEM OR ME.
THEY CHOSE THIS FATE.
THE TWO OF YOU SHOULD'VE NEVER MET.
I DON'T WANT TO DIE!!
STOP IT!!
HOW MANY TIMES DO I HAVE TO EXPLAIN THIS TO YOU?!
IT'S THEM OR ME!
THAT IS THE BASIC LAW OF SURVIVAL!
It seems...

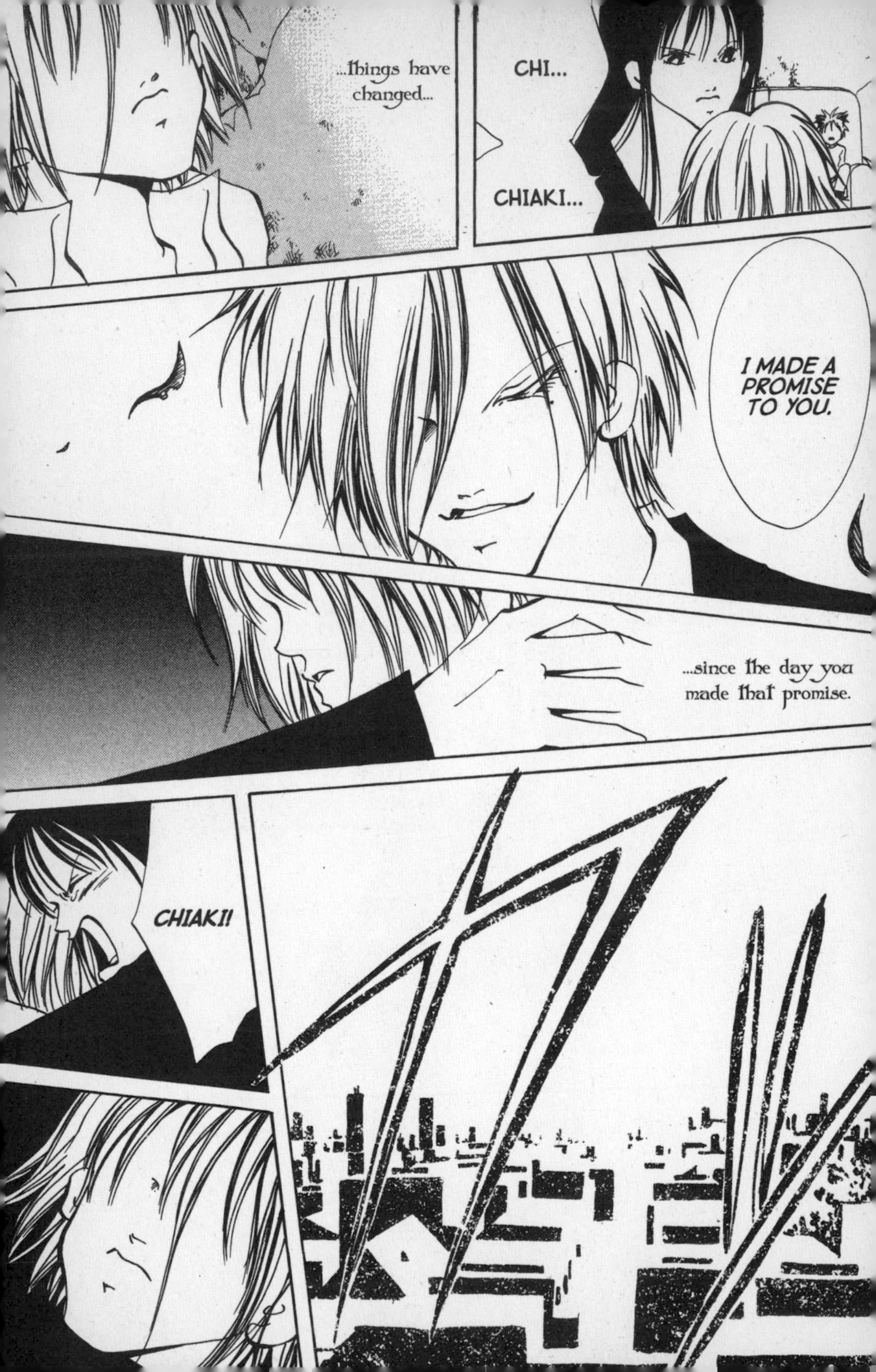
CHI...
CHIAKI...
...things have changed...
I MADE A PROMISE TO YOU.
...since the day you made that promise.
CHIAKI!

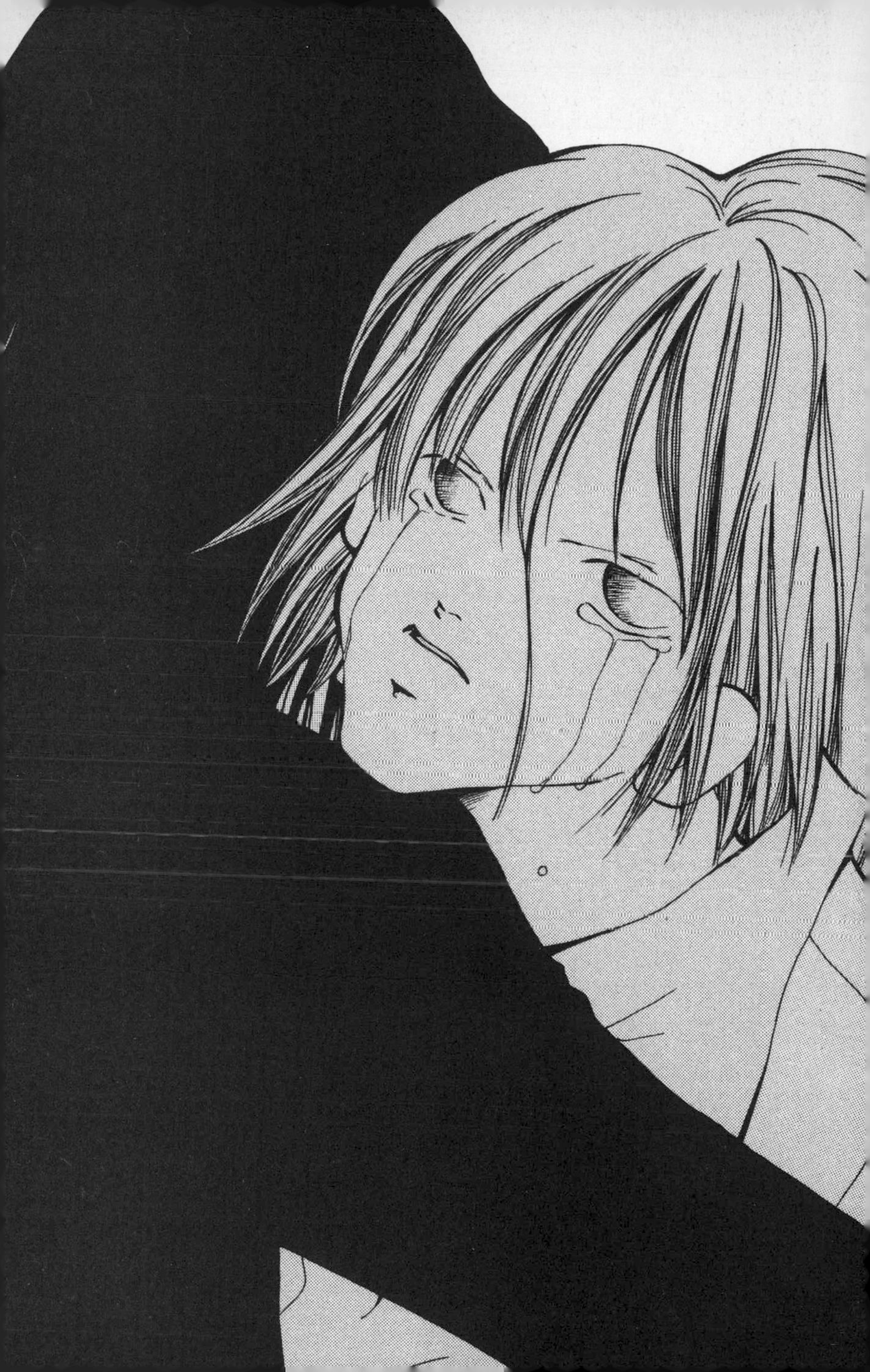

Changed way too much...

...to keep any promise.

THE BLOOD...

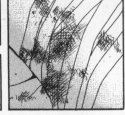

HE WON'T STOP BLEEDING.

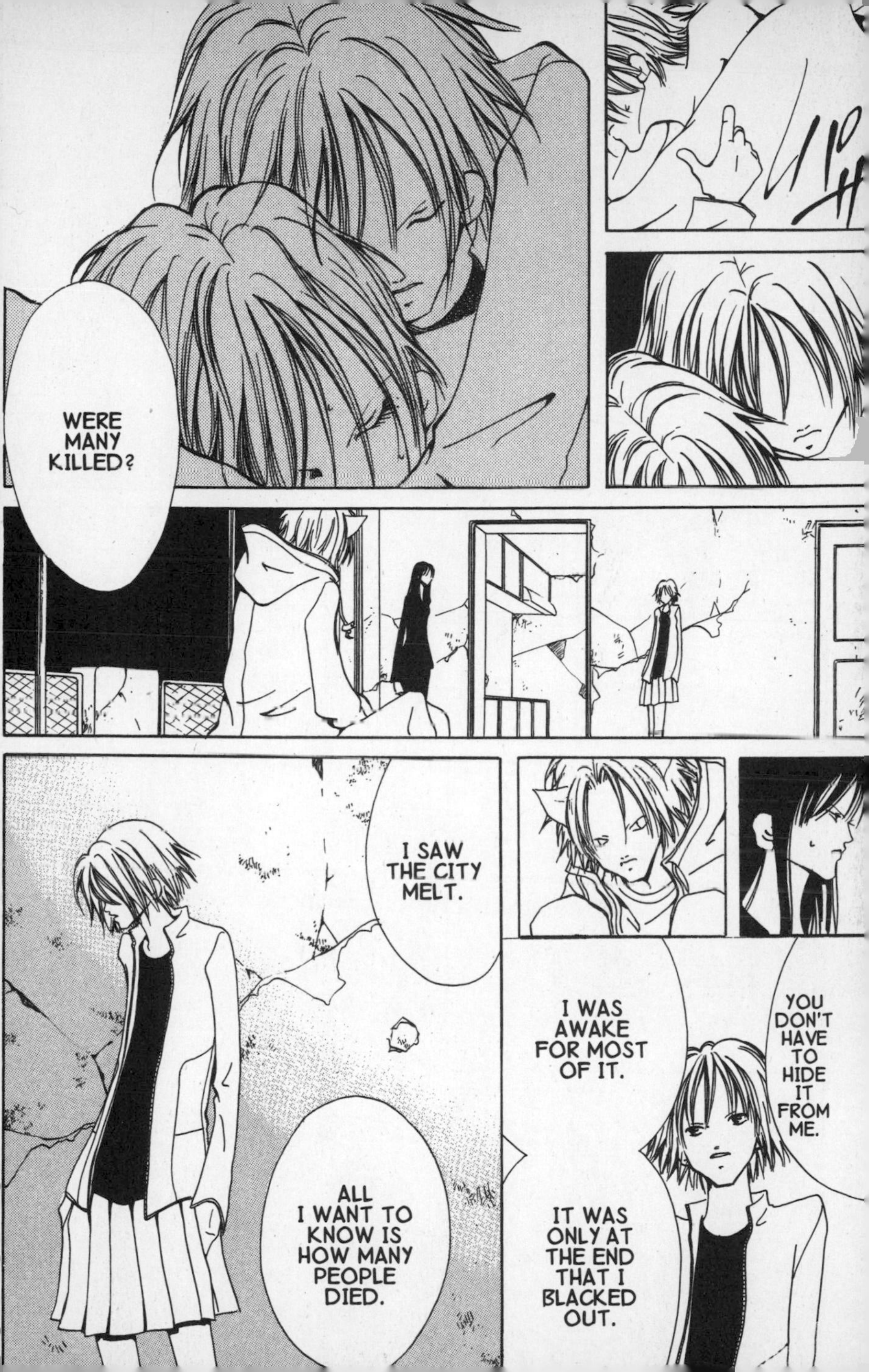

パサ
WERE MANY KILLED?
YOU DON'T HAVE TO HIDE IT FROM ME.
I WAS AWAKE FOR MOST OF IT.
IT WAS ONLY AT THE END THAT I BLACKED OUT.
I SAW THE CITY MELT.
ALL I WANT TO KNOW IS HOW MANY PEOPLE DIED.

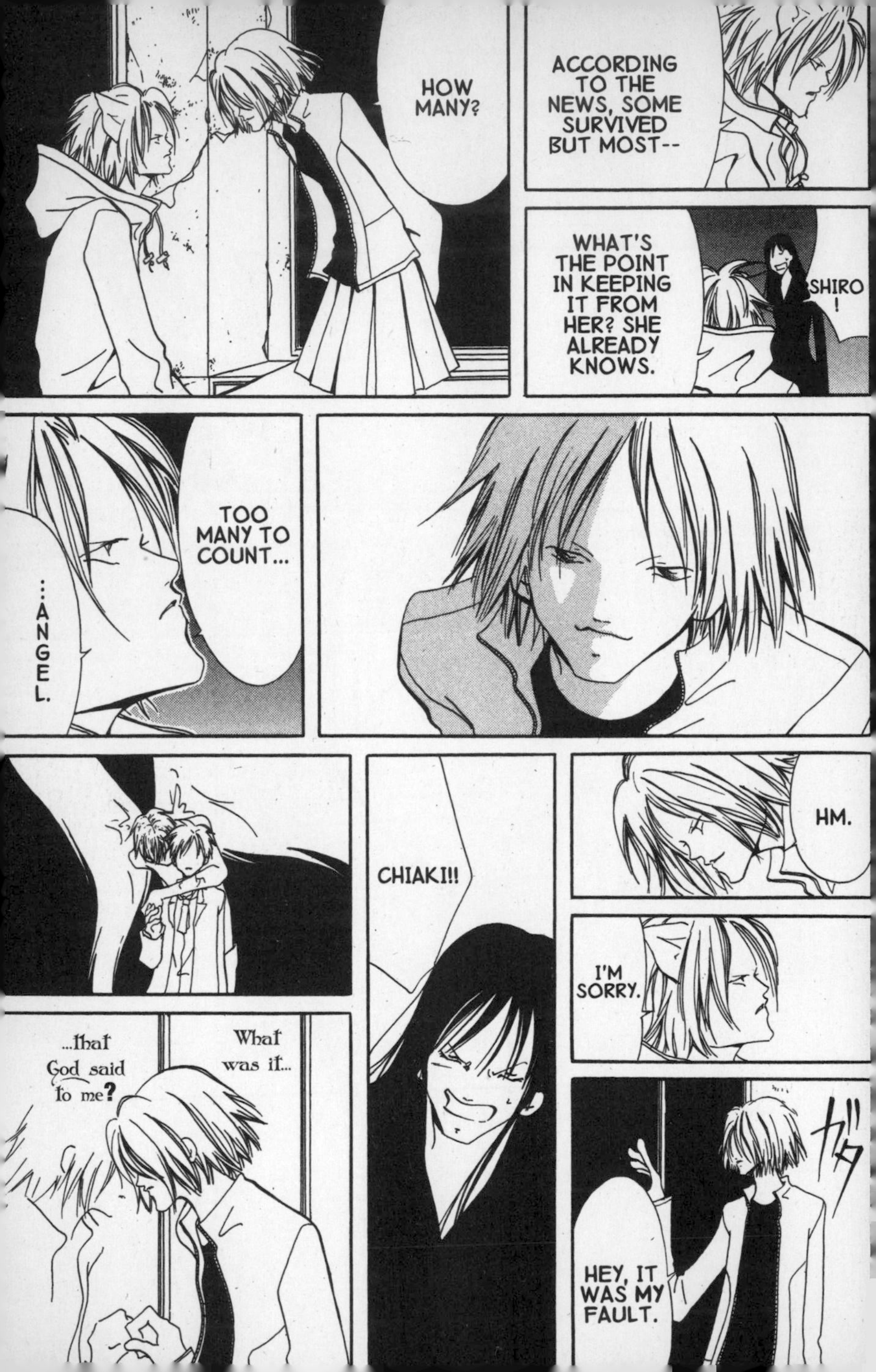
ACCORDING TO THE NEWS, SOME SURVIVED BUT MOST--
WHAT'S THE POINT IN KEEPING IT FROM HER? SHE ALREADY KNOWS.
SHIRO!
HOW MANY?
TOO MANY TO COUNT...
...ANGEL.
HM.
I'M SORRY.
ガタ
HEY, IT WAS MY FAULT.
CHIAKI!!
What was it...
...that God said to me?

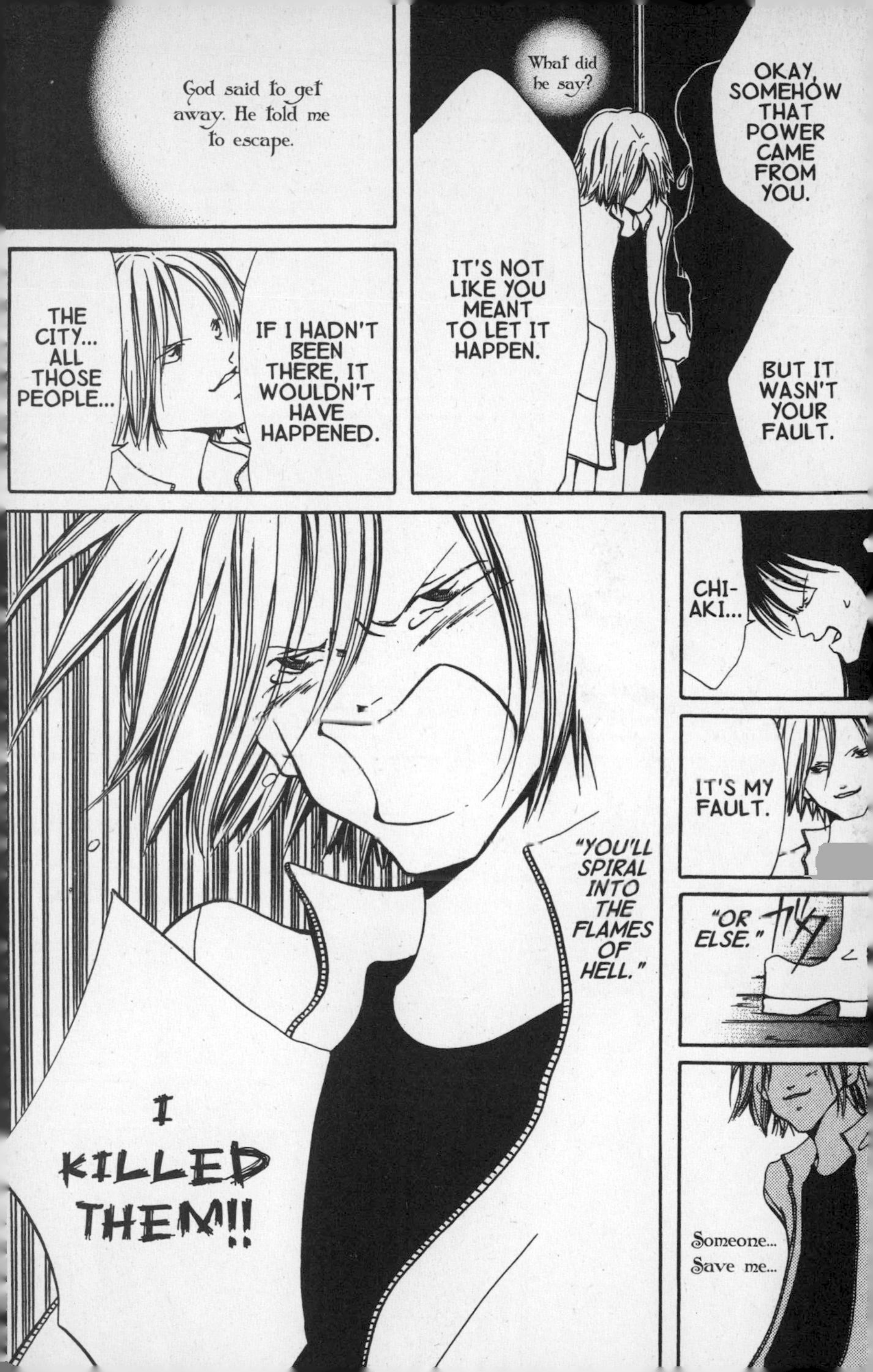
OKAY, SOMEHOW THAT POWER CAME FROM YOU.
What did he say?
IT'S NOT LIKE YOU MEANT TO LET IT HAPPEN.
BUT IT WASN'T YOUR FAULT.
God said to get away. He told me to escape.
IF I HADN'T BEEN THERE, IT WOULDN'T HAVE HAPPENED.
THE CITY... ALL THOSE PEOPLE...
CHI-AKI...
IT'S MY FAULT.
"OR ELSE."
Someone... Save me...
"YOU'LL SPIRAL INTO THE FLAMES OF HELL."
I KILLED THEM!!

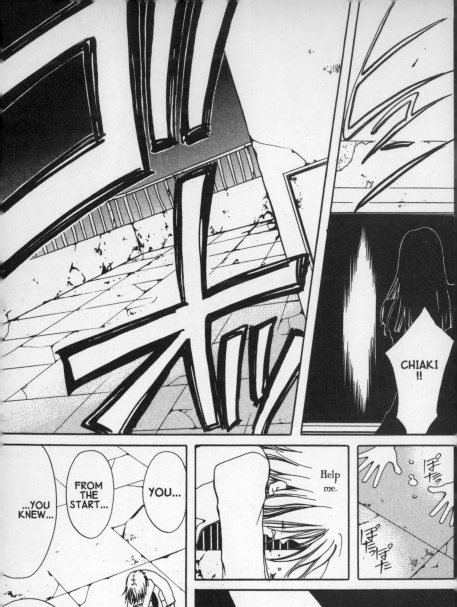

CHIAKI!!

...YOU KNEW...

FROM THE START...

YOU...

Help me.

...WHAT WAS GOING TO HAPPEN.

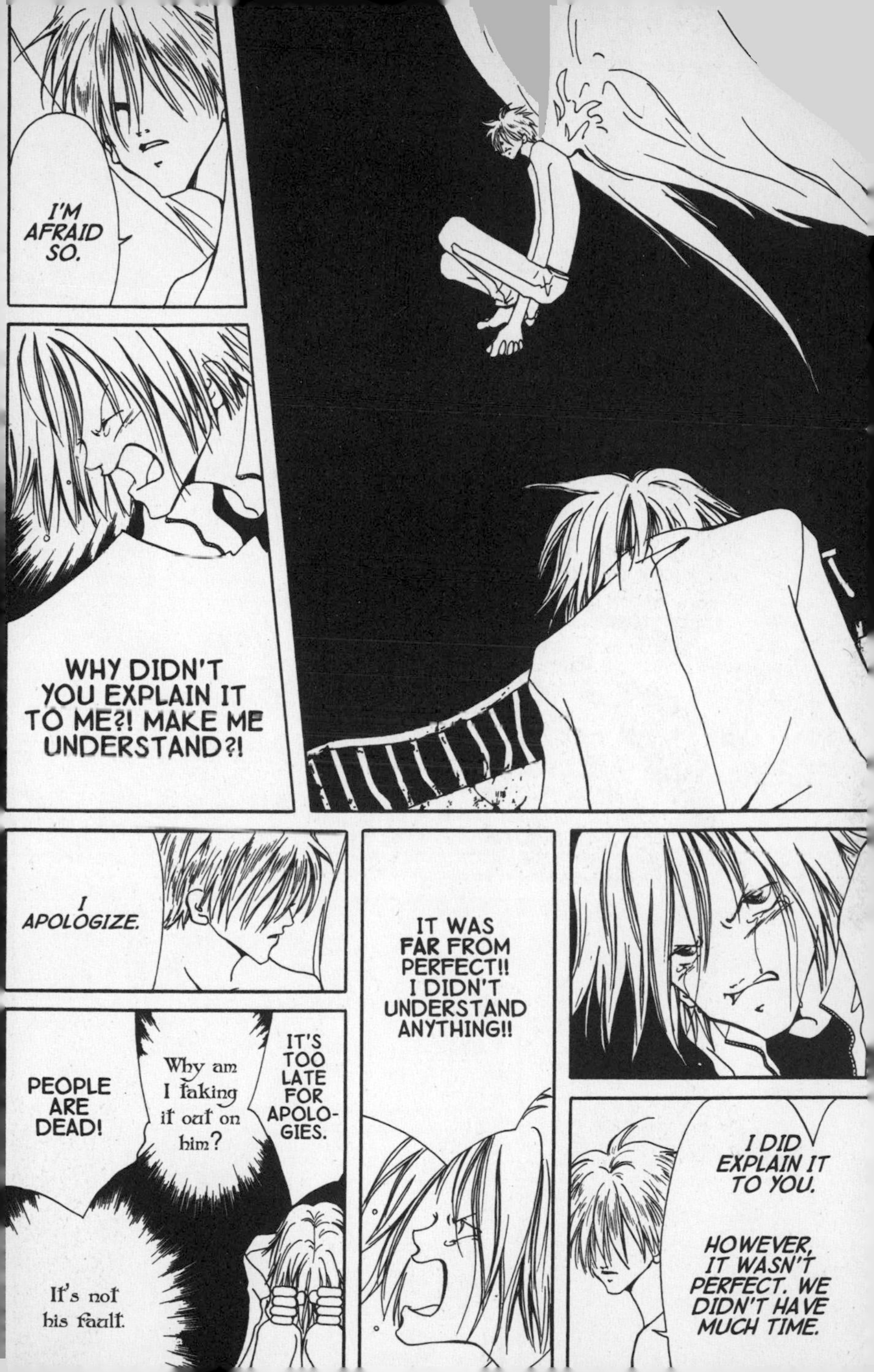
I'M AFRAID SO.
WHY DIDN'T YOU EXPLAIN IT TO ME?! MAKE ME UNDERSTAND?!
I DID EXPLAIN IT TO YOU.
HOWEVER, IT WASN'T PERFECT. WE DIDN'T HAVE MUCH TIME.
IT WAS FAR FROM PERFECT!! I DIDN'T UNDERSTAND ANYTHING!!
I APOLOGIZE.
IT'S TOO LATE FOR APOLOGIES.
Why am I taking it out on him?
PEOPLE ARE DEAD!
It's not his fault.

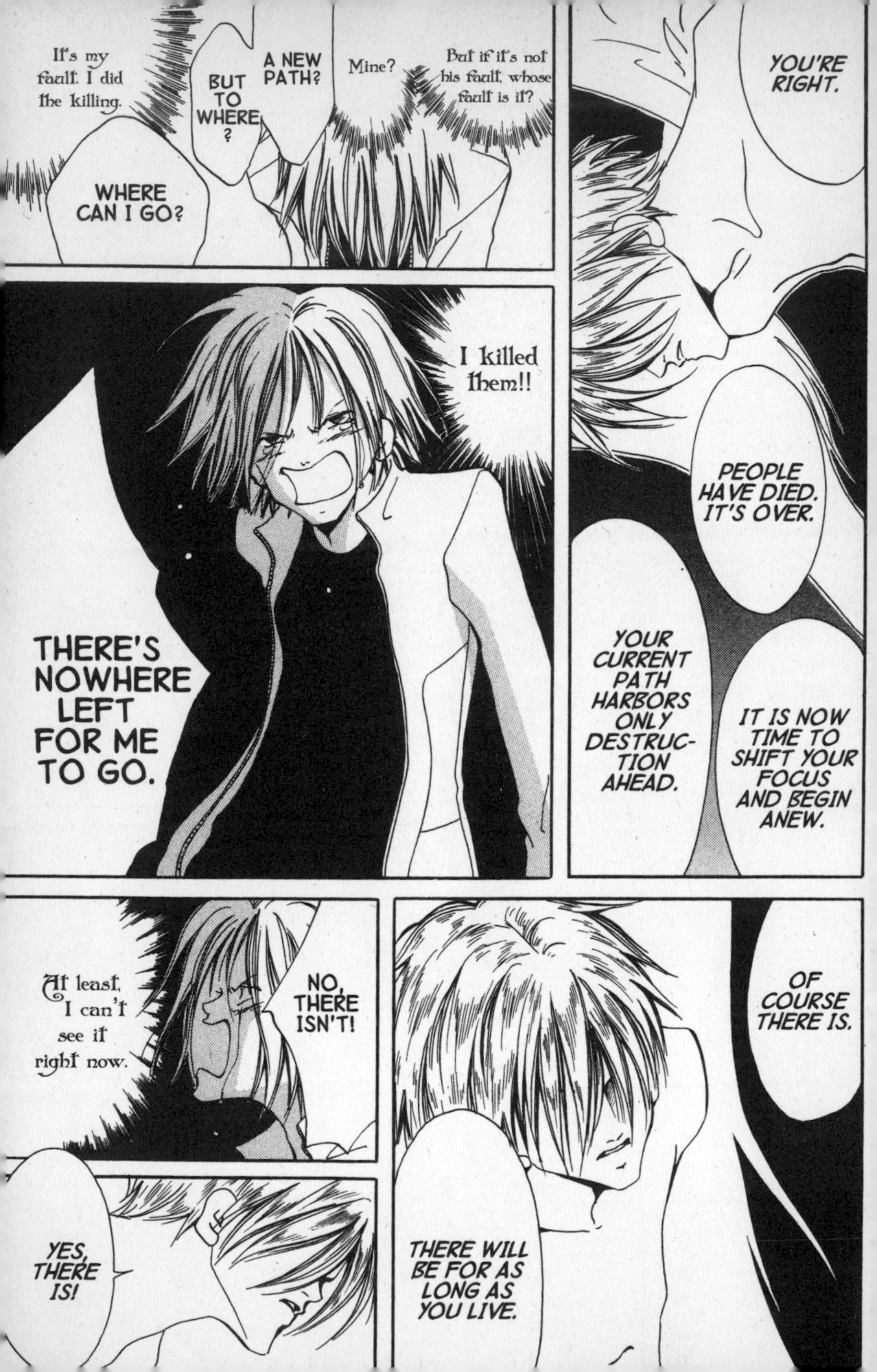
YOU'RE RIGHT.
PEOPLE HAVE DIED. IT'S OVER.
YOUR CURRENT PATH HARBORS ONLY DESTRUCTION AHEAD.
IT IS NOW TIME TO SHIFT YOUR FOCUS AND BEGIN ANEW.
But if it's not his fault, whose fault is it?
Mine?
A NEW PATH?
BUT TO WHERE?
It's my fault. I did the killing.
WHERE CAN I GO?
I killed them!!
THERE'S NOWHERE LEFT FOR ME TO GO.
OF COURSE THERE IS.
THERE WILL BE FOR AS LONG AS YOU LIVE.
NO, THERE ISN'T!
At least, I can't see it right now.
YES, THERE IS!

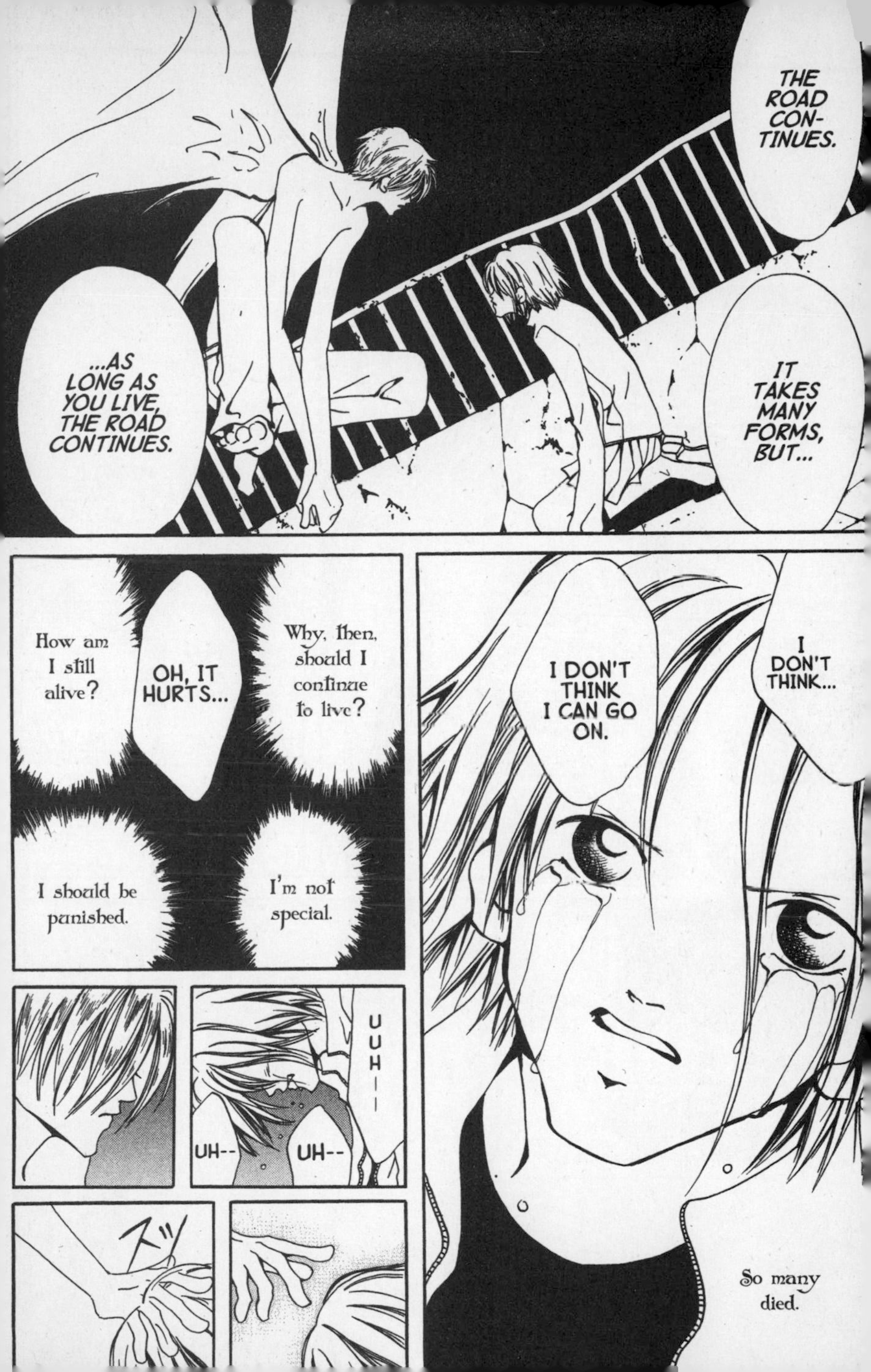
THE ROAD CON-TINUES.
IT TAKES MANY FORMS, BUT...
...AS LONG AS YOU LIVE, THE ROAD CONTINUES.
I DON'T THINK...
I DON'T THINK I CAN GO ON.
So many died.
Why, then, should I continue to live?
OH, IT HURTS...
How am I still alive?
I'm not special.
I should be punished.
UUH--
UH--
UH--
ズッ

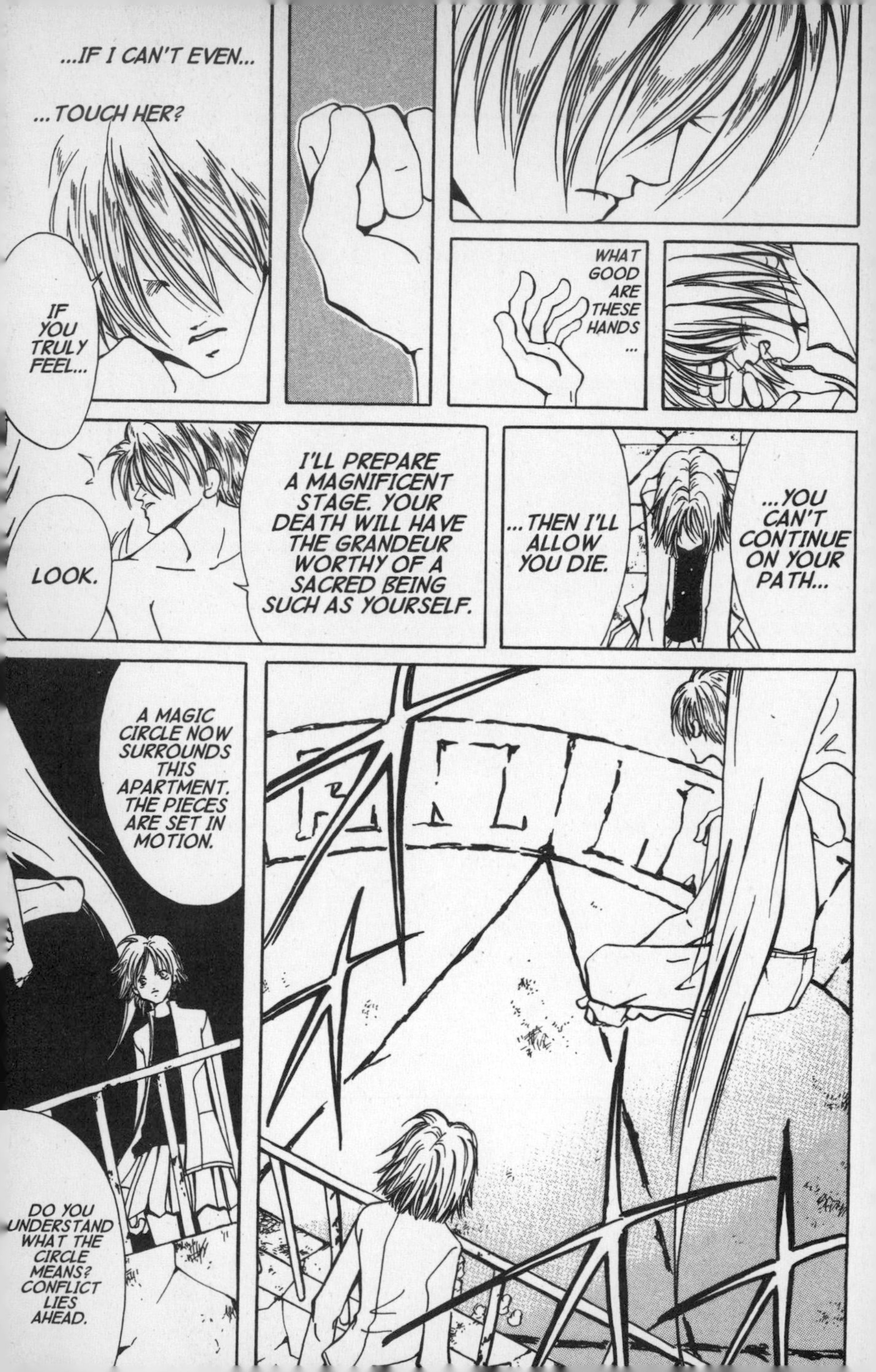
WHAT GOOD ARE THESE HANDS...
...IF I CAN'T EVEN...
...TOUCH HER?
IF YOU TRULY FEEL...
...YOU CAN'T CONTINUE ON YOUR PATH...
...THEN I'LL ALLOW YOU DIE.
I'LL PREPARE A MAGNIFICENT STAGE. YOUR DEATH WILL HAVE THE GRANDEUR WORTHY OF A SACRED BEING SUCH AS YOURSELF.
LOOK.
A MAGIC CIRCLE NOW SURROUNDS THIS APARTMENT. THE PIECES ARE SET IN MOTION.
DO YOU UNDERSTAND WHAT THE CIRCLE MEANS? CONFLICT LIES AHEAD.

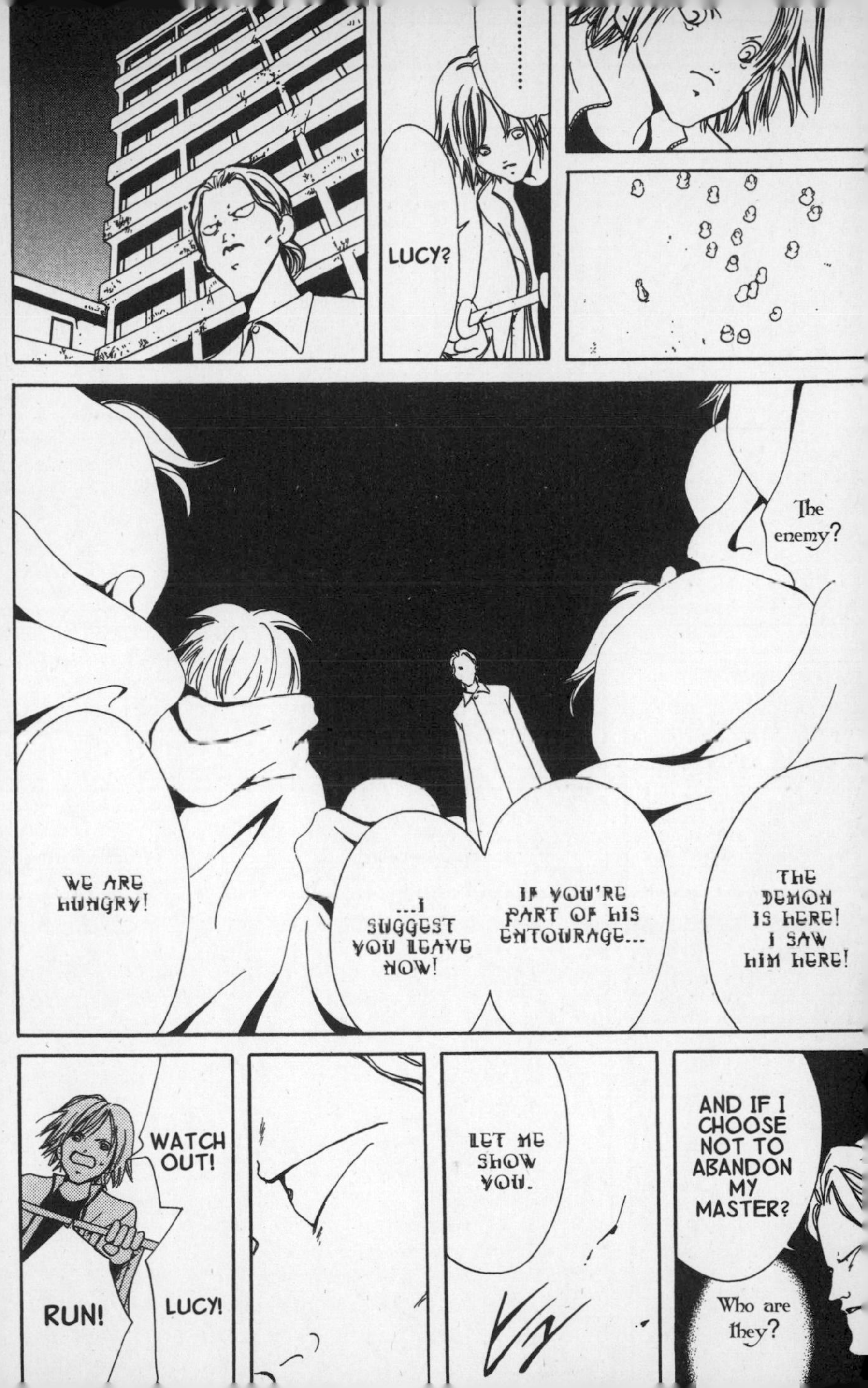
LUCY?
The enemy?
THE DEMON IS HERE! I SAW HIM HERE!
IF YOU'RE PART OF HIS ENTOURAGE...
...I SUGGEST YOU LEAVE NOW!
WE ARE HUNGRY!
AND IF I CHOOSE NOT TO ABANDON MY MASTER?
Who are they?
LET ME SHOW YOU.
WATCH OUT!
LUCY!
RUN!

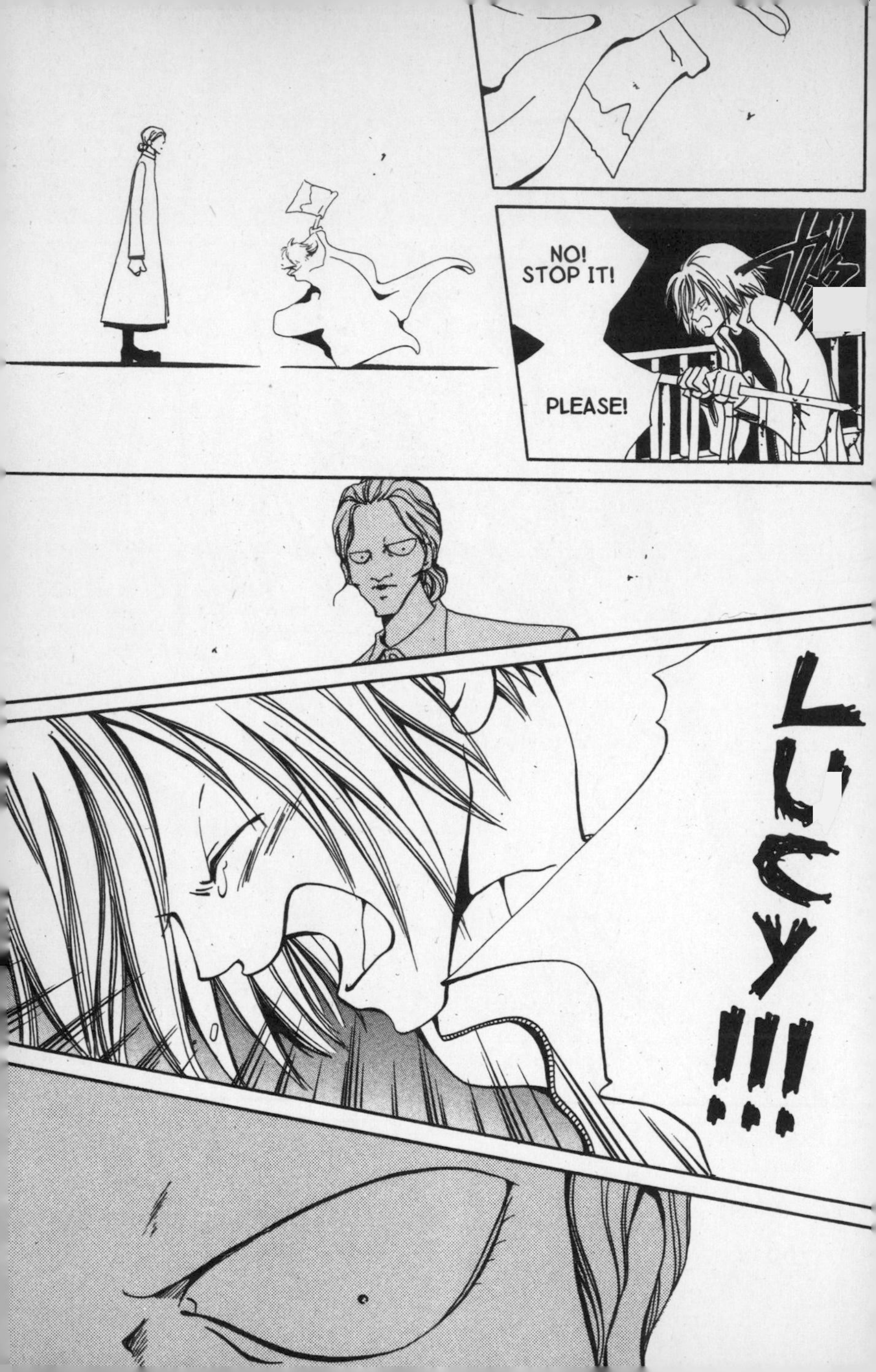
NO! STOP IT!
PLEASE!
LUCY!!!

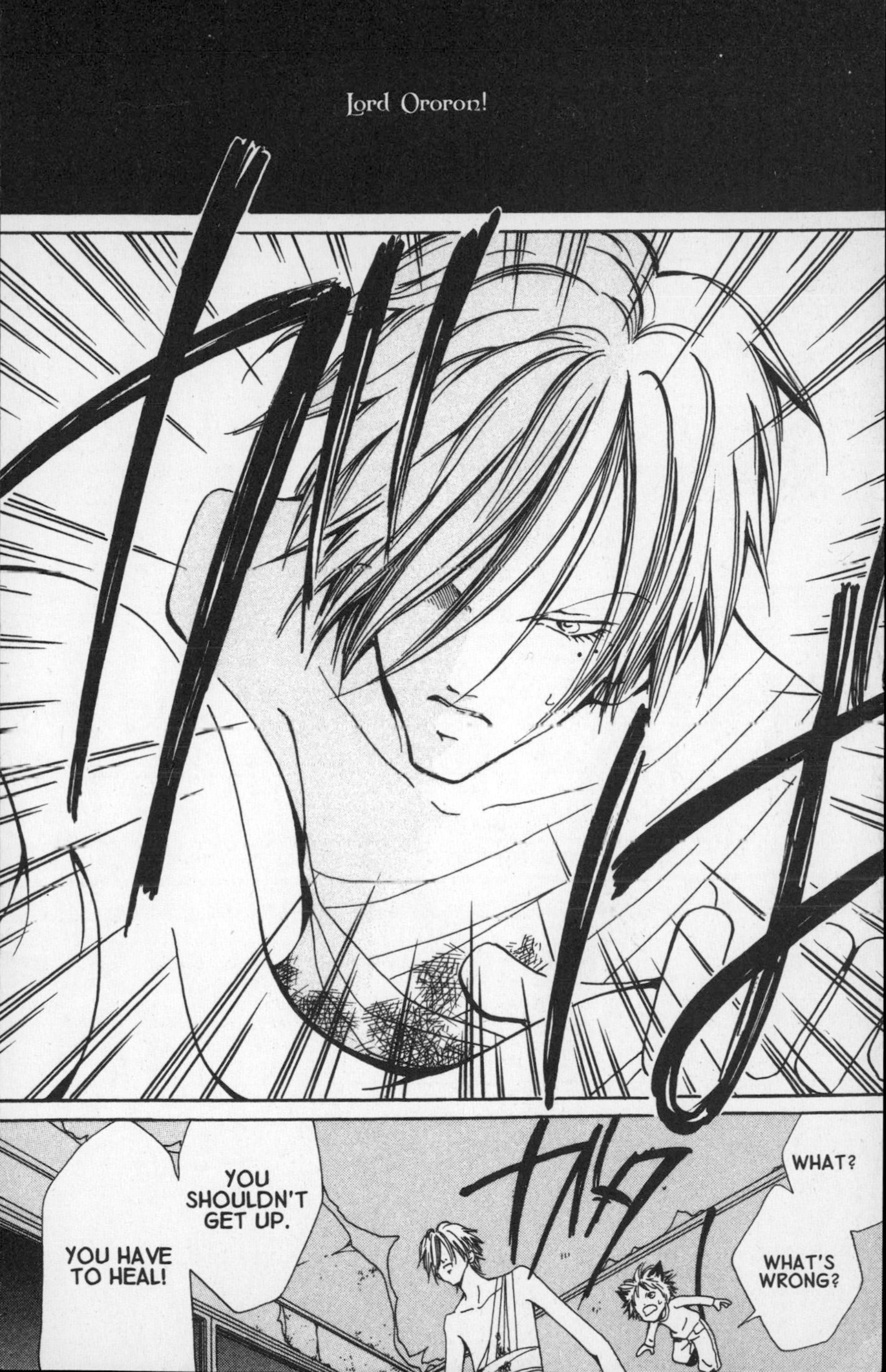
Lord Ororon!
WHAT?
WHAT'S WRONG?
YOU SHOULDN'T GET UP.
YOU HAVE TO HEAL!

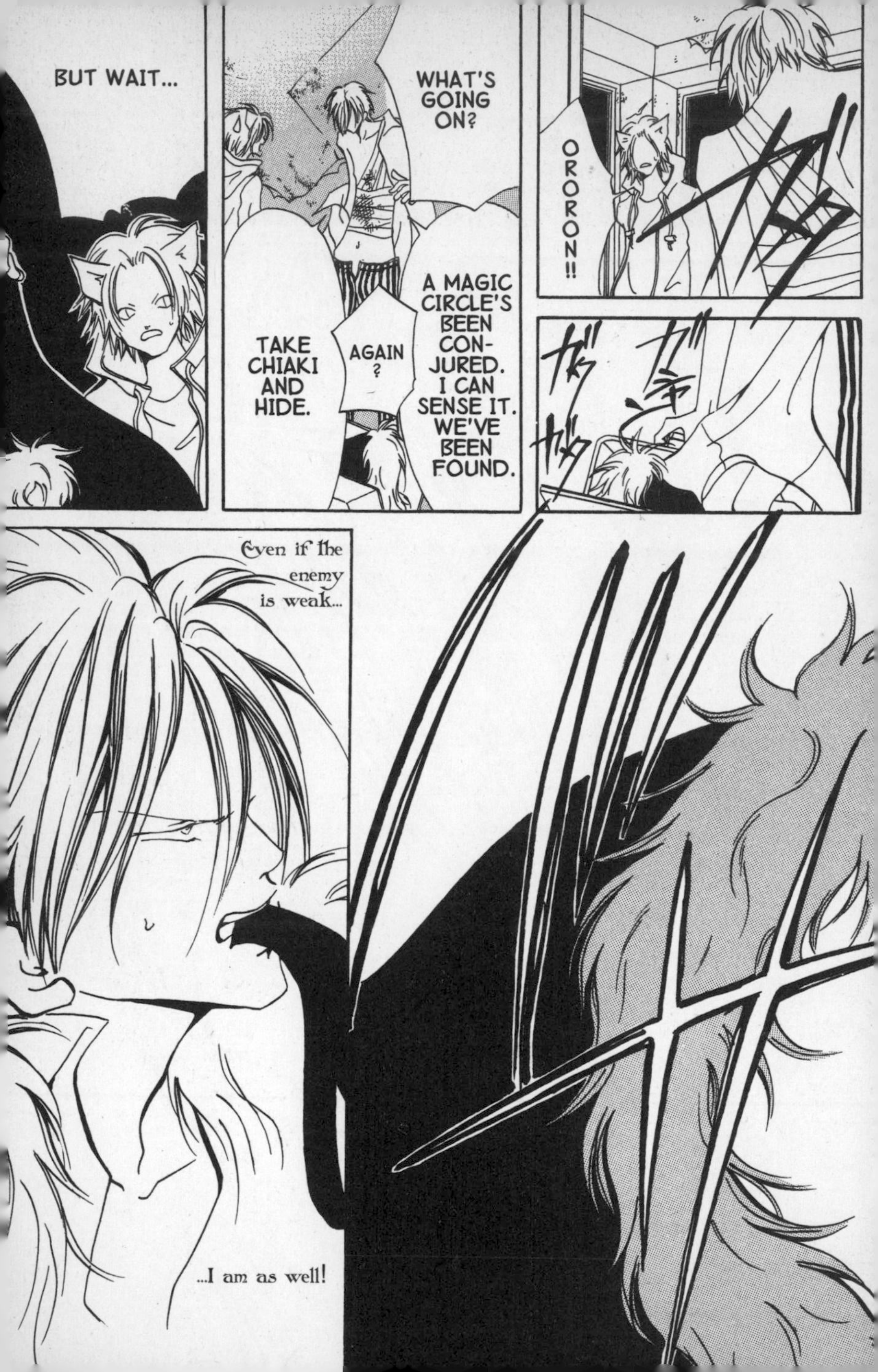
ORORON!!
WHAT'S GOING ON?
A MAGIC CIRCLE'S BEEN CON-JURED. I CAN SENSE IT. WE'VE BEEN FOUND.
AGAIN?
TAKE CHIAKI AND HIDE.
BUT WAIT...
Even if the enemy is weak...
...I am as well!

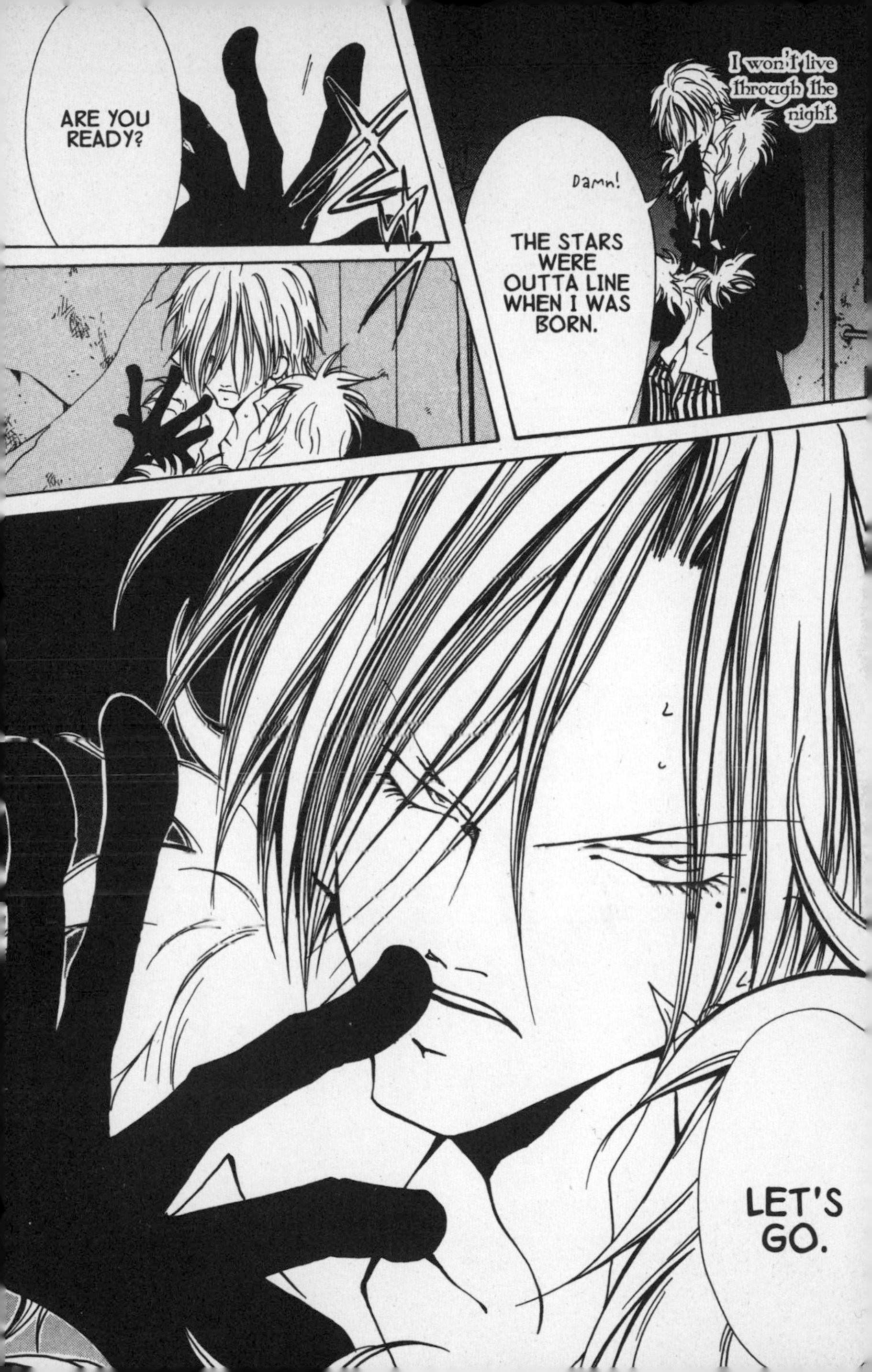
I won't live through the night.
Damn!
THE STARS WERE OUTTA LINE WHEN I WAS BORN.
ARE YOU READY?
LET'S GO.

-12-
STRANGE LOYALTY

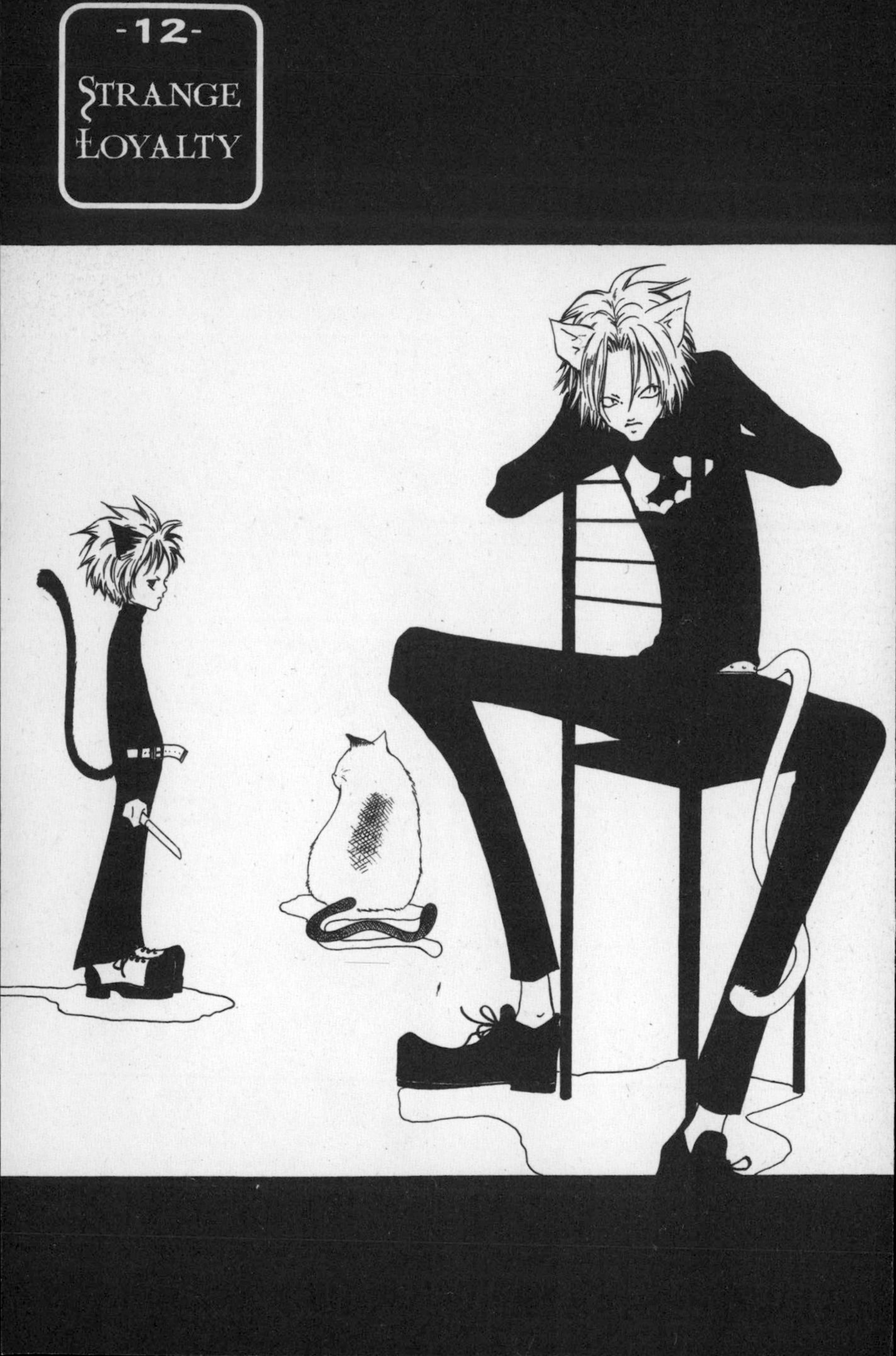

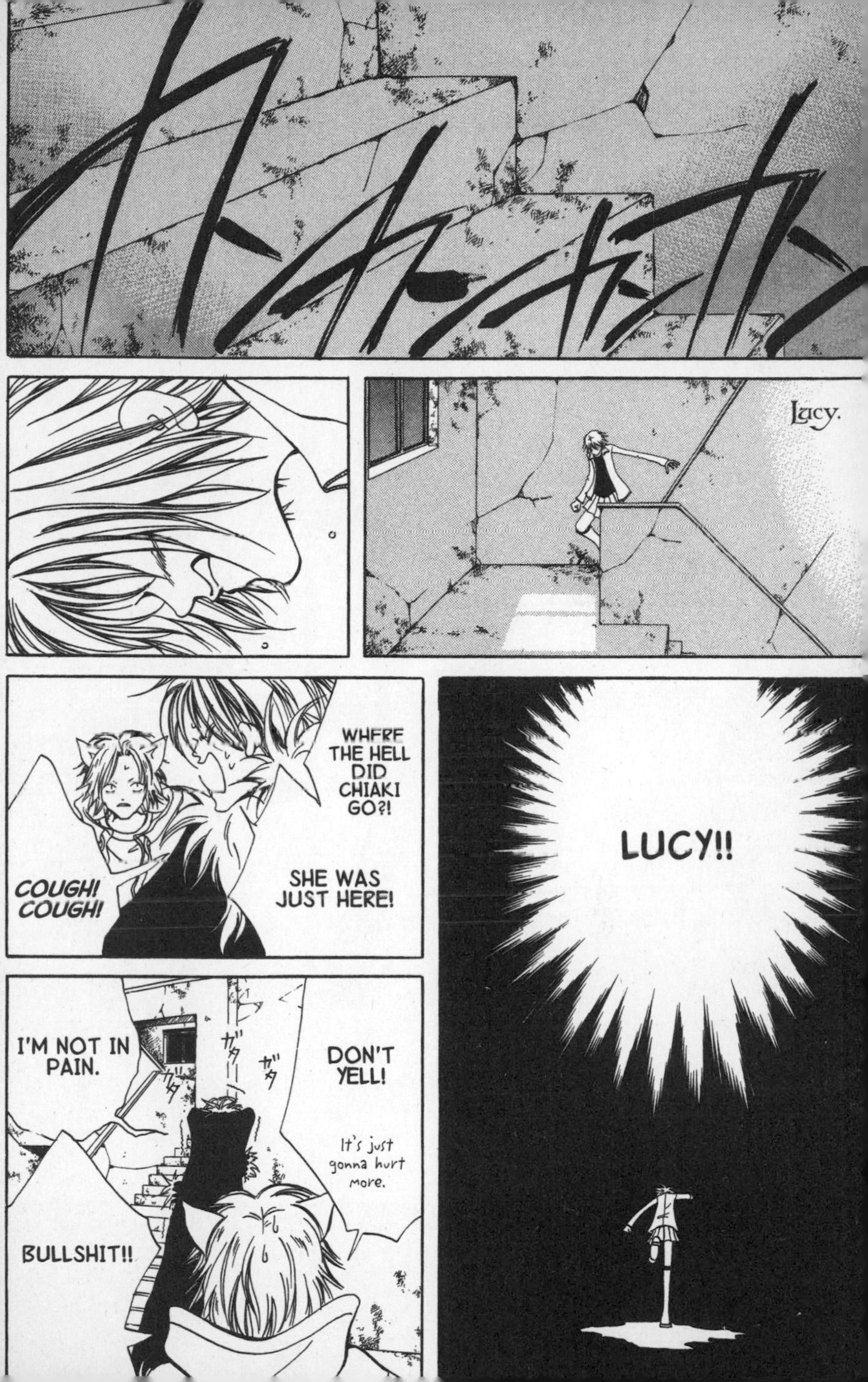
Lucy.
LUCY!!
WHERE THE HELL DID CHIAKI GO?!
SHE WAS JUST HERE!
COUGH! COUGH!
DON'T YELL!
It's just gonna hurt more.
ガタ ガタ
I'M NOT IN PAIN.
BULLSHIT!!

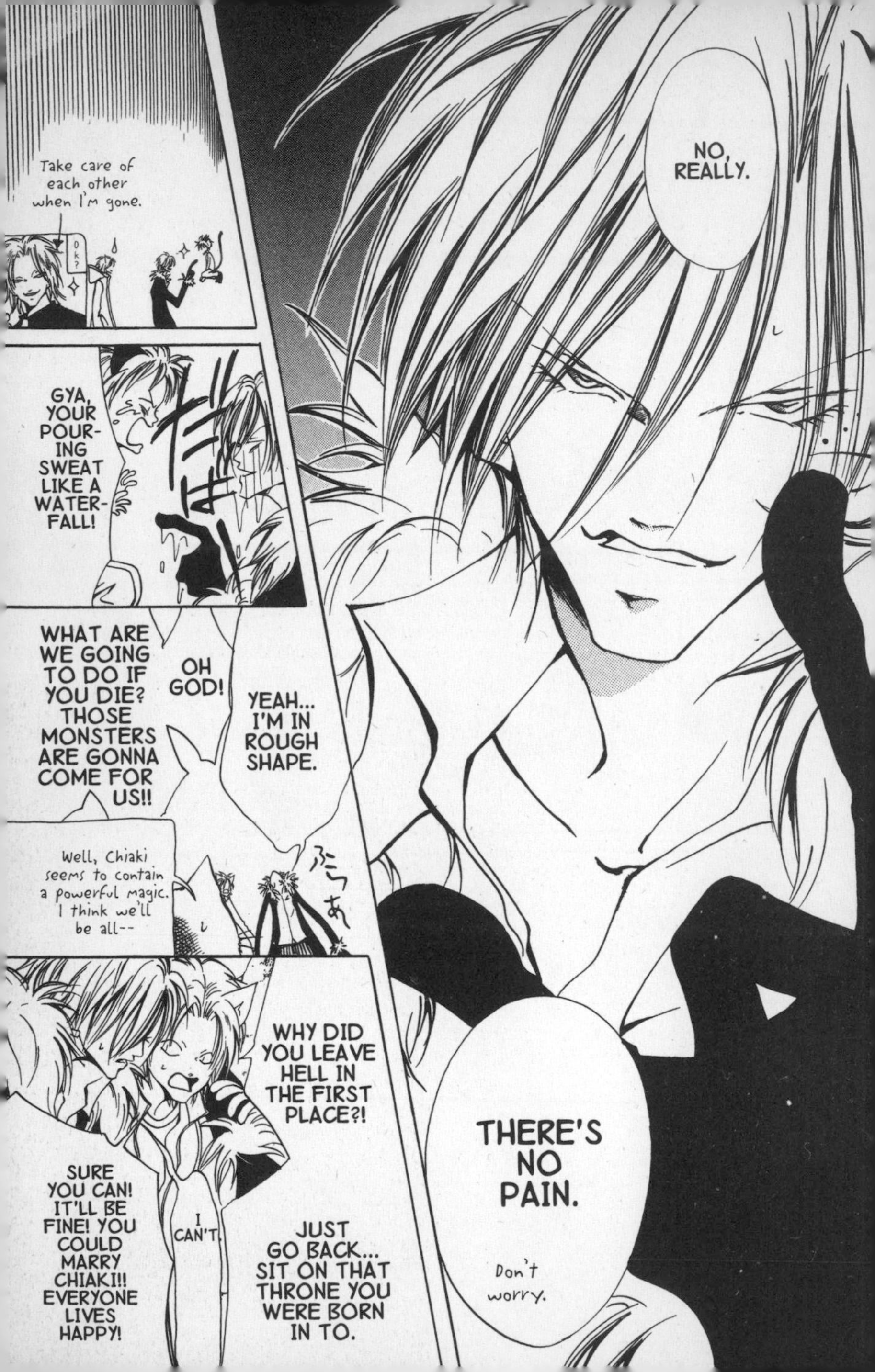
NO, REALLY.
THERE'S NO PAIN.
Don't worry.
Take care of each other when I'm gone.
Ok?
GYA, YOUR POURING SWEAT LIKE A WATERFALL!
YEAH... I'M IN ROUGH SHAPE.
OH GOD!
WHAT ARE WE GOING TO DO IF YOU DIE? THOSE MONSTERS ARE GONNA COME FOR US!!
ふらあ
Well, Chiaki seems to contain a powerful magic. I think we'll be all--
WHY DID YOU LEAVE HELL IN THE FIRST PLACE?!
JUST GO BACK... SIT ON THAT THRONE YOU WERE BORN IN TO.
I CAN'T.
SURE YOU CAN! IT'LL BE FINE! YOU COULD MARRY CHIAKI!! EVERYONE LIVES HAPPY!

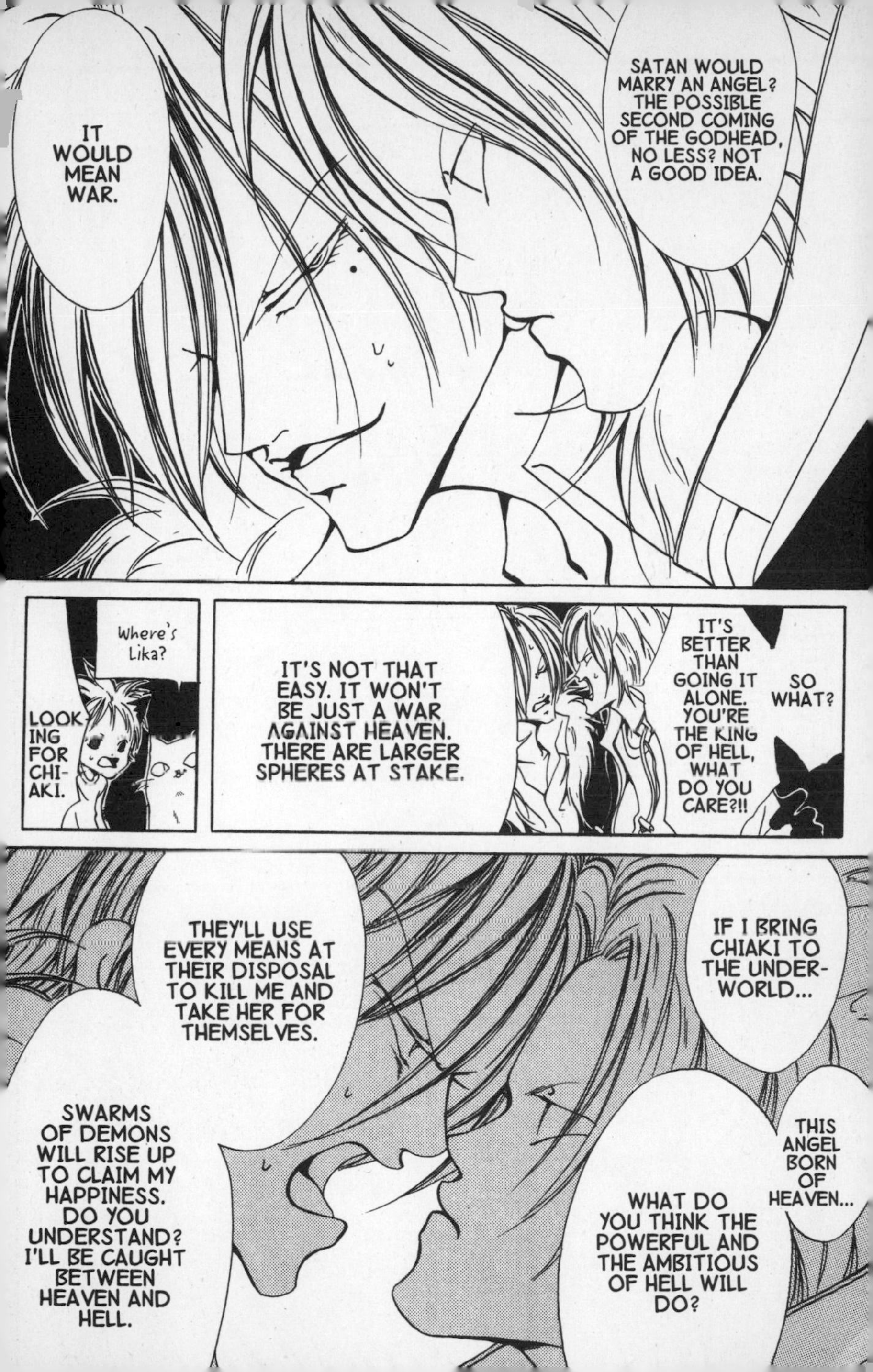
SATAN WOULD MARRY AN ANGEL? THE POSSIBLE SECOND COMING OF THE GODHEAD, NO LESS? NOT A GOOD IDEA.
IT WOULD MEAN WAR.
SO WHAT?
IT'S BETTER THAN GOING IT ALONE. YOU'RE THE KING OF HELL, WHAT DO YOU CARE?!!
IT'S NOT THAT EASY. IT WON'T BE JUST A WAR AGAINST HEAVEN. THERE ARE LARGER SPHERES AT STAKE.
Where's Lika?
LOOKING FOR CHIAKI.
IF I BRING CHIAKI TO THE UNDERWORLD...
THIS ANGEL BORN OF HEAVEN...
WHAT DO YOU THINK THE POWERFUL AND THE AMBITIOUS OF HELL WILL DO?
THEY'LL USE EVERY MEANS AT THEIR DISPOSAL TO KILL ME AND TAKE HER FOR THEMSELVES.
SWARMS OF DEMONS WILL RISE UP TO CLAIM MY HAPPINESS. DO YOU UNDERSTAND? I'LL BE CAUGHT BETWEEN HEAVEN AND HELL.

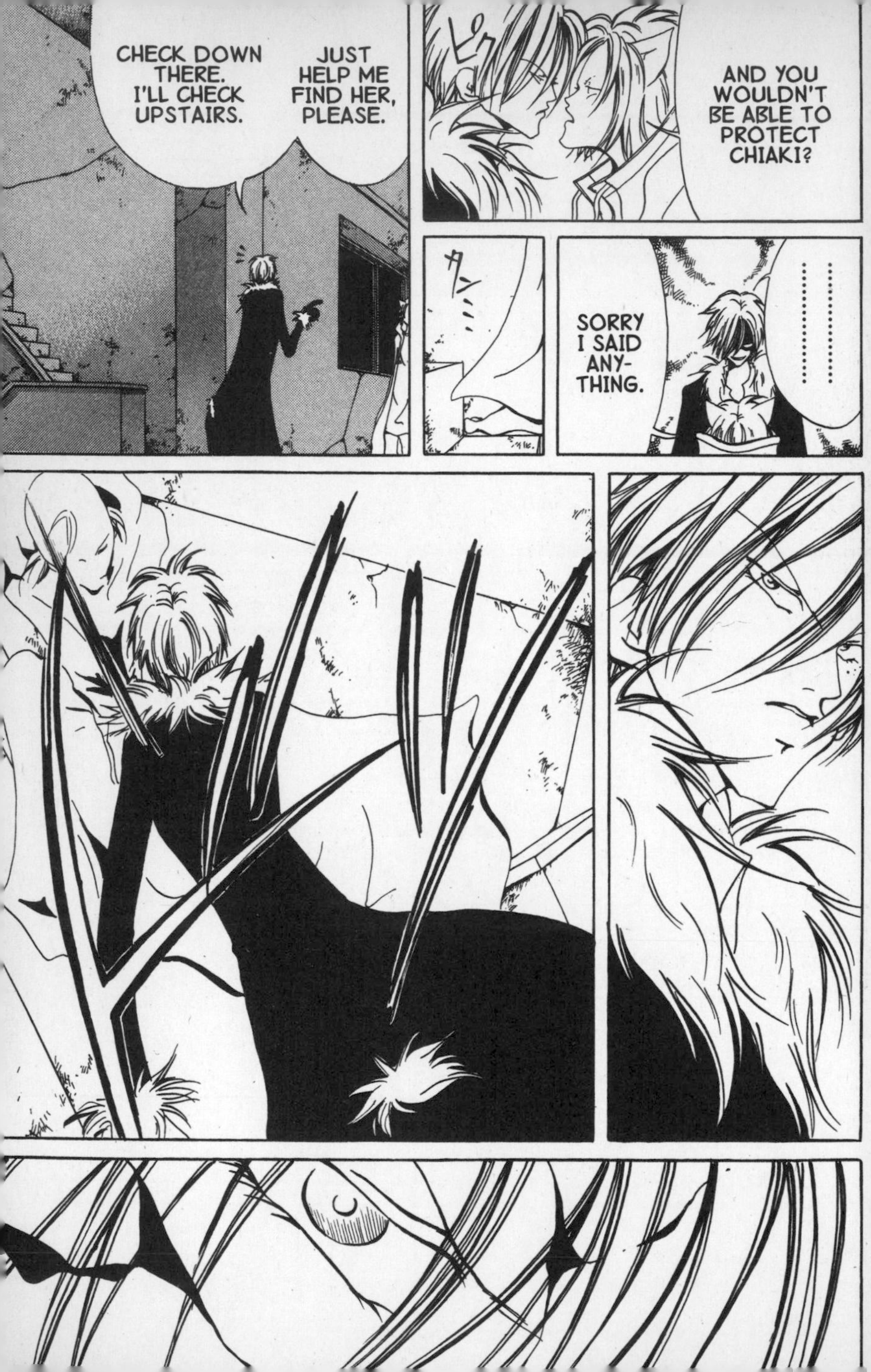
AND YOU WOULDN'T BE ABLE TO PROTECT CHIAKI?
......
SORRY I SAID ANYTHING.
JUST HELP ME FIND HER, PLEASE.
CHECK DOWN THERE. I'LL CHECK UPSTAIRS.

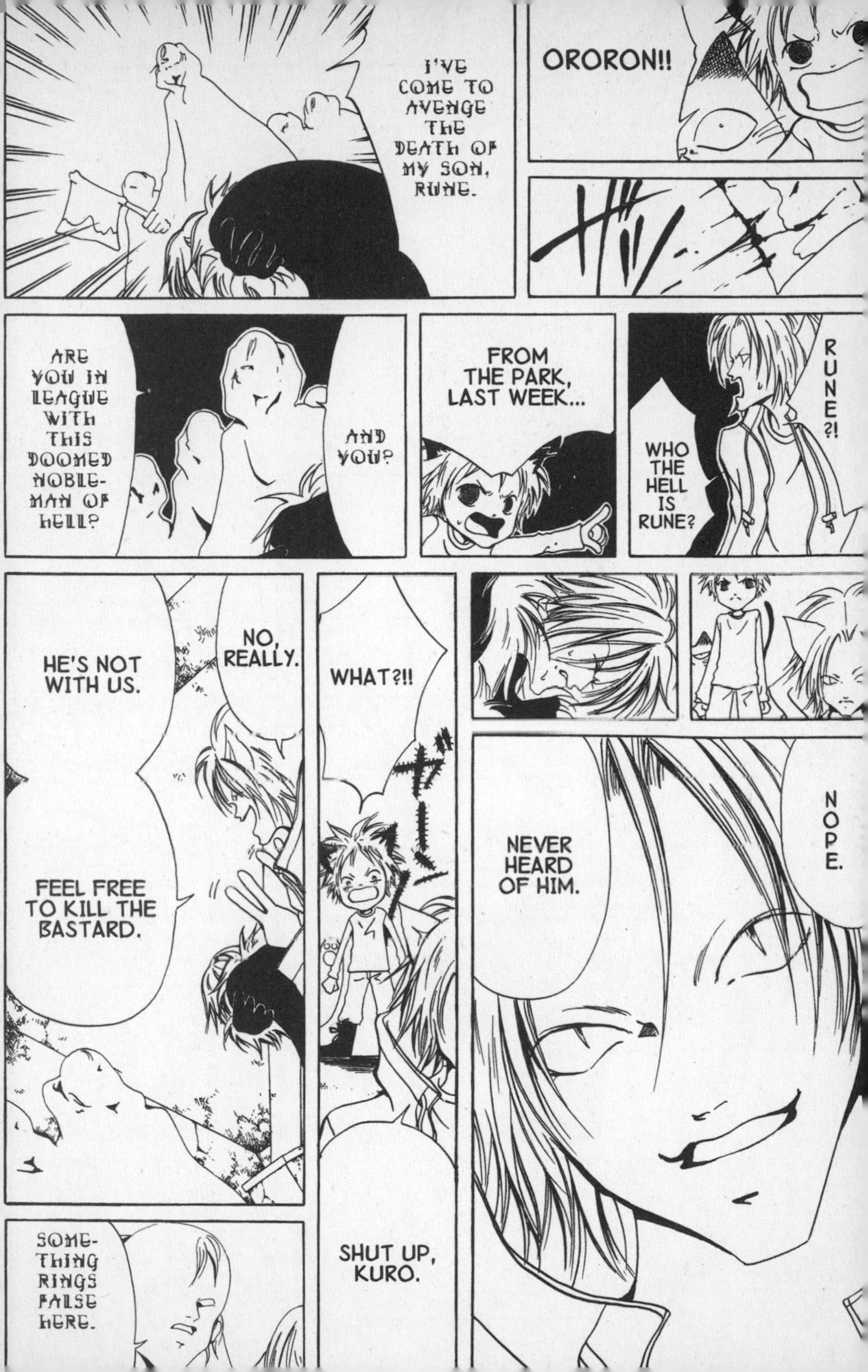
ORORON!!
I'VE COME TO AVENGE THE DEATH OF MY SON, RUNE.
RUNE?!
WHO THE HELL IS RUNE?
FROM THE PARK, LAST WEEK...
AND YOU?
ARE YOU IN LEAGUE WITH THIS DOOMED NOBLE-MAN OF HELL?
NOPE.
NEVER HEARD OF HIM.
WHAT?!!
SHUT UP, KURO.
NO, REALLY.
HE'S NOT WITH US.
FEEL FREE TO KILL THE BASTARD.
SOME-THING RINGS FALSE HERE.

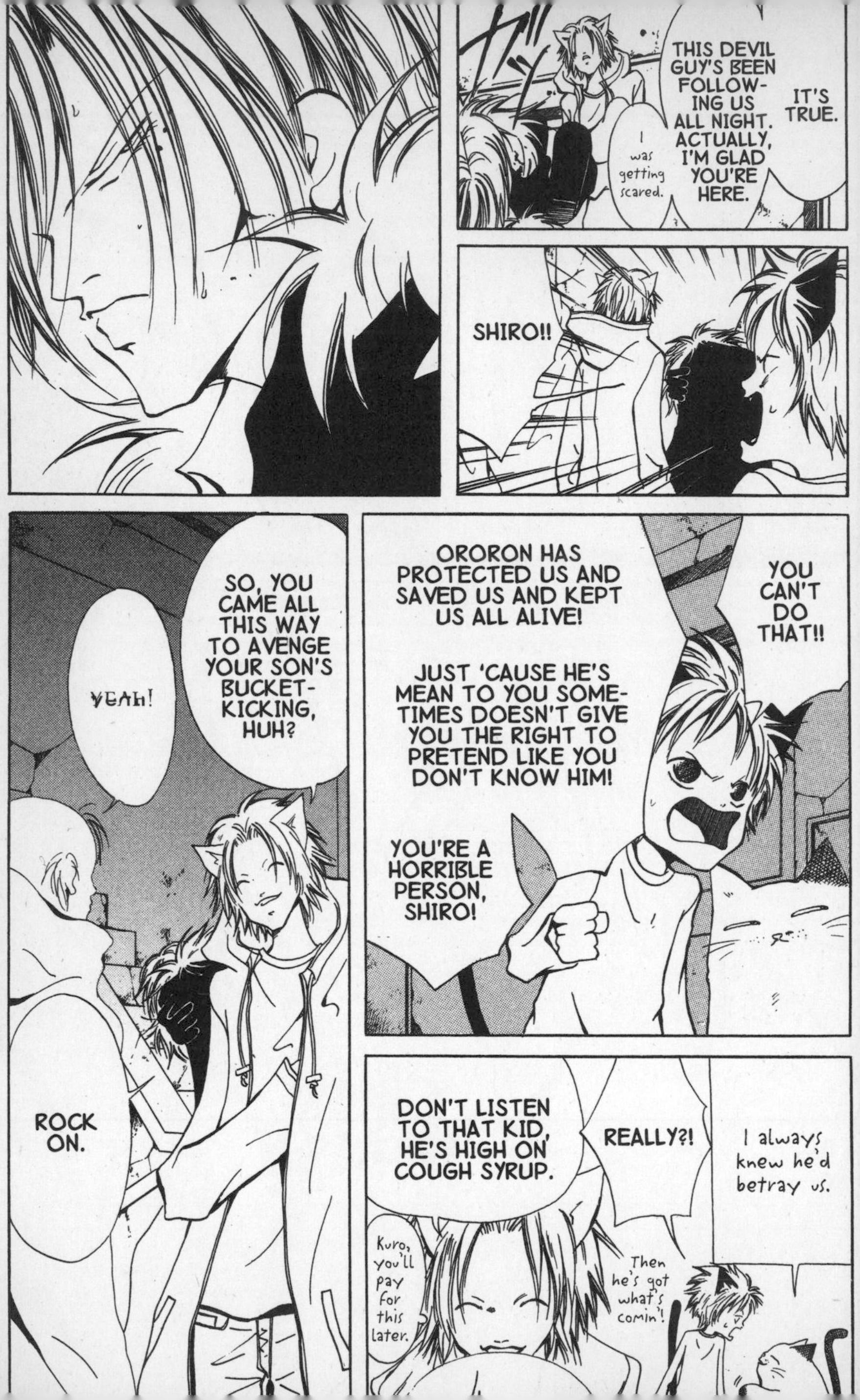
IT'S TRUE.
THIS DEVIL GUY'S BEEN FOLLOW-ING US ALL NIGHT. ACTUALLY, I'M GLAD YOU'RE HERE.
I was getting scared.
SHIRO!!
YOU CAN'T DO THAT!!
ORORON HAS PROTECTED US AND SAVED US AND KEPT US ALL ALIVE!
JUST 'CAUSE HE'S MEAN TO YOU SOME-TIMES DOESN'T GIVE YOU THE RIGHT TO PRETEND LIKE YOU DON'T KNOW HIM!
YOU'RE A HORRIBLE PERSON, SHIRO!
I always knew he'd betray us.
REALLY?!
DON'T LISTEN TO THAT KID, HE'S HIGH ON COUGH SYRUP.
Then he's got what's comin'!
Kuro, you'll pay for this later.
SO, YOU CAME ALL THIS WAY TO AVENGE YOUR SON'S BUCKET-KICKING, HUH?
YEAH!
ROCK ON.

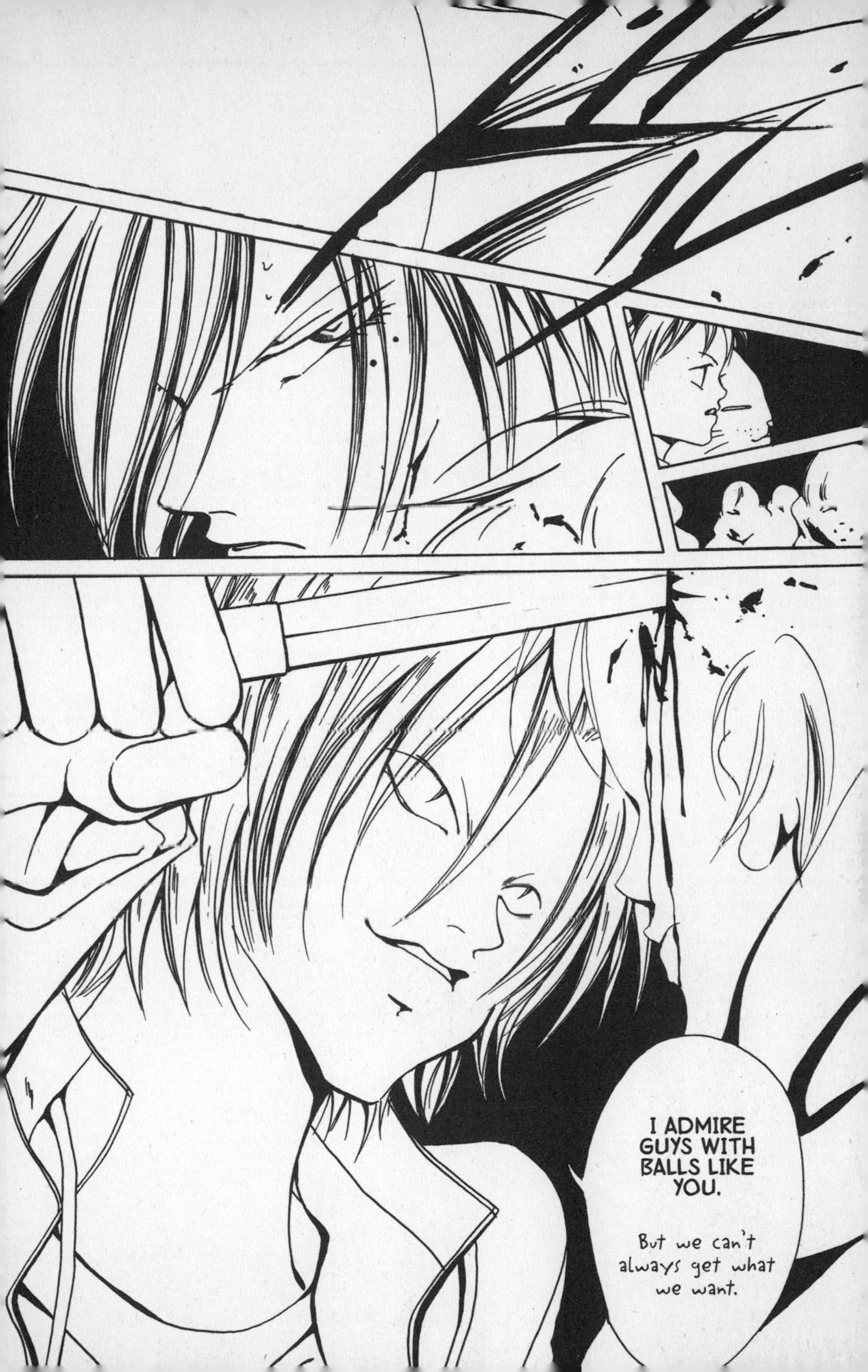
I ADMIRE GUYS WITH BALLS LIKE YOU.
But we can't always get what we want.

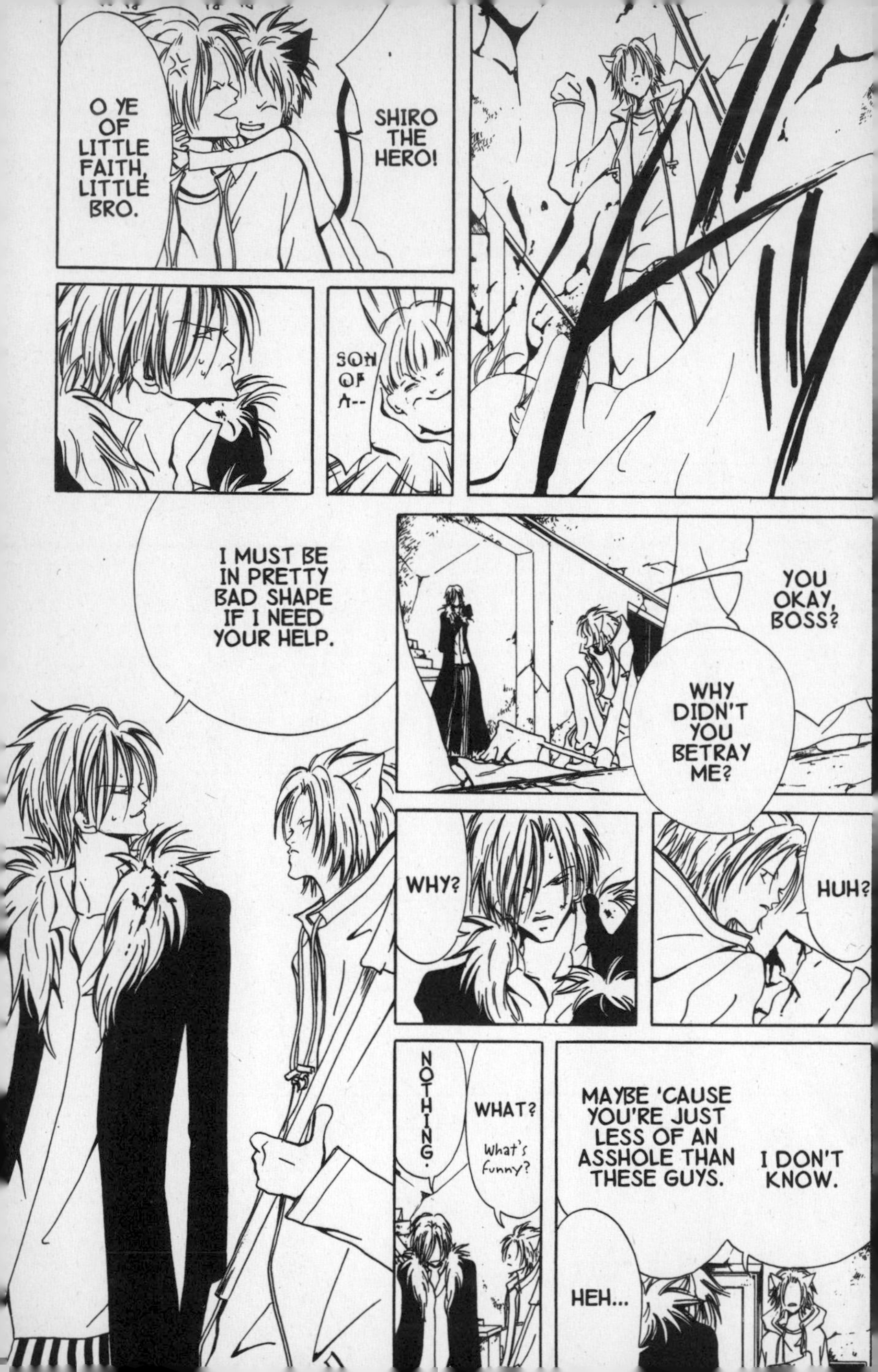
SHIRO THE HERO!
O YE OF LITTLE FAITH, LITTLE BRO.
SON OF A--
YOU OKAY, BOSS?
WHY DIDN'T YOU BETRAY ME?
HUH?
WHY?
I DON'T KNOW.
MAYBE 'CAUSE YOU'RE JUST LESS OF AN ASSHOLE THAN THESE GUYS.
HEH...
WHAT?
What's funny?
NOTHING.
I MUST BE IN PRETTY BAD SHAPE IF I NEED YOUR HELP.

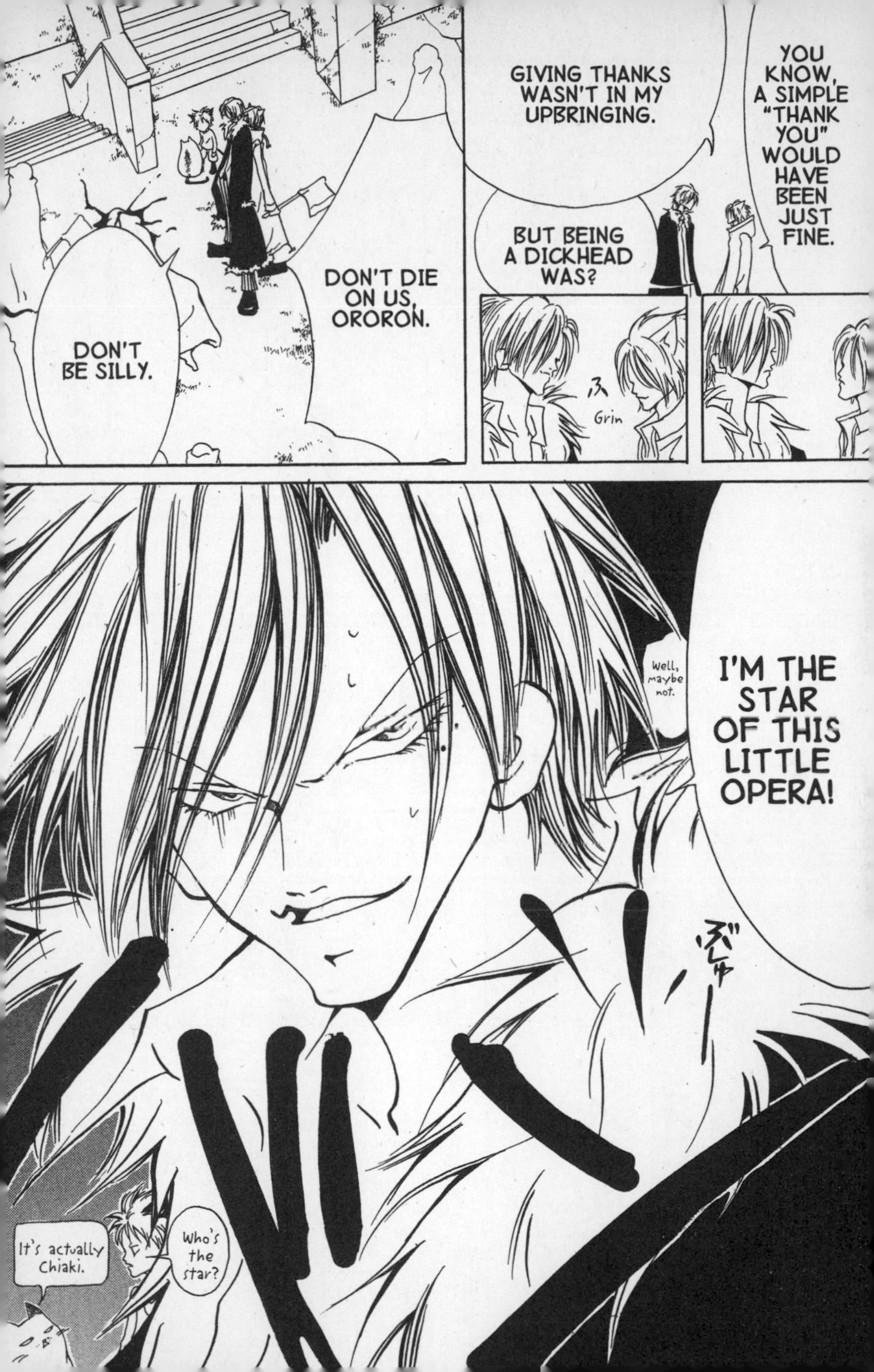
YOU KNOW, A SIMPLE "THANK YOU" WOULD HAVE BEEN JUST FINE.
GIVING THANKS WASN'T IN MY UPBRINGING.
BUT BEING A DICKHEAD WAS?
ふ
Grin
DON'T DIE ON US, ORORON.
DON'T BE SILLY.
I'M THE STAR OF THIS LITTLE OPERA!
Well, maybe not.
ぶしゅー
Who's the star?
It's actually Chiaki.

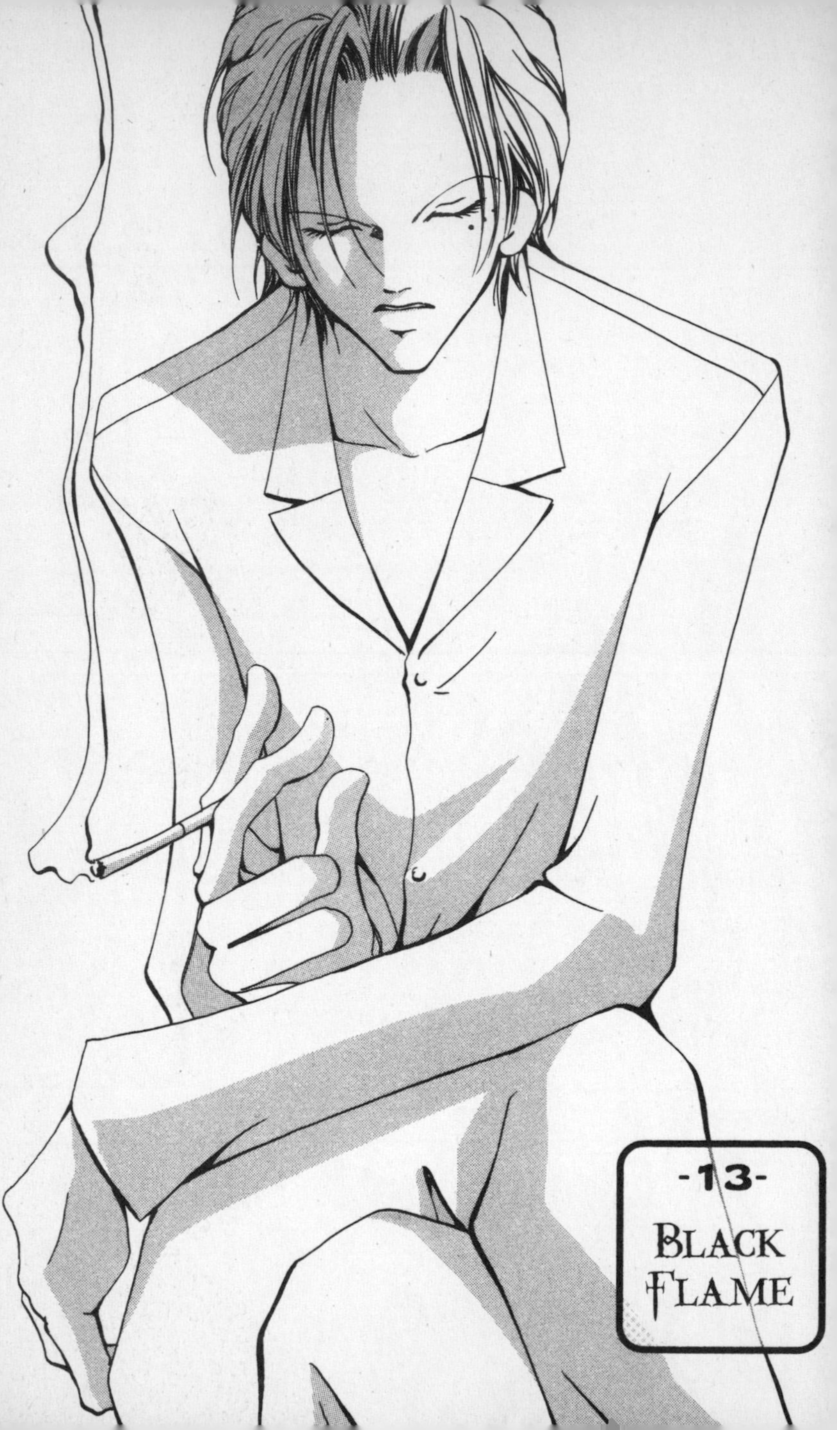
-13-
BLACK FLAME

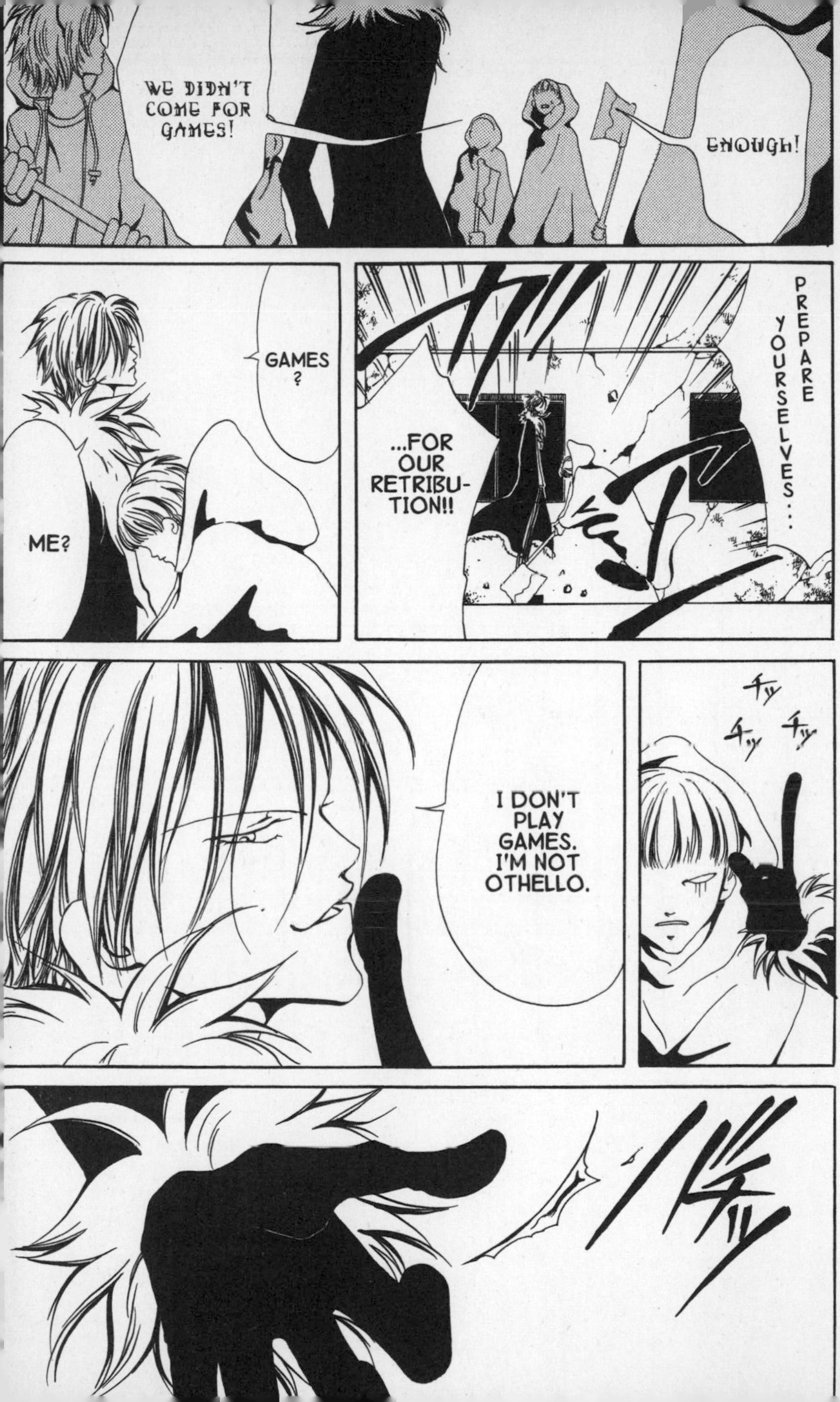
ENOUGH!
WE DIDN'T COME FOR GAMES!
PREPARE YOURSELVES...
...FOR OUR RETRIBUTION!!
GAMES?
ME?
チッ
チッ
チッ
I DON'T PLAY GAMES. I'M NOT OTHELLO.
バチッ

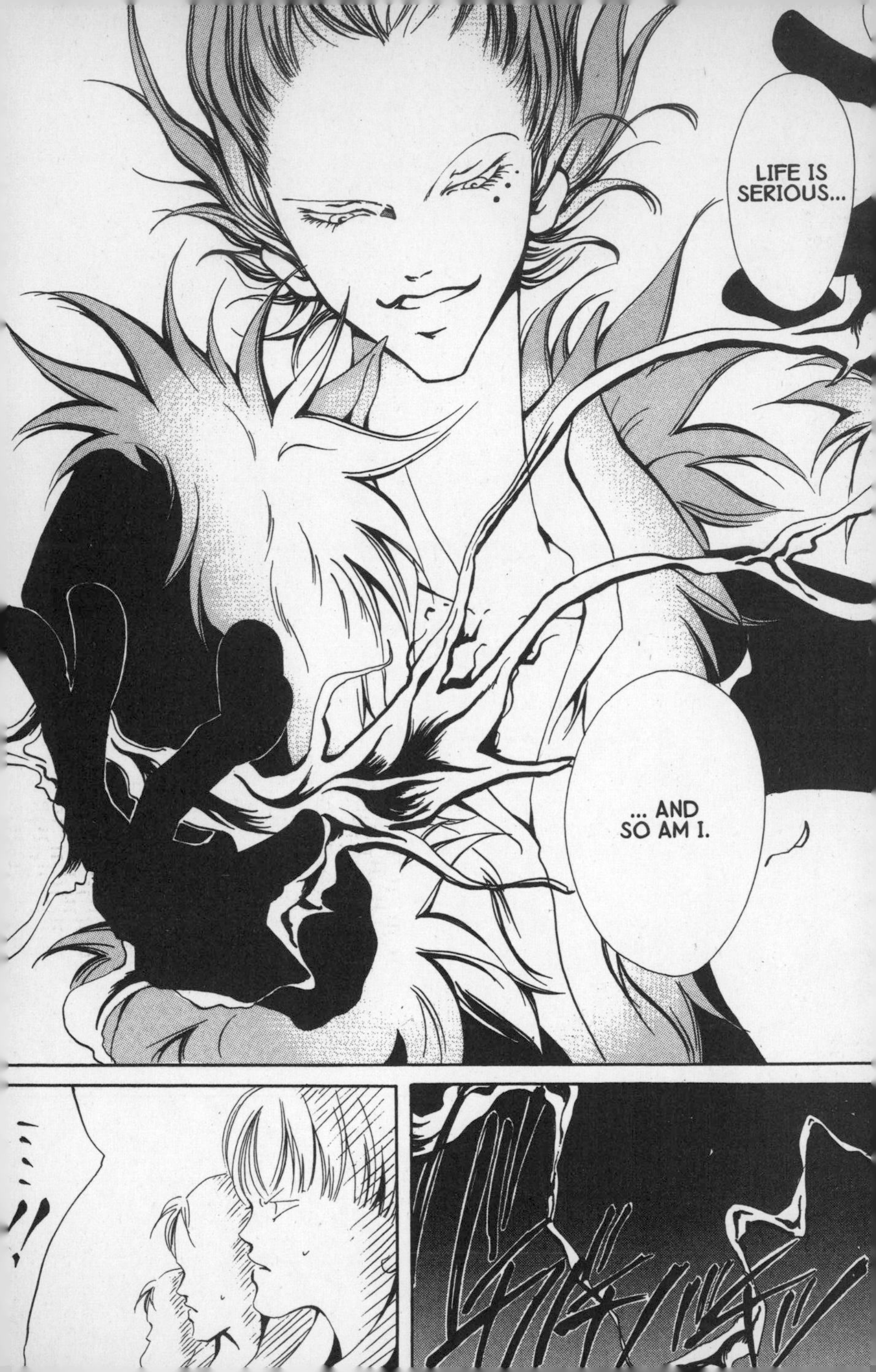
LIFE IS SERIOUS...
... AND SO AM I.

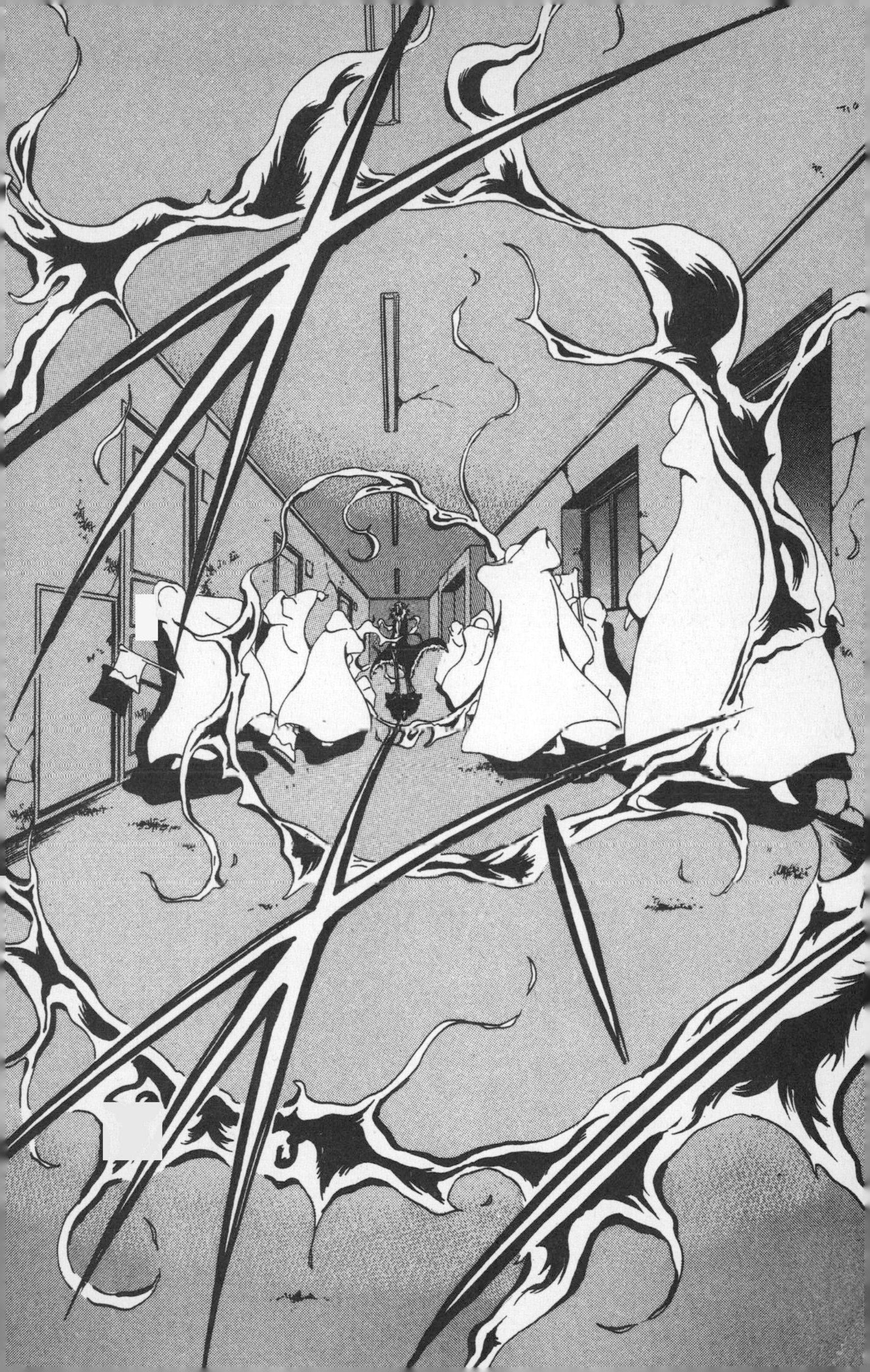

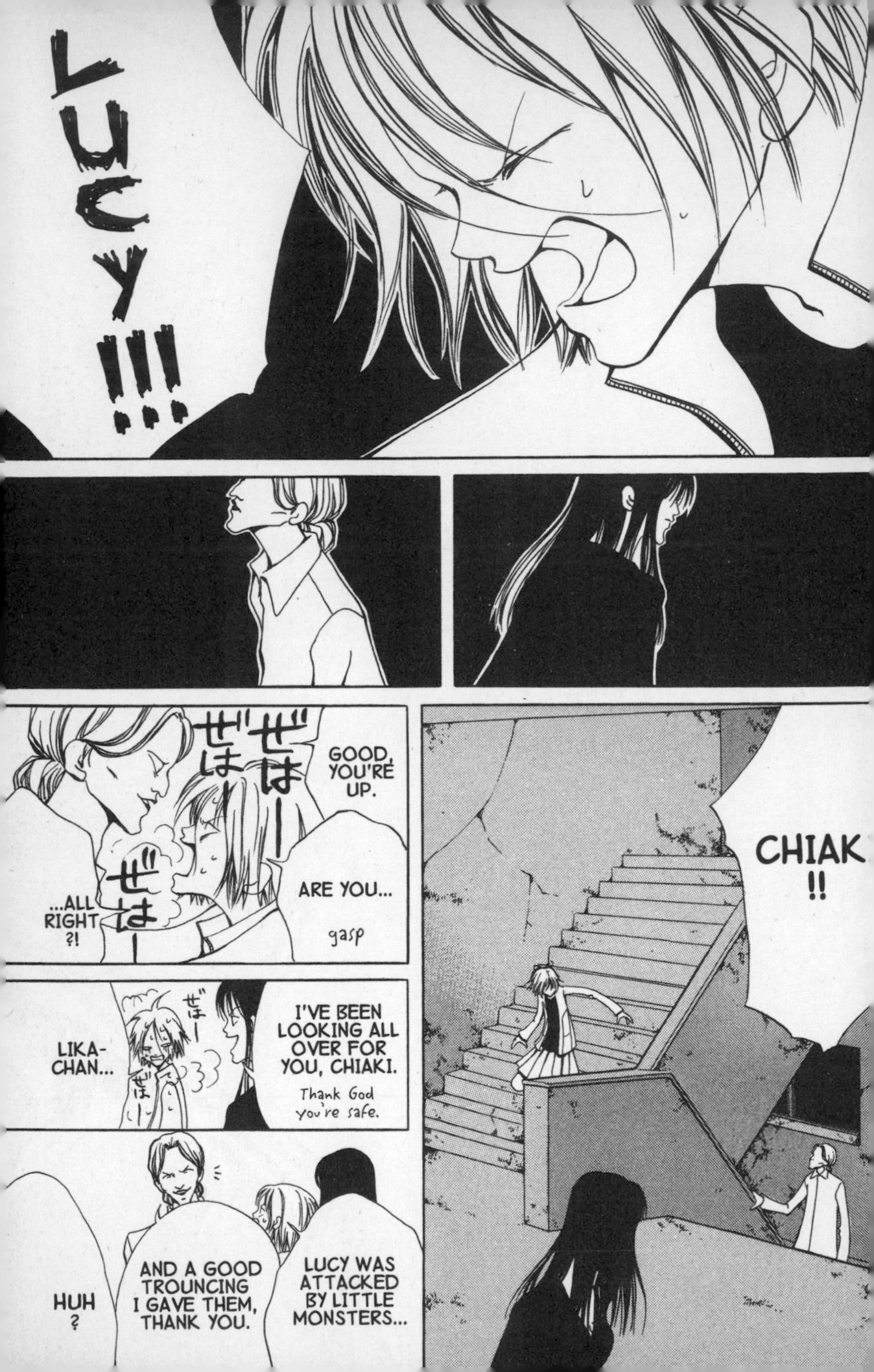
LUCY!!!
CHIAK !!
ぜはーぜはー
GOOD, YOU'RE UP.
ARE YOU...
gasp
ぜはー
...ALL RIGHT?!
I'VE BEEN LOOKING ALL OVER FOR YOU, CHIAKI.
Thank God you're safe.
LIKA-CHAN...
LUCY WAS ATTACKED BY LITTLE MONSTERS...
AND A GOOD TROUNCING I GAVE THEM, THANK YOU.
HUH?

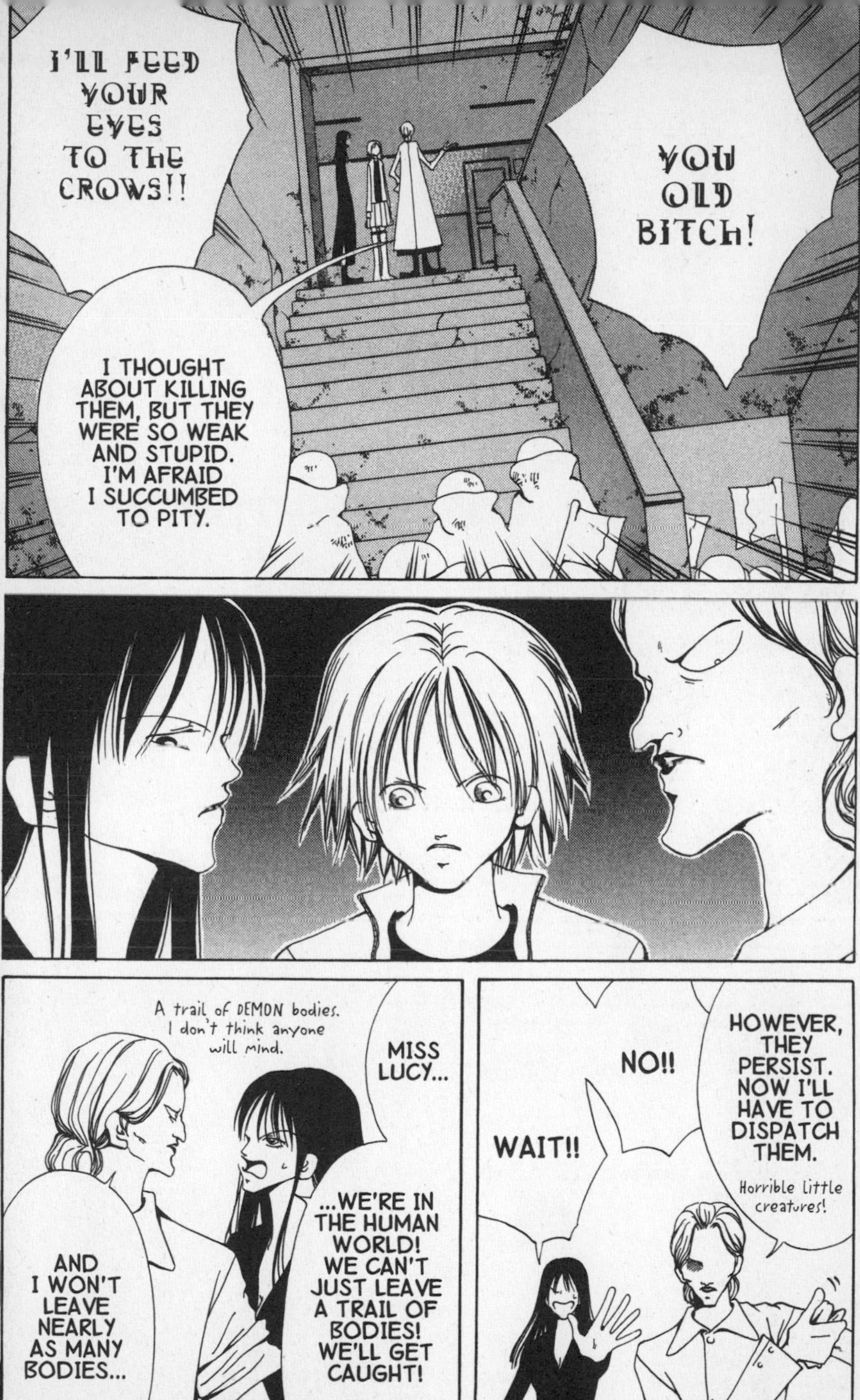
YOU OLD BITCH!
I'LL FEED YOUR EYES TO THE CROWS!!
I THOUGHT ABOUT KILLING THEM, BUT THEY WERE SO WEAK AND STUPID. I'M AFRAID I SUCCUMBED TO PITY.
HOWEVER, THEY PERSIST. NOW I'LL HAVE TO DISPATCH THEM.
Horrible little creatures!
NO!!
WAIT!!
MISS LUCY...
A trail of DEMON bodies. I don't think anyone will mind.
...WE'RE IN THE HUMAN WORLD! WE CAN'T JUST LEAVE A TRAIL OF BODIES! WE'LL GET CAUGHT!
AND I WON'T LEAVE NEARLY AS MANY BODIES...

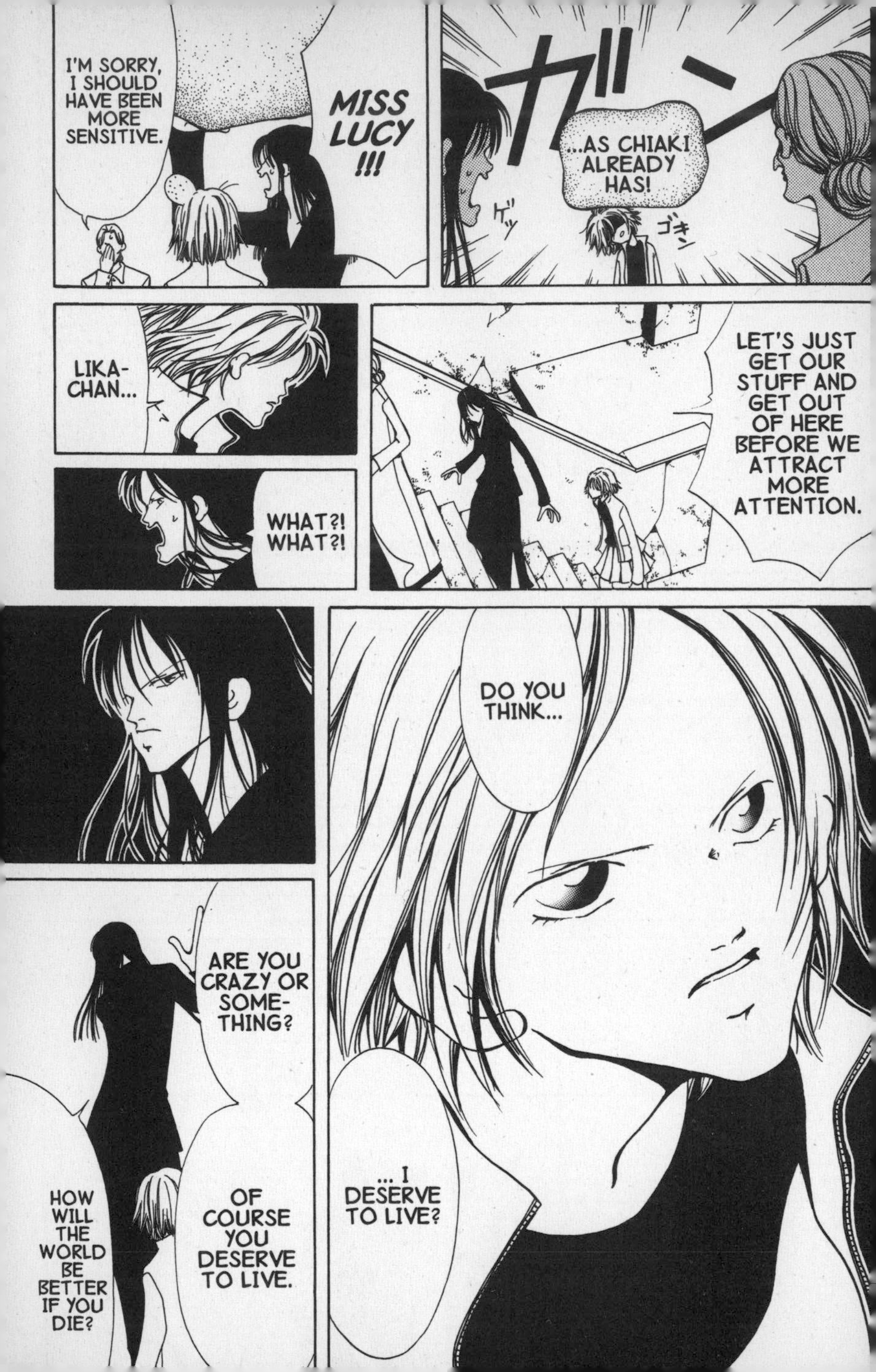
ガー
...AS CHIAKI ALREADY HAS!
ゲッ
ゴキン
MISS LUCY!!!
I'M SORRY, I SHOULD HAVE BEEN MORE SENSITIVE.
LET'S JUST GET OUR STUFF AND GET OUT OF HERE BEFORE WE ATTRACT MORE ATTENTION.
LIKA-CHAN...
WHAT?! WHAT?!
DO YOU THINK...
... I DESERVE TO LIVE?
ARE YOU CRAZY OR SOME-THING?
OF COURSE YOU DESERVE TO LIVE.
HOW WILL THE WORLD BE BETTER IF YOU DIE?

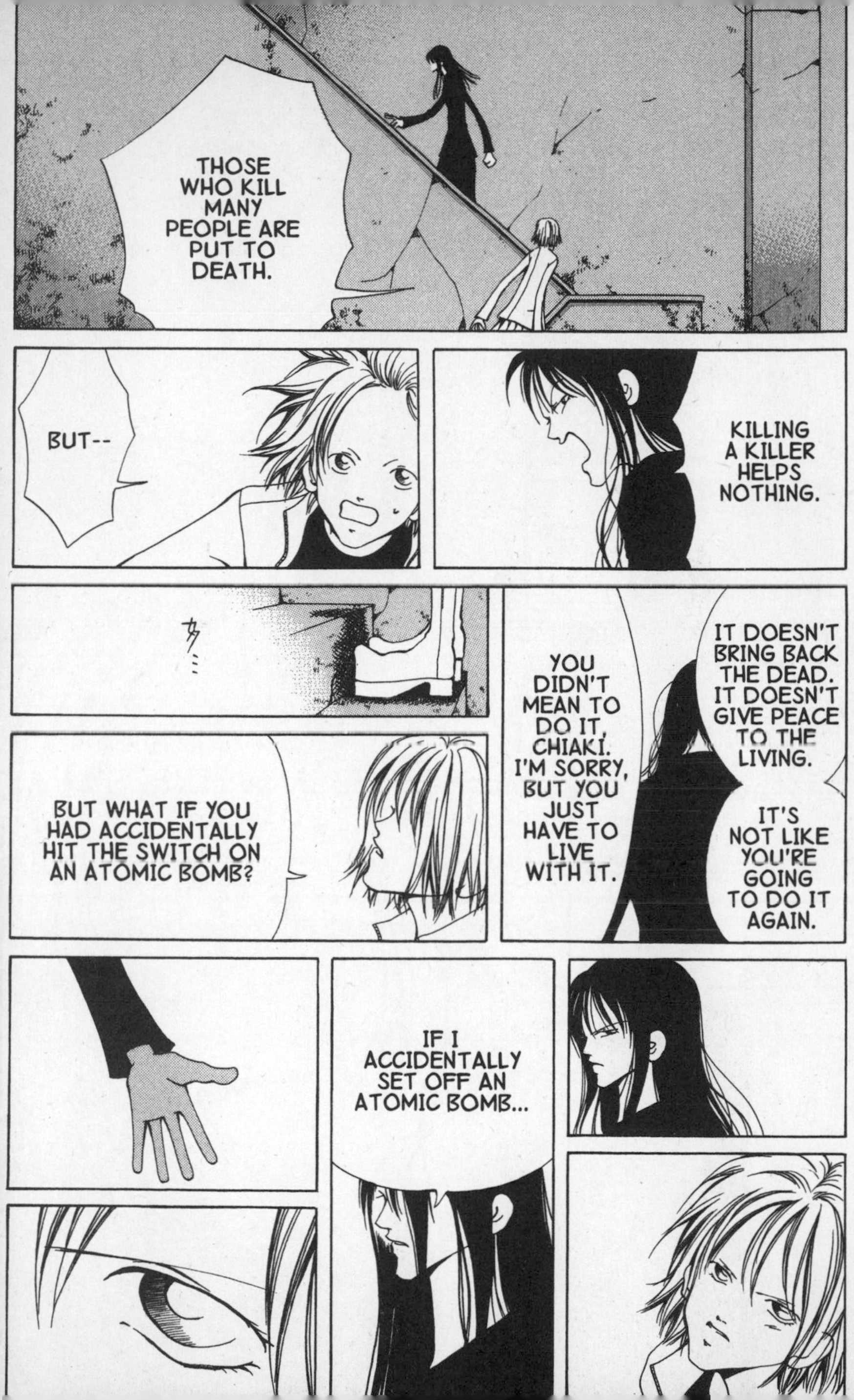
THOSE WHO KILL MANY PEOPLE ARE PUT TO DEATH.
KILLING A KILLER HELPS NOTHING.
BUT--
IT DOESN'T BRING BACK THE DEAD. IT DOESN'T GIVE PEACE TO THE LIVING.
IT'S NOT LIKE YOU'RE GOING TO DO IT AGAIN.
YOU DIDN'T MEAN TO DO IT, CHIAKI. I'M SORRY, BUT YOU JUST HAVE TO LIVE WITH IT.
BUT WHAT IF YOU HAD ACCIDENTALLY HIT THE SWITCH ON AN ATOMIC BOMB?
IF I ACCIDENTALLY SET OFF AN ATOMIC BOMB...

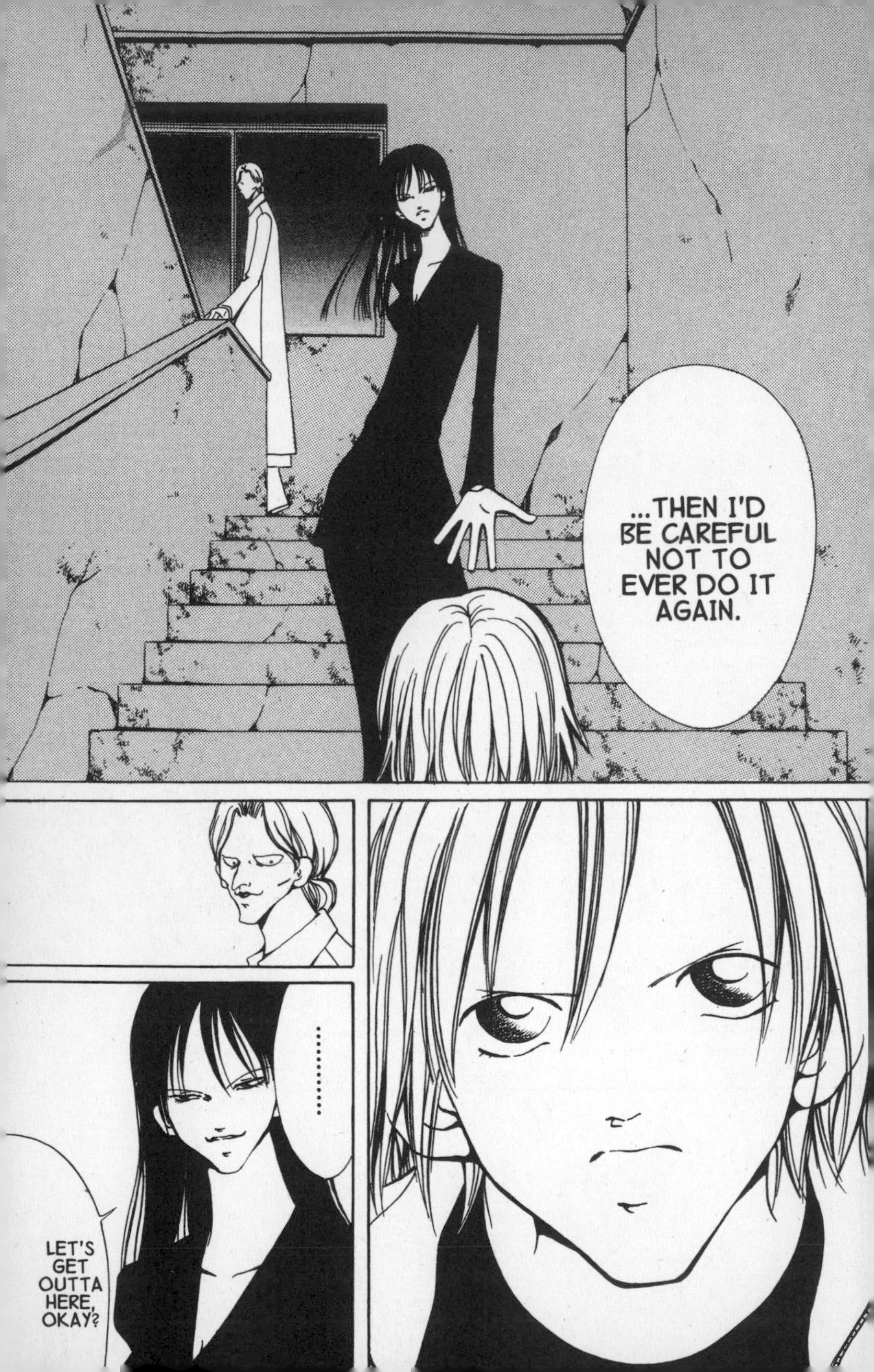
...THEN I'D BE CAREFUL NOT TO EVER DO IT AGAIN.
....
LET'S GET OUTTA HERE, OKAY?

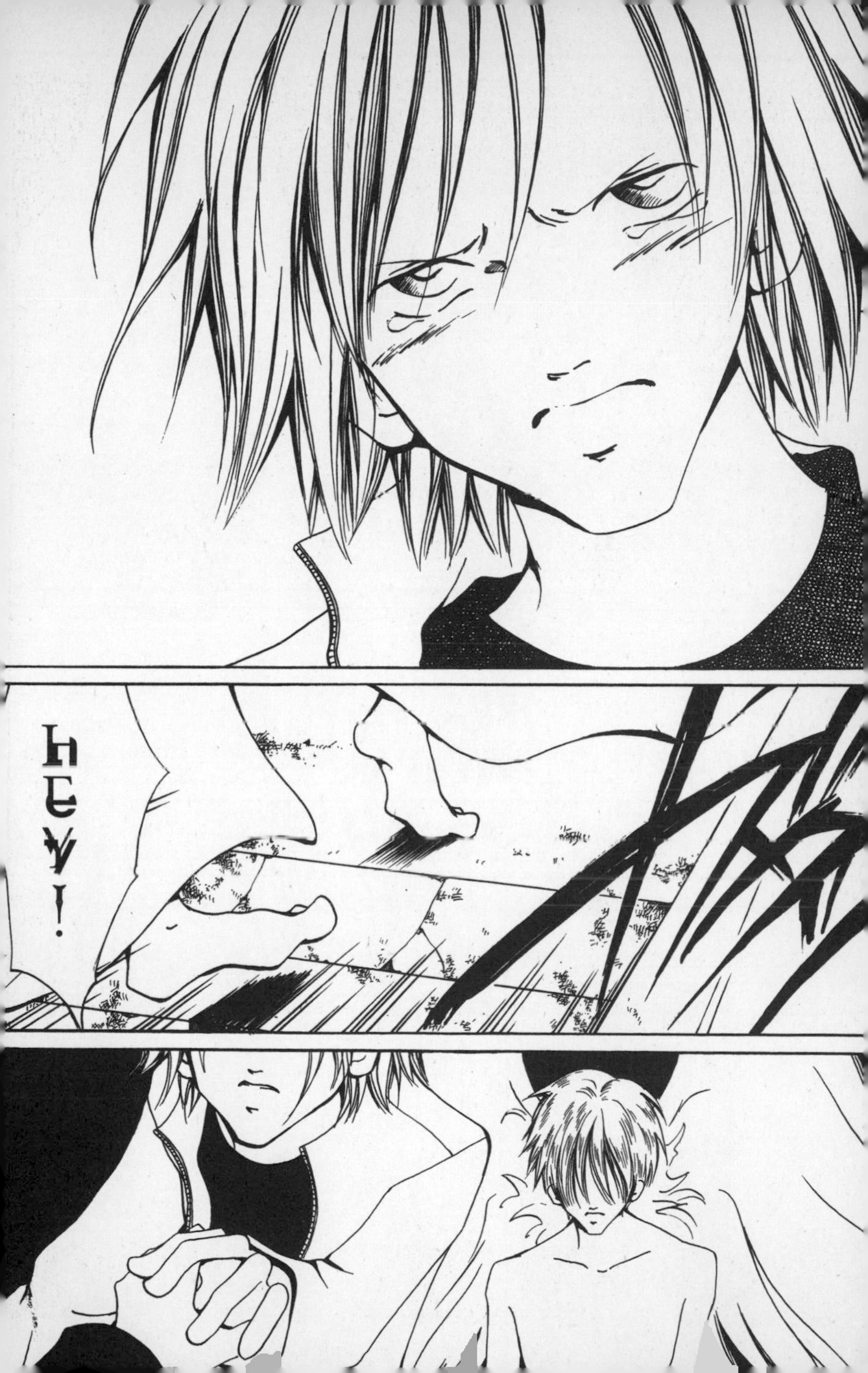
hey!

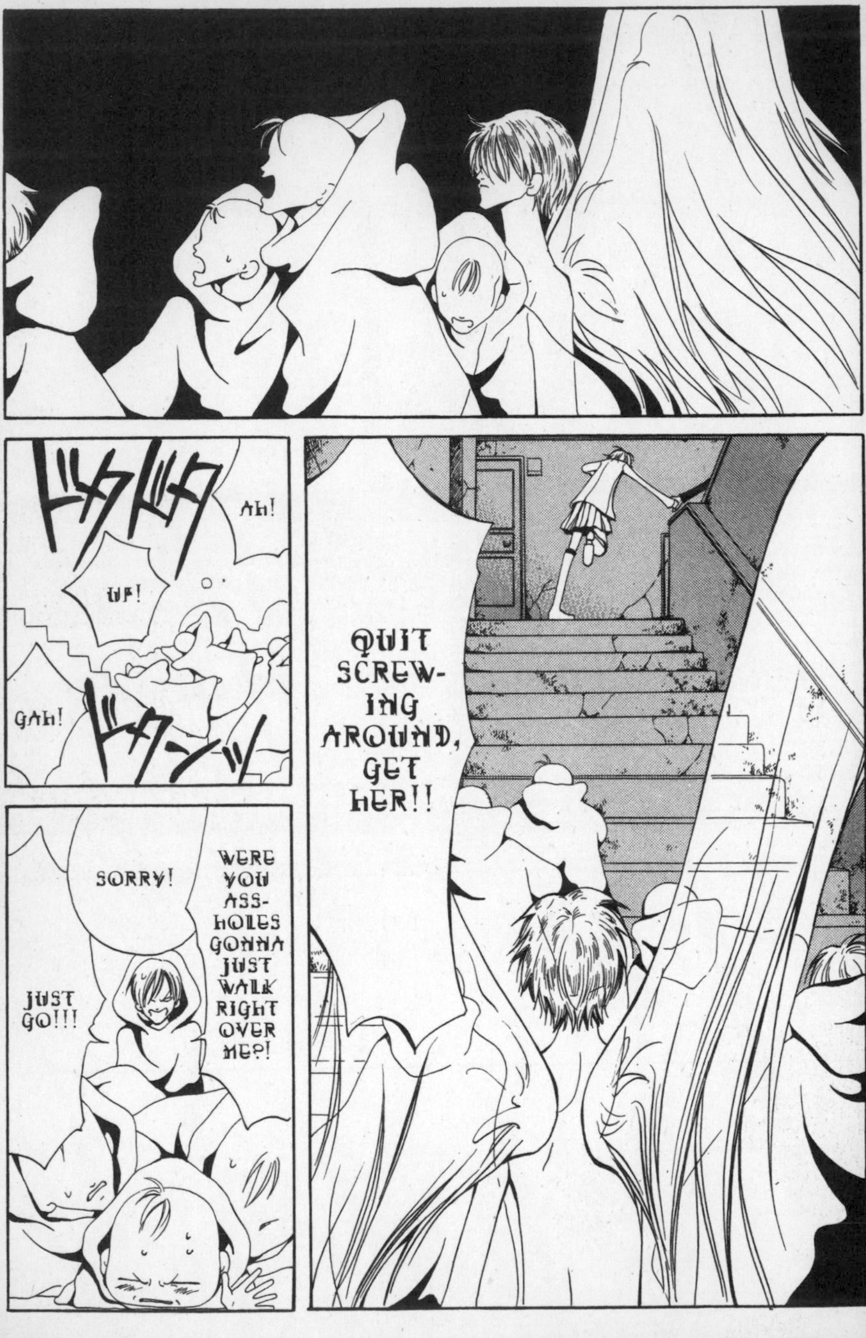
QUIT SCREWING AROUND, GET HER!!
ドタドタ
AH!
UF!
GAH!
ドターンッ
WERE YOU ASSHOLES GONNA JUST WALK RIGHT OVER ME?!
SORRY!
JUST GO!!!

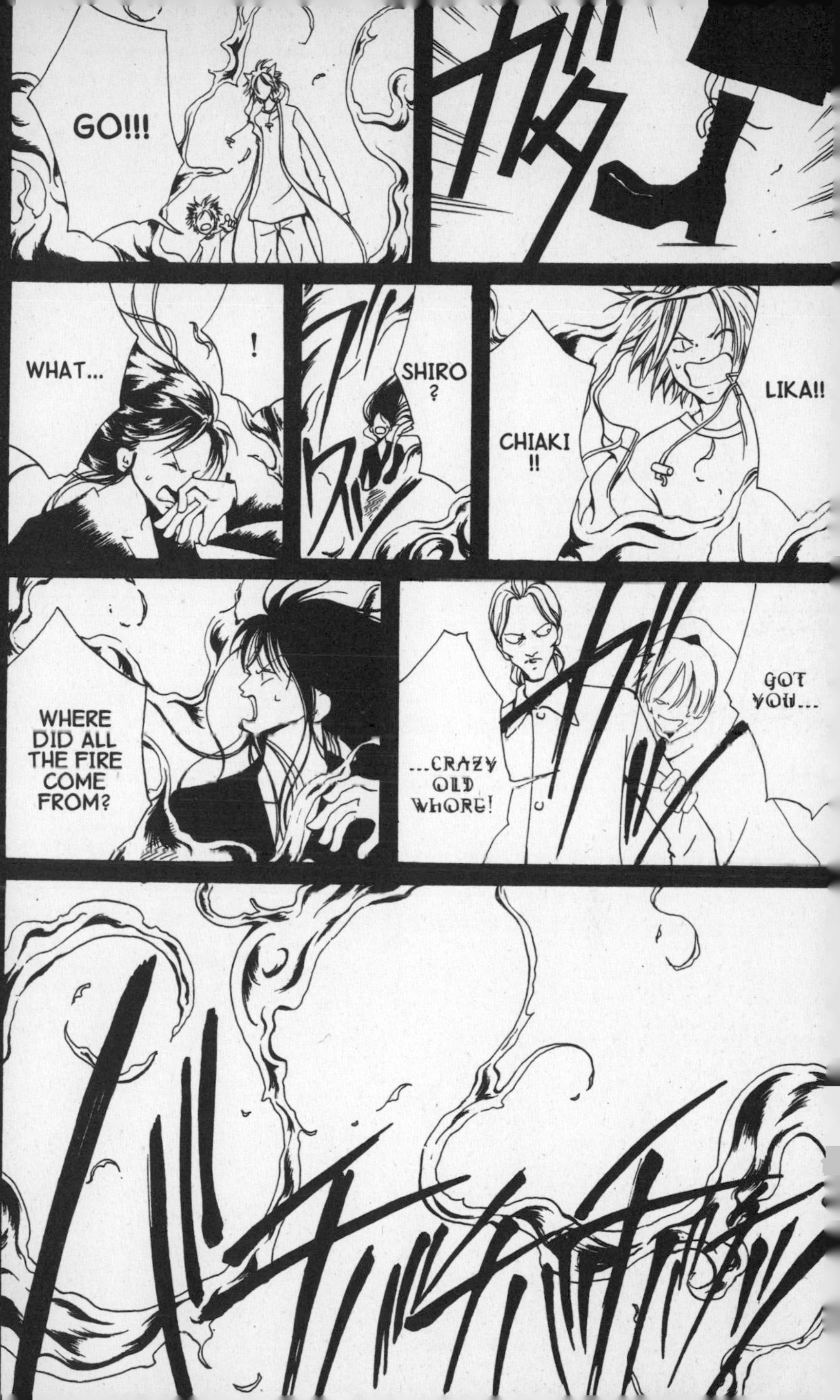
GO!!!
LIKA!!
CHIAKI !!
SHIRO ?
!
WHAT...
GOT YOU...
...CRAZY OLD WHORE!
WHERE DID ALL THE FIRE COME FROM?

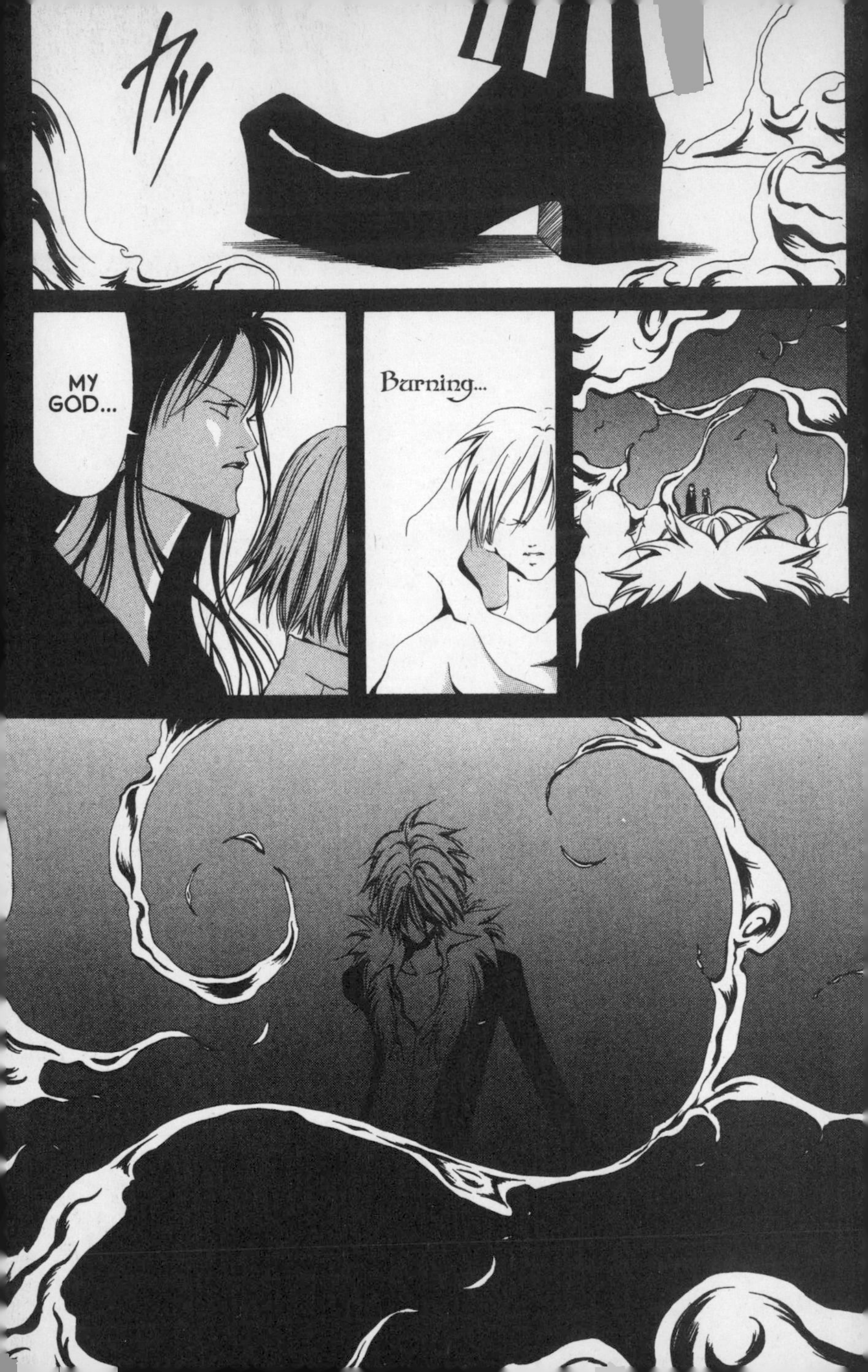
カッ
Burning...
MY GOD...

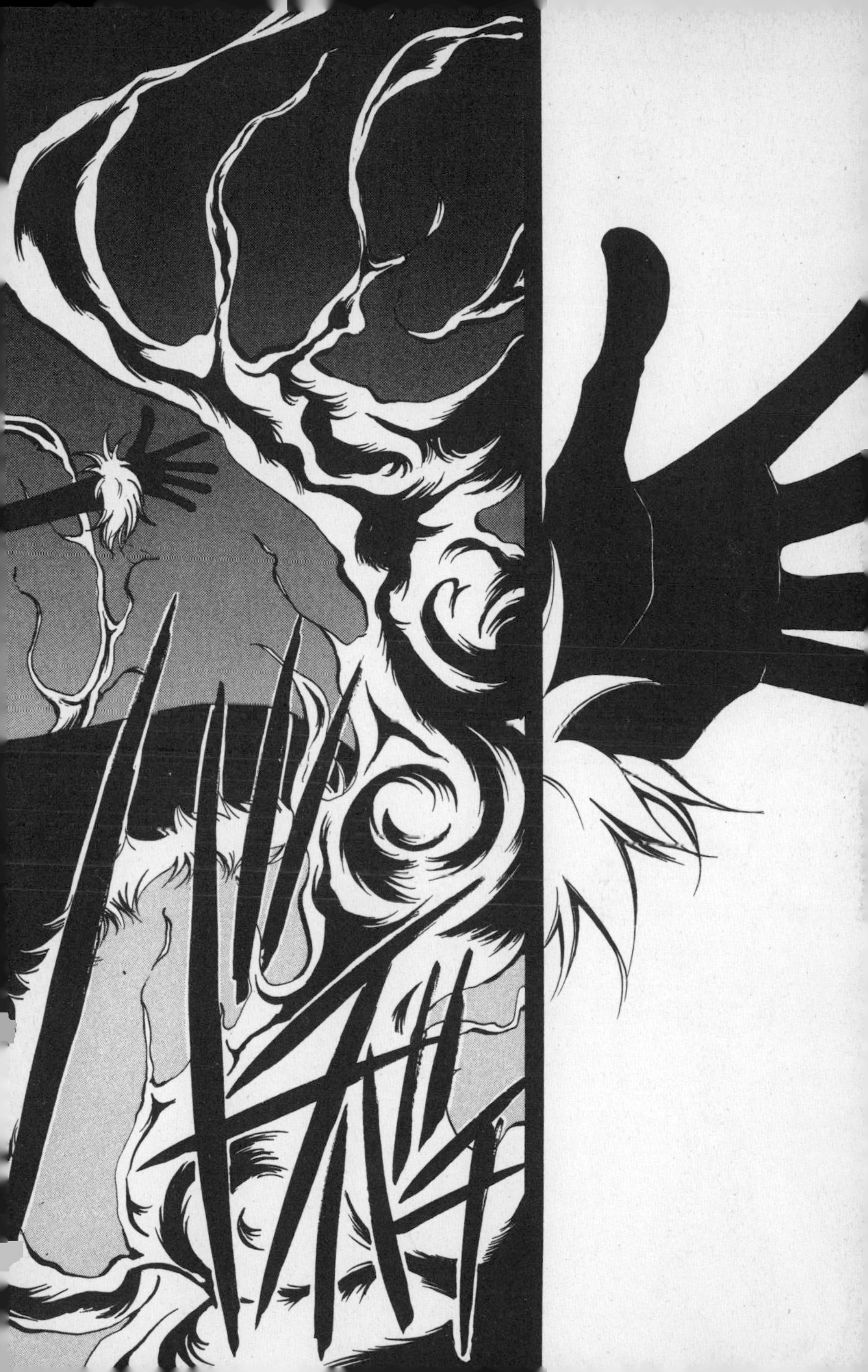

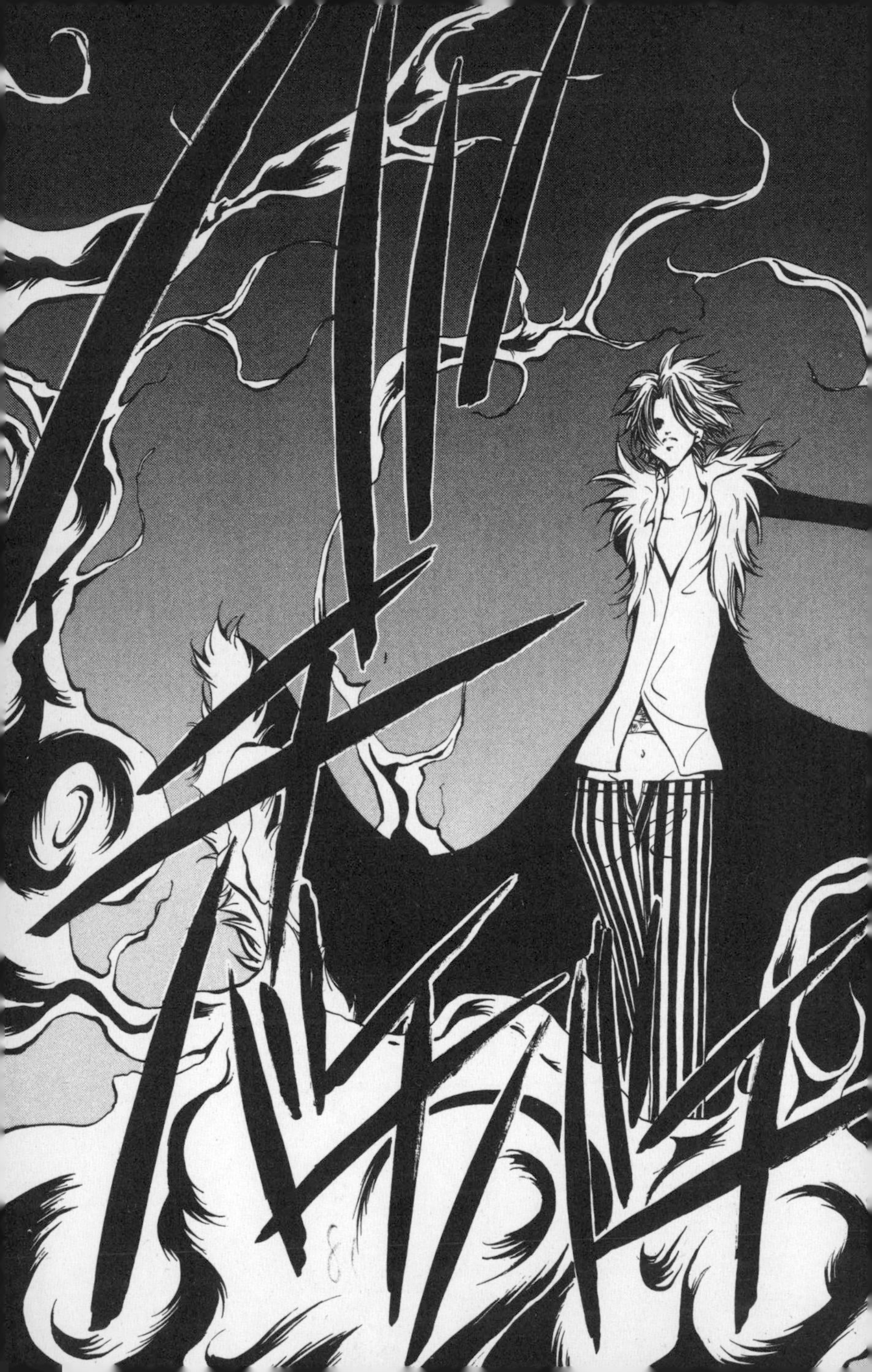

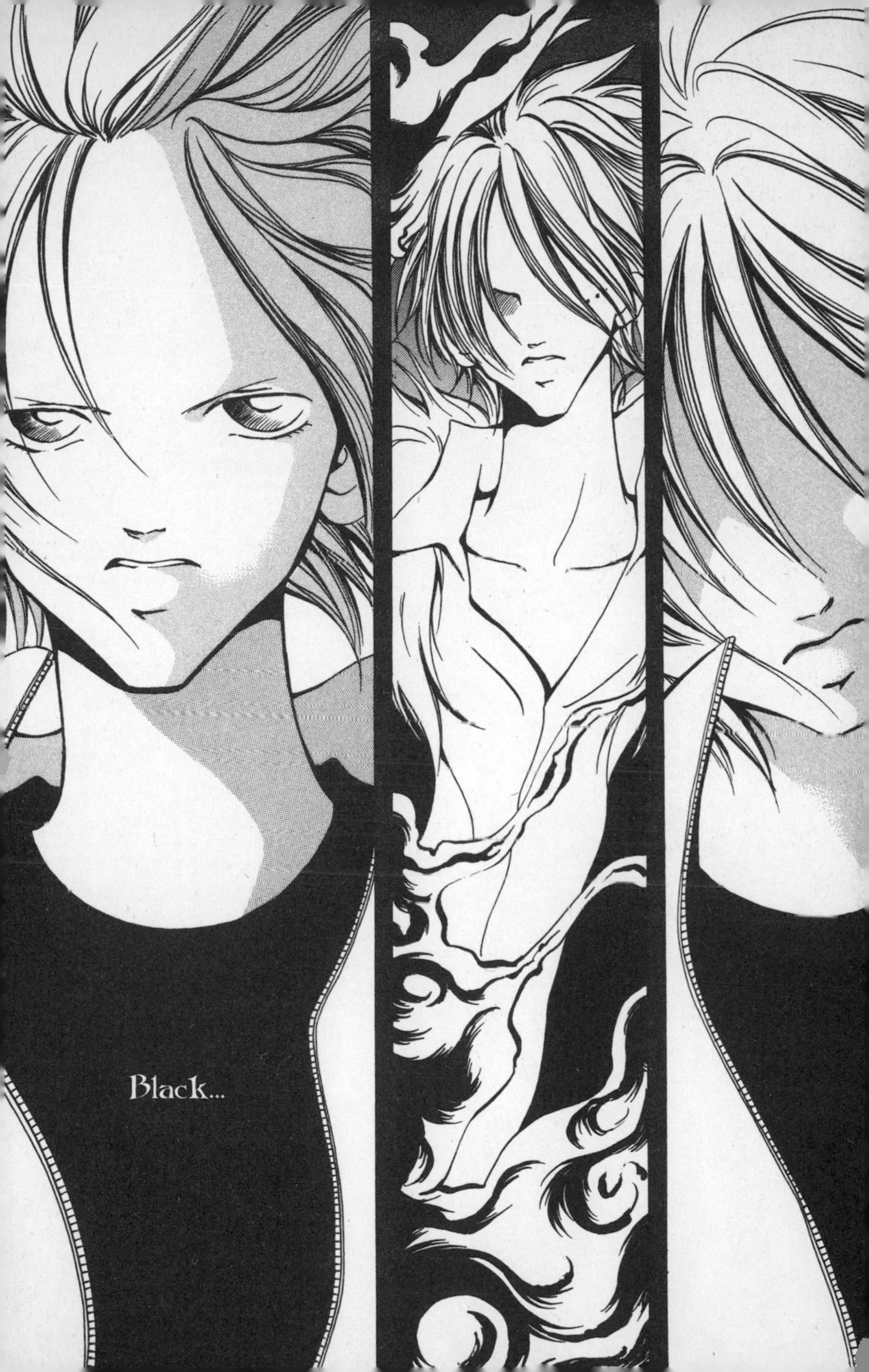
Black...

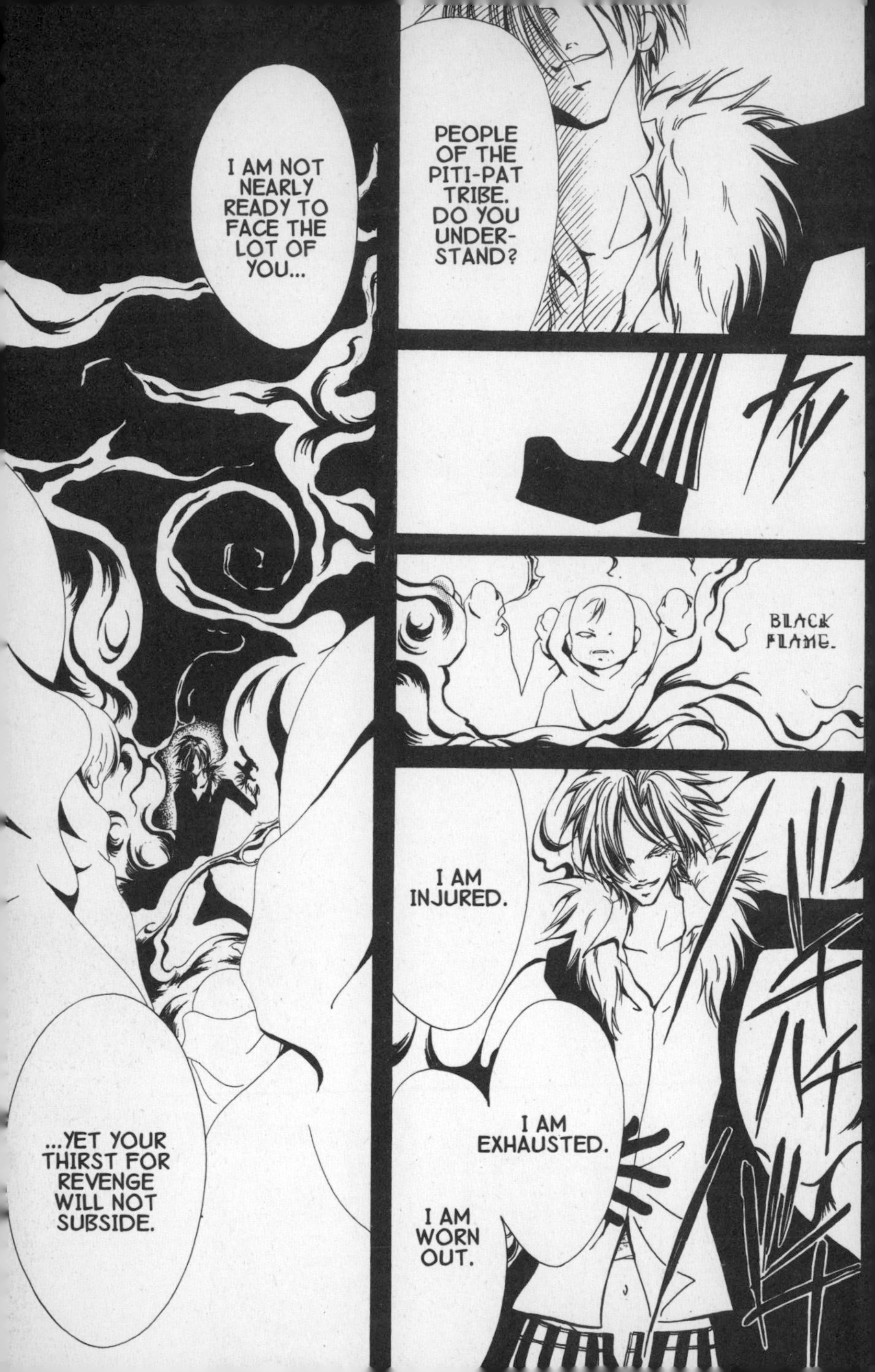
PEOPLE OF THE PITI-PAT TRIBE. DO YOU UNDER-STAND?
BLACK FLAME.
I AM INJURED.
I AM EXHAUSTED.
I AM WORN OUT.
I AM NOT NEARLY READY TO FACE THE LOT OF YOU...
...YET YOUR THIRST FOR REVENGE WILL NOT SUBSIDE.

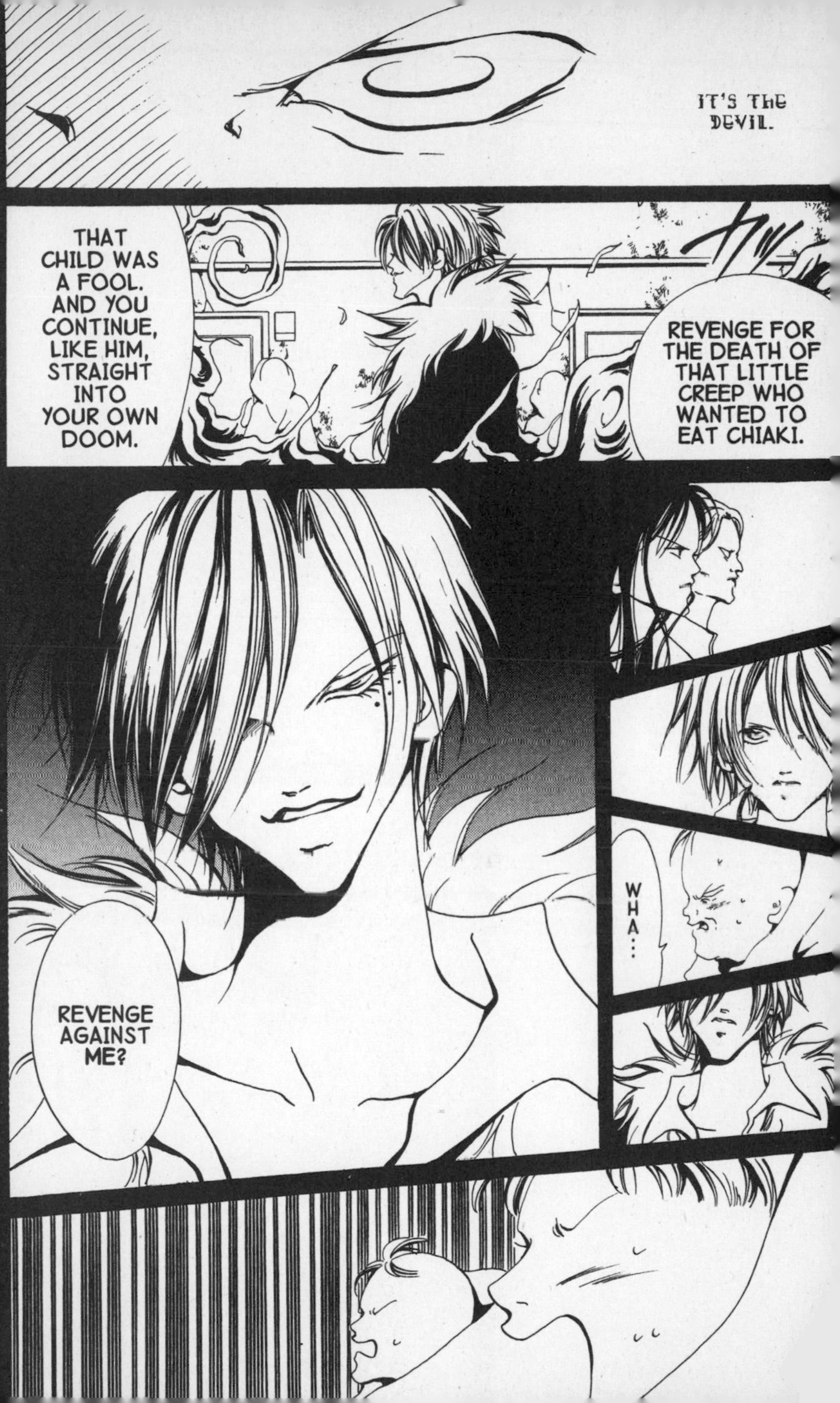
IT'S THE DEVIL.
REVENGE FOR THE DEATH OF THAT LITTLE CREEP WHO WANTED TO EAT CHIAKI.
THAT CHILD WAS A FOOL. AND YOU CONTINUE, LIKE HIM, STRAIGHT INTO YOUR OWN DOOM.
WHA...
REVENGE AGAINST ME?

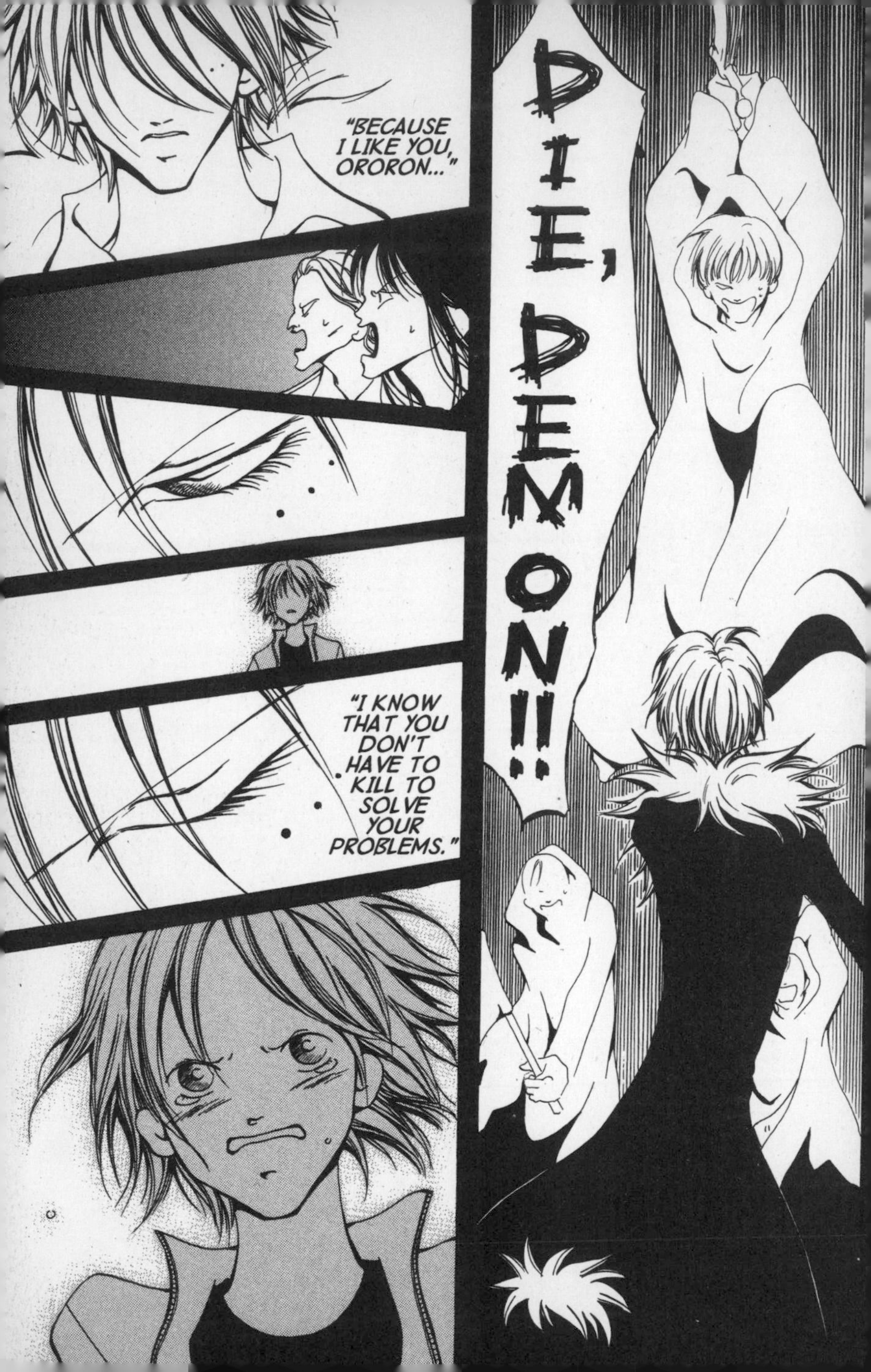
DIE, DEMON!!
"BECAUSE I LIKE YOU, ORORON..."
"I KNOW THAT YOU DON'T HAVE TO KILL TO SOLVE YOUR PROBLEMS."

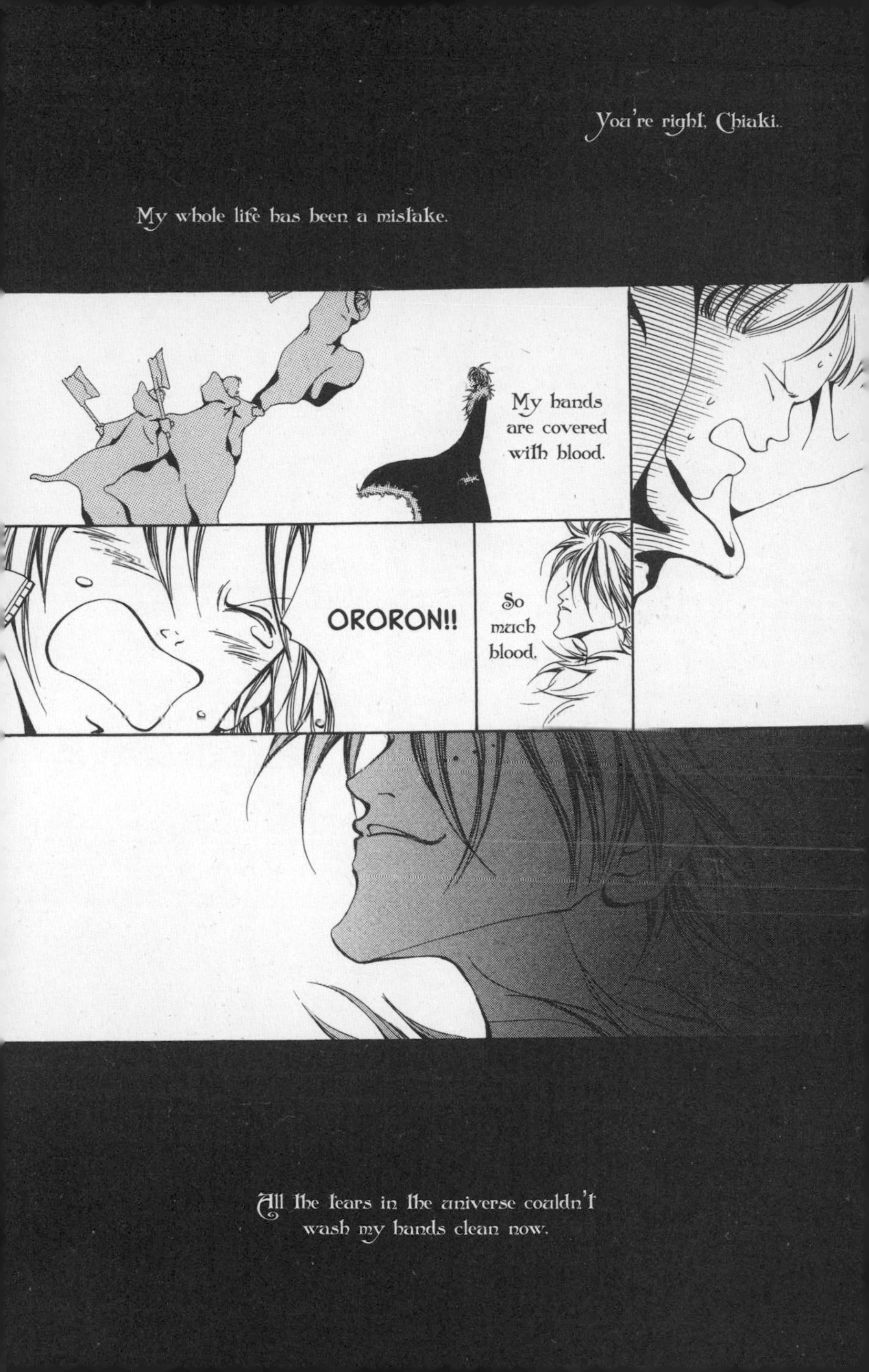
You're right, Chiaki.
My whole life has been a mistake.
My hands are covered with blood.
So much blood.
ORORON!!
All the tears in the universe couldn't wash my hands clean now.

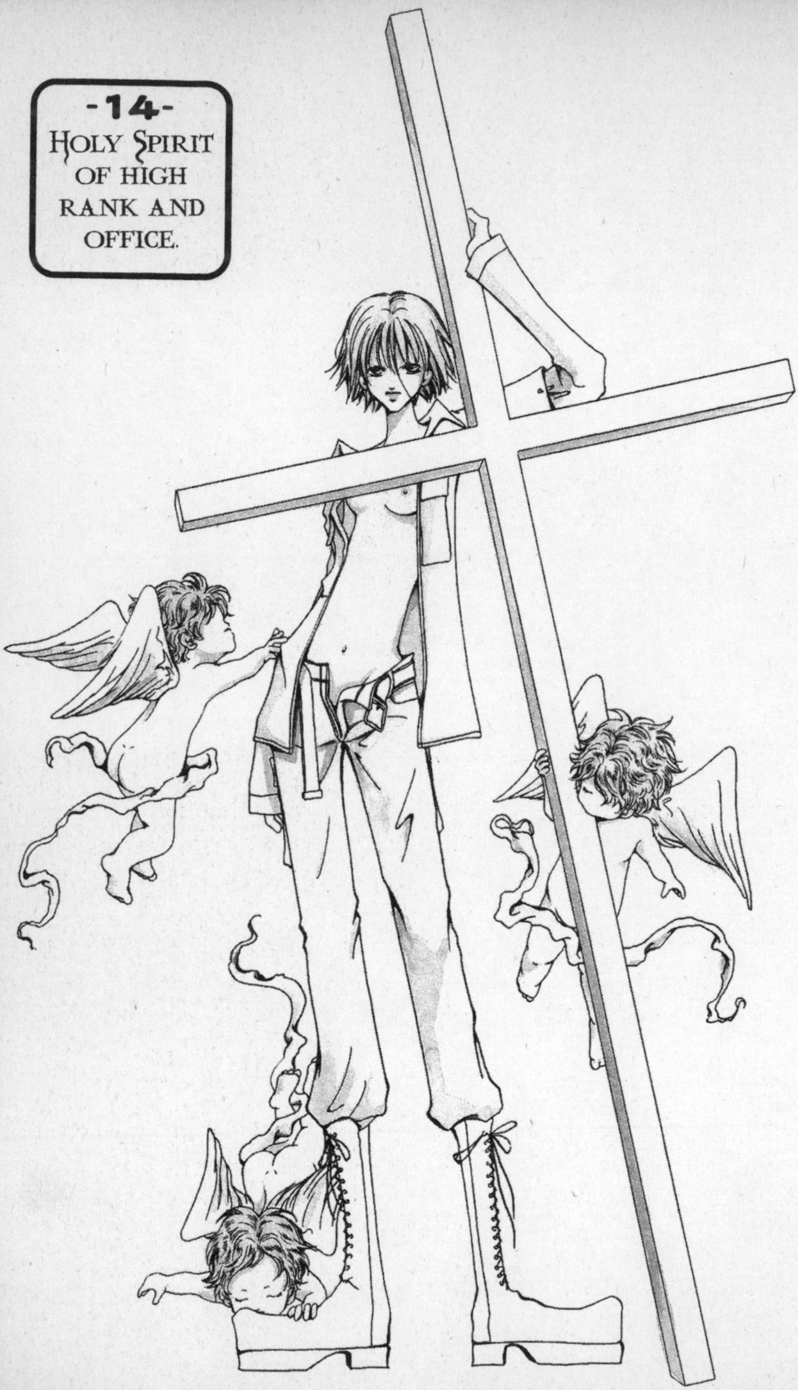
-14-
HOLY SPIRIT
OF HIGH
RANK AND
OFFICE.

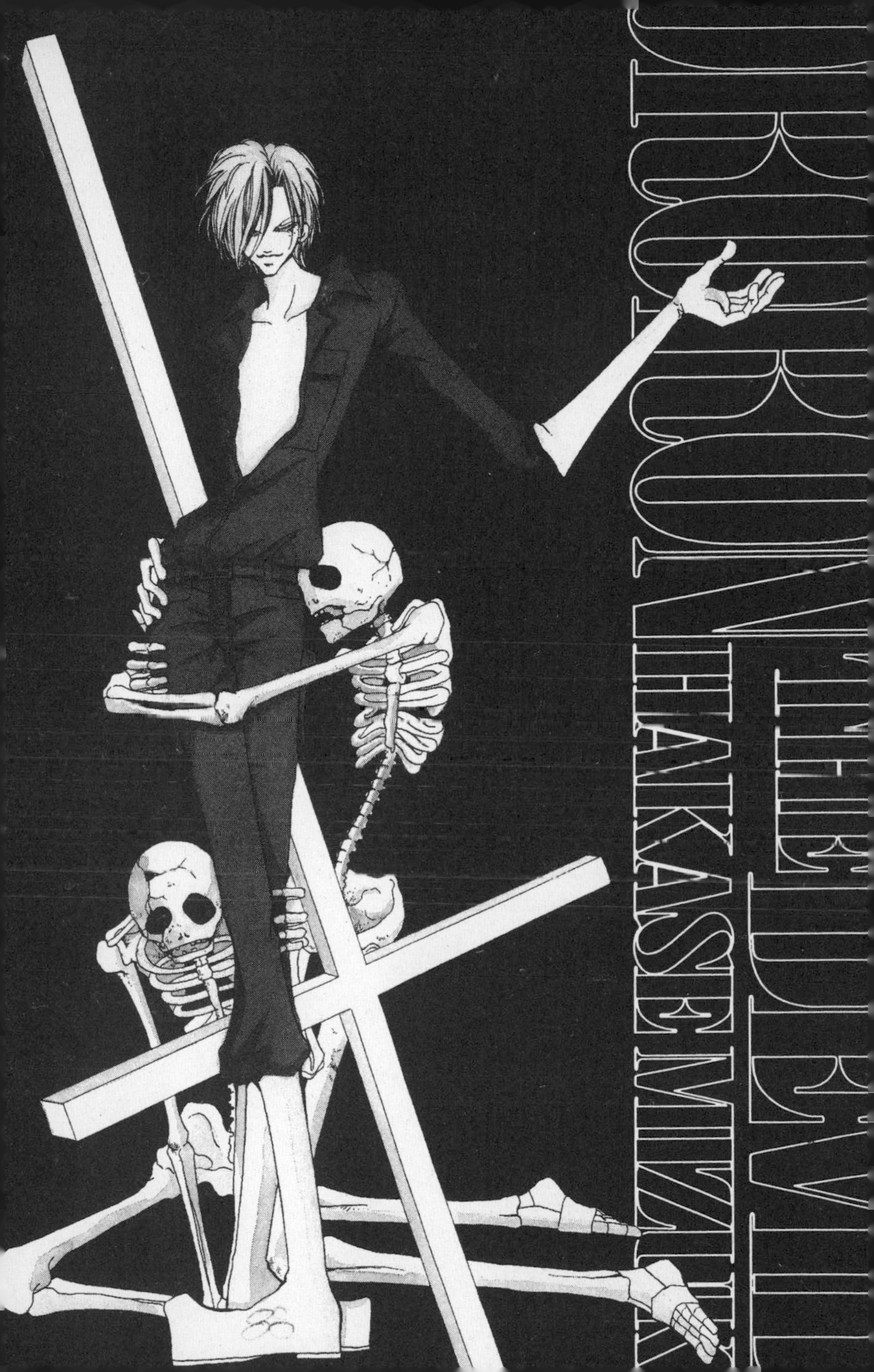
RON THE DEVIL
HAKASE MIZUK

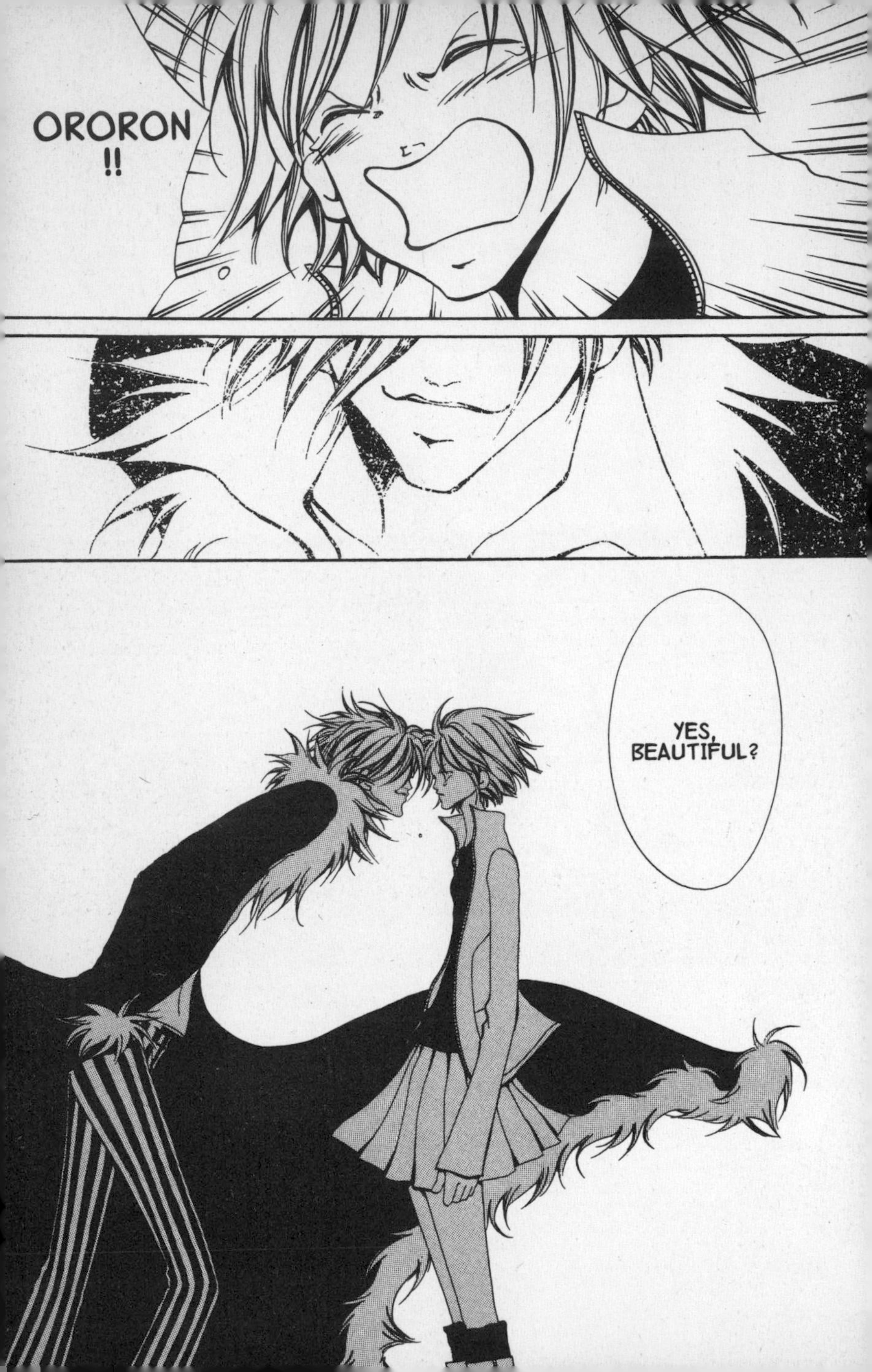
ORORON !!
YES, BEAUTIFUL?

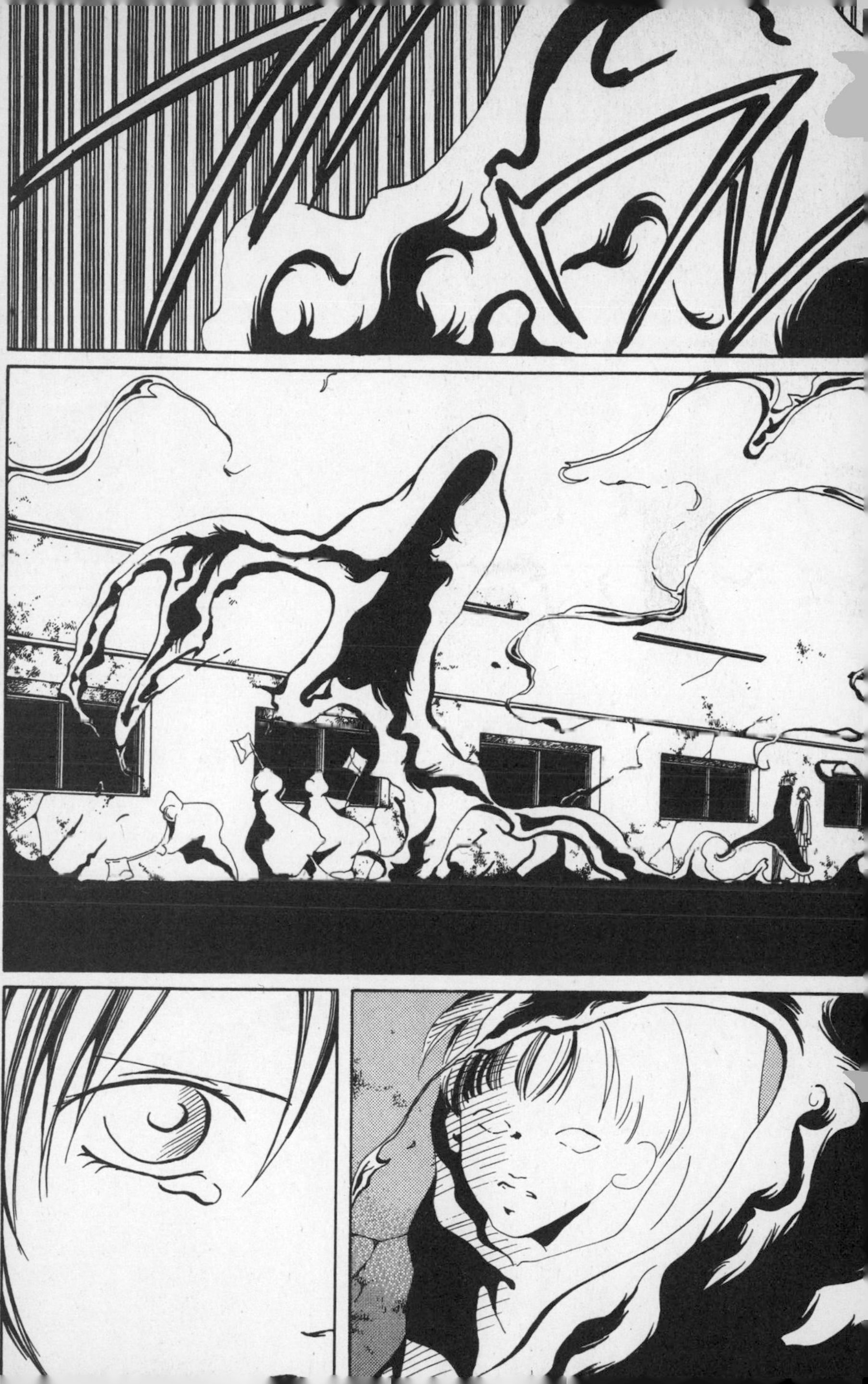

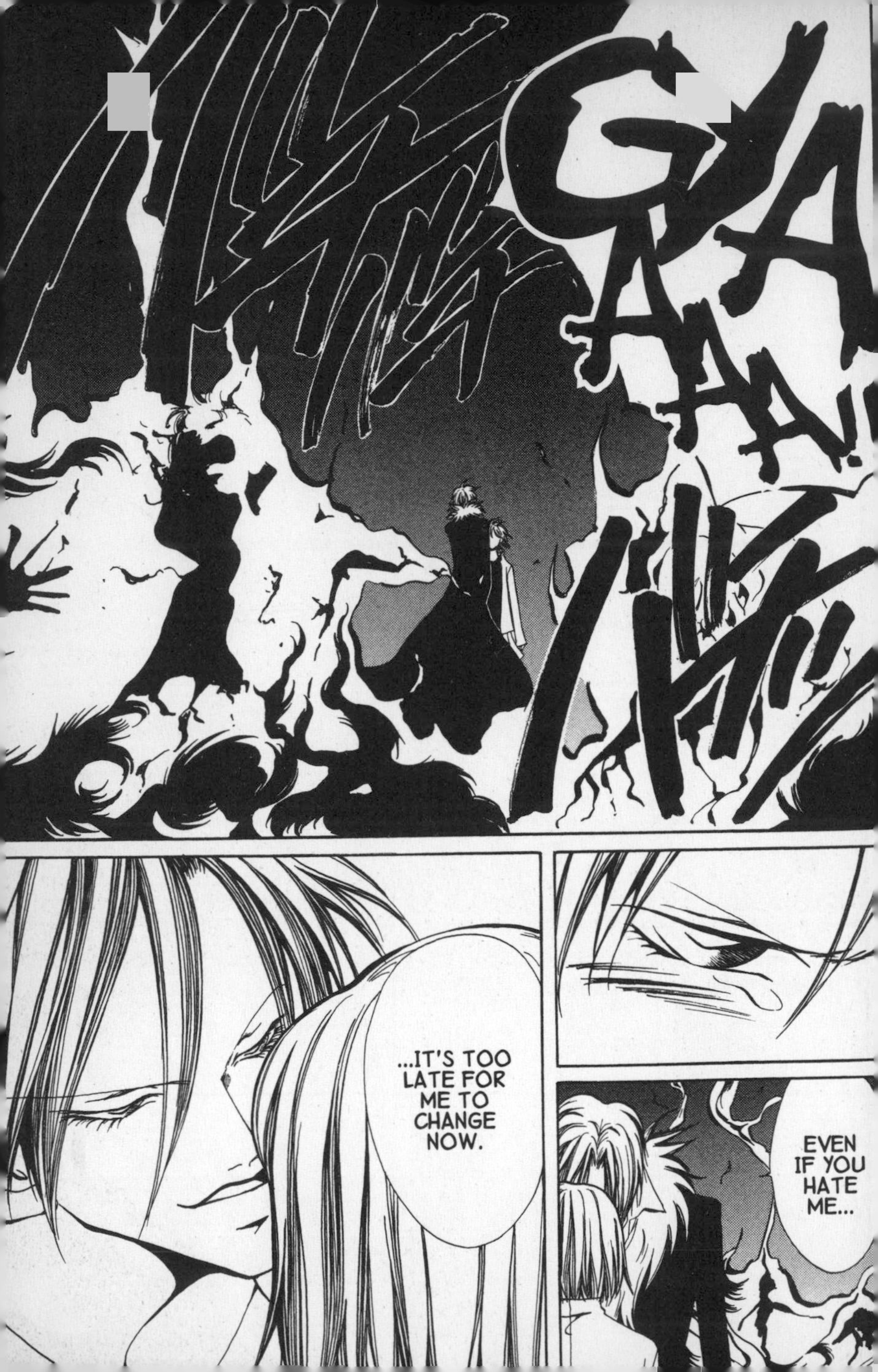
GYAAAN!
EVEN IF YOU HATE ME...
...IT'S TOO LATE FOR ME TO CHANGE NOW.

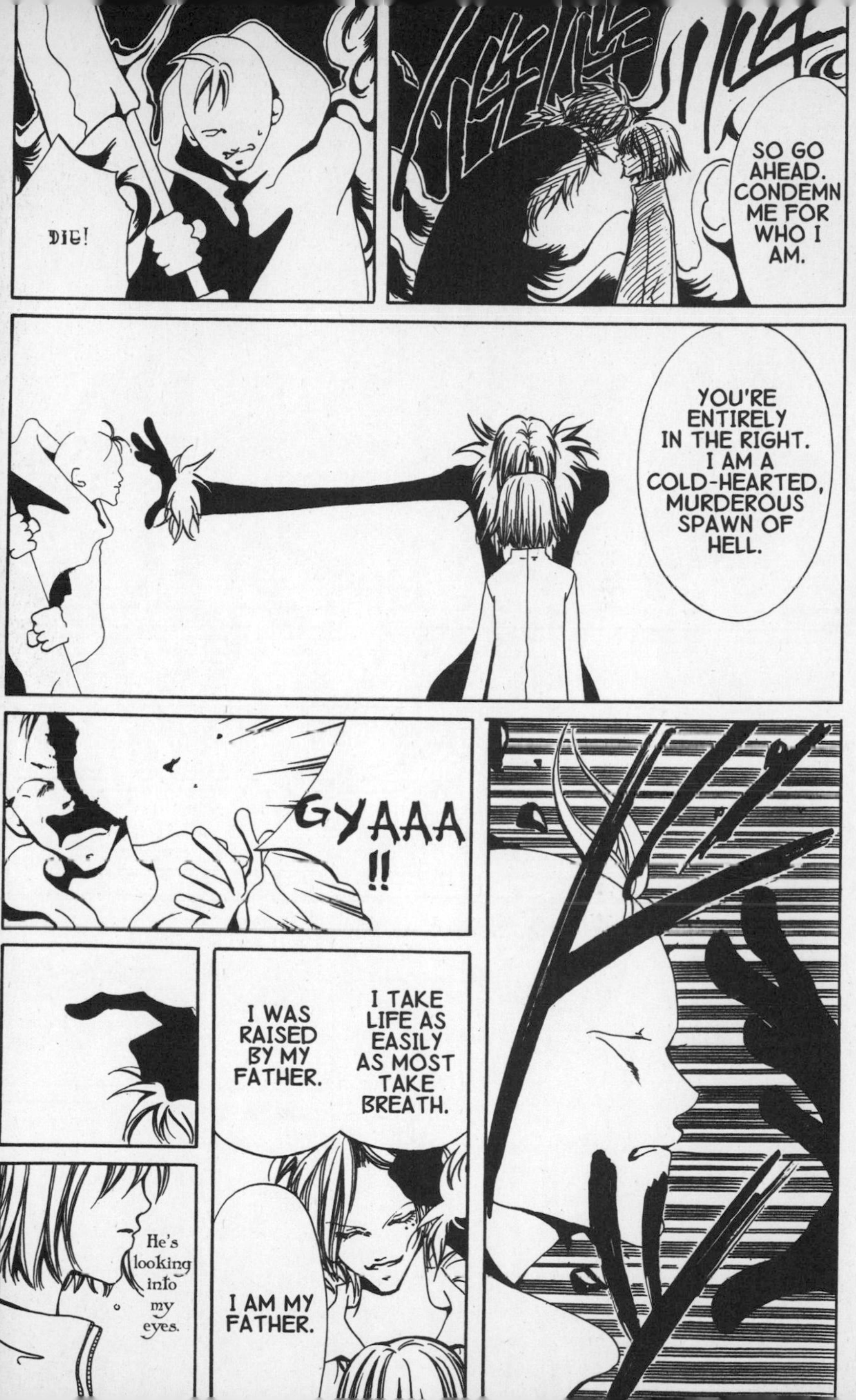
SO GO AHEAD. CONDEMN ME FOR WHO I AM.
DIE!
YOU'RE ENTIRELY IN THE RIGHT. I AM A COLD-HEARTED, MURDEROUS SPAWN OF HELL.
GYAAA!!
I TAKE LIFE AS EASILY AS MOST TAKE BREATH.
I WAS RAISED BY MY FATHER.
I AM MY FATHER.
He's looking into my eyes.

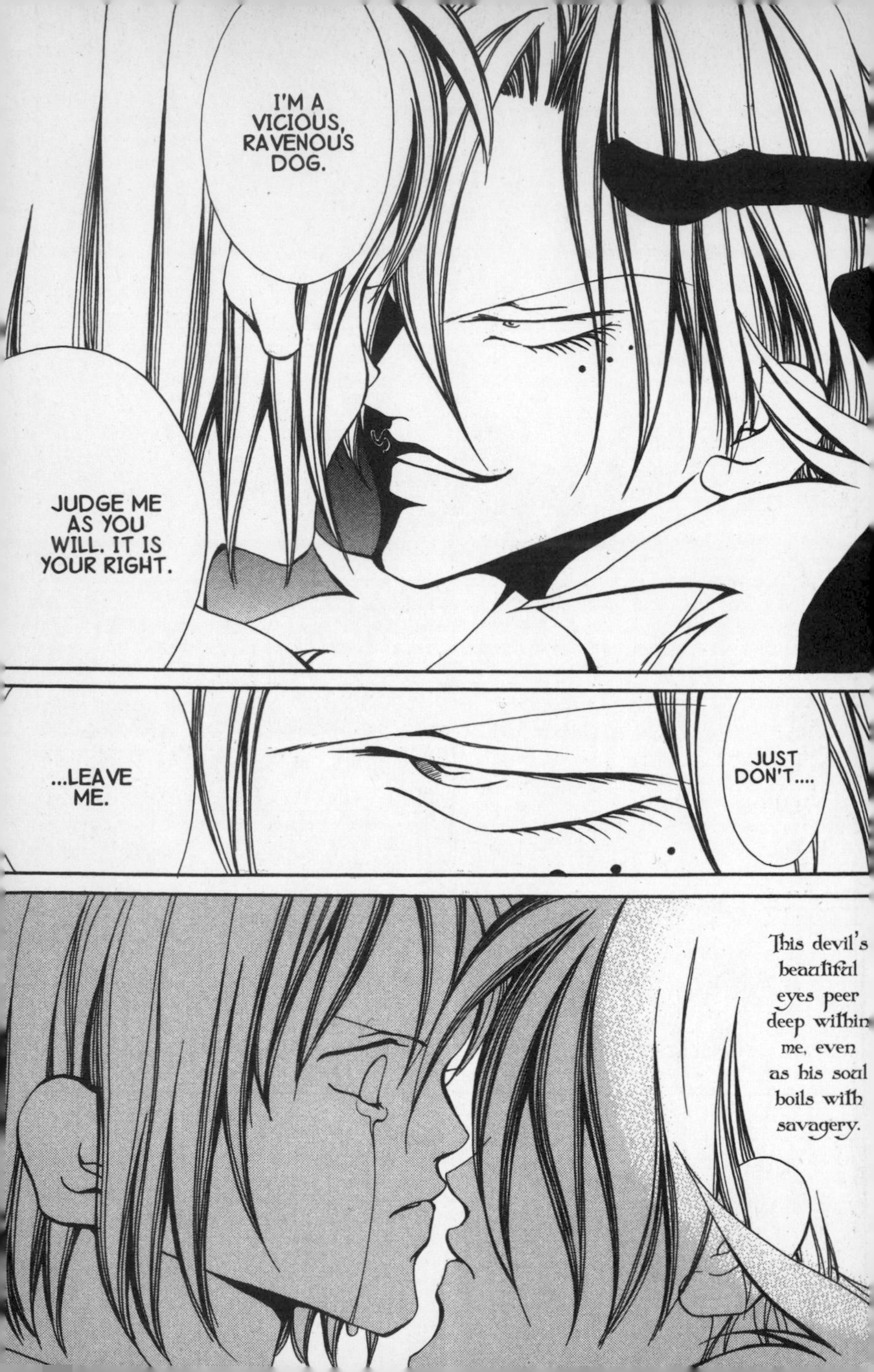
I'M A VICIOUS, RAVENOUS DOG.
JUDGE ME AS YOU WILL. IT IS YOUR RIGHT.
JUST DON'T....
...LEAVE ME.
This devil's beautiful eyes peer deep within me, even as his soul boils with savagery.

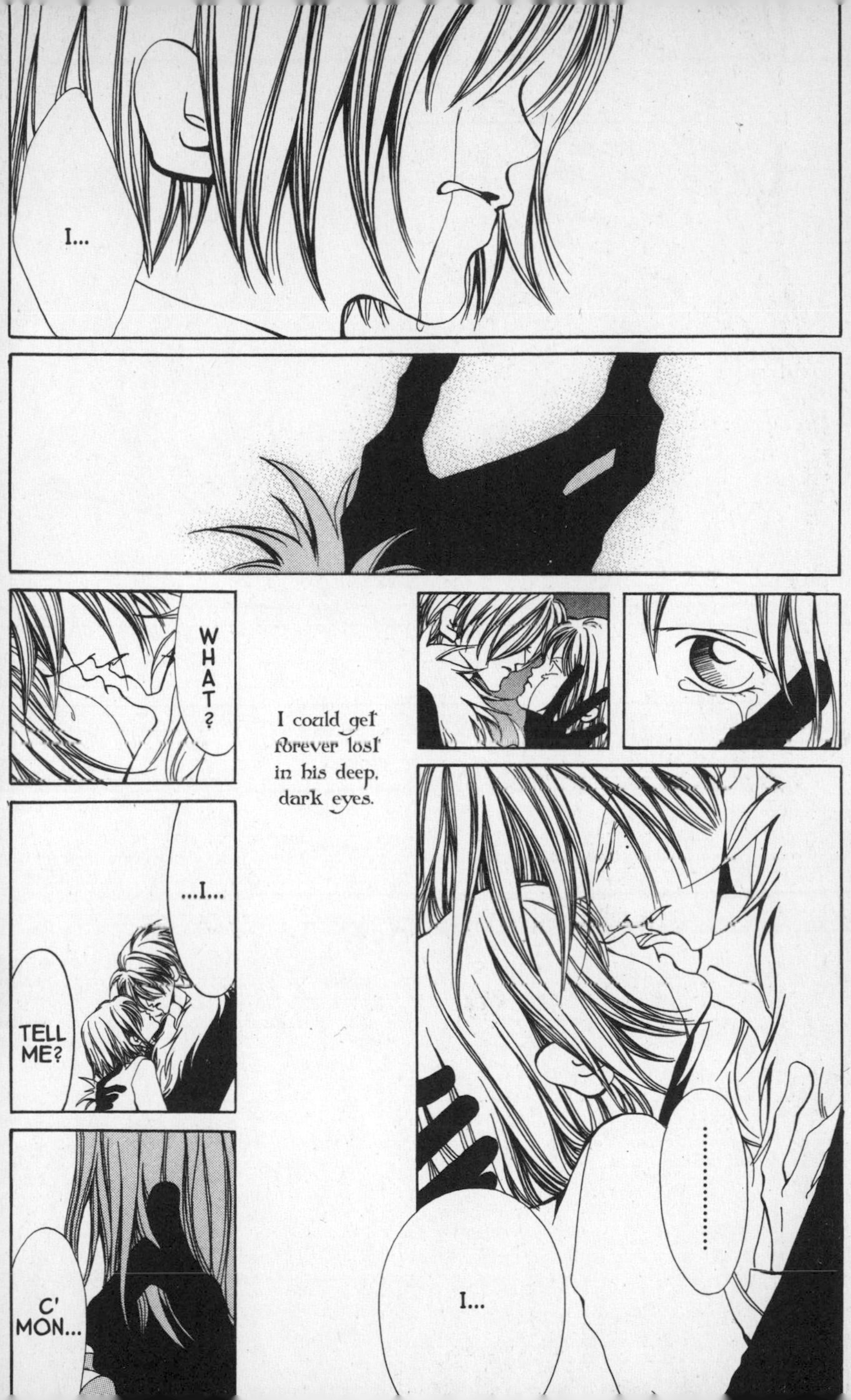
I...
......
I...
I could get forever lost in his deep, dark eyes.
WHAT?
...I...
TELL ME?
C' MON...

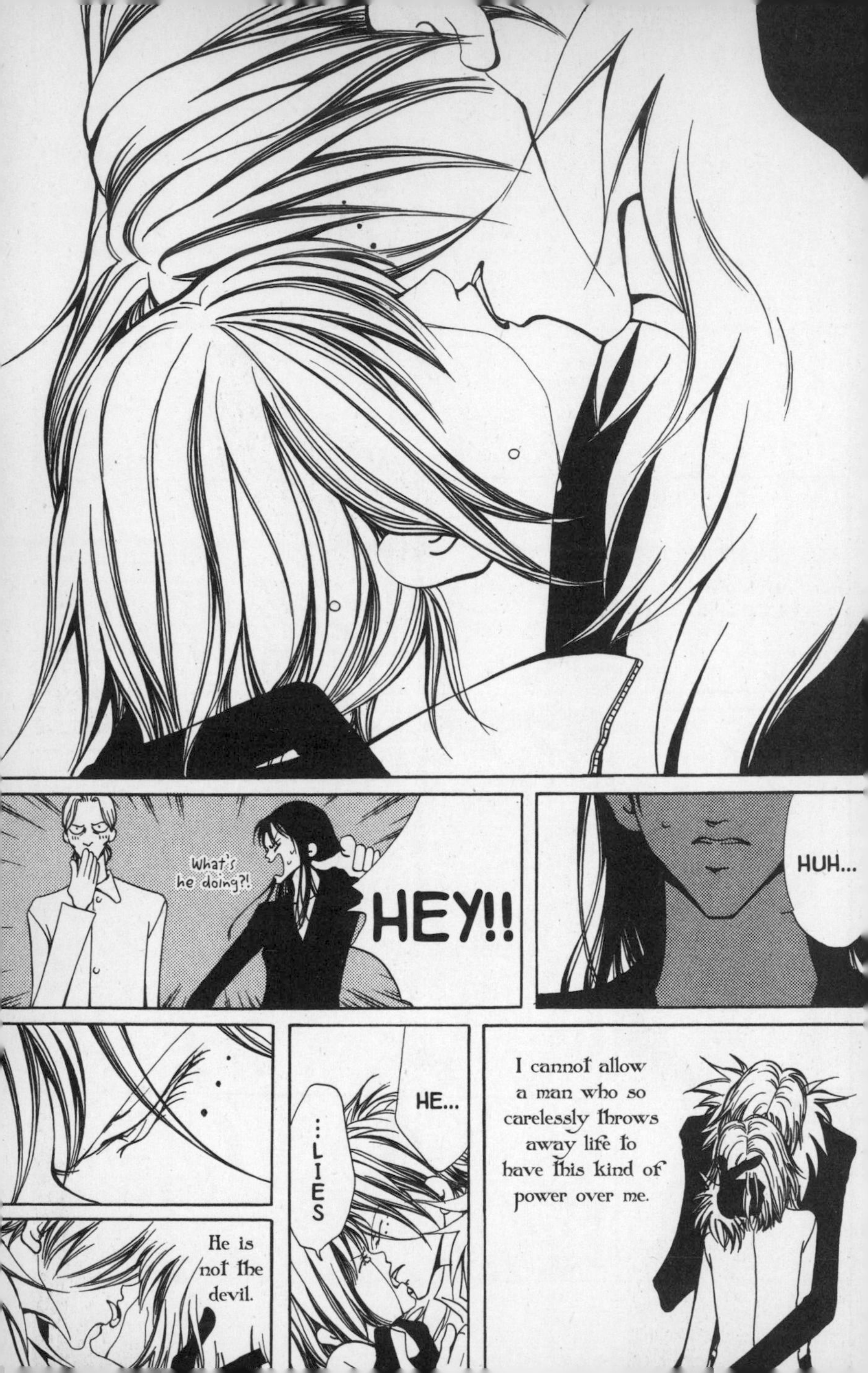
HUH...
HEY!!
What's he doing?!
I cannot allow a man who so carelessly throws away life to have this kind of power over me.
HE...
...LIES
He is not the devil.

I see sorrow in his eyes, a sorrow that's been there a long time.

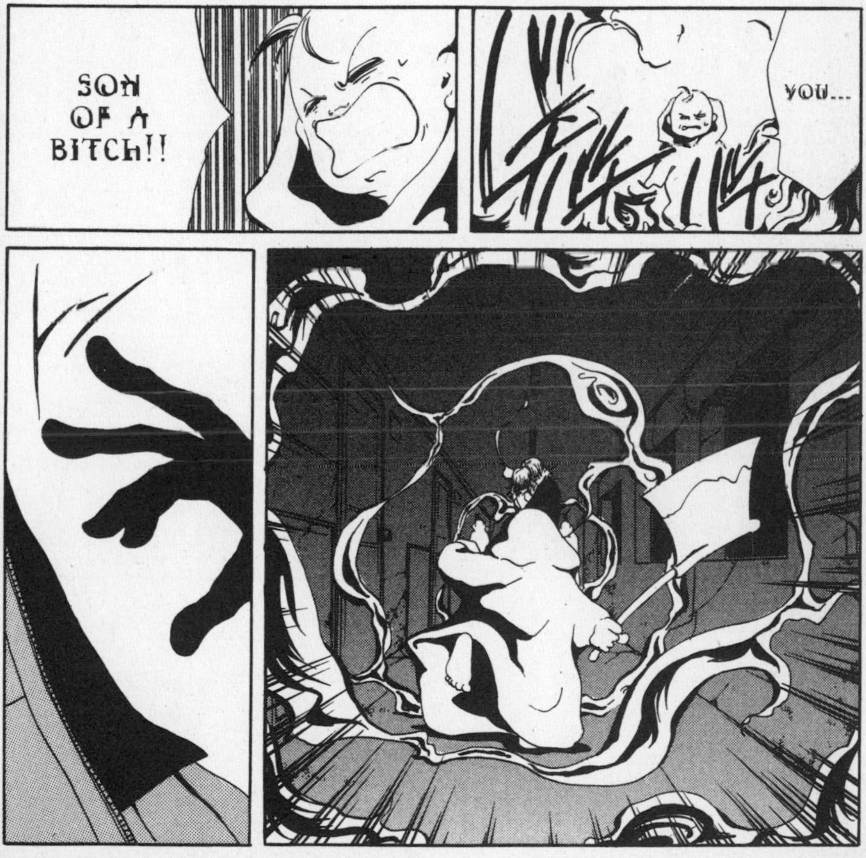
YOU...
SON OF A BITCH!!

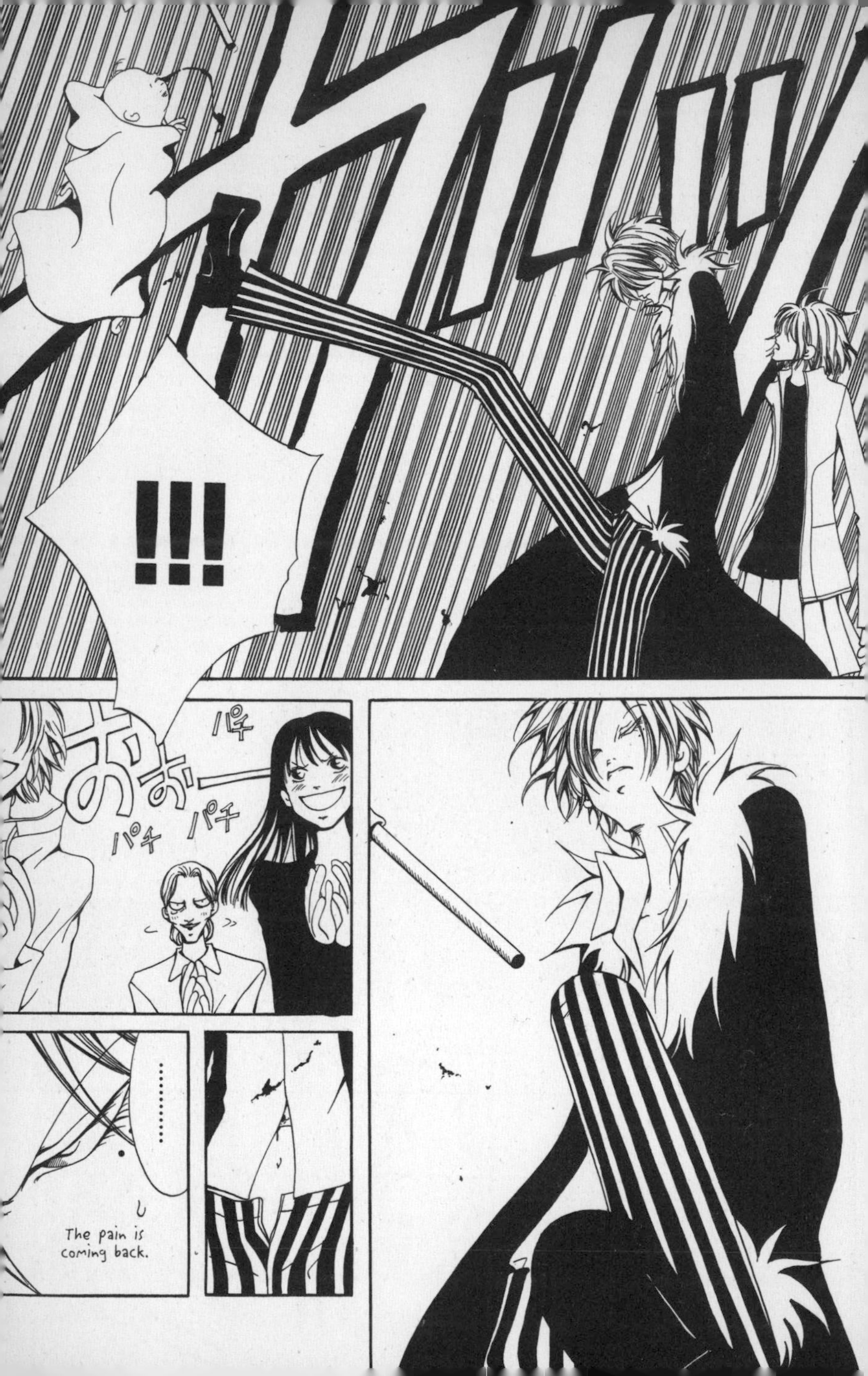
!!!
おおー
パチ
パチ
パチ
……
The pain is coming back.

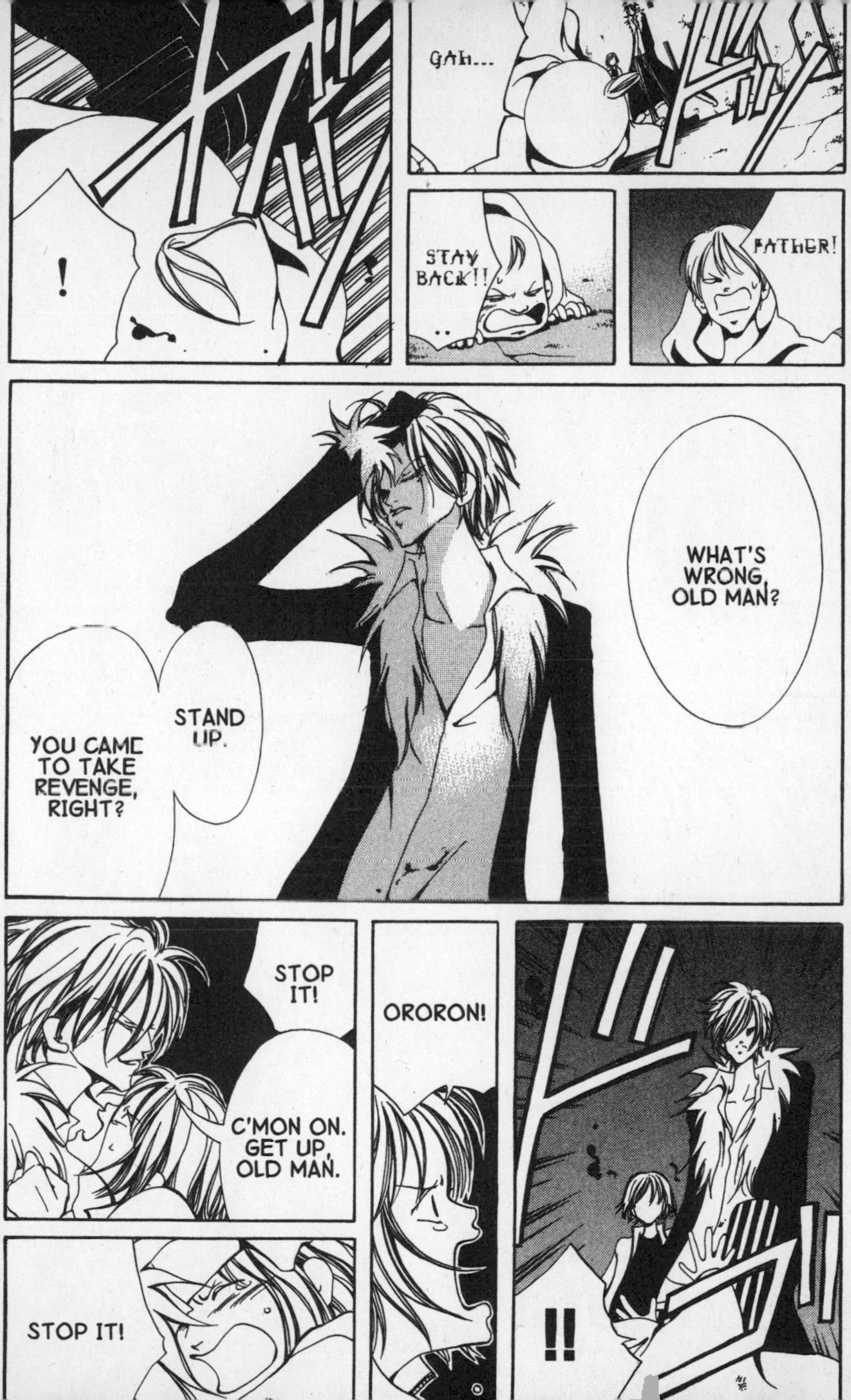
GAH...
FATHER!
STAY BACK!!
..
!
WHAT'S WRONG, OLD MAN?
STAND UP.
YOU CAME TO TAKE REVENGE, RIGHT?
!!
ORORON!
STOP IT!
C'MON ON. GET UP, OLD MAN.
STOP IT!

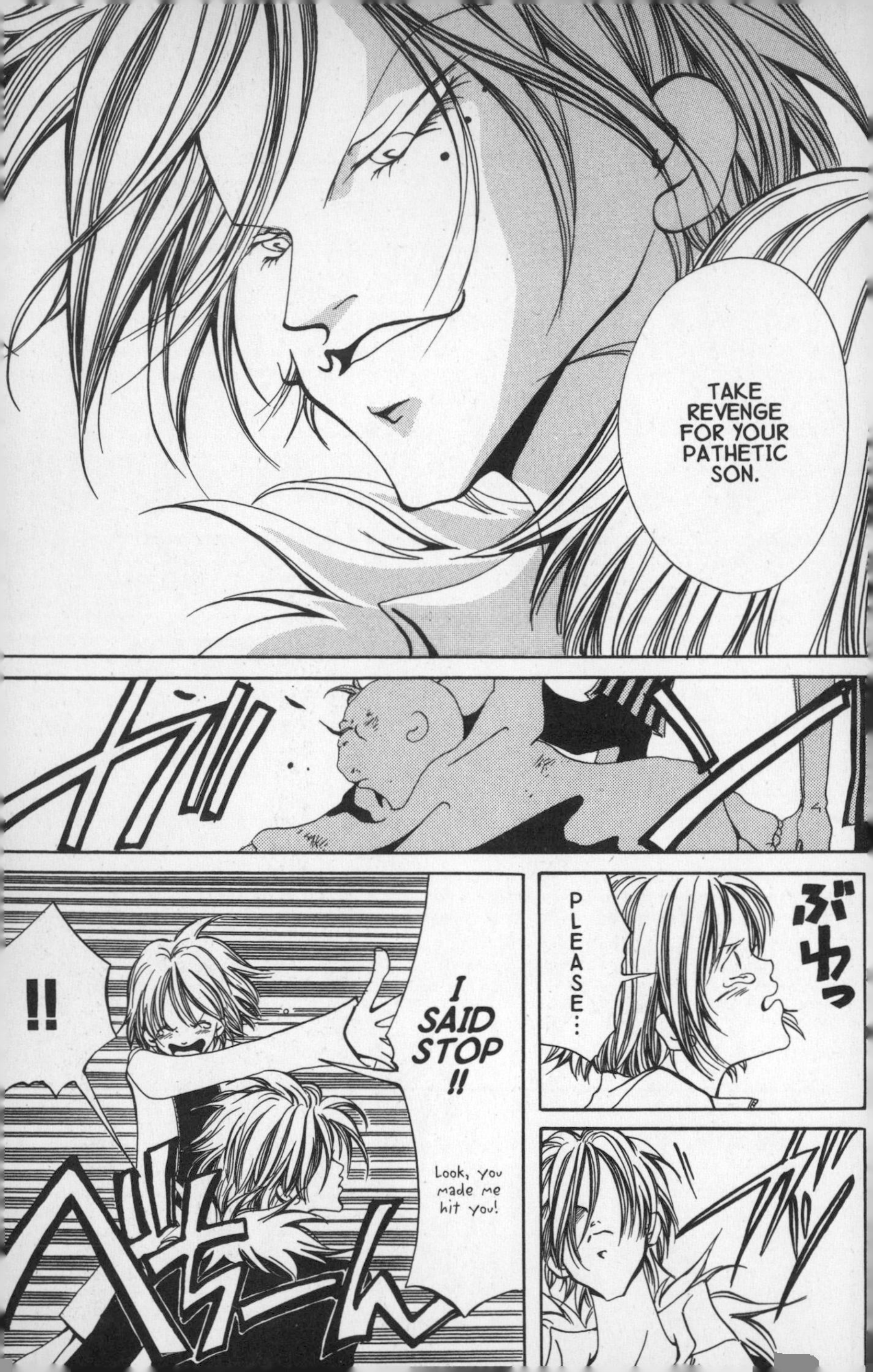
TAKE REVENGE FOR YOUR PATHETIC SON.
PLEASE...
!!
I SAID STOP !!
Look, you made me hit you!

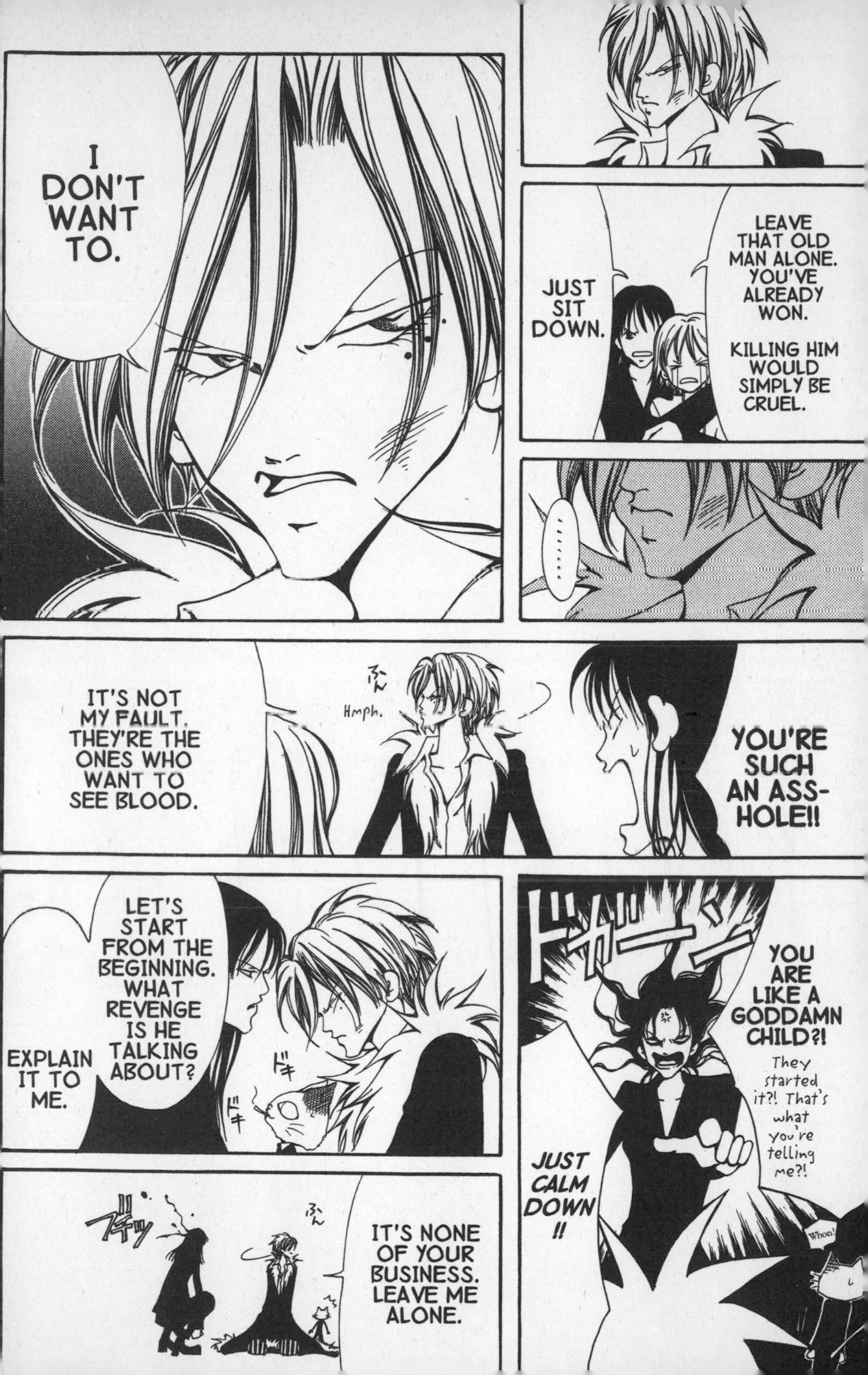
LEAVE THAT OLD MAN ALONE. YOU'VE ALREADY WON.
KILLING HIM WOULD SIMPLY BE CRUEL.
JUST SIT DOWN.
......
I DON'T WANT TO.
YOU'RE SUCH AN ASS-HOLE!!
ふん Hmph.
IT'S NOT MY FAULT. THEY'RE THE ONES WHO WANT TO SEE BLOOD.
ドガーン
YOU ARE LIKE A GODDAMN CHILD?!
They started it?! That's what you're telling me?!
JUST CALM DOWN !!
Whoa!
LET'S START FROM THE BEGINNING. WHAT REVENGE IS HE TALKING ABOUT?
ドキ ドキ
EXPLAIN IT TO ME.
IT'S NONE OF YOUR BUSINESS. LEAVE ME ALONE.
ふん
ブチッ

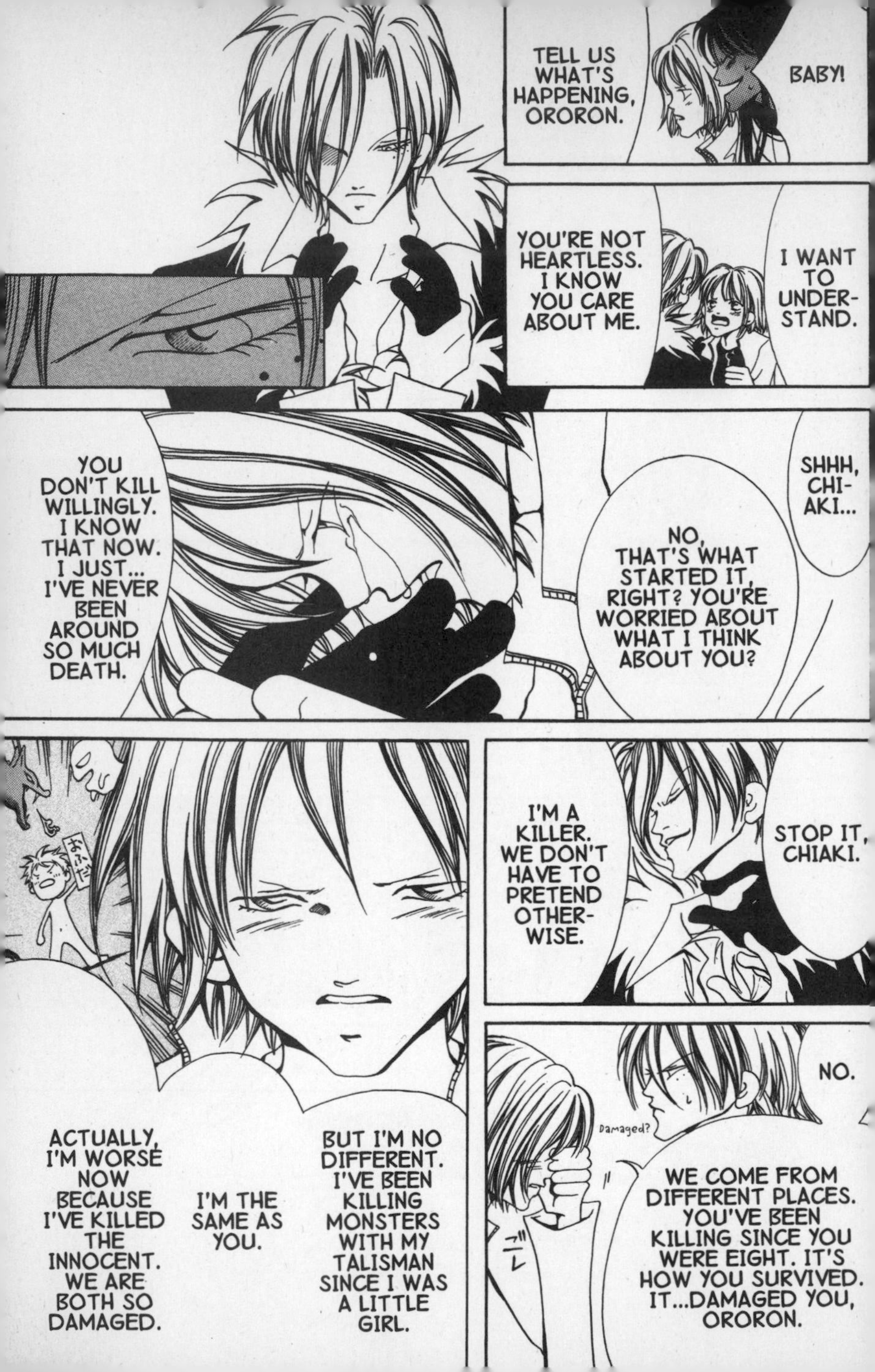
BABY!
TELL US WHAT'S HAPPENING, ORORON.
I WANT TO UNDER-STAND.
YOU'RE NOT HEARTLESS. I KNOW YOU CARE ABOUT ME.
SHHH, CHI-AKI...
NO, THAT'S WHAT STARTED IT, RIGHT? YOU'RE WORRIED ABOUT WHAT I THINK ABOUT YOU?
YOU DON'T KILL WILLINGLY. I KNOW THAT NOW. I JUST... I'VE NEVER BEEN AROUND SO MUCH DEATH.
STOP IT, CHIAKI.
I'M A KILLER. WE DON'T HAVE TO PRETEND OTHER-WISE.
NO.
Damaged?
WE COME FROM DIFFERENT PLACES. YOU'VE BEEN KILLING SINCE YOU WERE EIGHT. IT'S HOW YOU SURVIVED. IT...DAMAGED YOU, ORORON.
おふだ
BUT I'M NO DIFFERENT. I'VE BEEN KILLING MONSTERS WITH MY TALISMAN SINCE I WAS A LITTLE GIRL.
I'M THE SAME AS YOU.
ACTUALLY, I'M WORSE NOW BECAUSE I'VE KILLED THE INNOCENT. WE ARE BOTH SO DAMAGED.

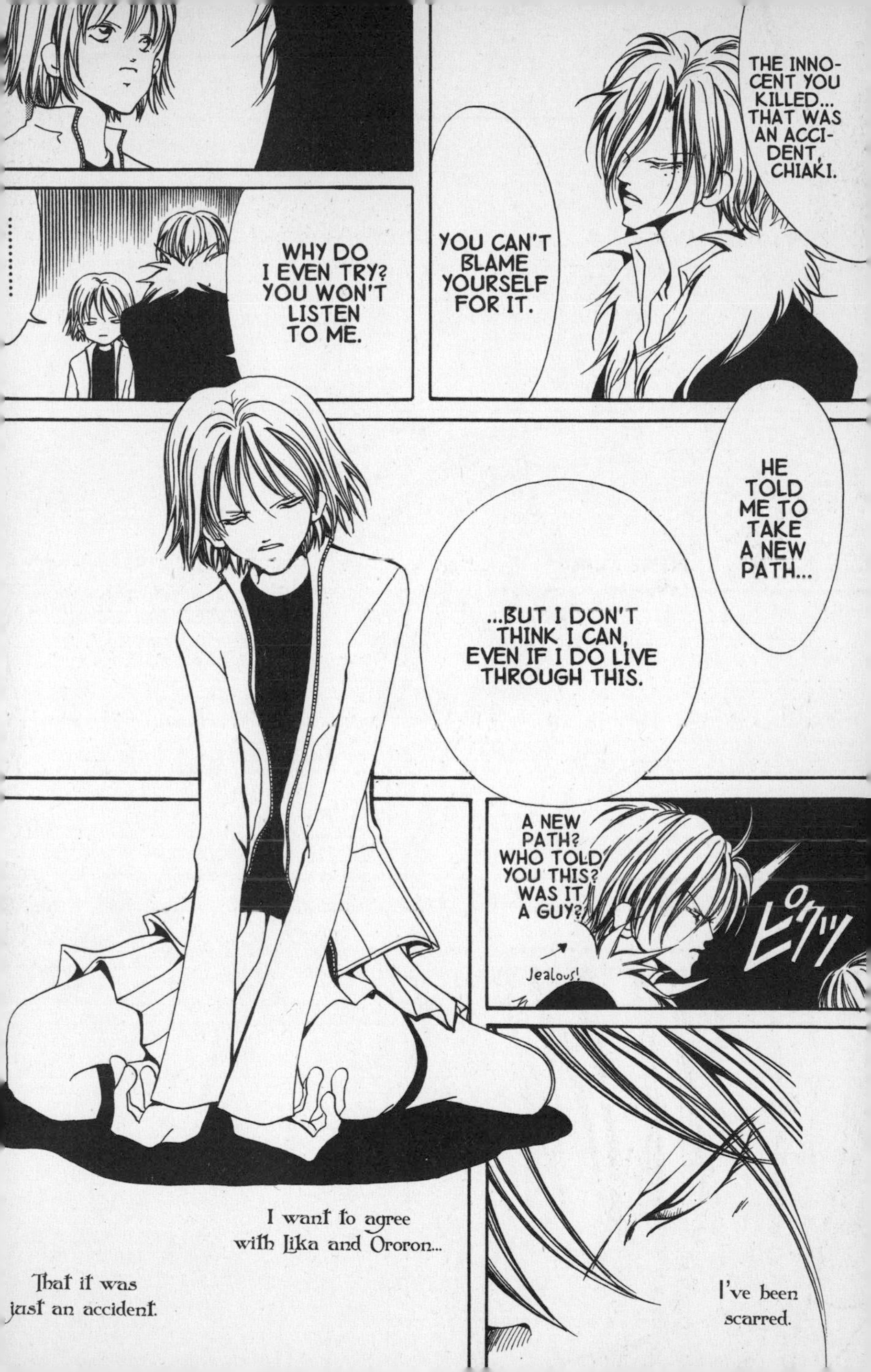
THE INNOCENT YOU KILLED... THAT WAS AN ACCIDENT, CHIAKI.
YOU CAN'T BLAME YOURSELF FOR IT.
WHY DO I EVEN TRY? YOU WON'T LISTEN TO ME.
HE TOLD ME TO TAKE A NEW PATH...
...BUT I DON'T THINK I CAN, EVEN IF I DO LIVE THROUGH THIS.
A NEW PATH? WHO TOLD YOU THIS? WAS IT A GUY?
Jealous!
ピクッ
I've been scarred.
I want to agree with Lika and Ororon...
That it was just an accident.

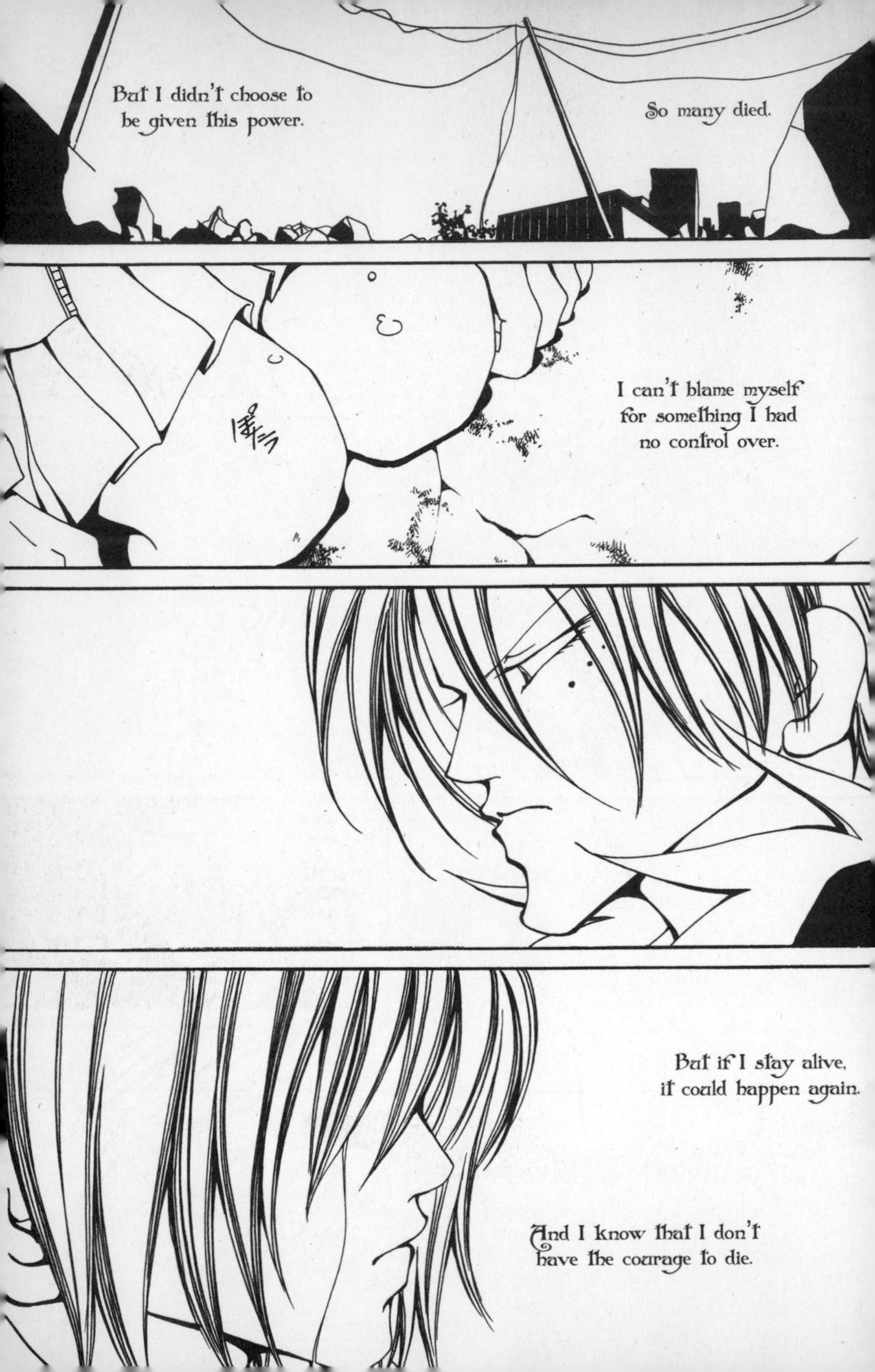
So many died.
But I didn't choose to be given this power.
I can't blame myself for something I had no control over.
But if I stay alive, it could happen again.
And I know that I don't have the courage to die.

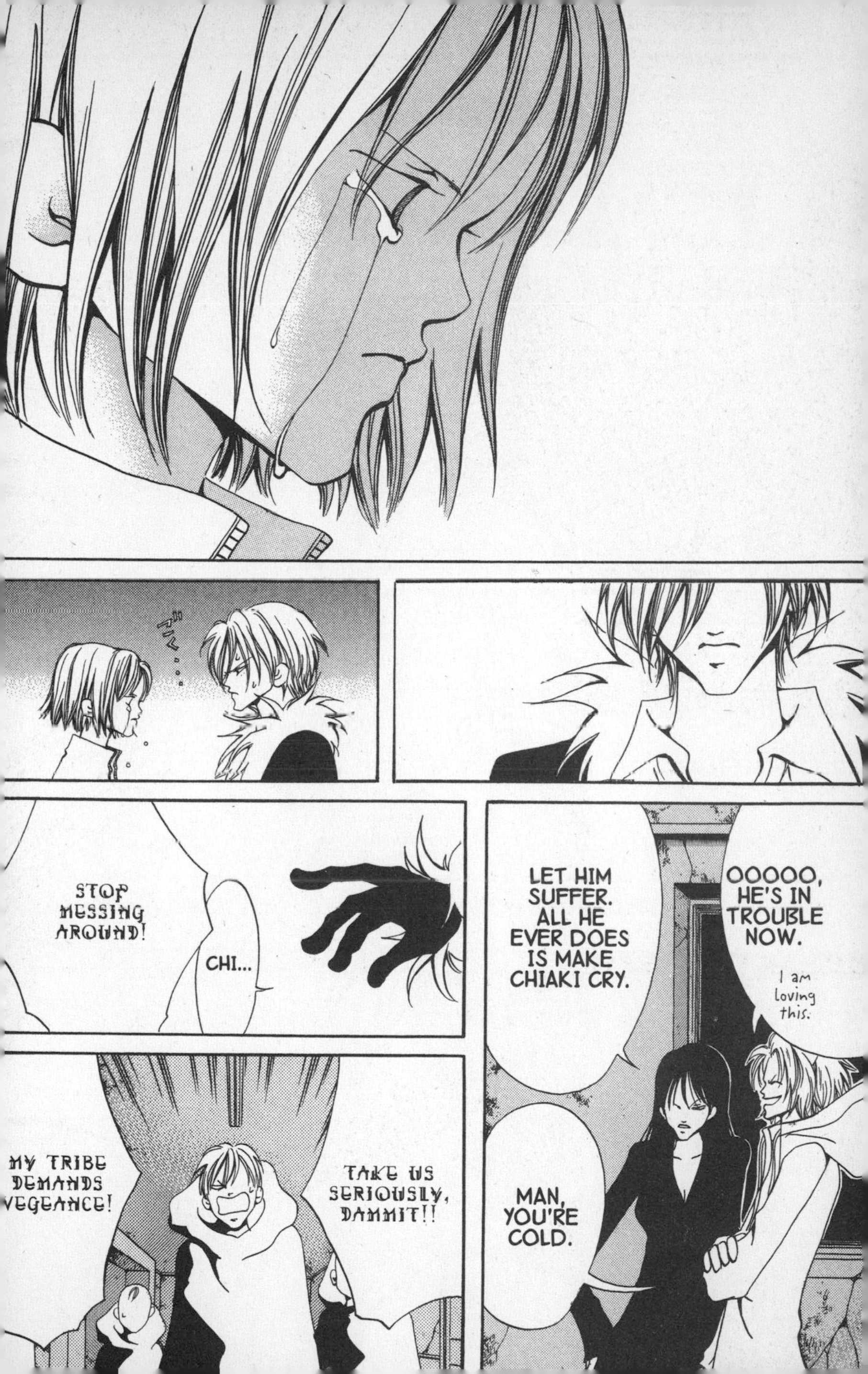
OOOOO, HE'S IN TROUBLE NOW.
I am loving this.
LET HIM SUFFER. ALL HE EVER DOES IS MAKE CHIAKI CRY.
MAN, YOU'RE COLD.
CHI...
STOP MESSING AROUND!
TAKE US SERIOUSLY, DAMMIT!!
MY TRIBE DEMANDS VEGEANCE!

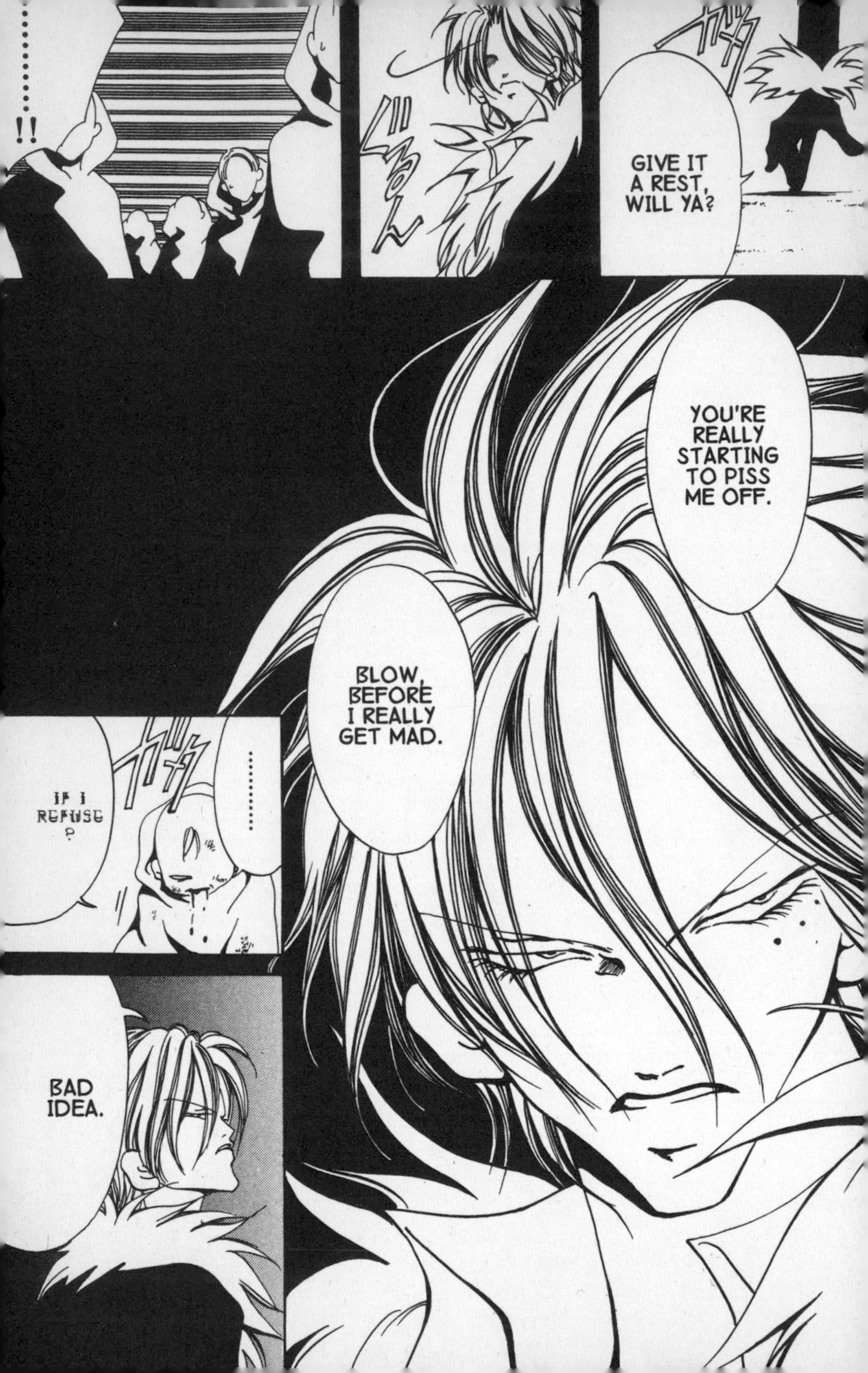
GIVE IT A REST, WILL YA?
......!!
YOU'RE REALLY STARTING TO PISS ME OFF.
BLOW, BEFORE I REALLY GET MAD.
......
IF I REFUSE?
BAD IDEA.

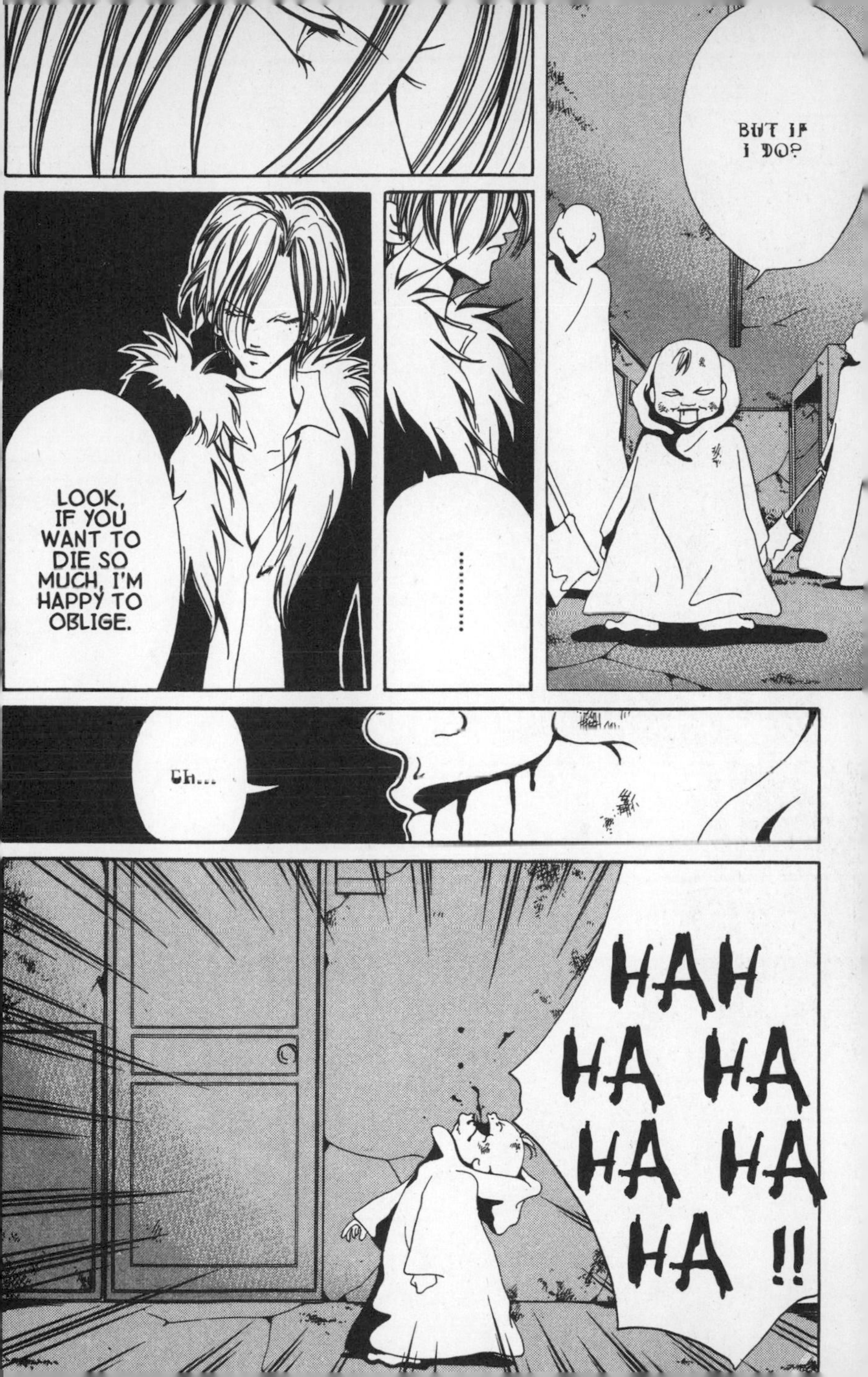
BUT IF I DO?
....
LOOK, IF YOU WANT TO DIE SO MUCH, I'M HAPPY TO OBLIGE.
Uh...
HAH HA HA HA HA HA HA HA !!

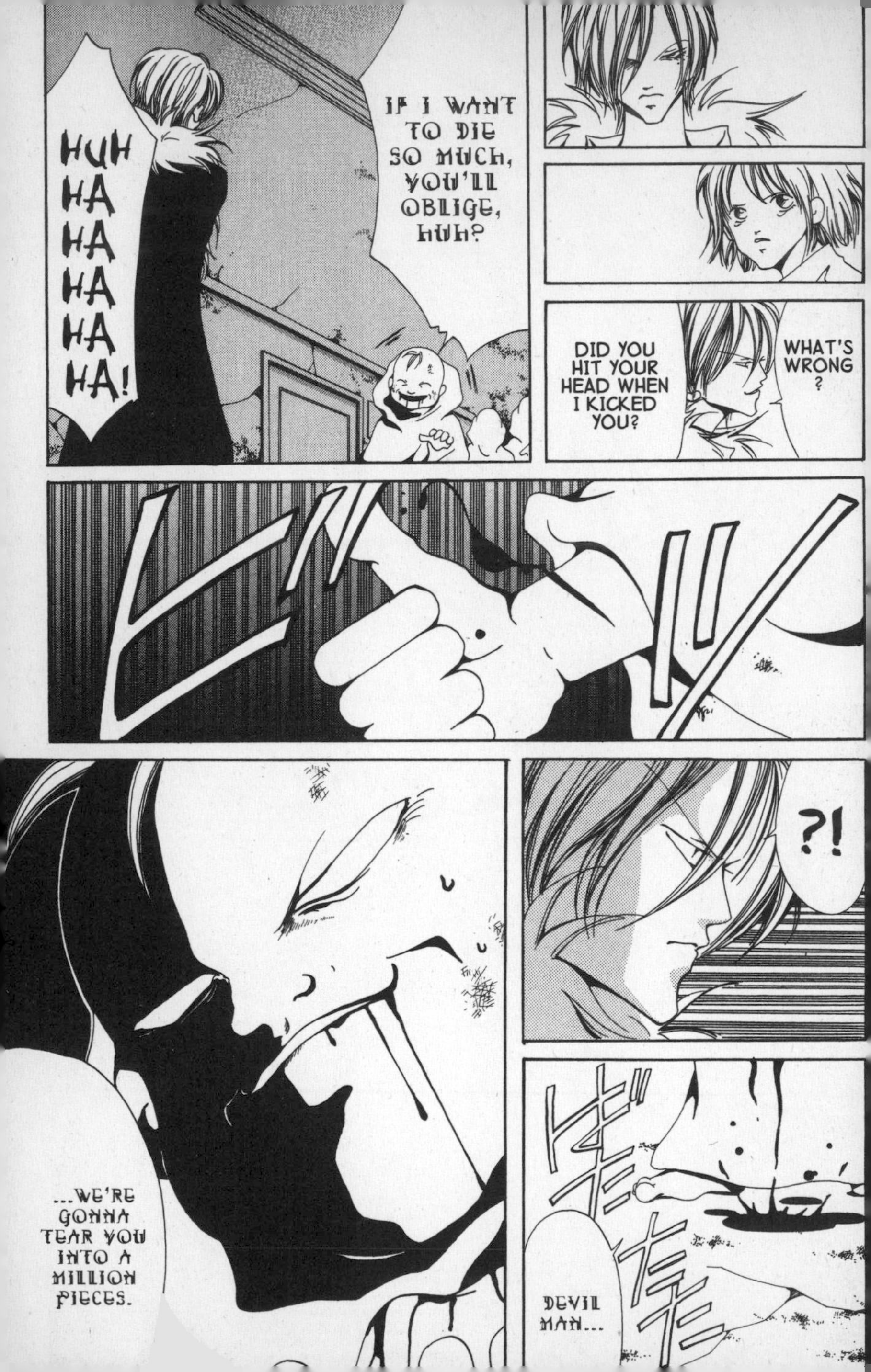
WHAT'S WRONG?
DID YOU HIT YOUR HEAD WHEN I KICKED YOU?
IF I WANT TO DIE SO MUCH, YOU'LL OBLIGE, HUH?
HUH HA HA HA HA HA HA!
?!
DEVIL MAN...
...WE'RE GONNA TEAR YOU INTO A MILLION PIECES.

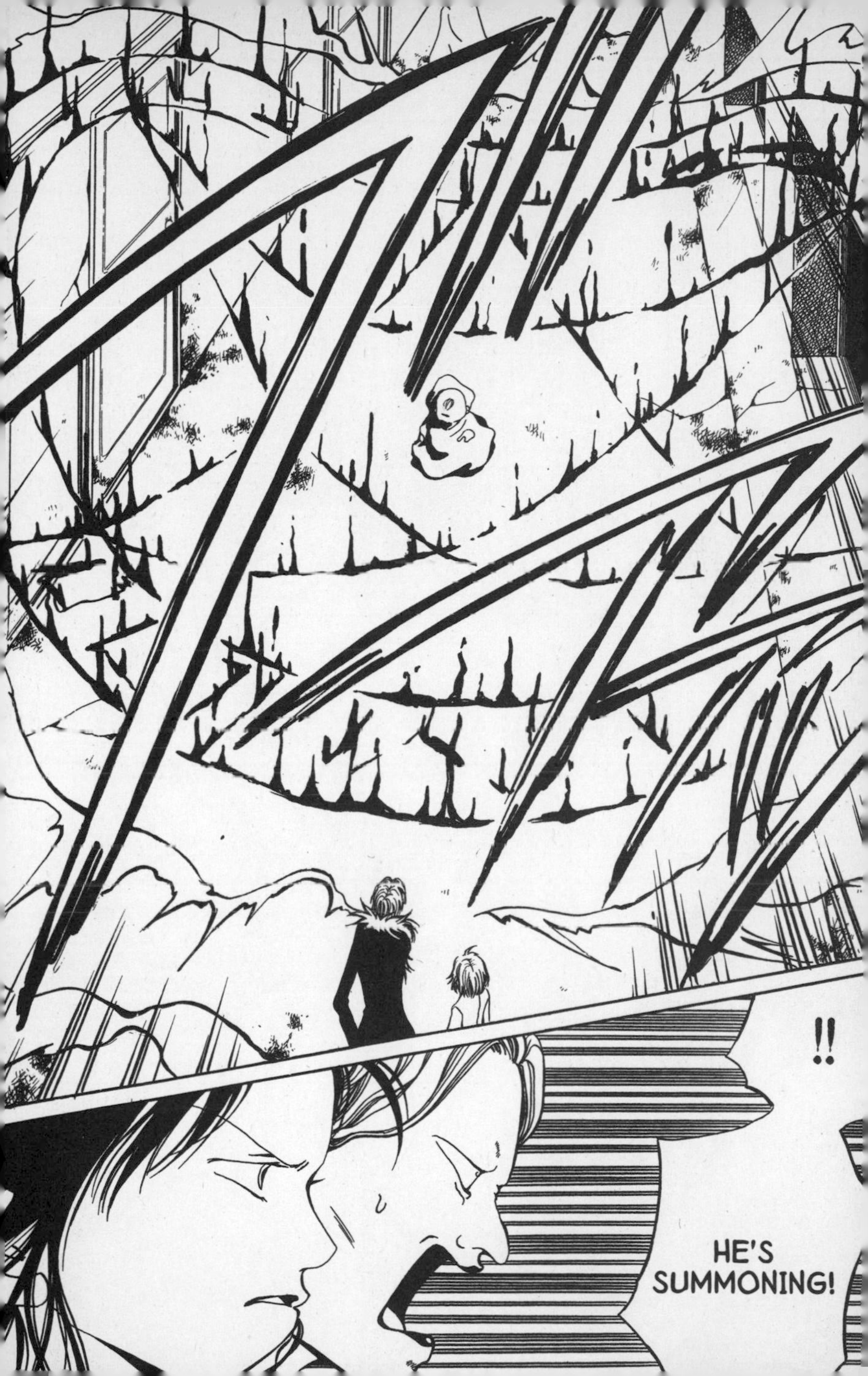
!!
HE'S SUMMONING!

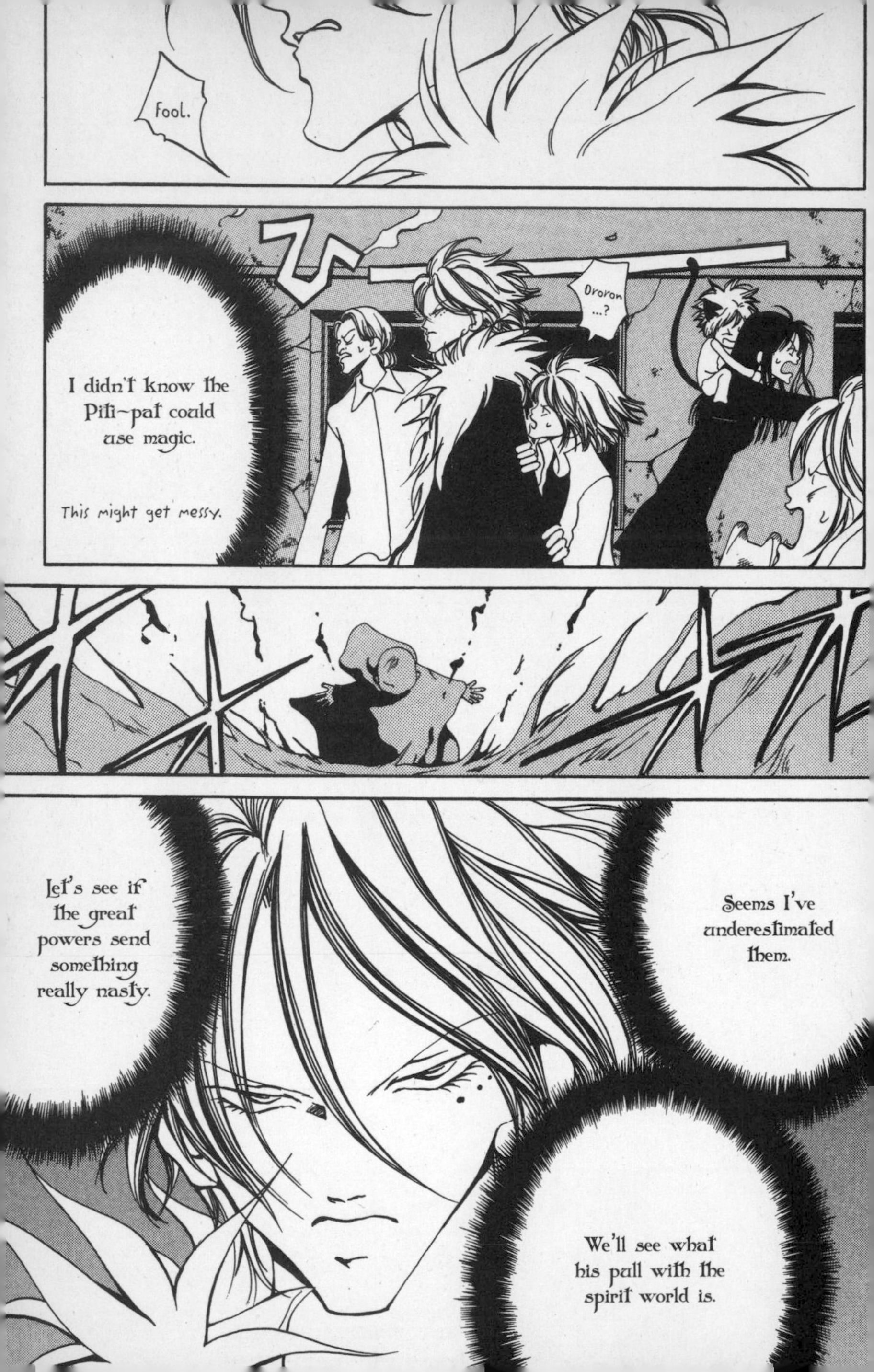
Fool.
Ororon ...?
I didn't know the Pili~pat could use magic.
This might get messy.
Seems I've underestimated them.
Let's see if the great powers send something really nasty.
We'll see what his pull with the spirit world is.

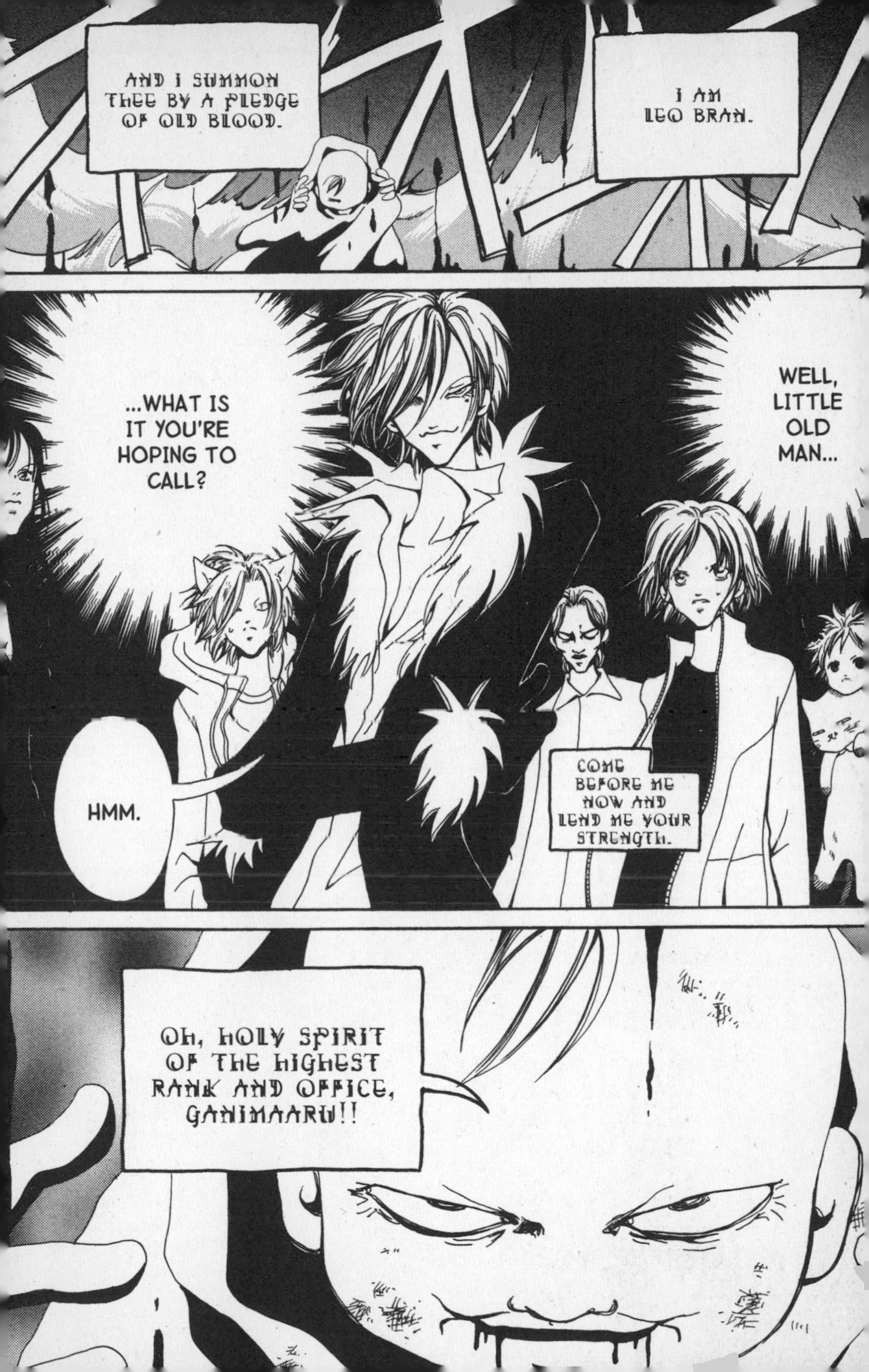
I AM LEO BRAN.
AND I SUMMON THEE BY A PLEDGE OF OLD BLOOD.
WELL, LITTLE OLD MAN...
...WHAT IS IT YOU'RE HOPING TO CALL?
COME BEFORE ME NOW AND LEND ME YOUR STRENGTH.
HMM.
OH, HOLY SPIRIT OF THE HIGHEST RANK AND OFFICE, GANIMAARU!!

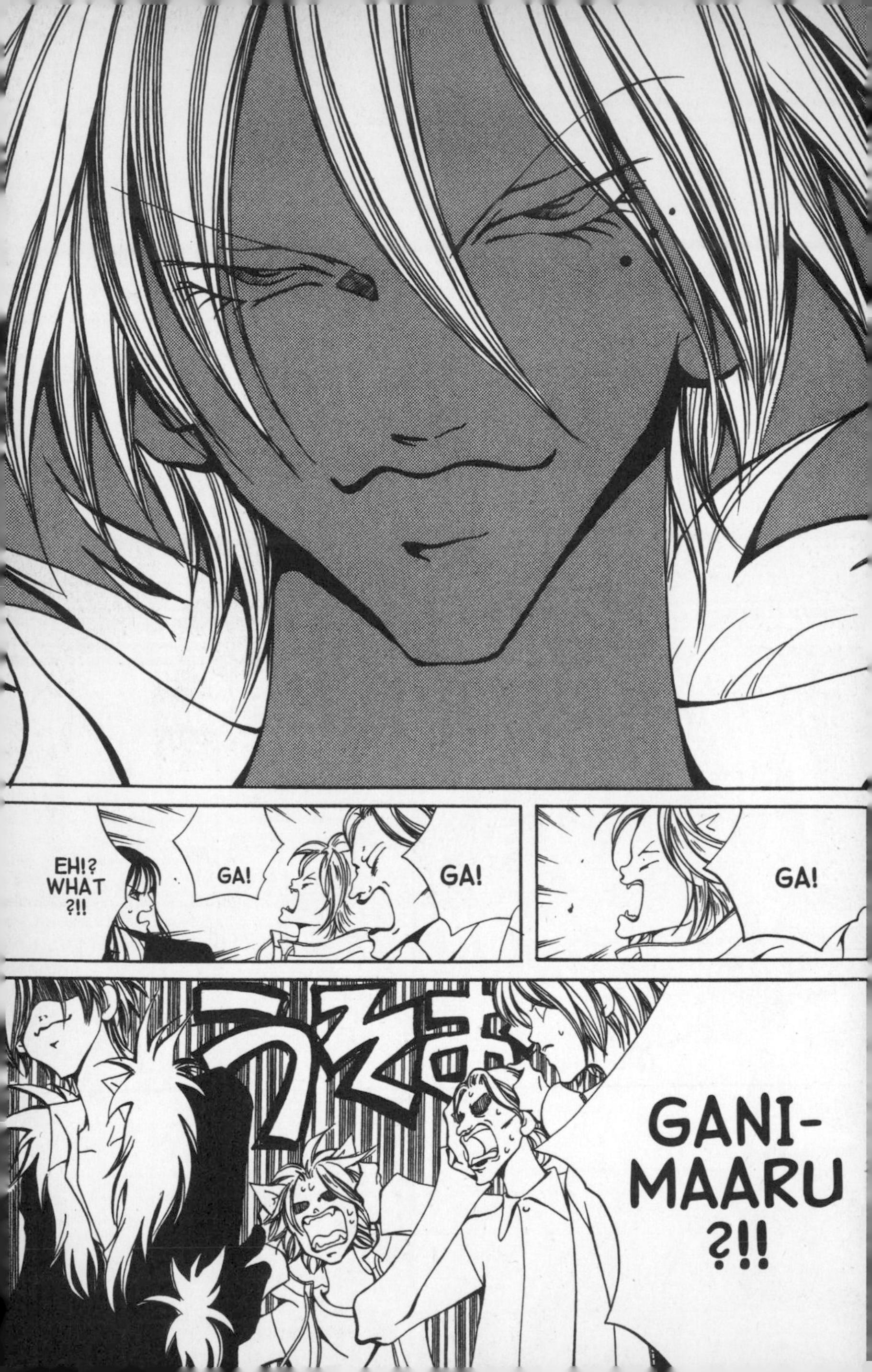
GA!
GA!
GA!
EH!? WHAT ?!!
GANI-MAARU ?!!
うえあ

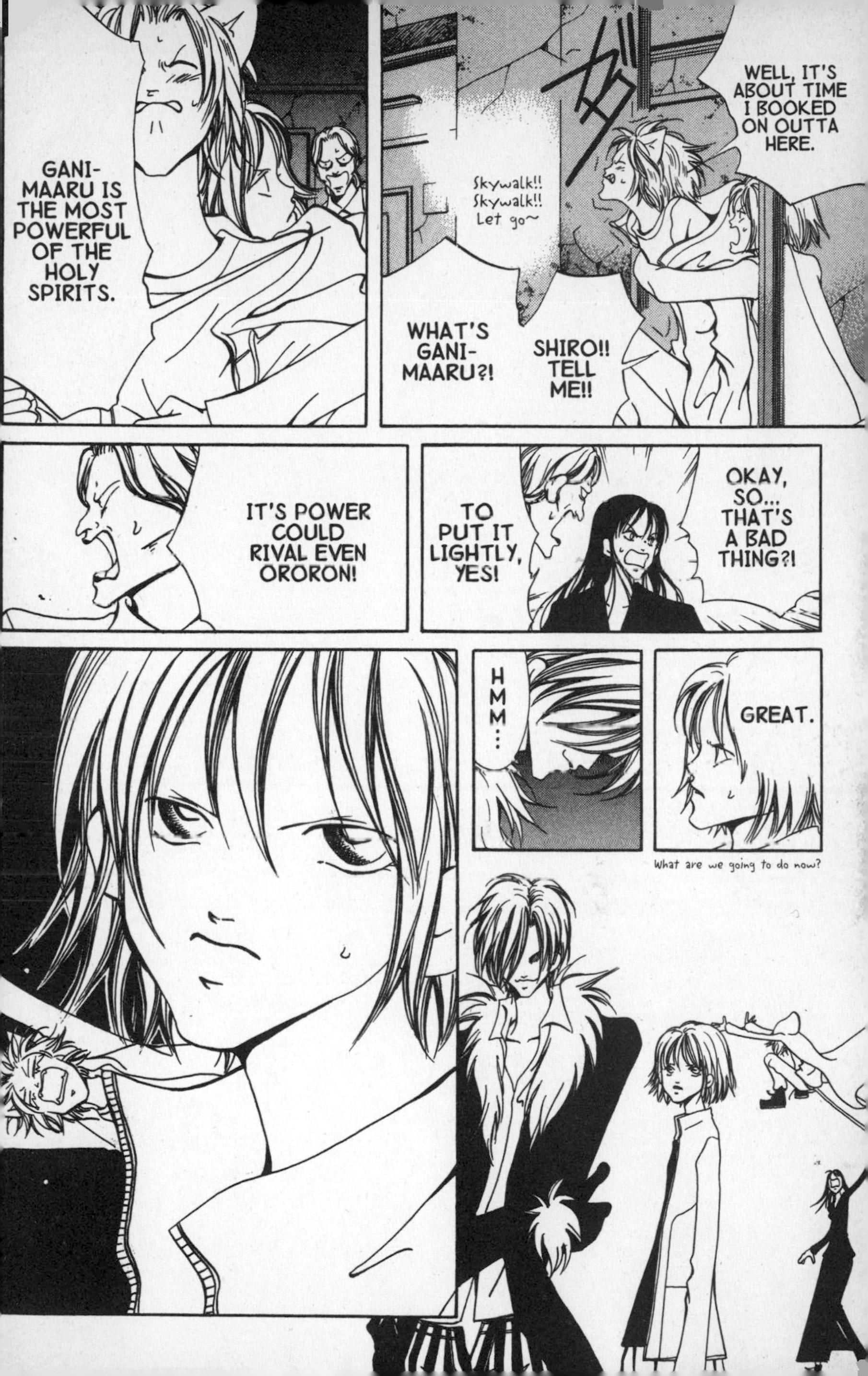
WELL, IT'S ABOUT TIME I BOOKED ON OUTTA HERE.
Skywalk!! Skywalk!! Let go~
SHIRO!! TELL ME!!
WHAT'S GANI-MAARU?!
GANI-MAARU IS THE MOST POWERFUL OF THE HOLY SPIRITS.
OKAY, SO... THAT'S A BAD THING?!
TO PUT IT LIGHTLY, YES!
IT'S POWER COULD RIVAL EVEN ORORON!
GREAT.
HMM...
What are we going to do now?

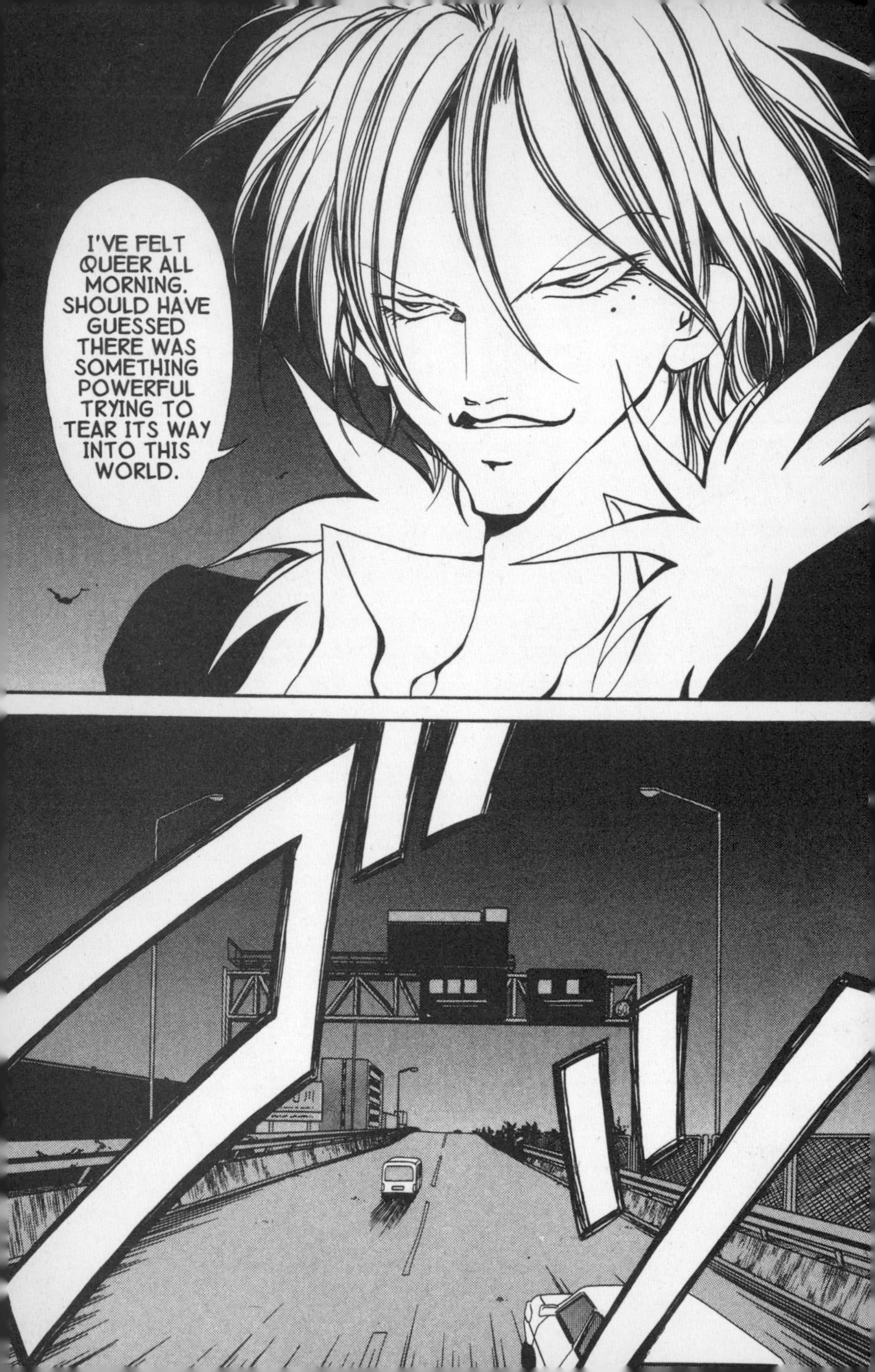
I'VE FELT QUEER ALL MORNING. SHOULD HAVE GUESSED THERE WAS SOMETHING POWERFUL TRYING TO TEAR ITS WAY INTO THIS WORLD.

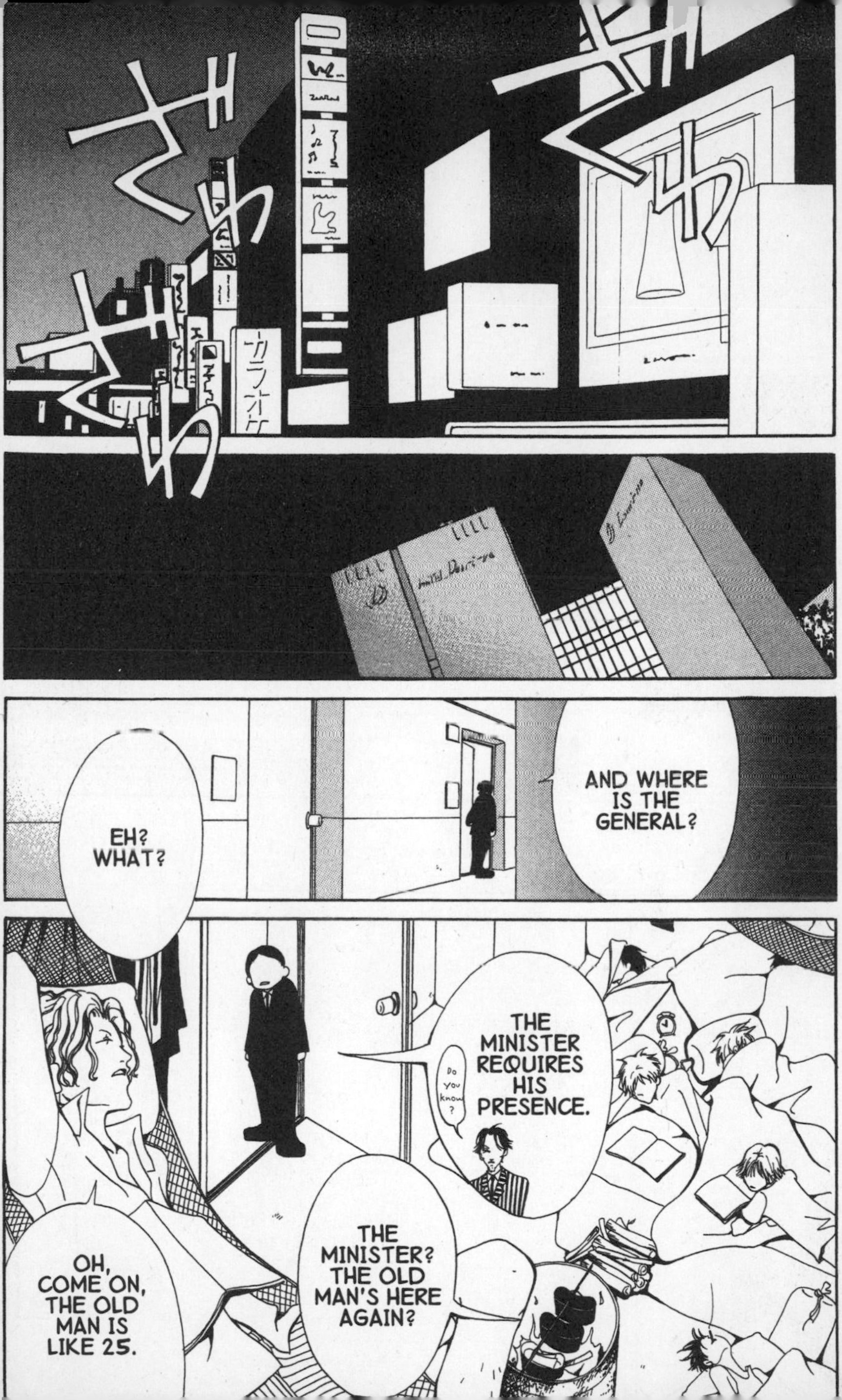
ざわ
ざわざわ
カラオケ
AND WHERE IS THE GENERAL?
EH? WHAT?
THE MINISTER REQUIRES HIS PRESENCE.
Do you know?
THE MINISTER? THE OLD MAN'S HERE AGAIN?
OH, COME ON, THE OLD MAN IS LIKE 25.

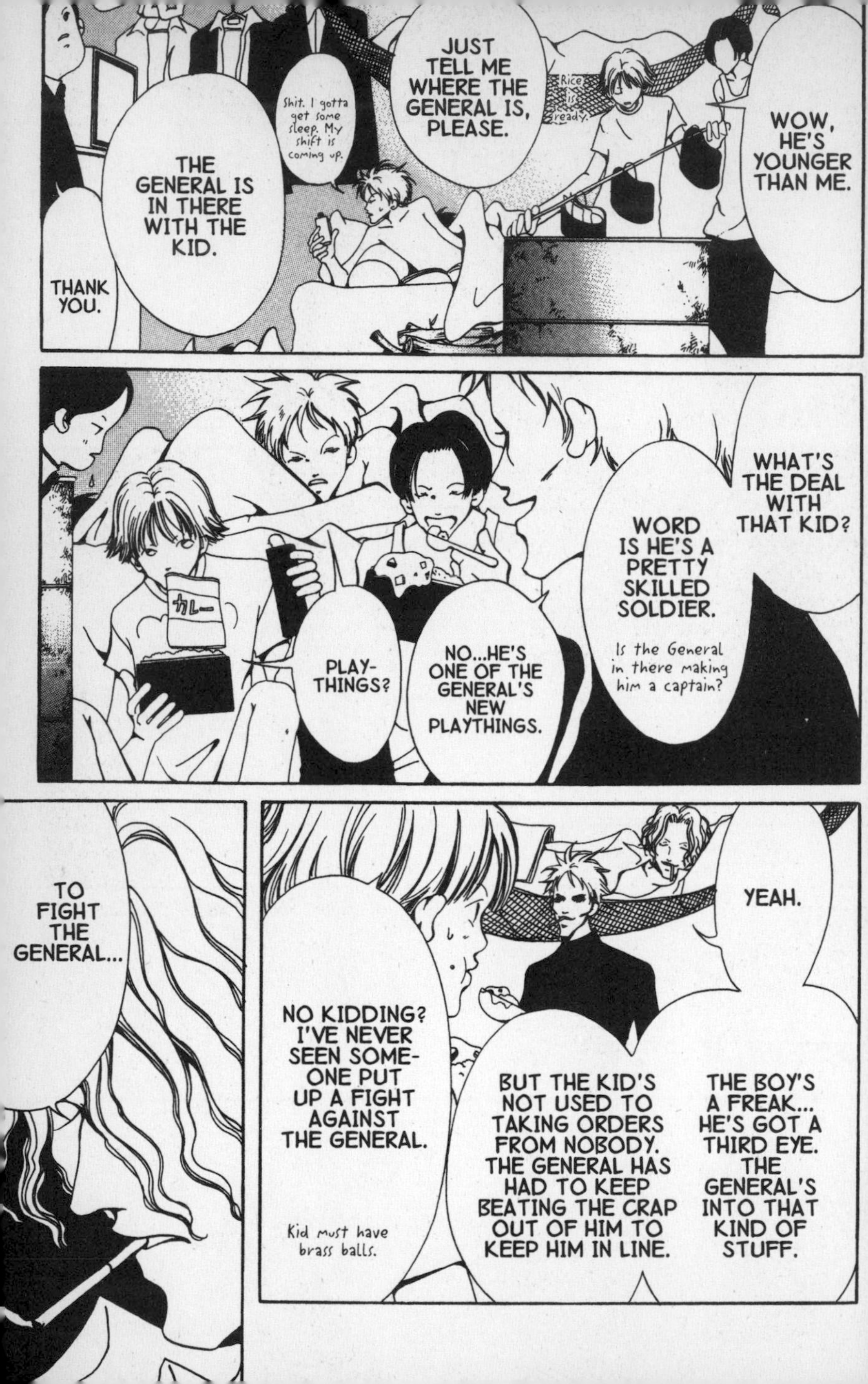
WOW, HE'S YOUNGER THAN ME.
Rice is ready.
JUST TELL ME WHERE THE GENERAL IS, PLEASE.
Shit. I gotta get some sleep. My shift is coming up.
THE GENERAL IS IN THERE WITH THE KID.
THANK YOU.
WHAT'S THE DEAL WITH THAT KID?
WORD IS HE'S A PRETTY SKILLED SOLDIER.
Is the General in there making him a captain?
NO...HE'S ONE OF THE GENERAL'S NEW PLAYTHINGS.
PLAY-THINGS?
YEAH.
THE BOY'S A FREAK... HE'S GOT A THIRD EYE. THE GENERAL'S INTO THAT KIND OF STUFF.
BUT THE KID'S NOT USED TO TAKING ORDERS FROM NOBODY. THE GENERAL HAS HAD TO KEEP BEATING THE CRAP OUT OF HIM TO KEEP HIM IN LINE.
NO KIDDING? I'VE NEVER SEEN SOME-ONE PUT UP A FIGHT AGAINST THE GENERAL.
Kid must have brass balls.
TO FIGHT THE GENERAL...

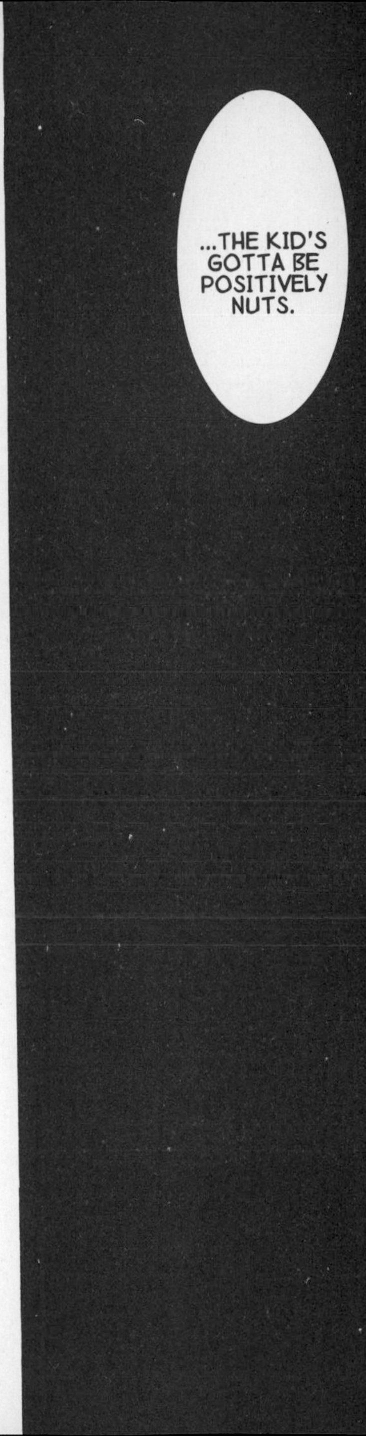
...THE KID'S GOTTA BE POSITIVELY NUTS.
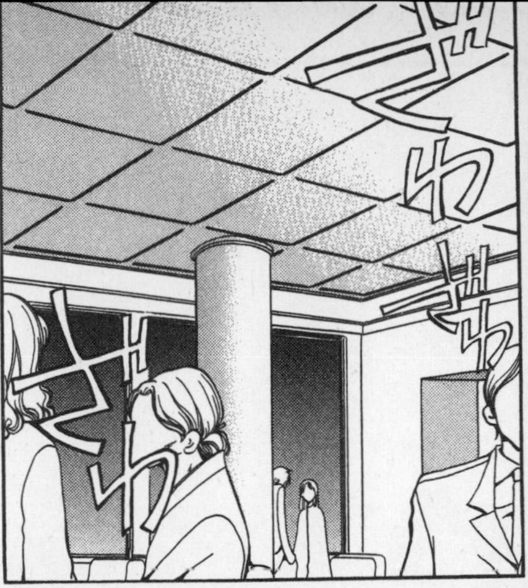
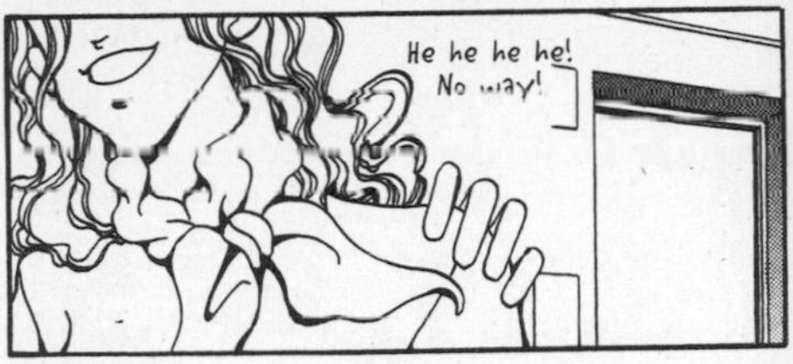
He he he he! No way!

Human cities are too noisy.

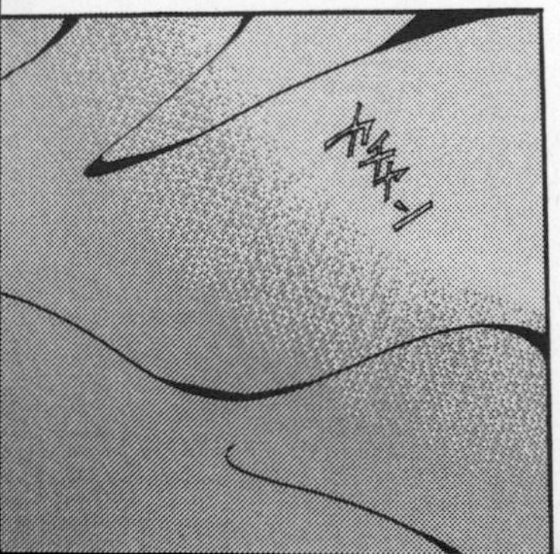

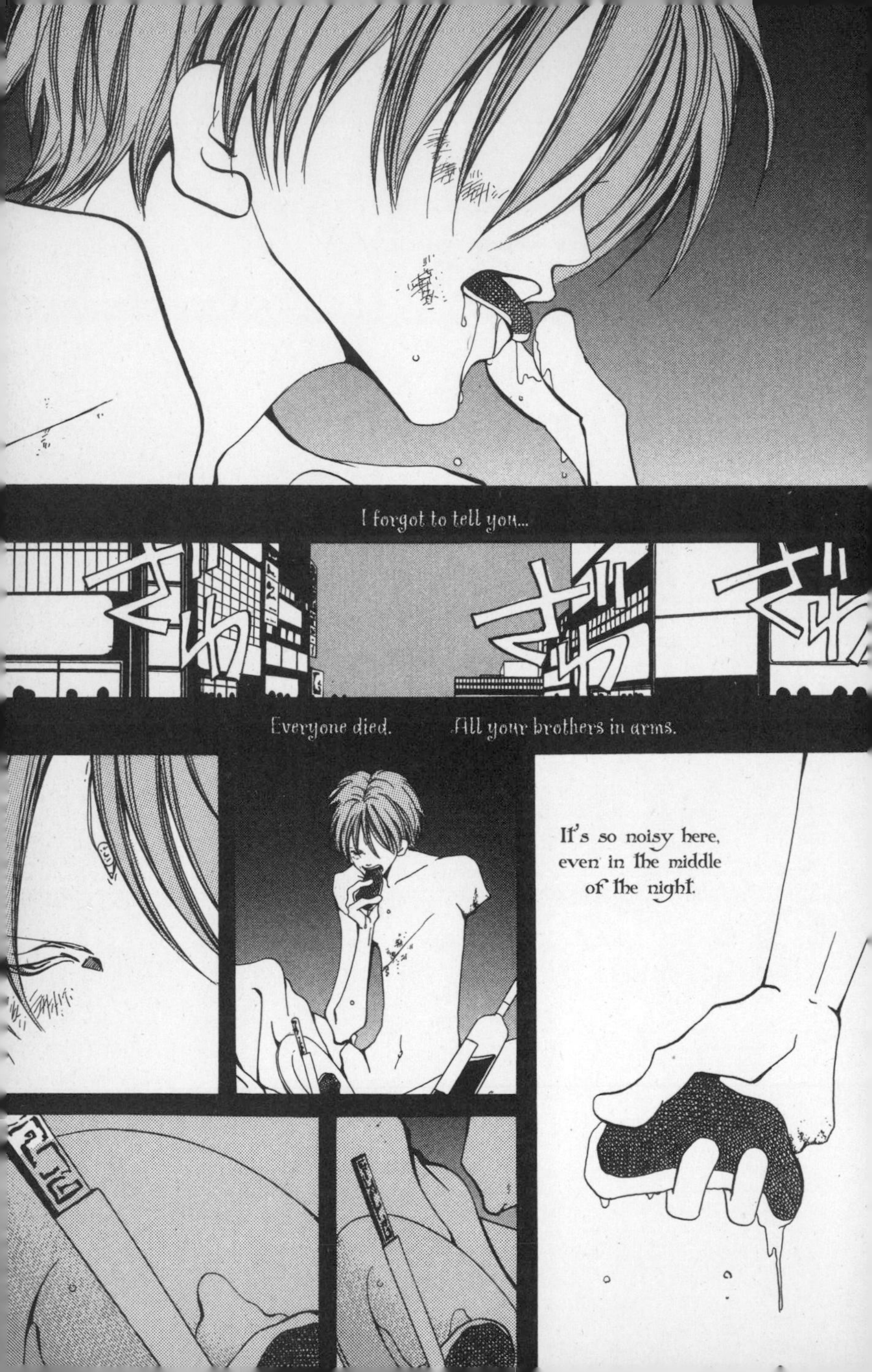
I forgot to tell you...
ざわ
ざわ
さわ
Everyone died.
All your brothers in arms.
It's so noisy here, even in the middle of the night.

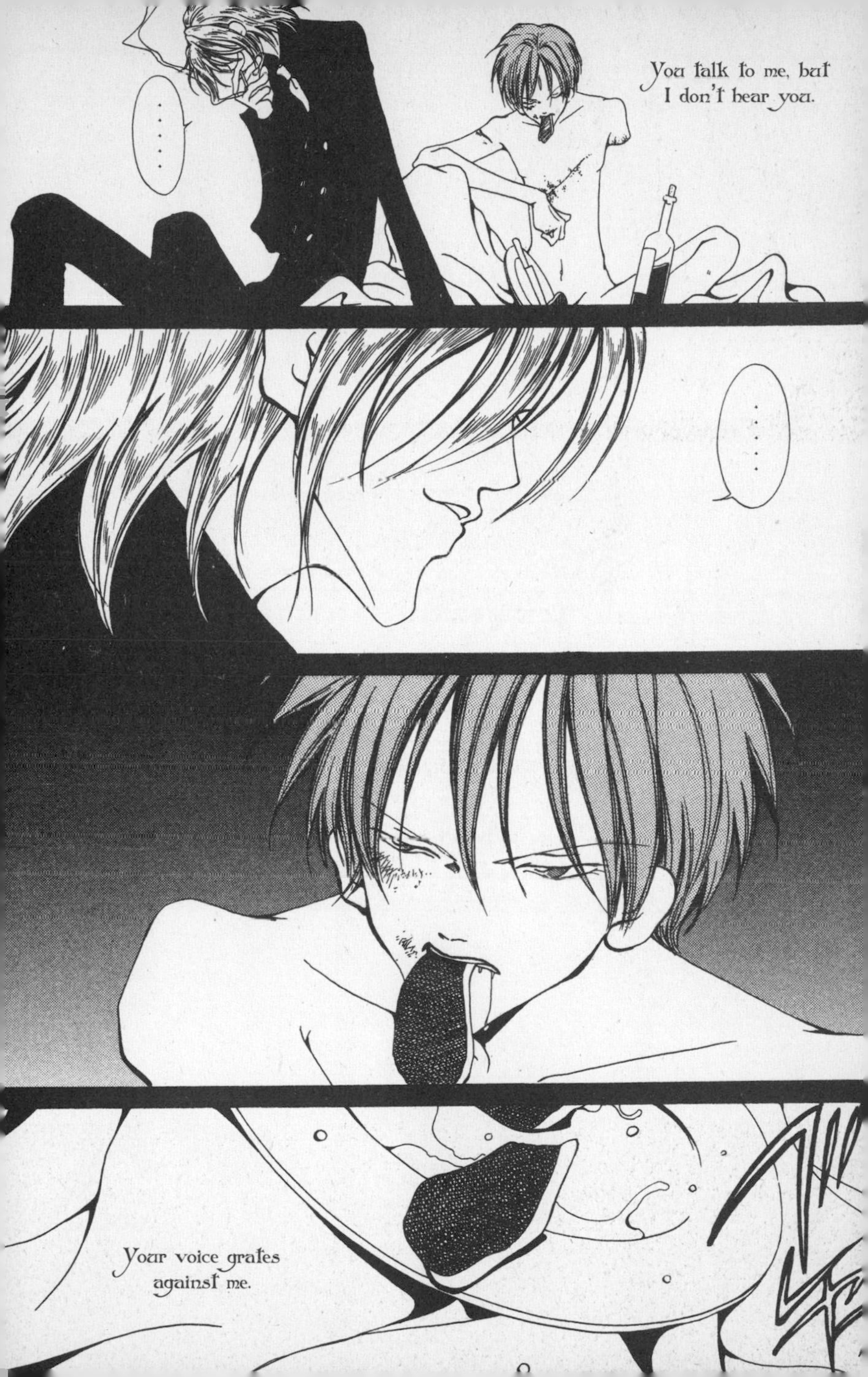
You talk to me, but I don't hear you.
Your voice grates against me.

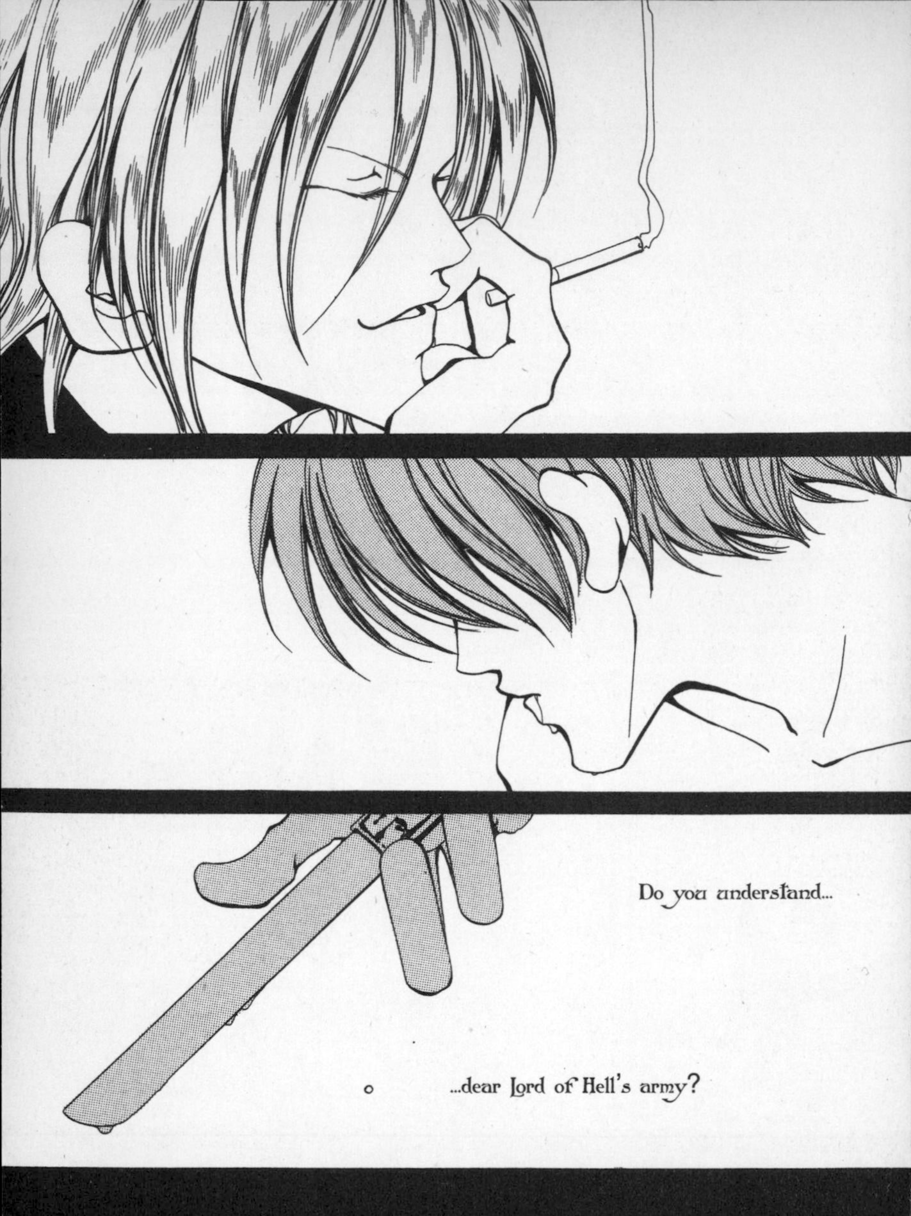
Do you understand...
...dear Lord of Hell's army?

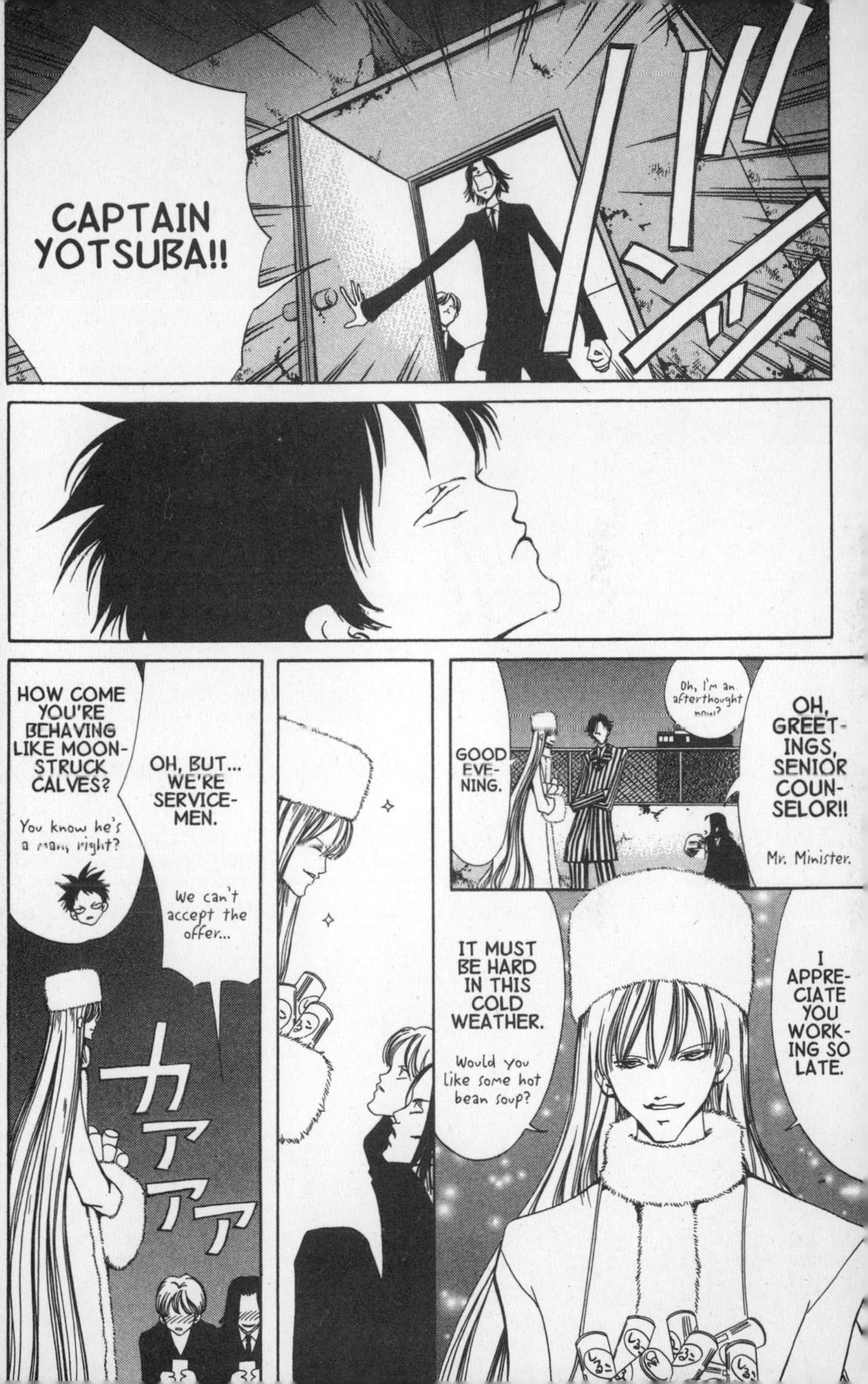
CAPTAIN YOTSUBA!!
OH, GREETINGS, SENIOR COUNSELOR!!
Mr. Minister.
Oh, I'm an afterthought now?
GOOD EVENING.
I APPRECIATE YOU WORKING SO LATE.
IT MUST BE HARD IN THIS COLD WEATHER.
Would you like some hot bean soup?
OH, BUT... WE'RE SERVICEMEN.
We can't accept the offer...
HOW COME YOU'RE BEHAVING LIKE MOONSTRUCK CALVES?
You know he's a man, right?
カァァァ

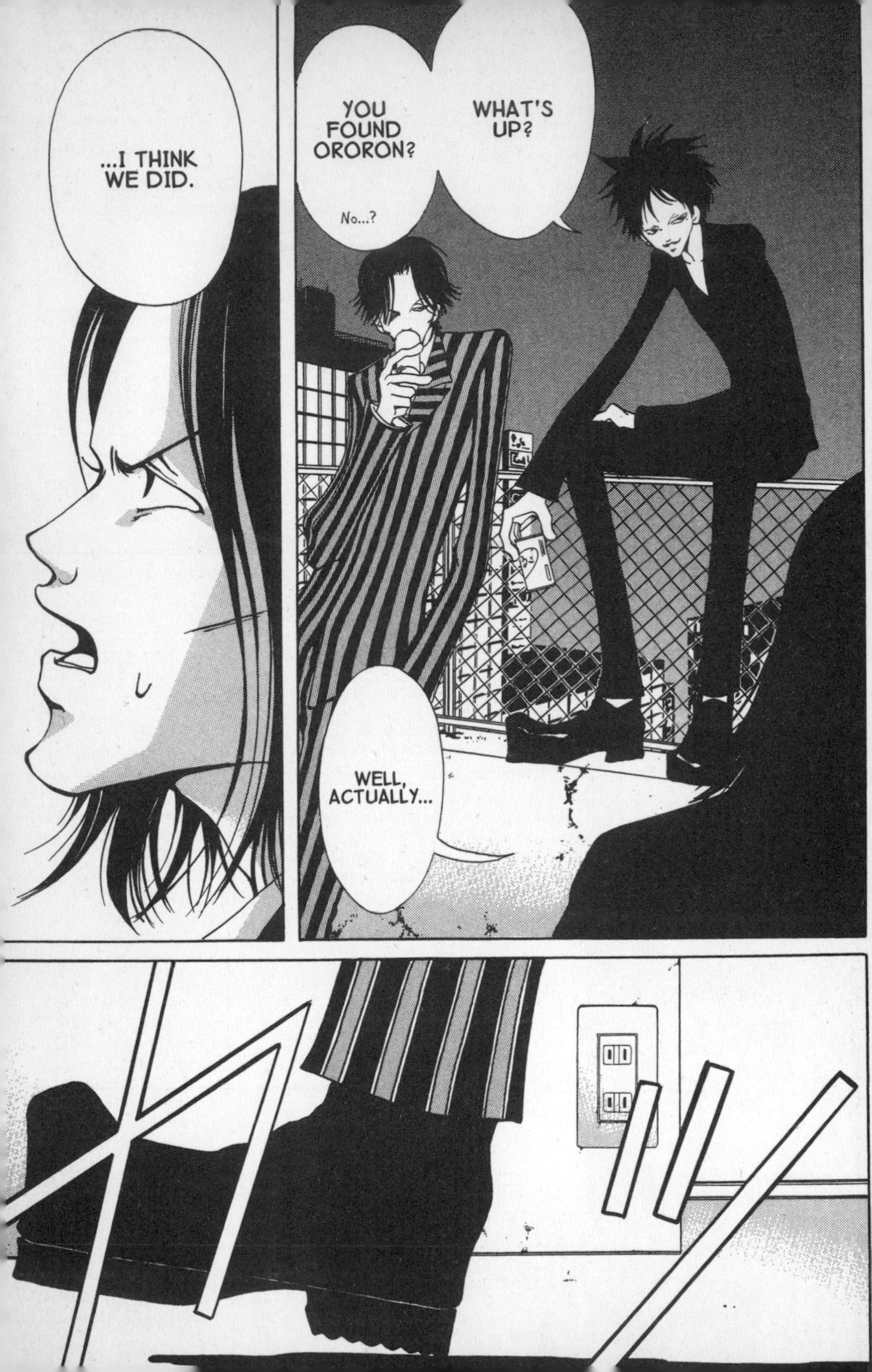
WHAT'S UP?
YOU FOUND ORORON?
No...?
WELL, ACTUALLY...
...I THINK WE DID.

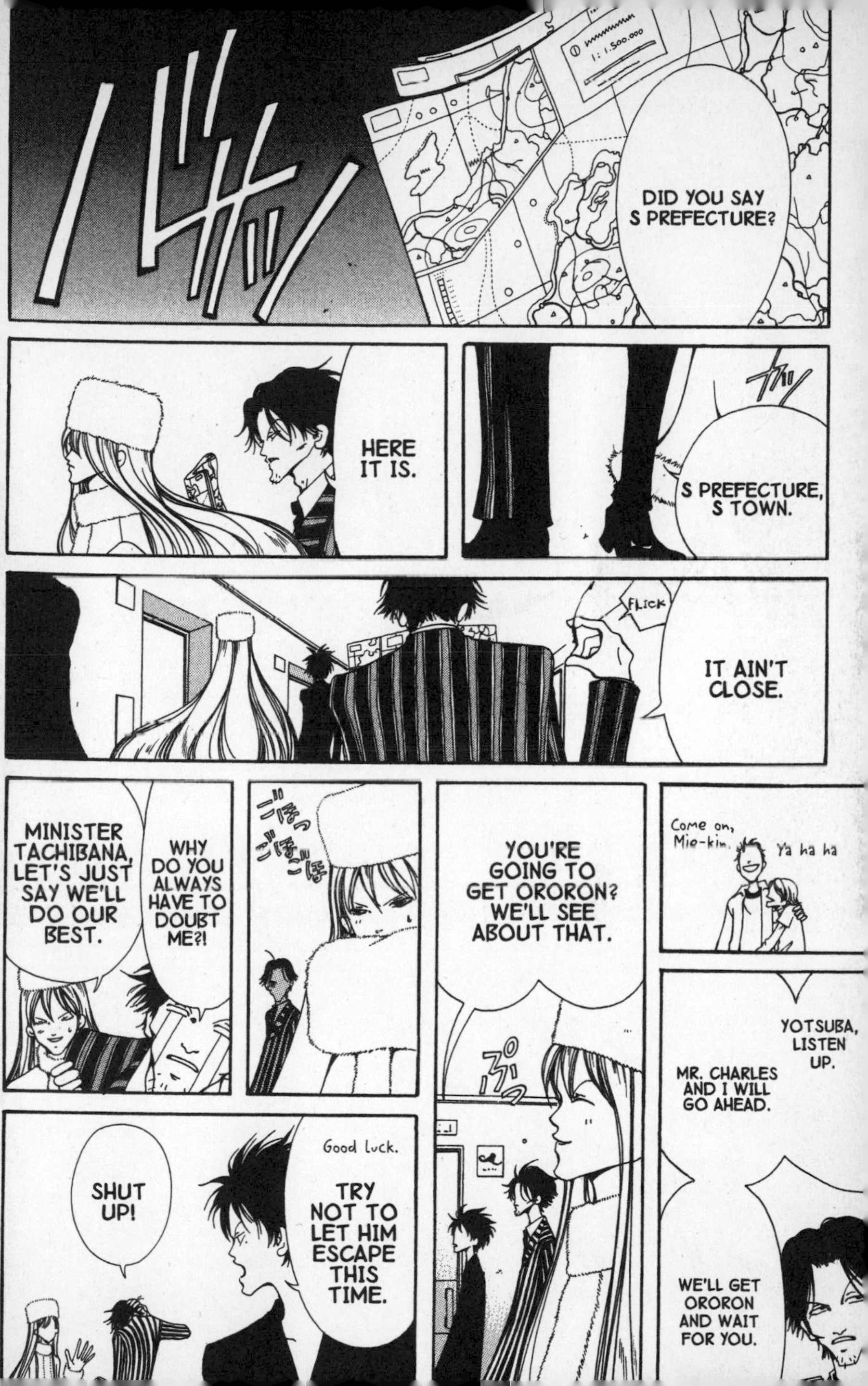
1: 1.500.000
DID YOU SAY S PREFECTURE?
S PREFECTURE, S TOWN.
HERE IT IS.
FLICK
IT AIN'T CLOSE.
Come on, Mio-kin.
Ya ha ha
YOTSUBA, LISTEN UP.
MR. CHARLES AND I WILL GO AHEAD.
WE'LL GET ORORON AND WAIT FOR YOU.
YOU'RE GOING TO GET ORORON? WE'LL SEE ABOUT THAT.
ごほっ ごほっ ごほ
WHY DO YOU ALWAYS HAVE TO DOUBT ME?!
MINISTER TACHIBANA, LET'S JUST SAY WE'LL DO OUR BEST.
Good luck.
TRY NOT TO LET HIM ESCAPE THIS TIME.
SHUT UP!

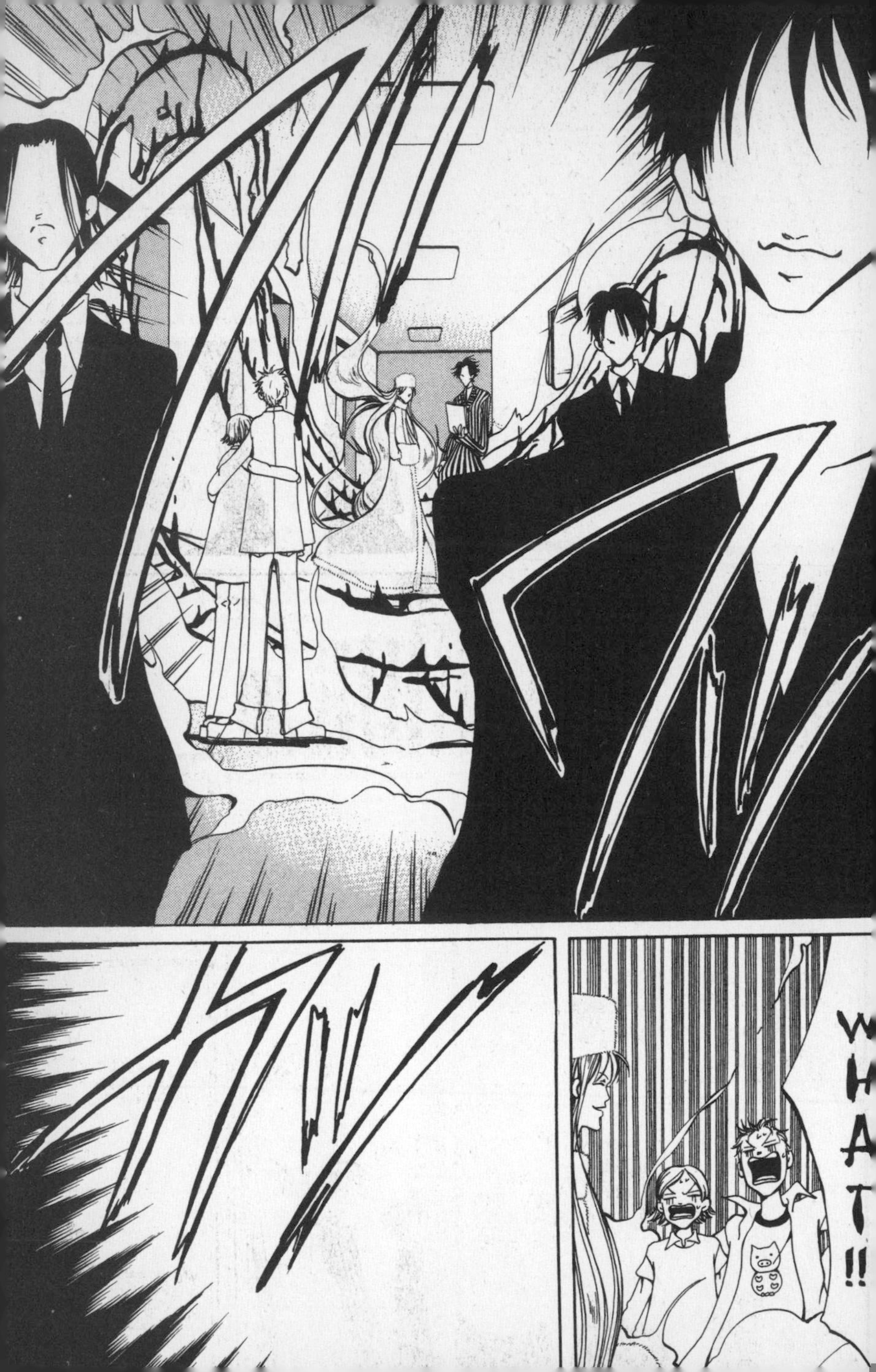
WHAT!!

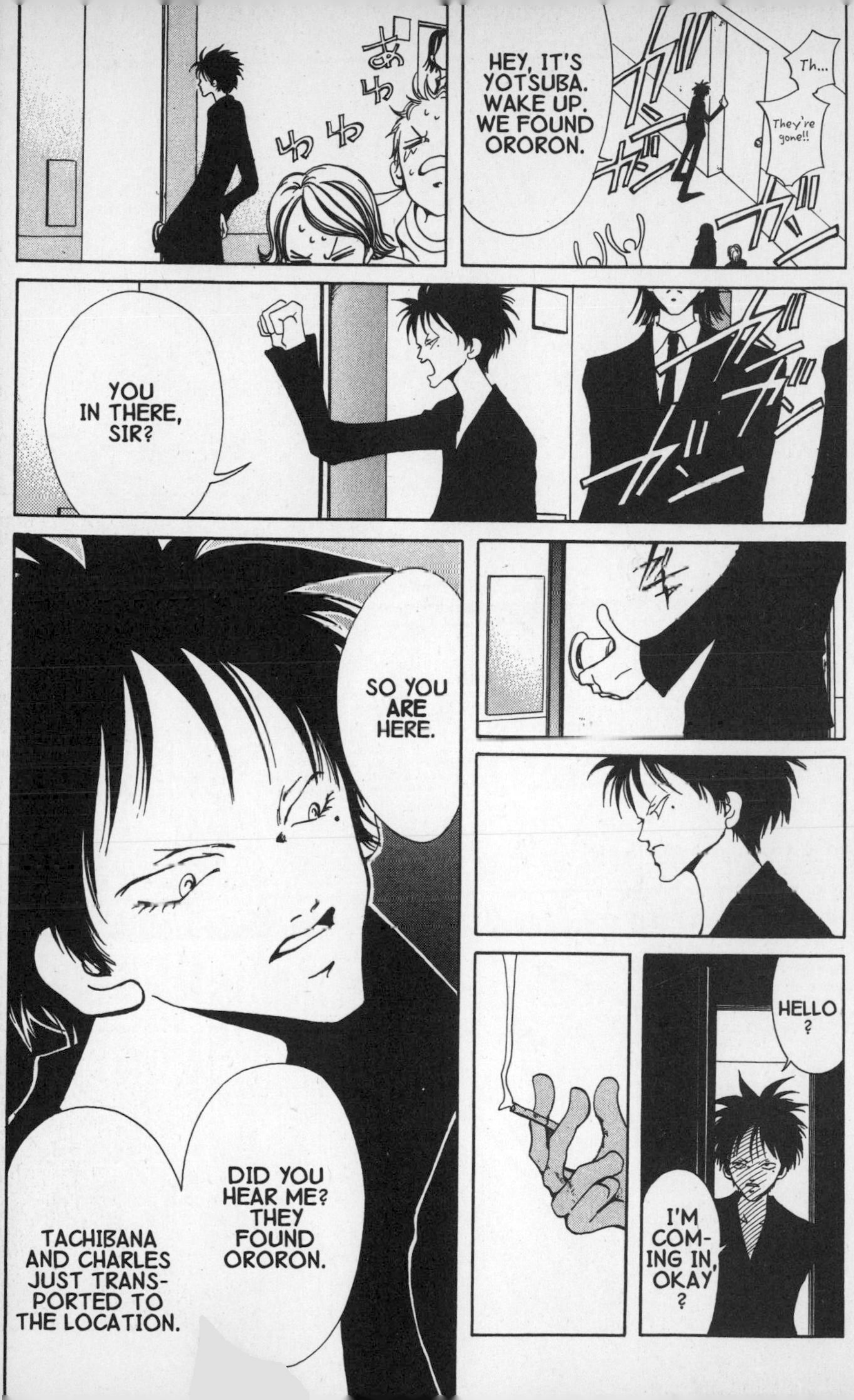
Th...
They're gone!!
HEY, IT'S YOTSUBA. WAKE UP. WE FOUND ORORON.
YOU IN THERE, SIR?
HELLO?
I'M COMING IN, OKAY?
SO YOU ARE HERE.
DID YOU HEAR ME? THEY FOUND ORORON.
TACHIBANA AND CHARLES JUST TRANSPORTED TO THE LOCATION.

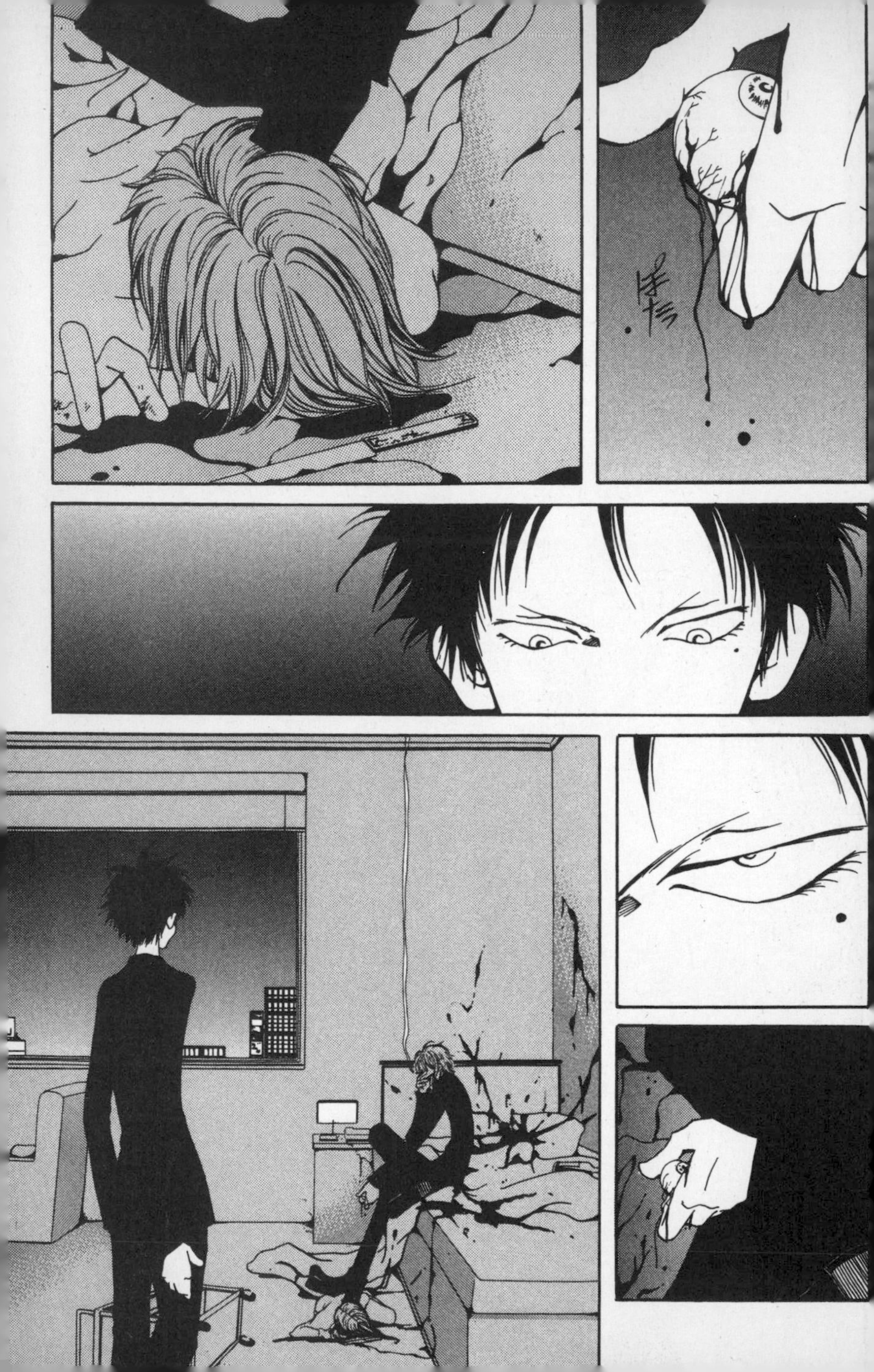
ぽた

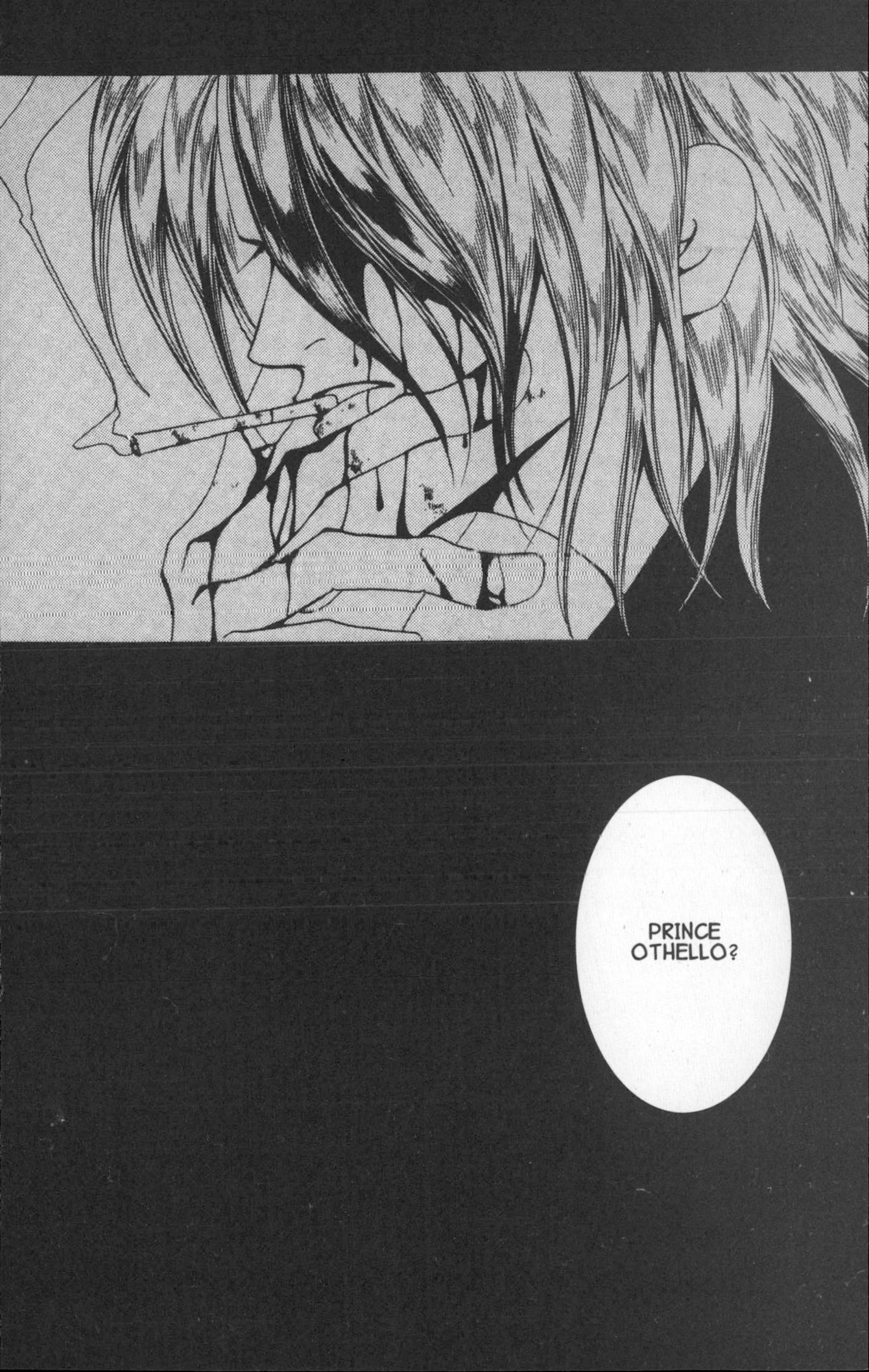
PRINCE OTHELLO?

-15-

BREAKING THE CIRCLE

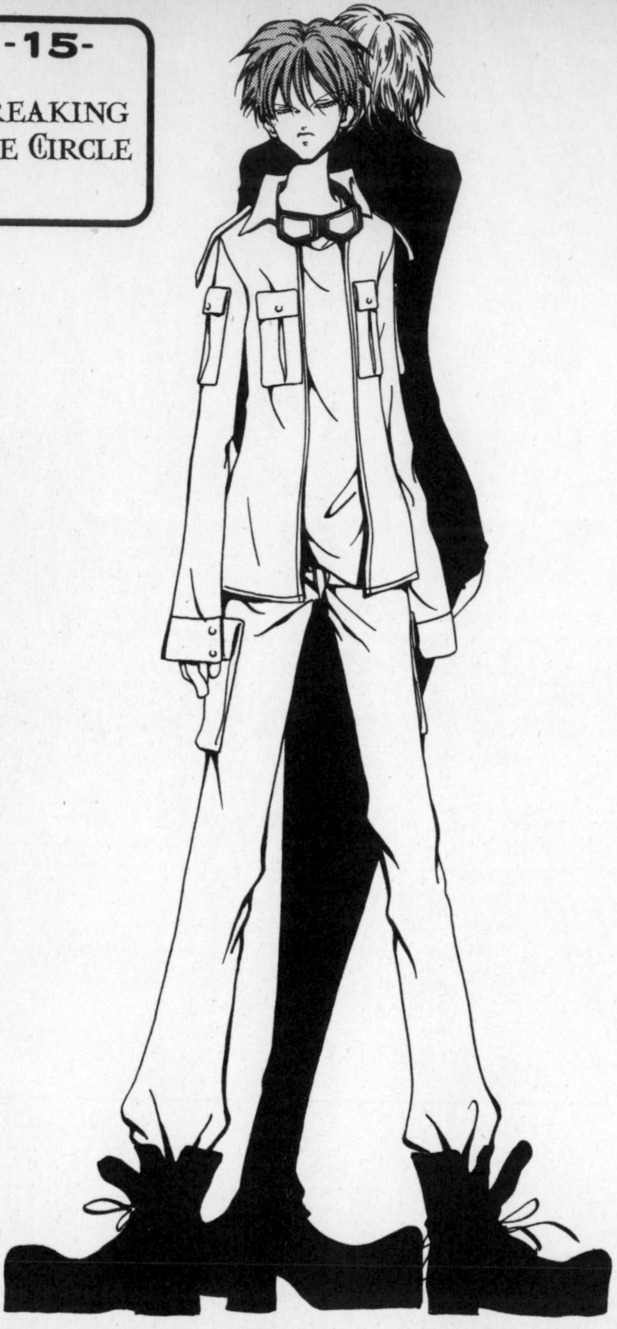

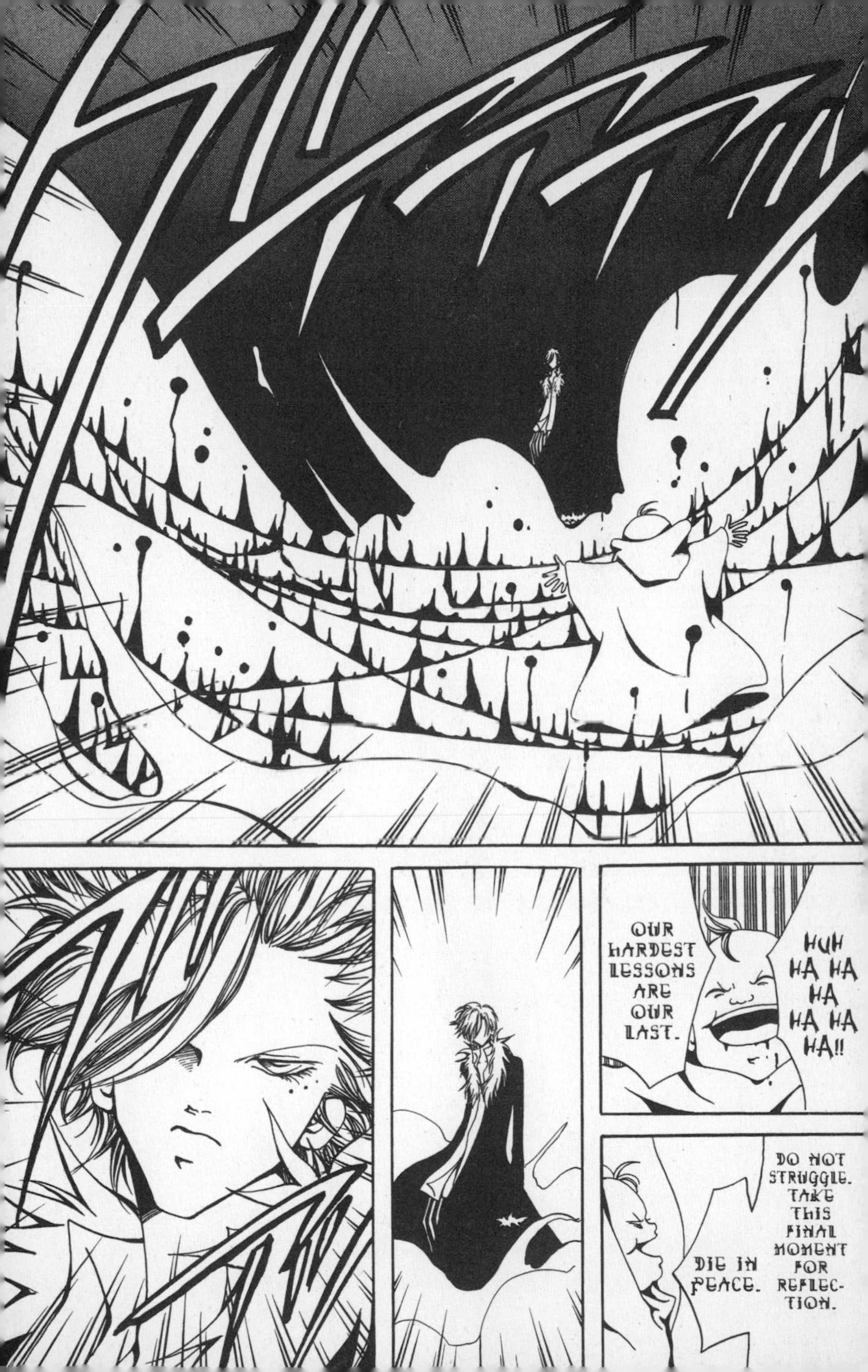
HUH HA HA HA HA HA HA!!
OUR HARDEST LESSONS ARE OUR LAST.
DO NOT STRUGGLE. TAKE THIS FINAL MOMENT FOR REFLECTION.
DIE IN PEACE.

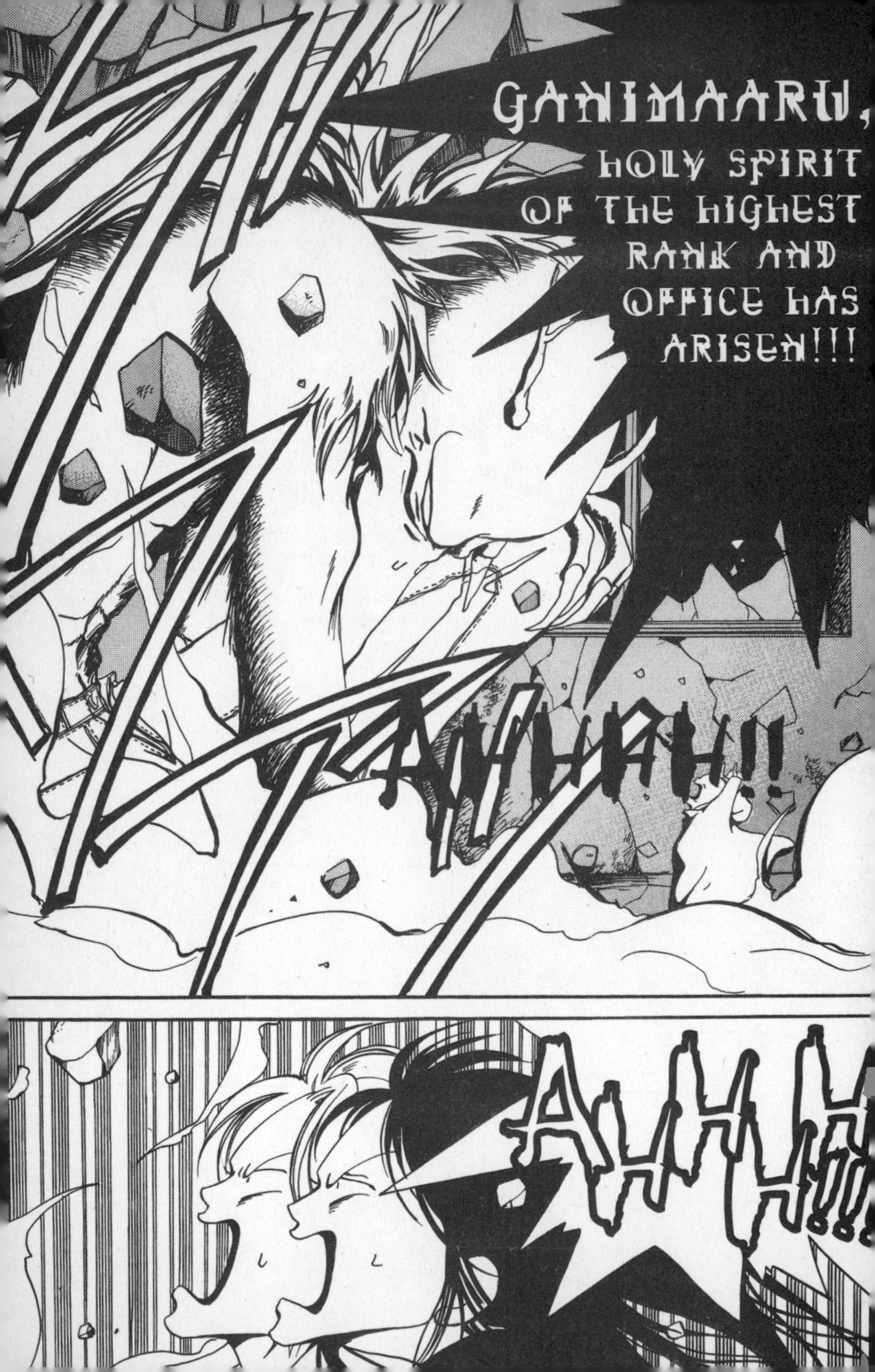
GANIMAARU, HOLY SPIRIT OF THE HIGHEST RANK AND OFFICE HAS ARISEN!!!
AHHAH!!
AHHH

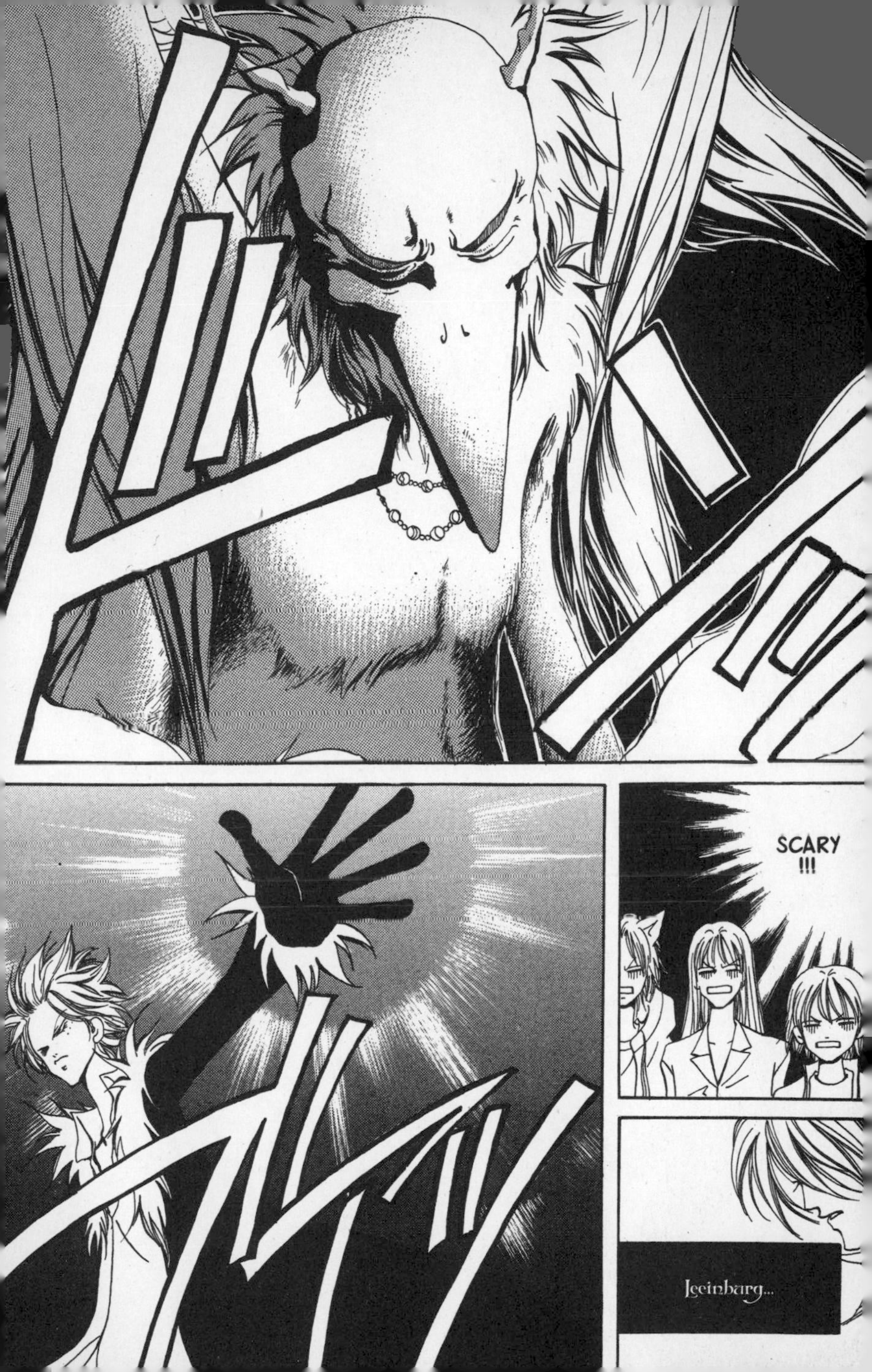
SCARY !!!
Leinburg...

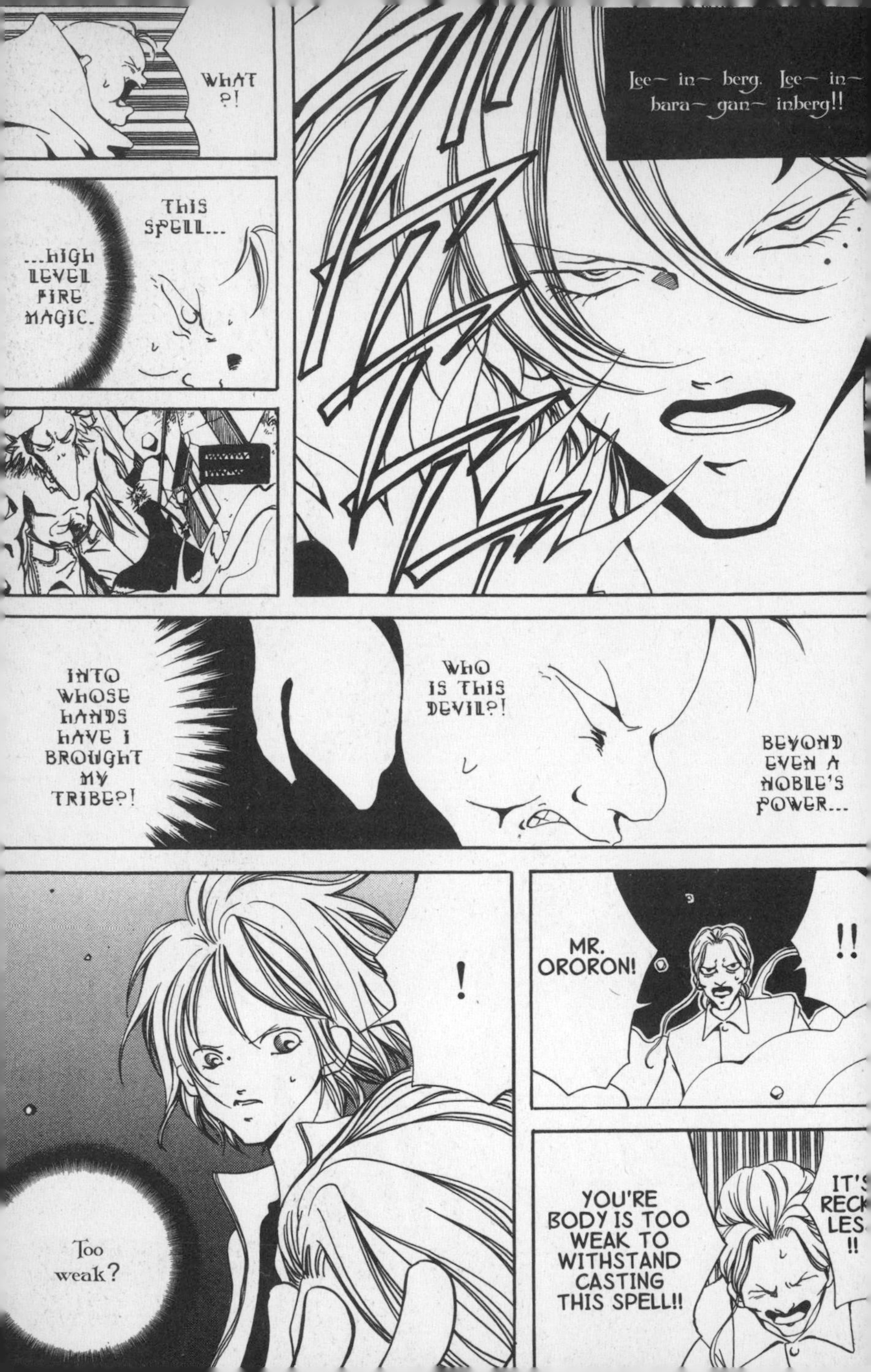

Lee~ in~ berg. Lee~ in~ bara~ gan~ inberg!!
WHAT?!
THIS SPELL...
...HIGH LEVEL FIRE MAGIC.
BEYOND EVEN A NOBLE'S POWER...
WHO IS THIS DEVIL?!
INTO WHOSE HANDS HAVE I BROUGHT MY TRIBE?!
!!
MR. ORORON!
IT'S RECK LES !!
YOU'RE BODY IS TOO WEAK TO WITHSTAND CASTING THIS SPELL!!
!
Too weak?

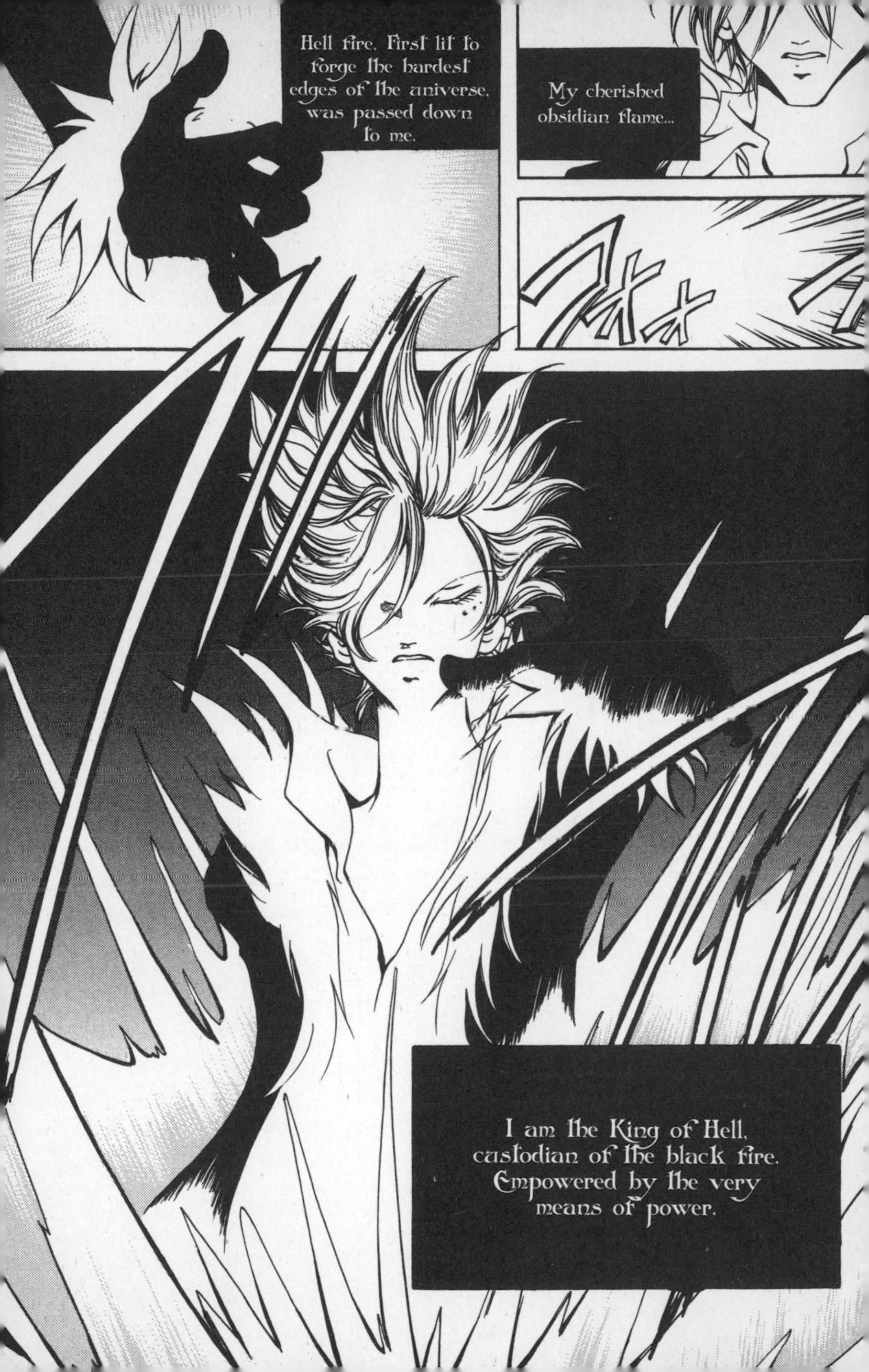
My cherished obsidian flame...
フォォ
Hell fire. First lit to forge the hardest edges of the universe, was passed down to me.
I am the King of Hell, custodian of the black fire. Empowered by the very means of power.

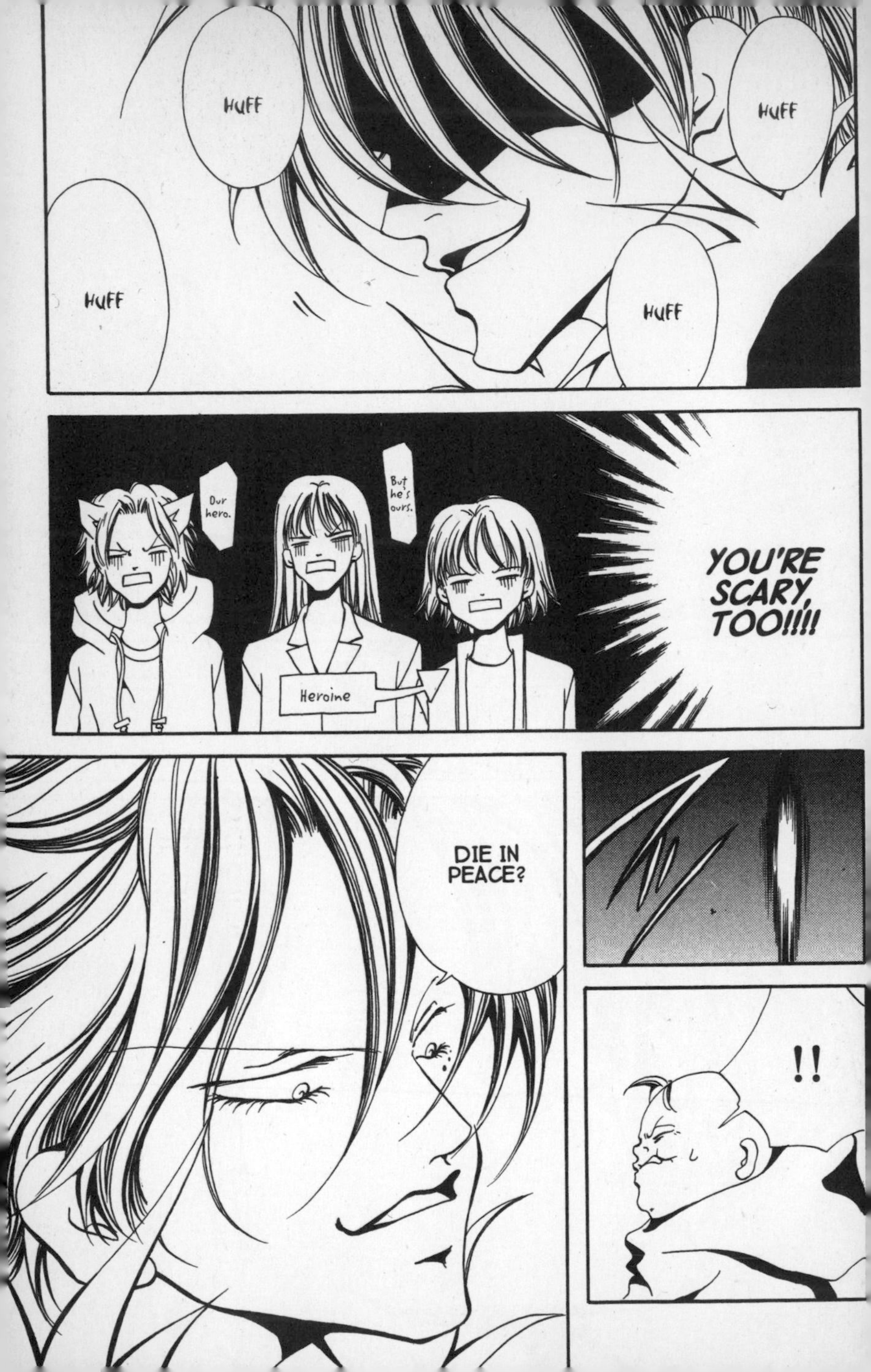
HUFF
HUFF
HUFF
HUFF
YOU'RE SCARY, TOO!!!!
But he's ours.
Our hero.
Heroine
!!
DIE IN PEACE?

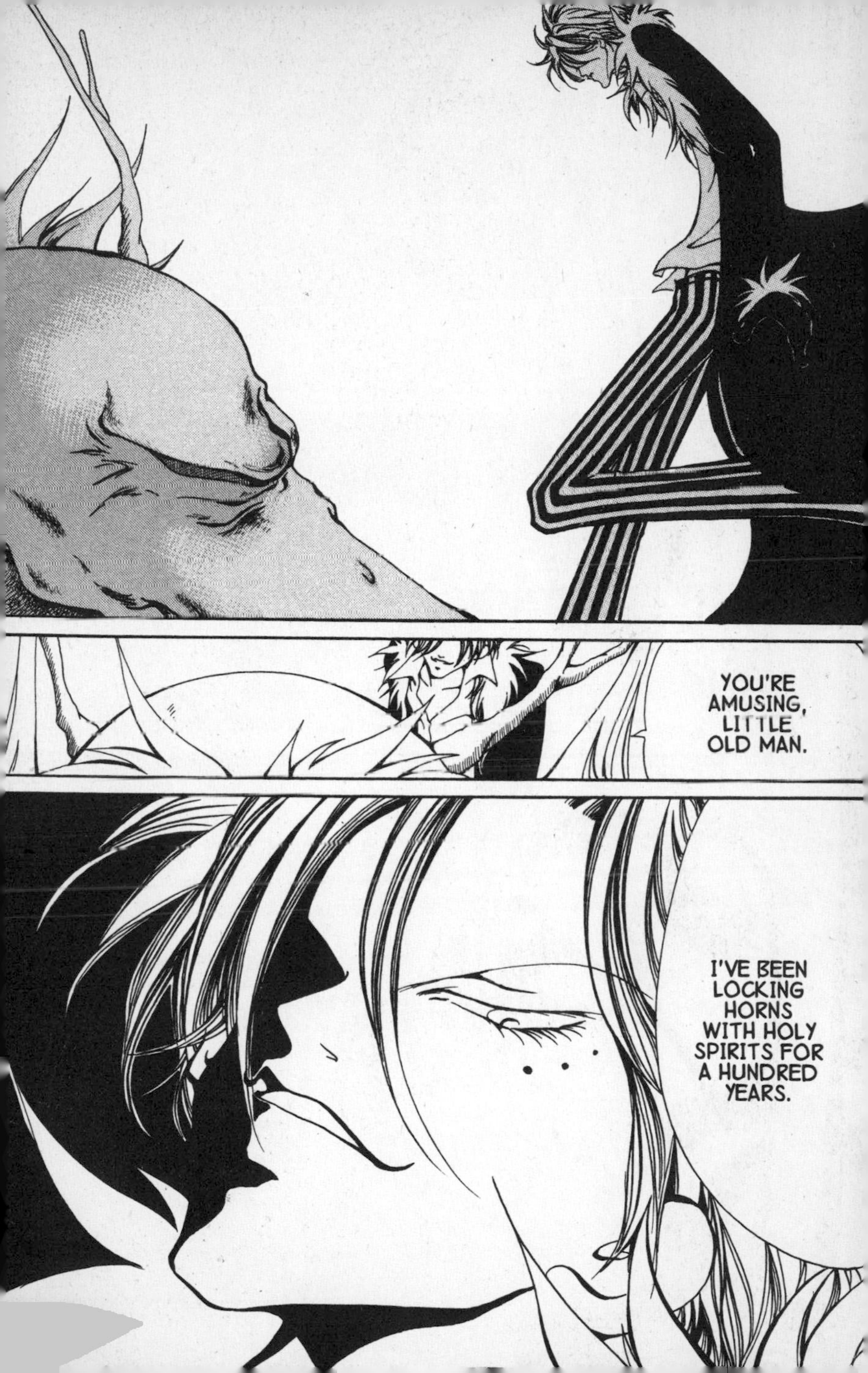
YOU'RE AMUSING, LITTLE OLD MAN.
I'VE BEEN LOCKING HORNS WITH HOLY SPIRITS FOR A HUNDRED YEARS.

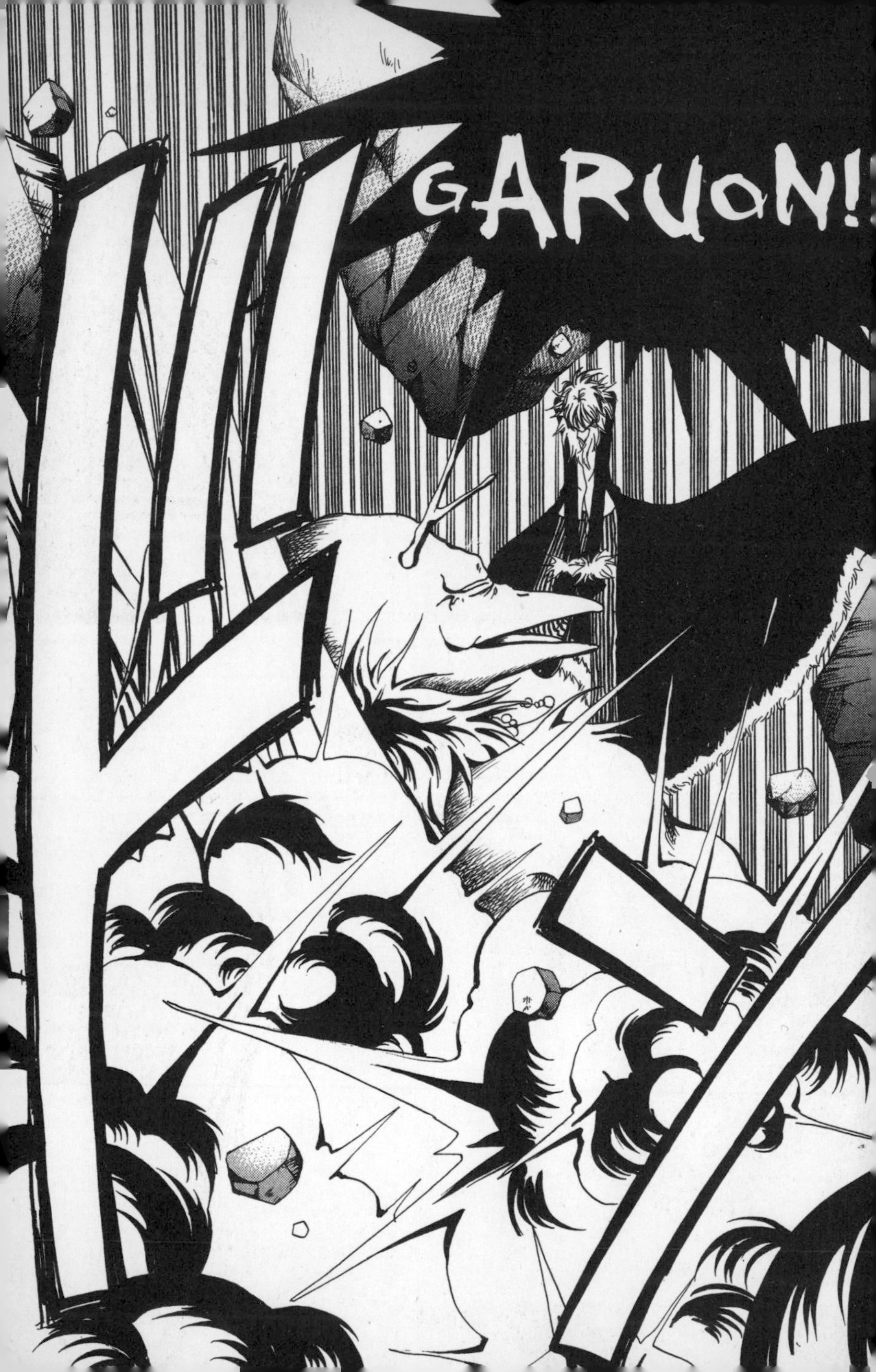
GARUON!!

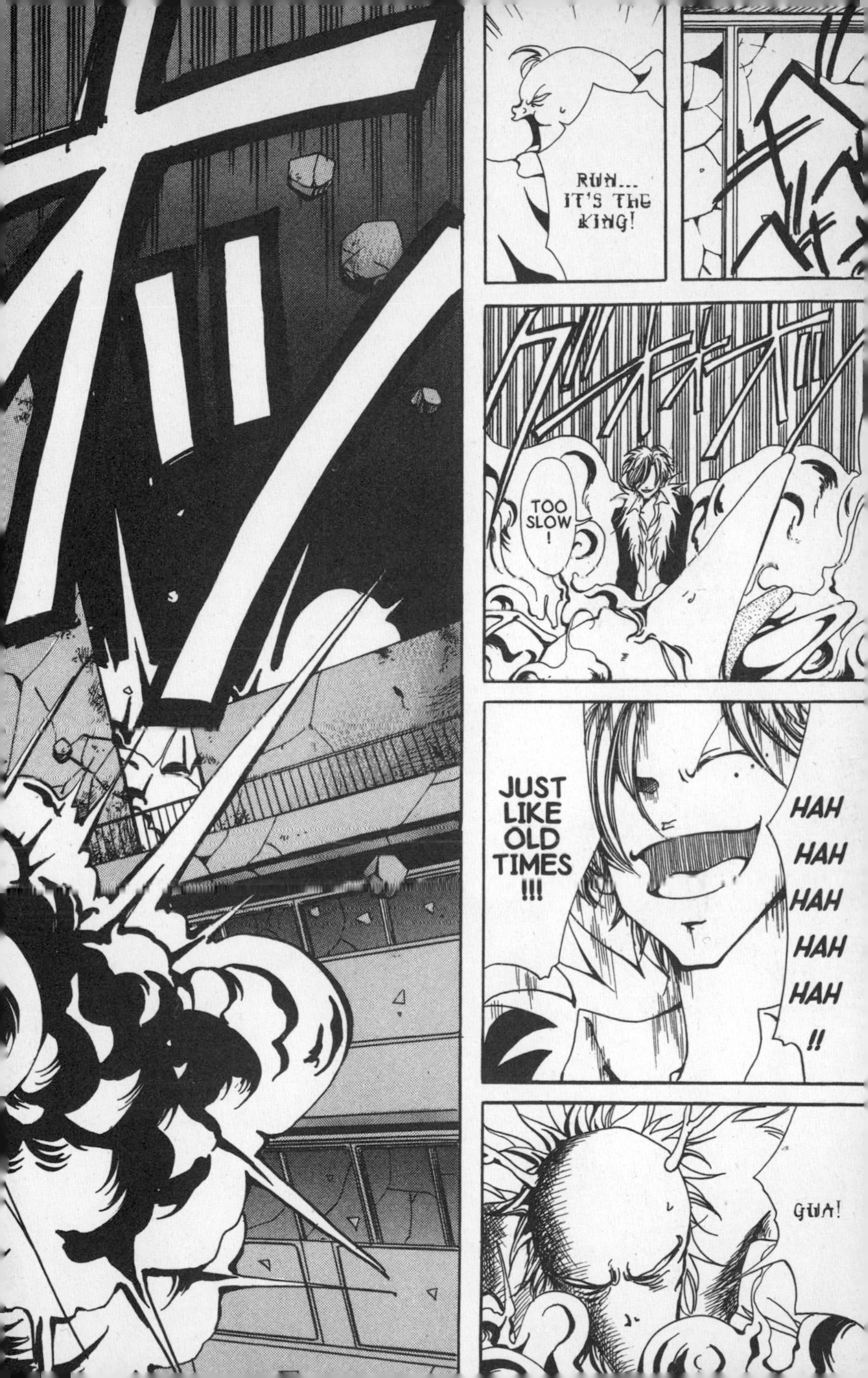
RUN... IT'S THE KING!
TOO SLOW!
HAH HAH HAH HAH HAH!!
JUST LIKE OLD TIMES!!!
GUA!

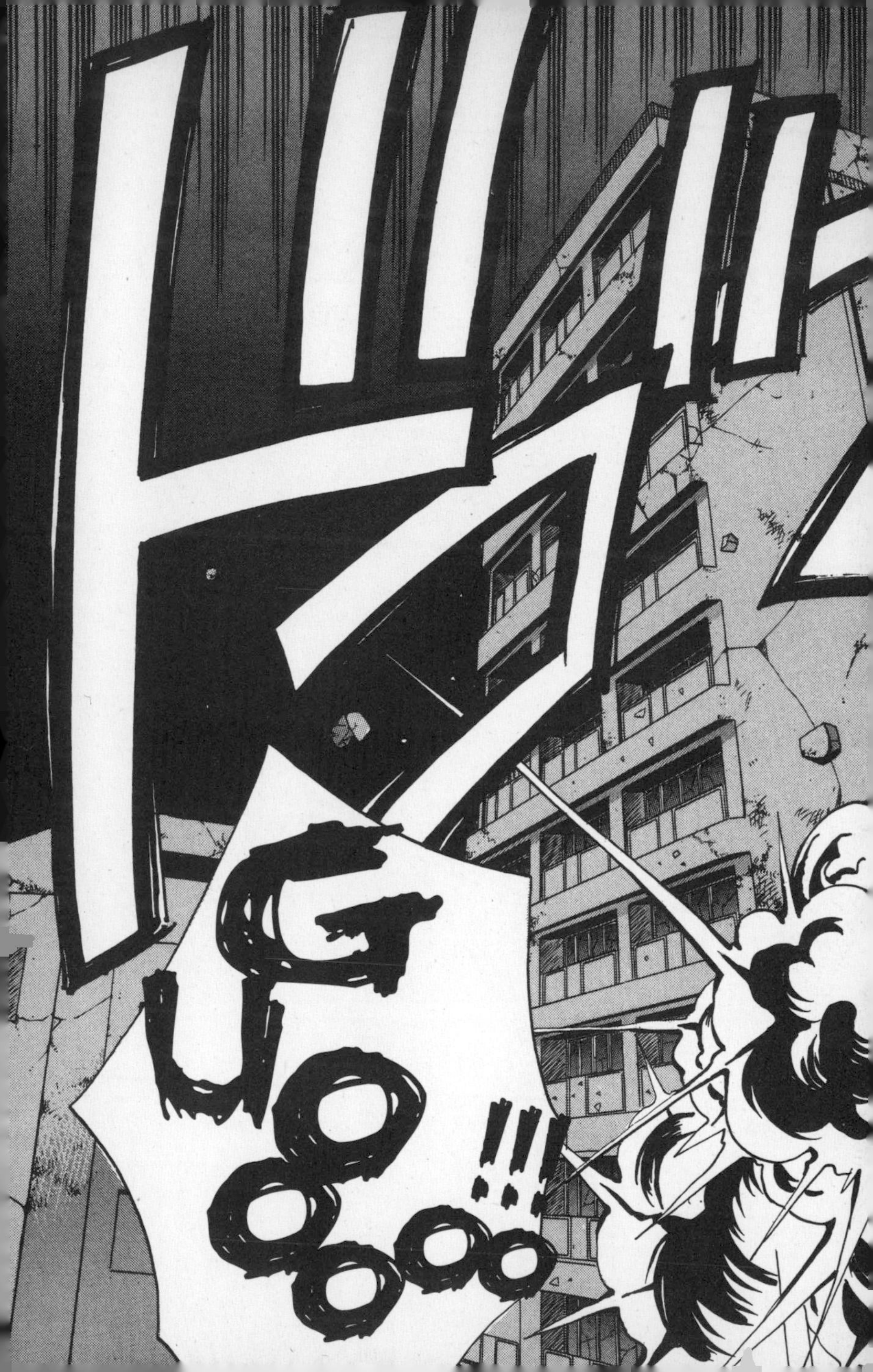
GUOOOOO!!!

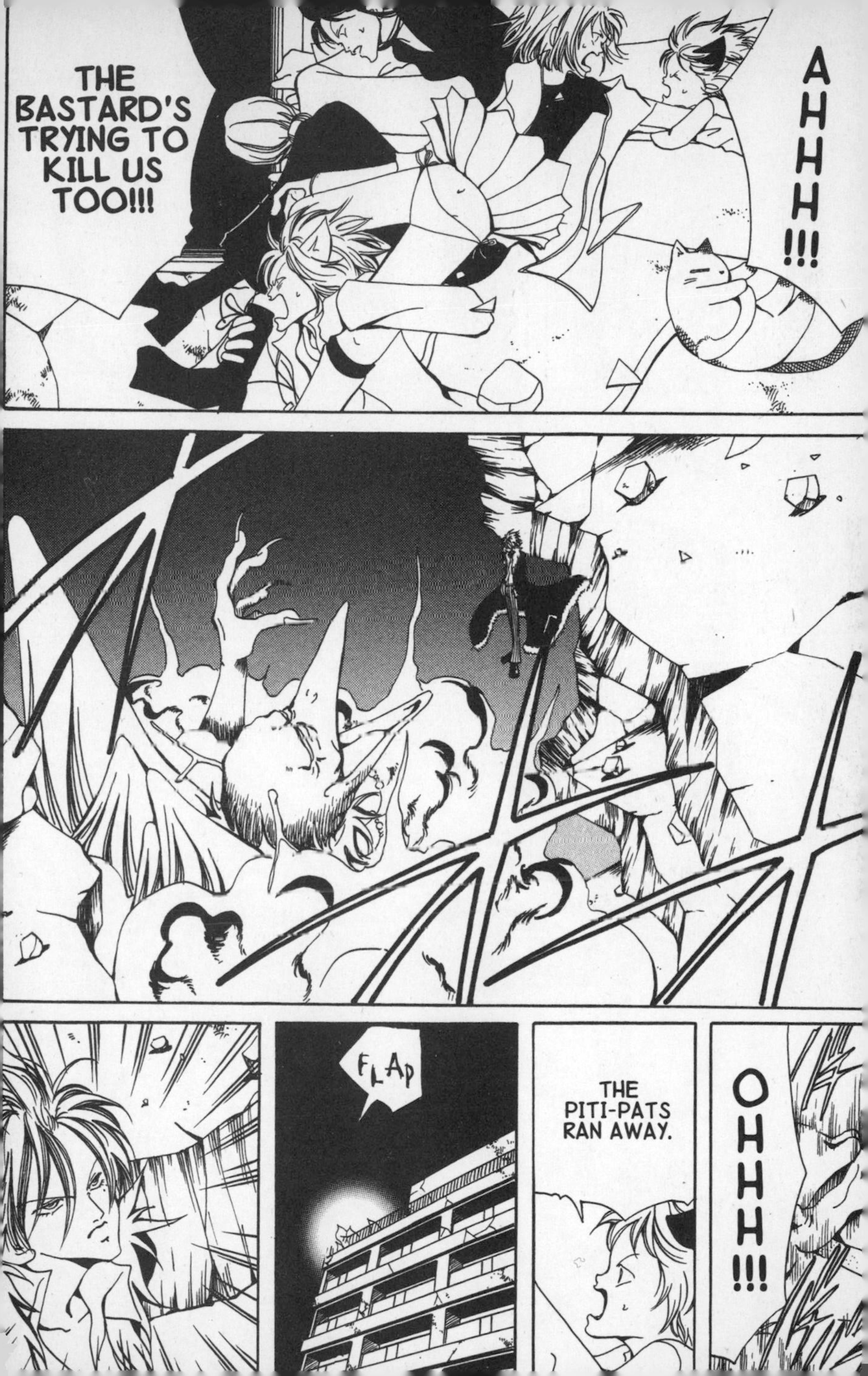
AHHH!!!
THE BASTARD'S TRYING TO KILL US TOO!!!
OHHH!!!
THE PITI-PATS RAN AWAY.
FLAP

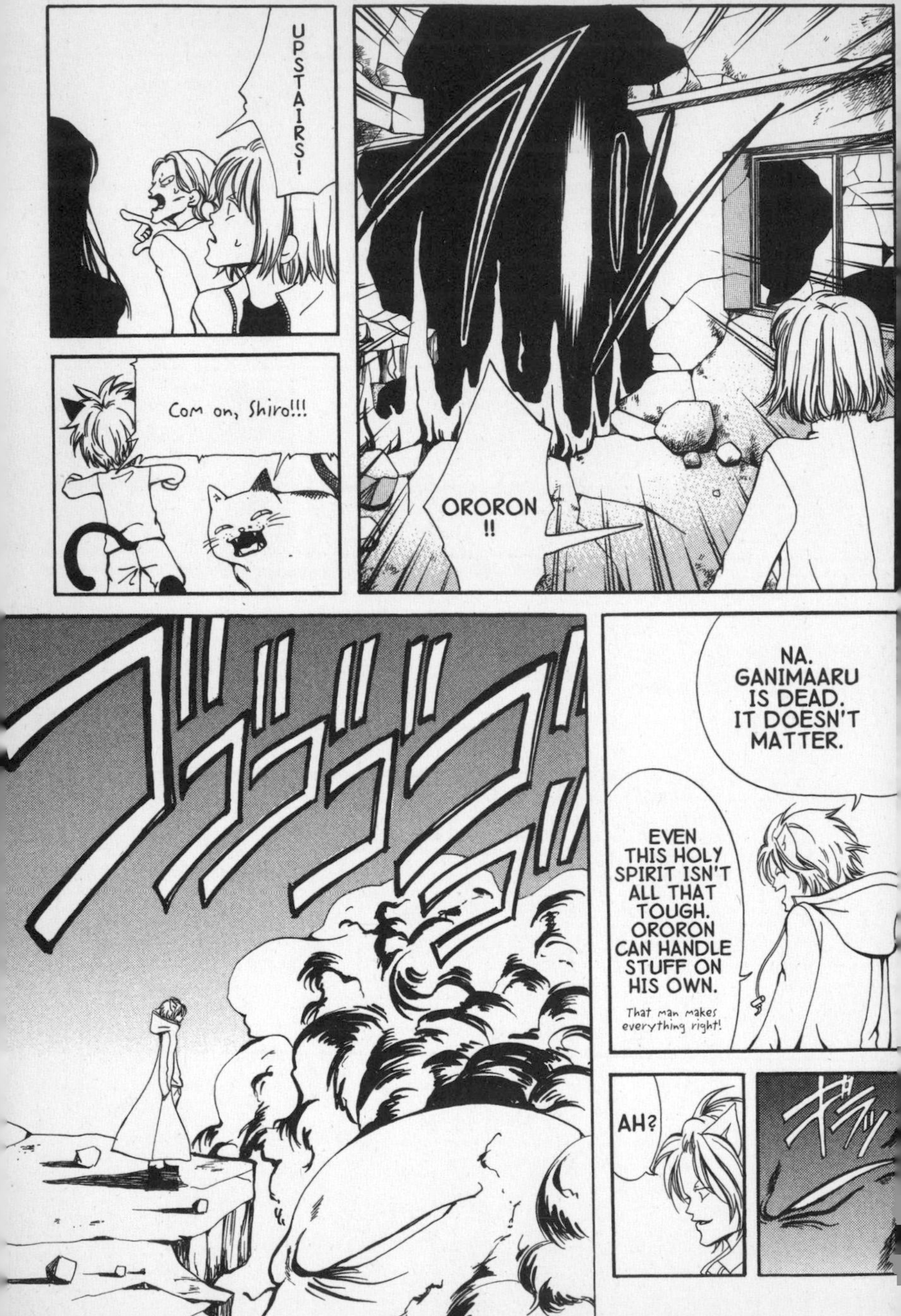
ORORON !!
UPSTAIRS!
Com on, Shiro!!!
NA. GANIMAARU IS DEAD. IT DOESN'T MATTER.
EVEN THIS HOLY SPIRIT ISN'T ALL THAT TOUGH. ORORON CAN HANDLE STUFF ON HIS OWN.
That man makes everything right!
AH?

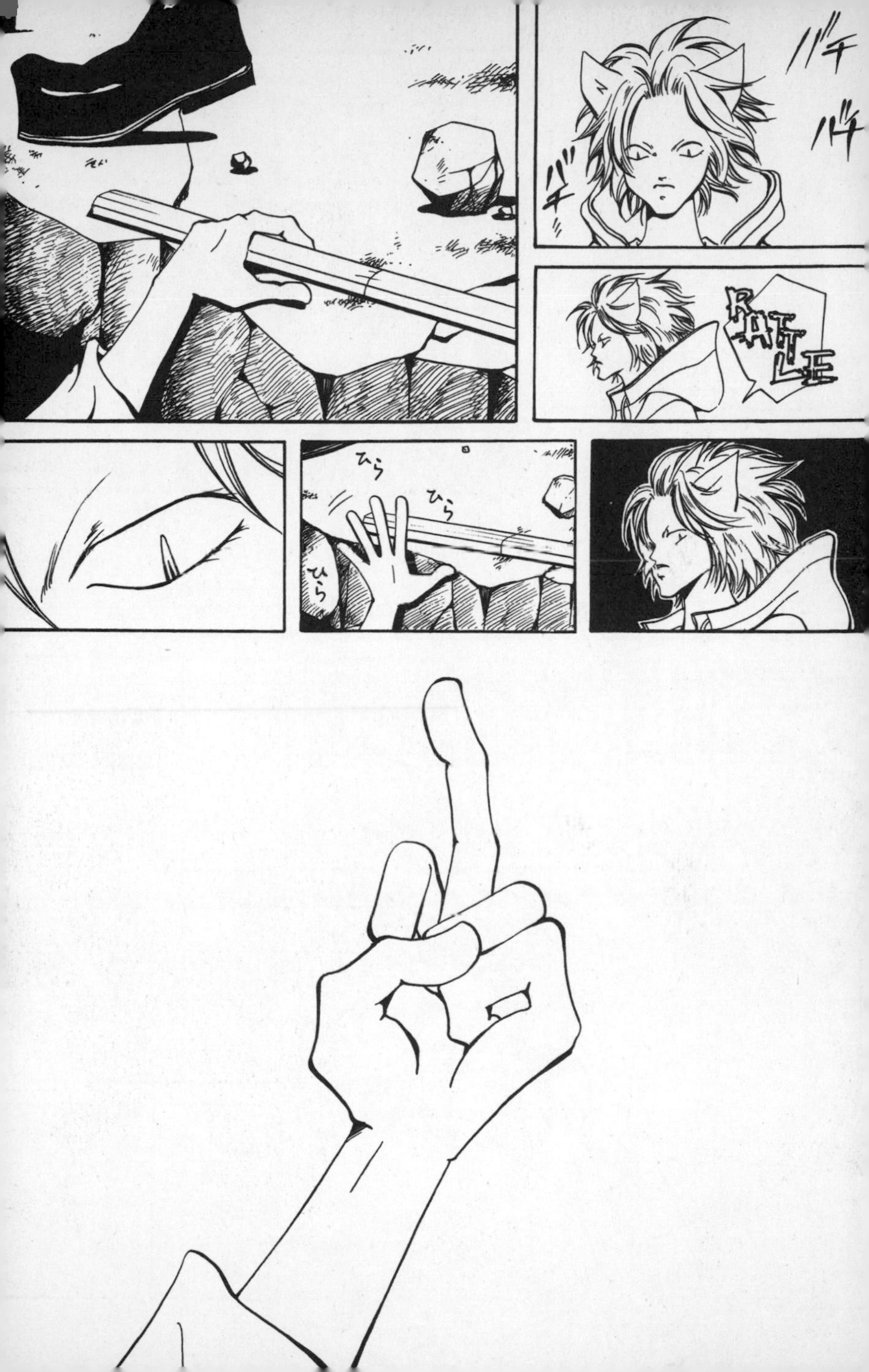
バチ
バチ
バチ
RATTLE
ひら
ひら
ひら

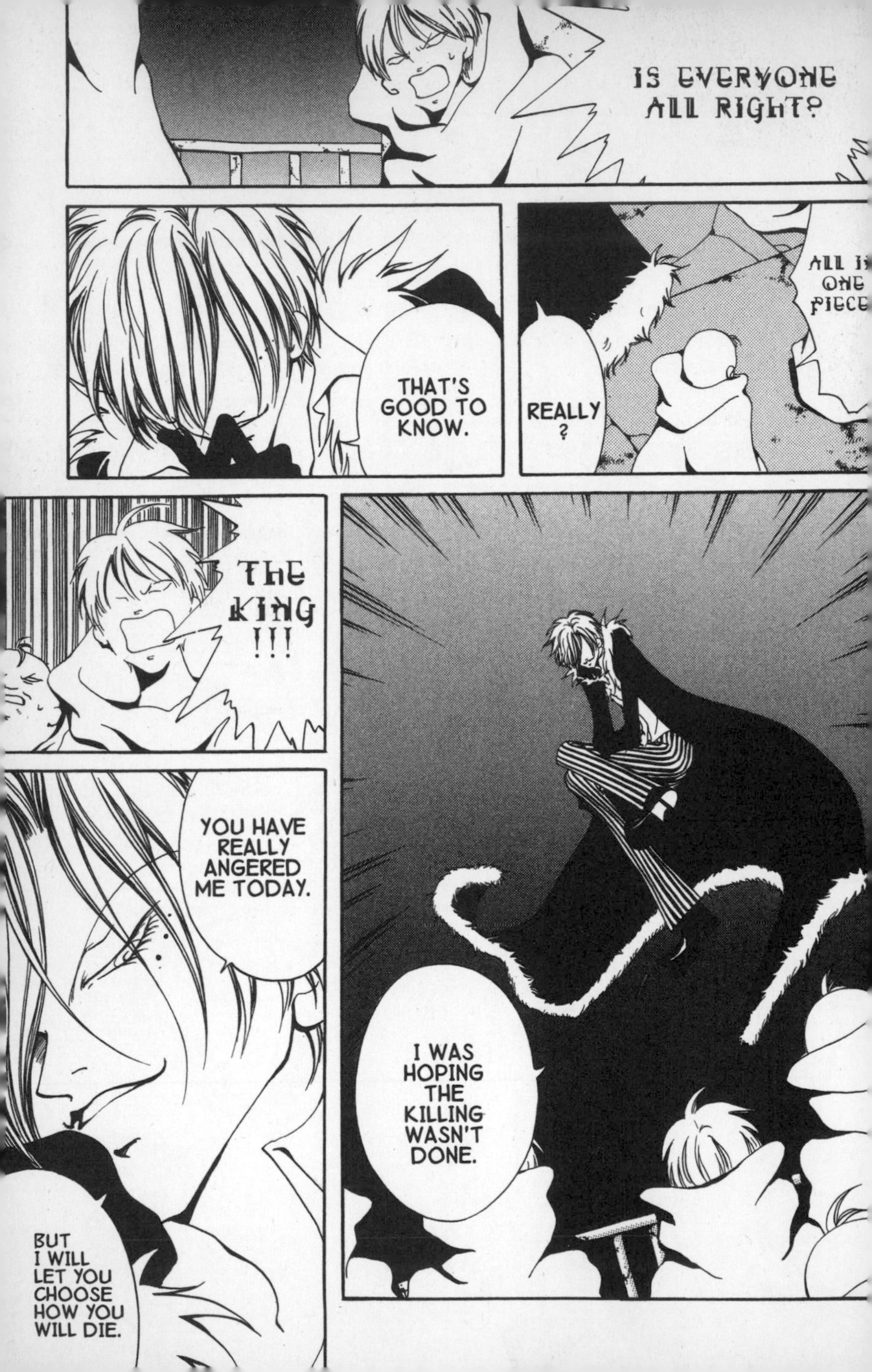
IS EVERYONE ALL RIGHT?
ALL I ONE PIECE
REALLY?
THAT'S GOOD TO KNOW.
I WAS HOPING THE KILLING WASN'T DONE.
THE KING!!!
YOU HAVE REALLY ANGERED ME TODAY.
BUT I WILL LET YOU CHOOSE HOW YOU WILL DIE.

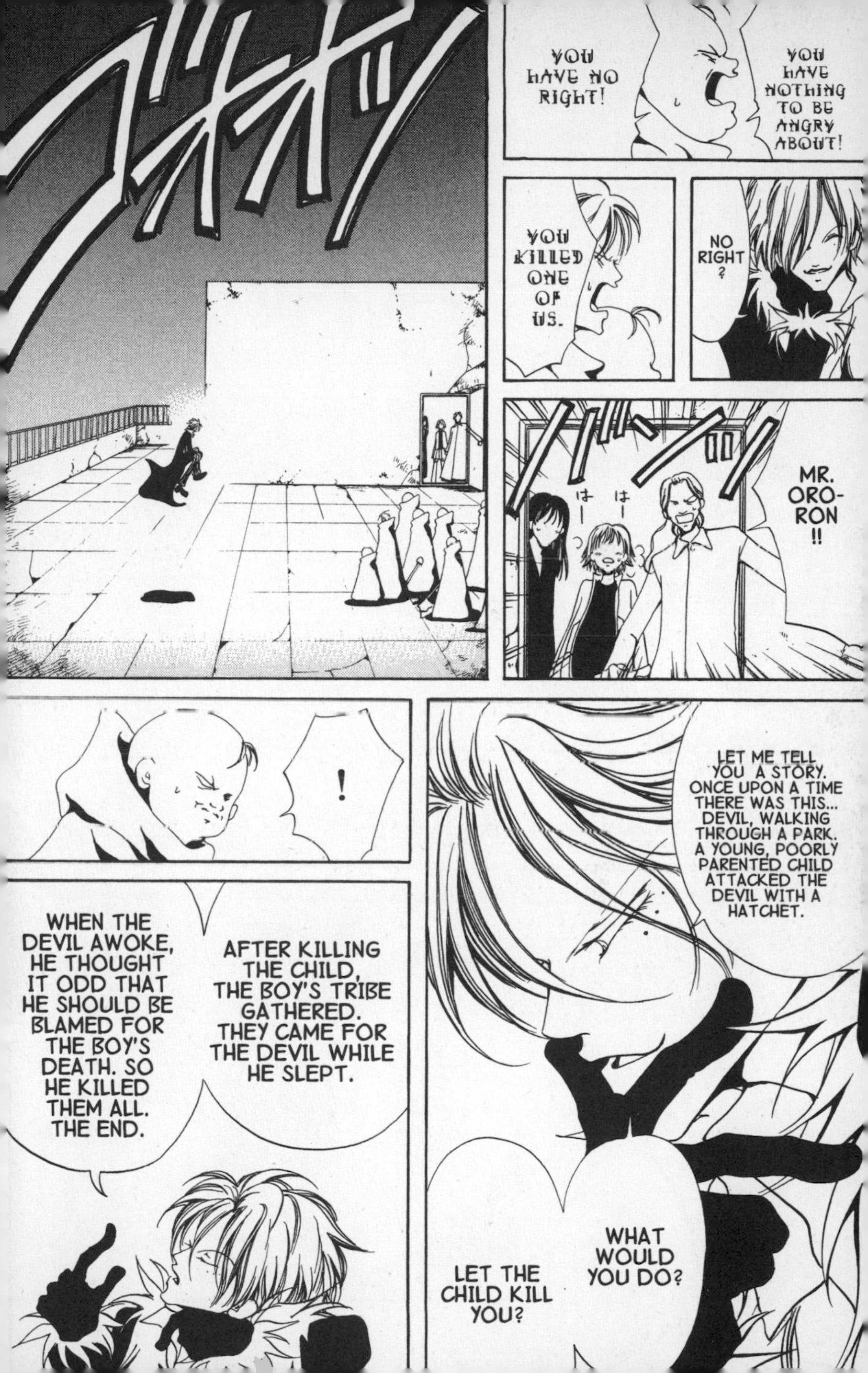
YOU HAVE NOTHING TO BE ANGRY ABOUT!
YOU HAVE NO RIGHT!
NO RIGHT?
YOU KILLED ONE OF US.
MR. ORO-RON!!
はー はー
LET ME TELL YOU A STORY. ONCE UPON A TIME THERE WAS THIS... DEVIL, WALKING THROUGH A PARK. A YOUNG, POORLY PARENTED CHILD ATTACKED THE DEVIL WITH A HATCHET.
WHAT WOULD YOU DO?
LET THE CHILD KILL YOU?
!
AFTER KILLING THE CHILD, THE BOY'S TRIBE GATHERED. THEY CAME FOR THE DEVIL WHILE HE SLEPT.
WHEN THE DEVIL AWOKE, HE THOUGHT IT ODD THAT HE SHOULD BE BLAMED FOR THE BOY'S DEATH. SO HE KILLED THEM ALL. THE END.

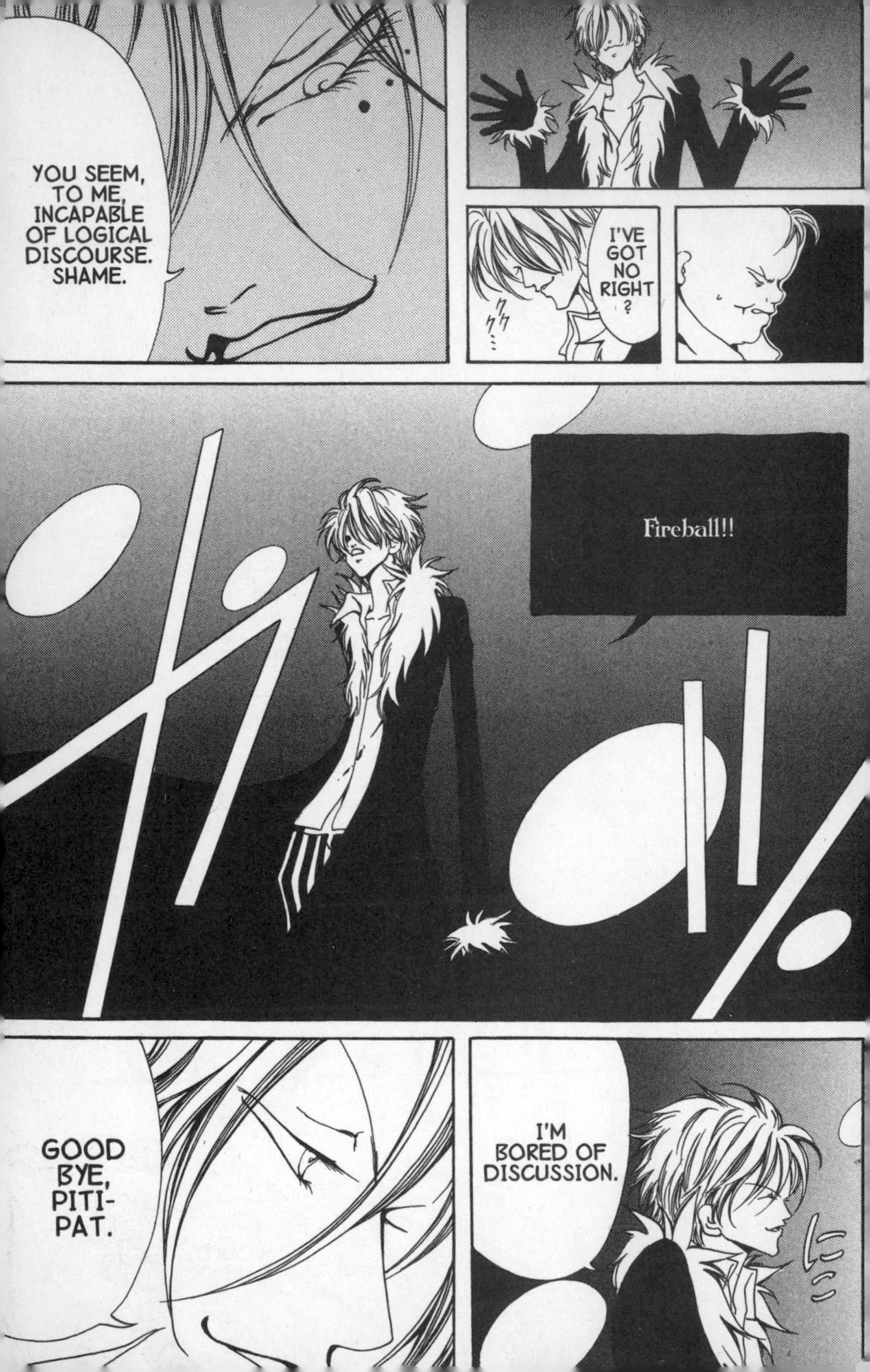
I'VE GOT NO RIGHT?
ククク…
YOU SEEM, TO ME, INCAPABLE OF LOGICAL DISCOURSE. SHAME.
Fireball!!
I'M BORED OF DISCUSSION.
にこ
GOOD BYE, PITI-PAT.

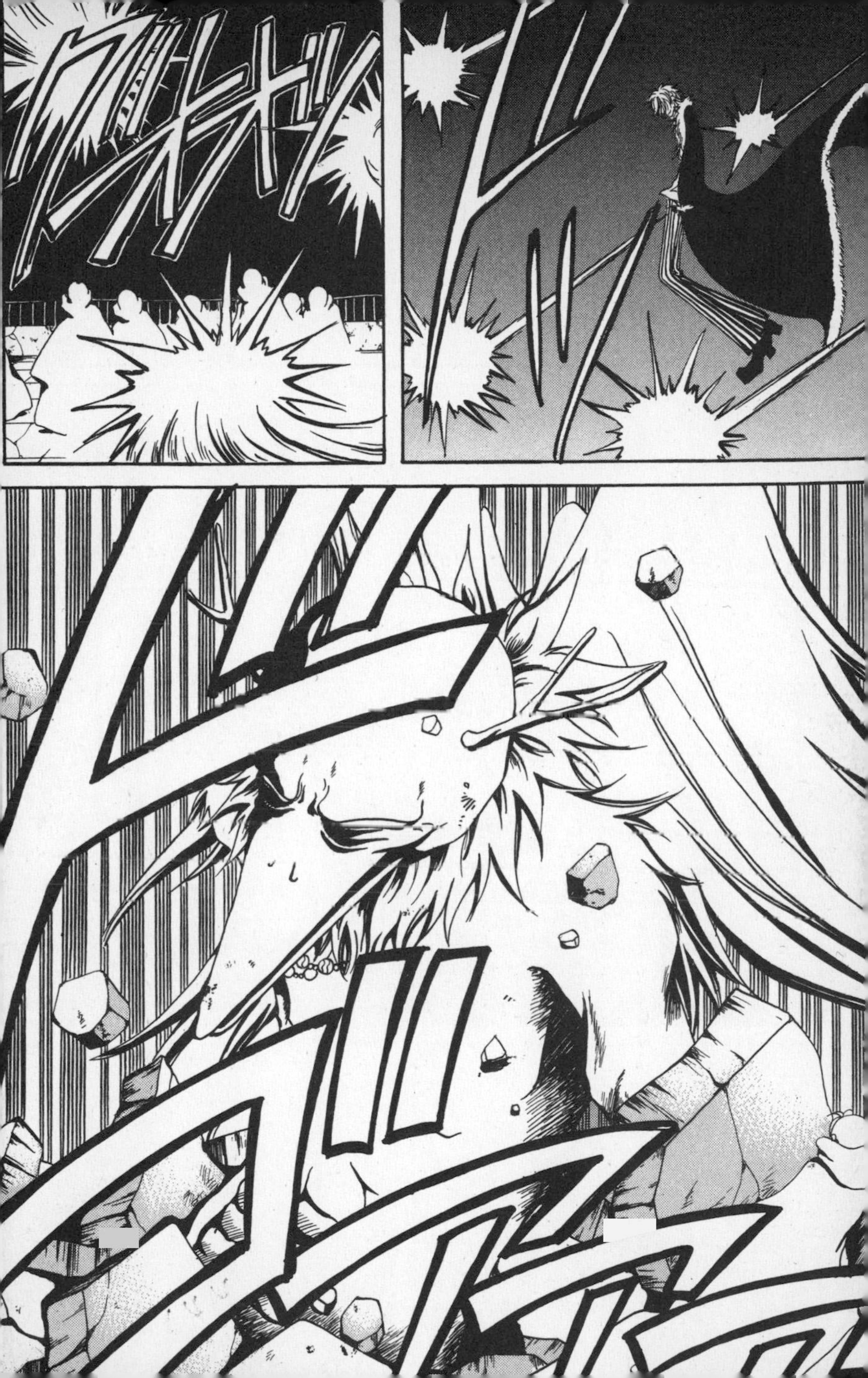

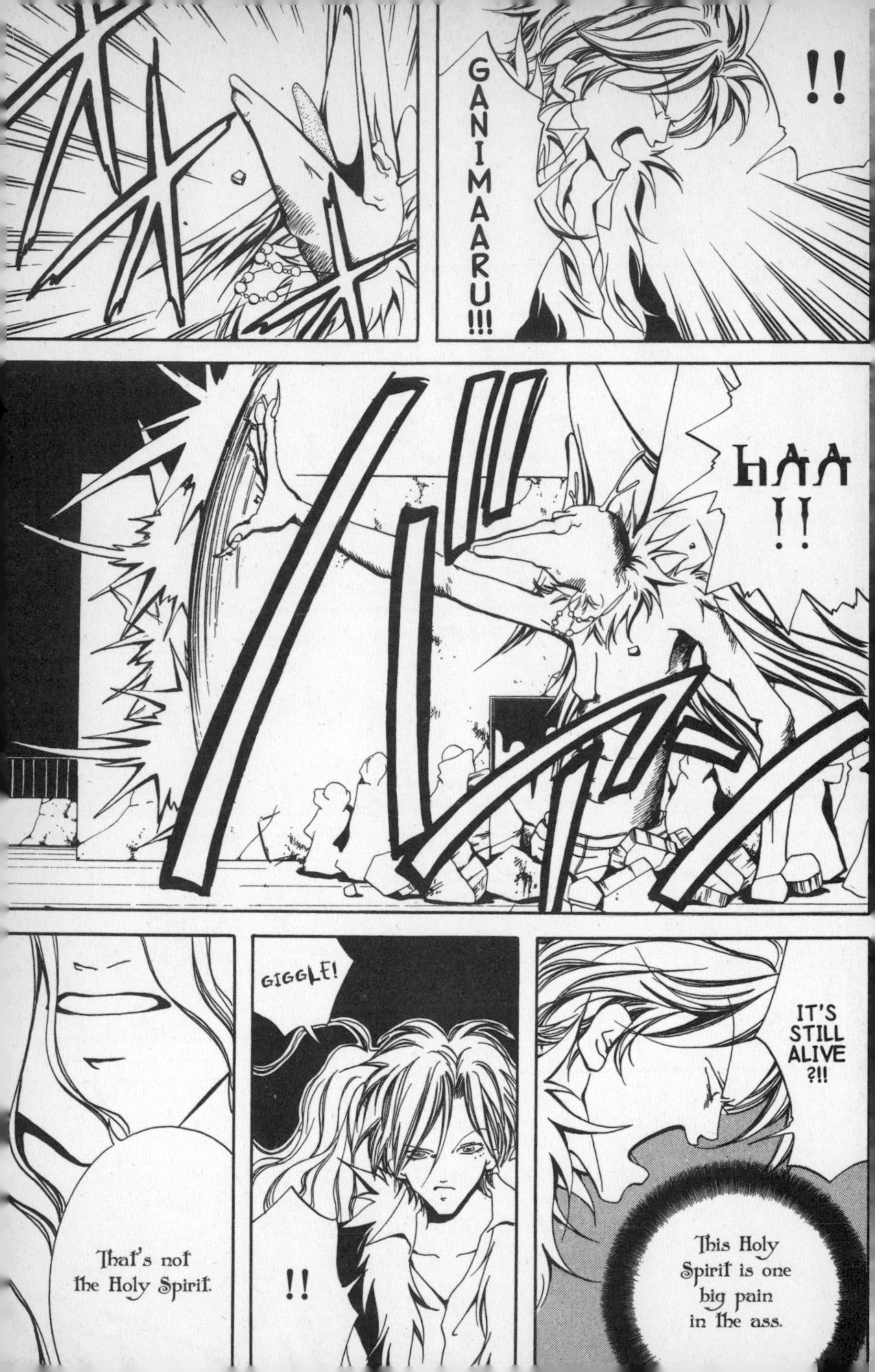
!!
GANIMAARU!!!
HAA!!
IT'S STILL ALIVE?!!
This Holy Spirit is one big pain in the ass.
GIGGLE!
!!
That's not the Holy Spirit.

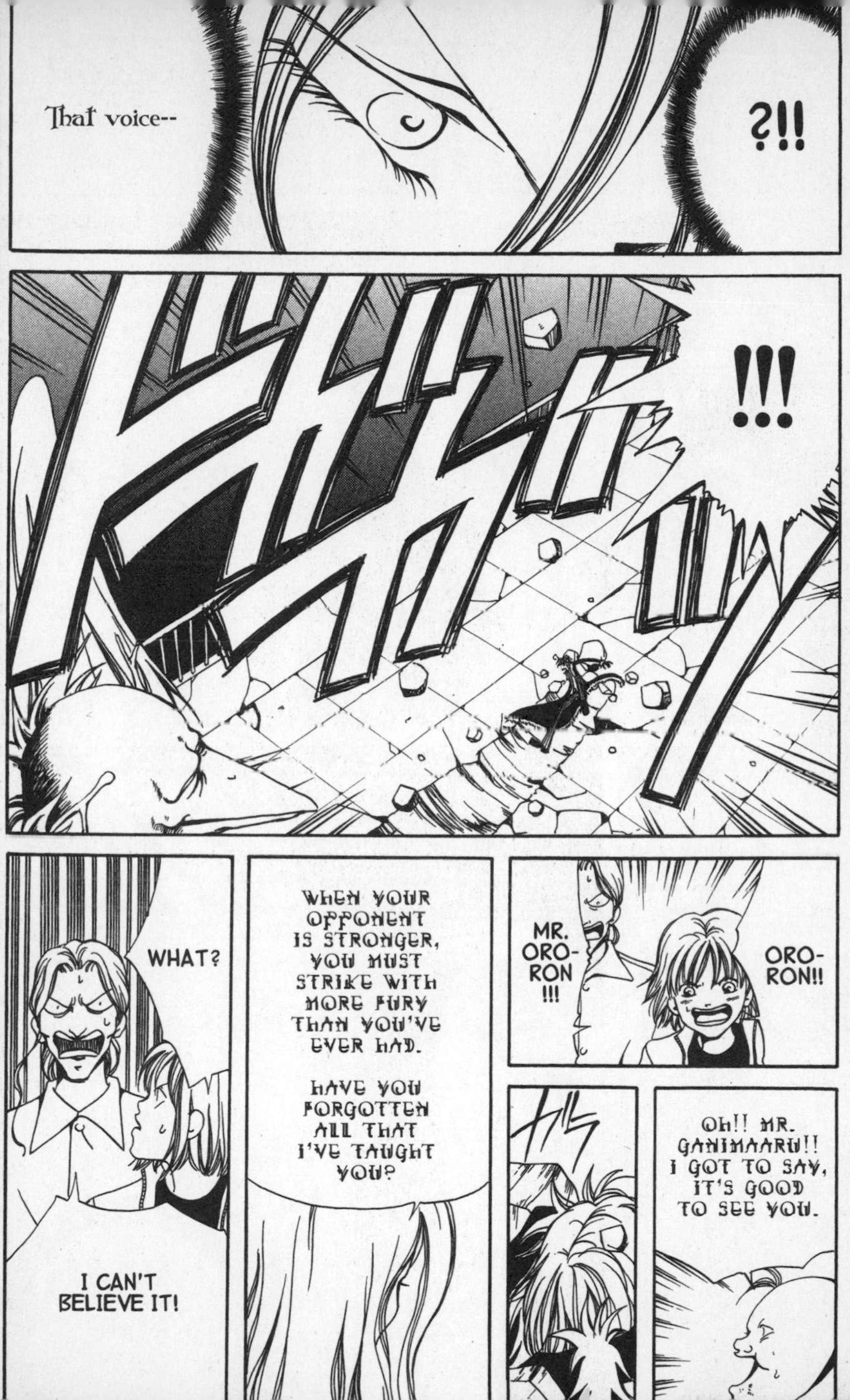
?!!
That voice--
!!!
ORO-RON!!
MR. ORO-RON !!!
OH!! MR. GANIMAARU!! I GOT TO SAY, IT'S GOOD TO SEE YOU.
WHEN YOUR OPPONENT IS STRONGER, YOU MUST STRIKE WITH MORE FURY THAN YOU'VE EVER HAD.
HAVE YOU FORGOTTEN ALL THAT I'VE TAUGHT YOU?
WHAT?
I CAN'T BELIEVE IT!

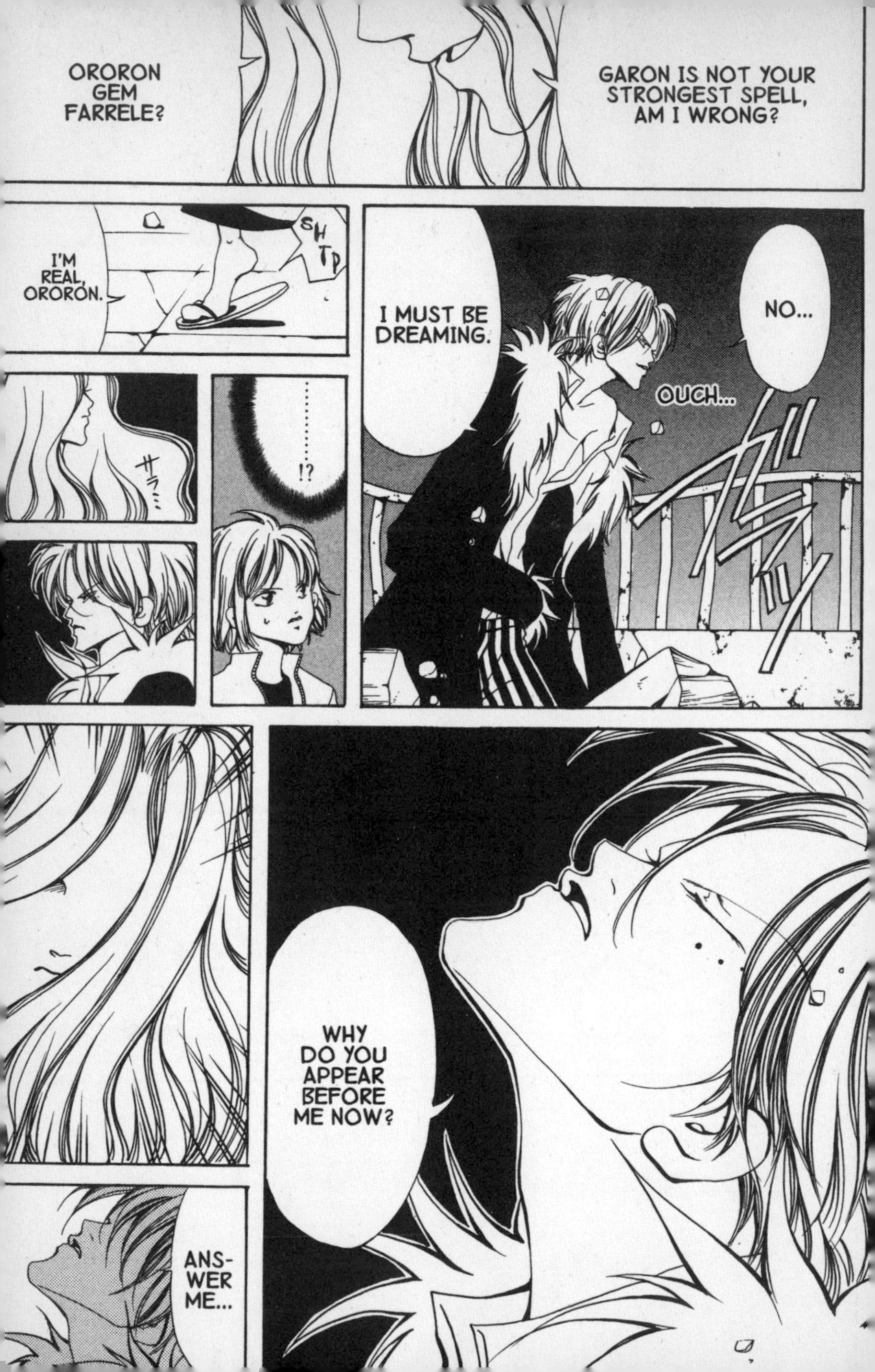
GARON IS NOT YOUR STRONGEST SPELL, AM I WRONG?
ORORON GEM FARRELE?
NO...
OUCH...
I MUST BE DREAMING.
SH TP
I'M REAL, ORORON.
......!?
サラ…
WHY DO YOU APPEAR BEFORE ME NOW?
ANS-WER ME...

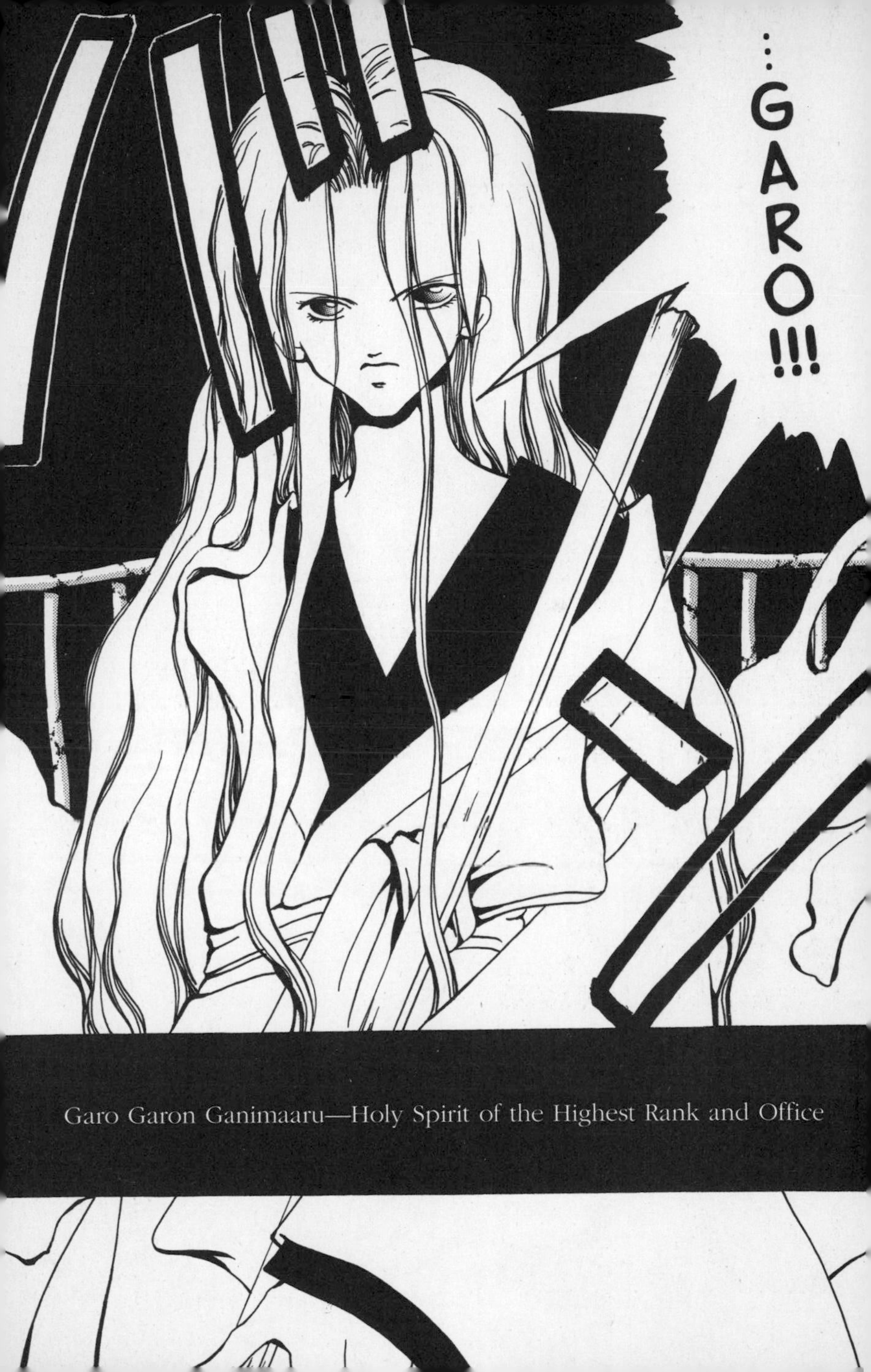
...GARO!!!
Garo Garon Ganimaaru—Holy Spirit of the Highest Rank and Office

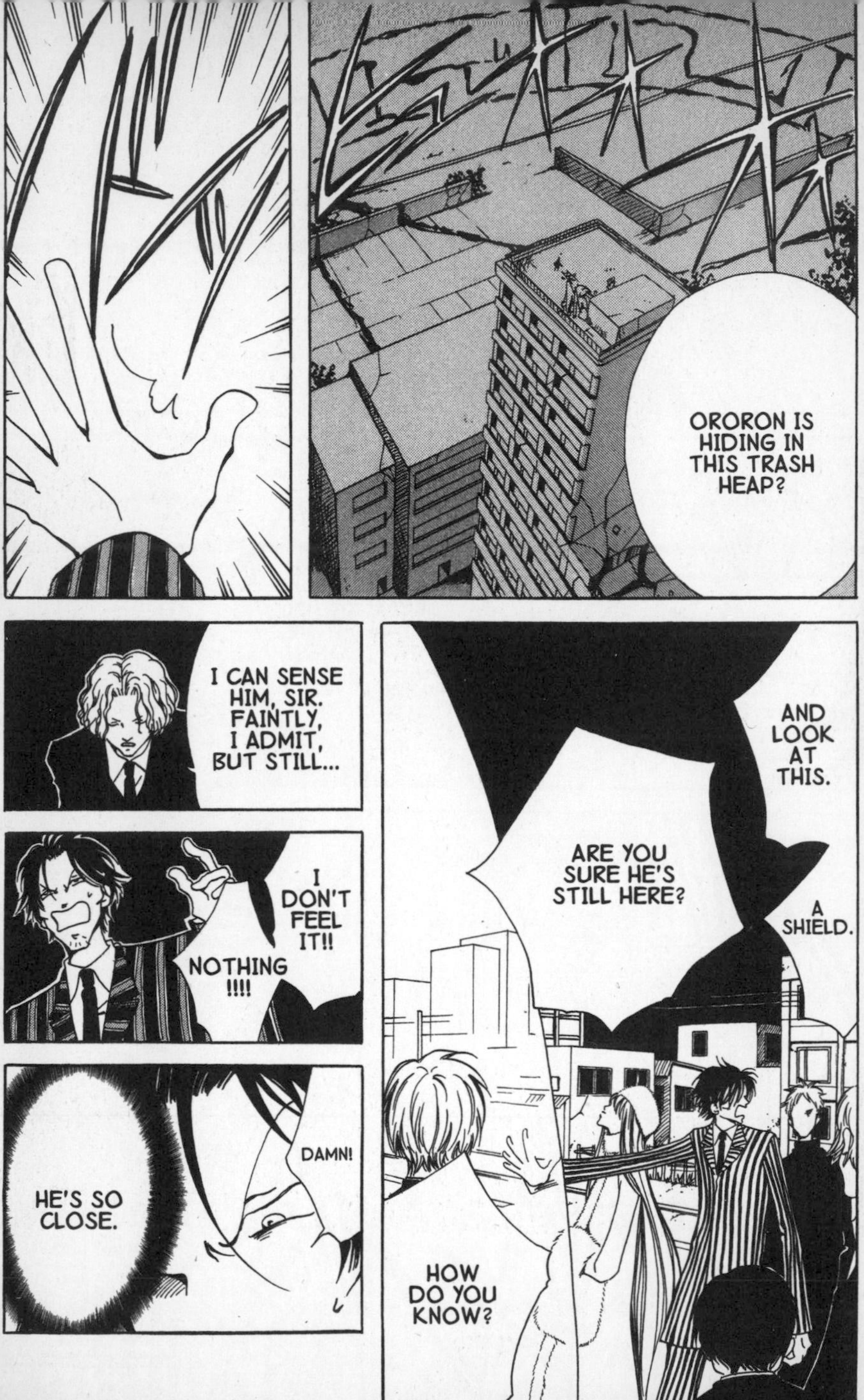
ORORON IS HIDING IN THIS TRASH HEAP?
AND LOOK AT THIS.
ARE YOU SURE HE'S STILL HERE?
A SHIELD.
HOW DO YOU KNOW?
I CAN SENSE HIM, SIR. FAINTLY, I ADMIT, BUT STILL...
I DON'T FEEL IT!!
NOTHING !!!!
DAMN!
HE'S SO CLOSE.

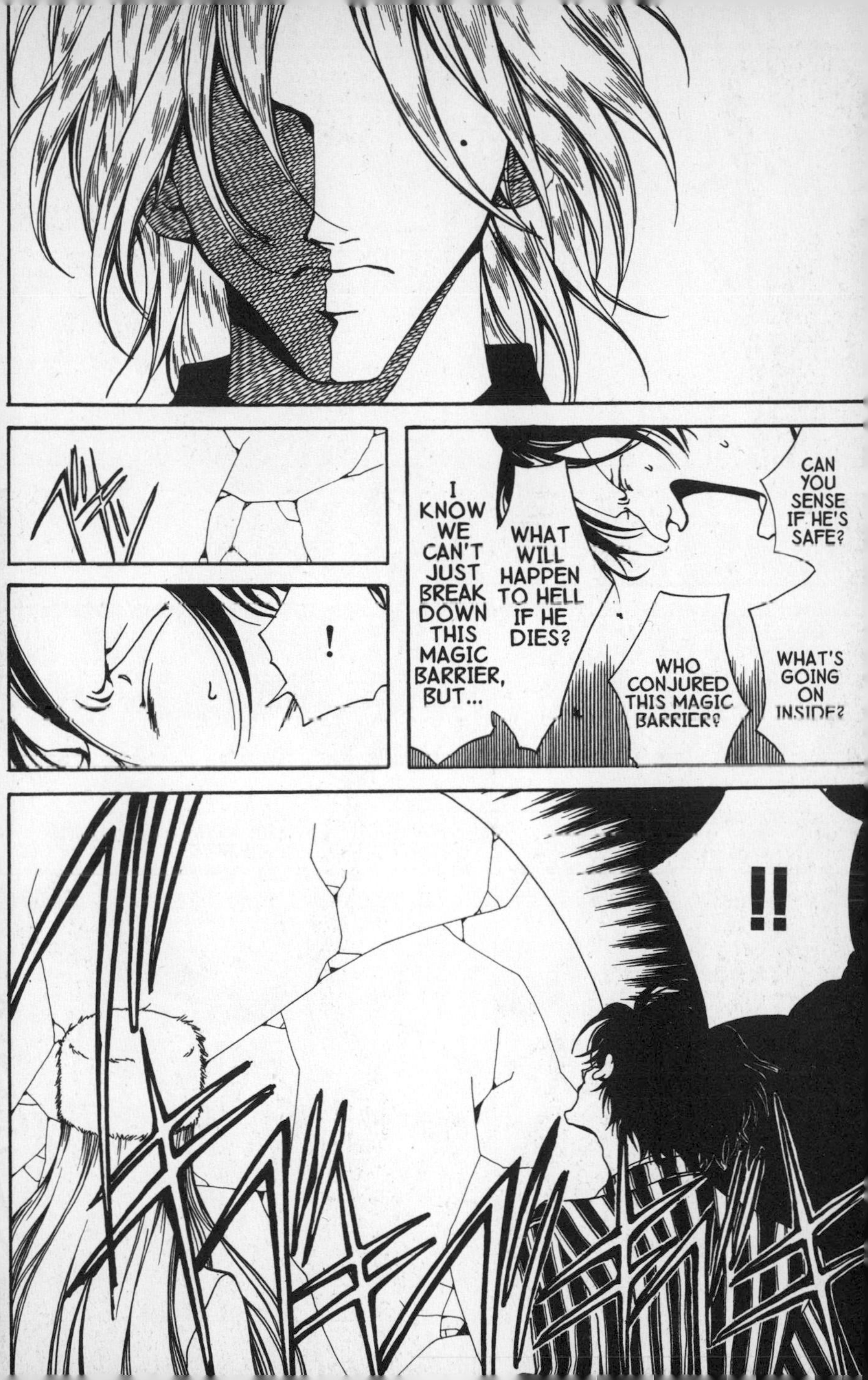
CAN YOU SENSE IF HE'S SAFE?
WHAT'S GOING ON INSIDE?
WHO CONJURED THIS MAGIC BARRIER?
WHAT WILL HAPPEN TO HELL IF HE DIES?
I KNOW WE CAN'T JUST BREAK DOWN THIS MAGIC BARRIER, BUT...
!
!!

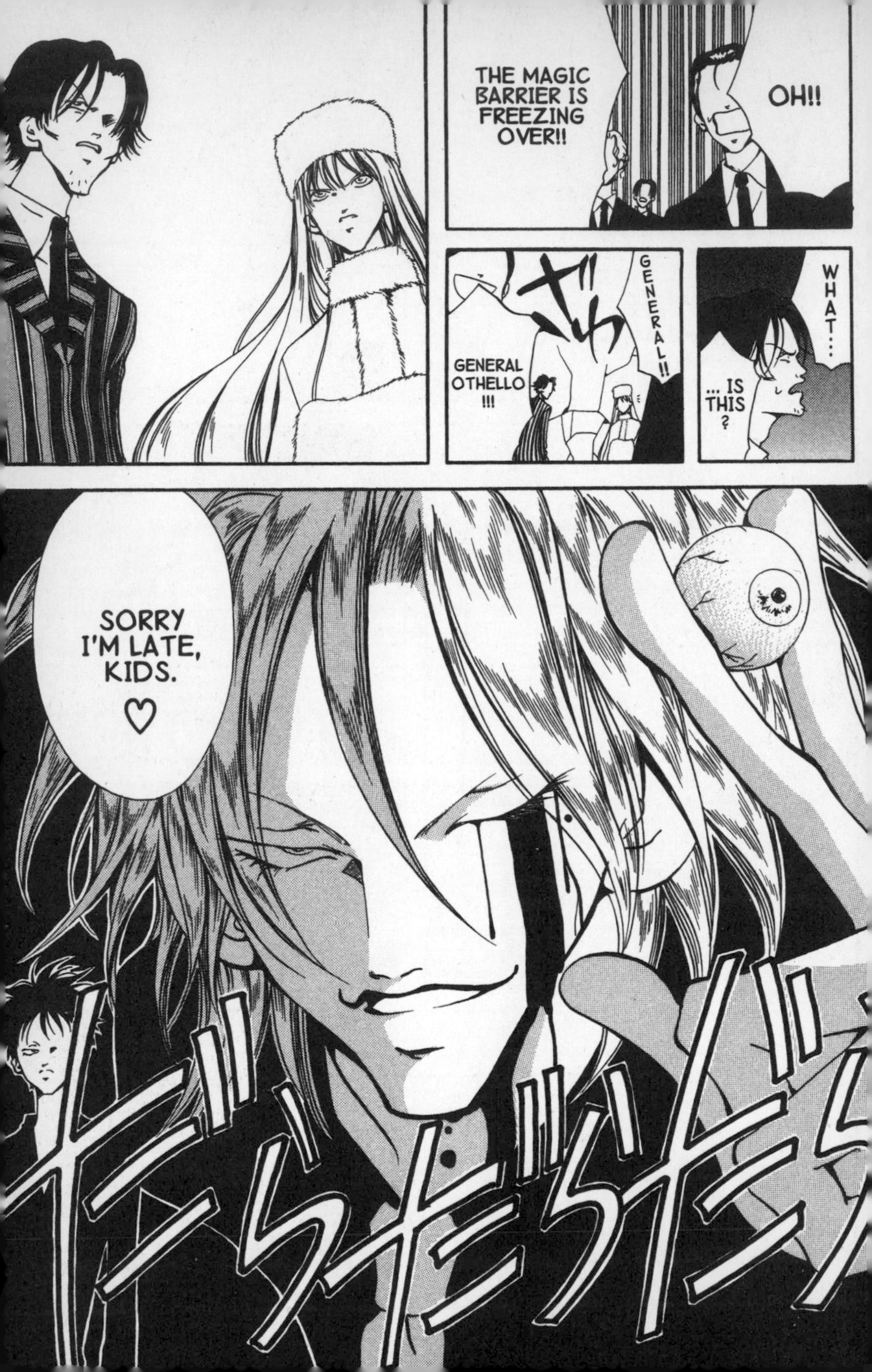
OH!!
THE MAGIC BARRIER IS FREEZING OVER!!
WHAT...
...IS THIS?
GENERAL!!
GENERAL OTHELLO!!!
SORRY I'M LATE, KIDS. ♡

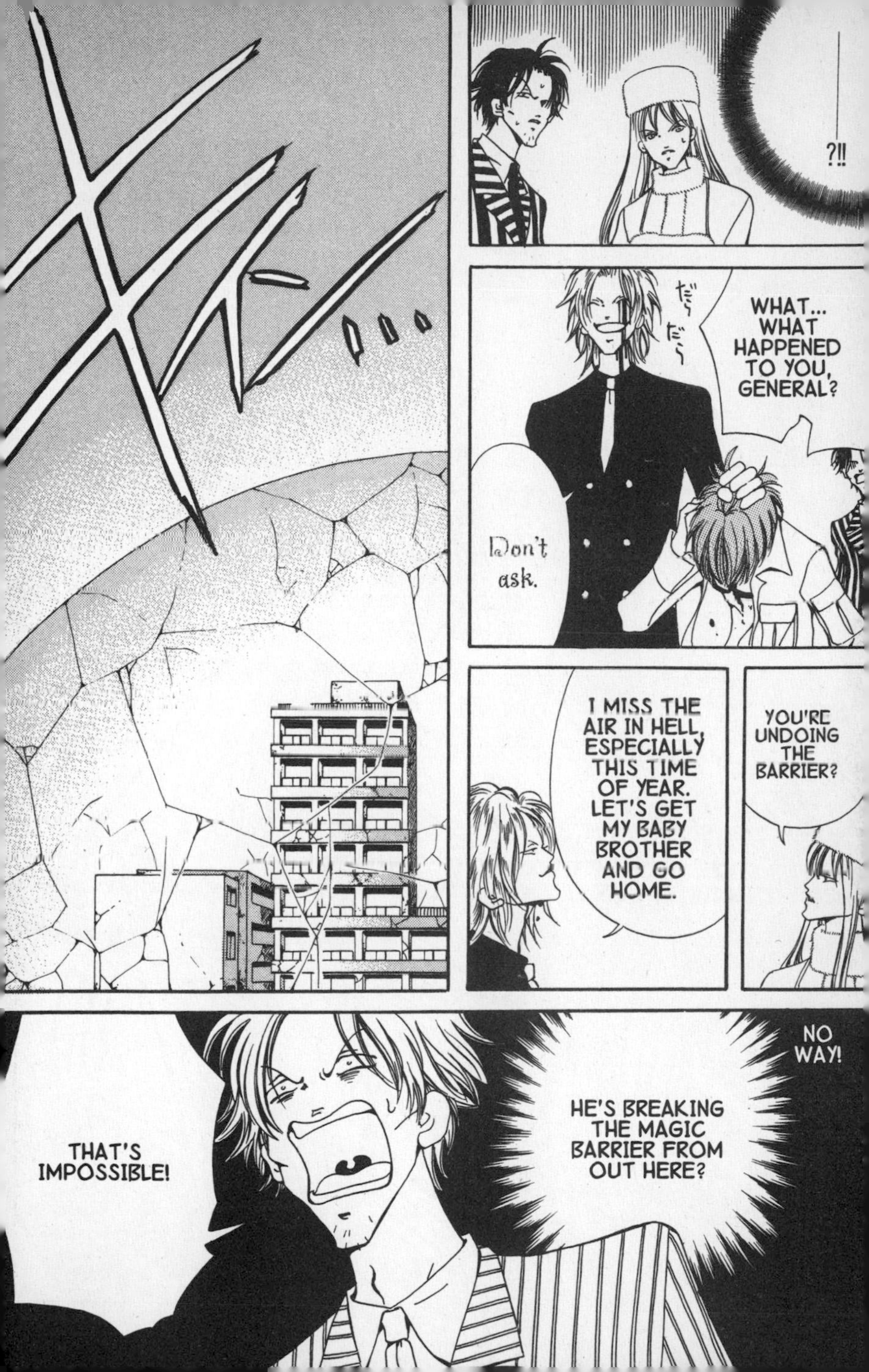
?!!
だら だら
WHAT... WHAT HAPPENED TO YOU, GENERAL?
Don't ask.
YOU'RE UNDOING THE BARRIER?
I MISS THE AIR IN HELL, ESPECIALLY THIS TIME OF YEAR. LET'S GET MY BABY BROTHER AND GO HOME.
NO WAY!
HE'S BREAKING THE MAGIC BARRIER FROM OUT HERE?
THAT'S IMPOSSIBLE!

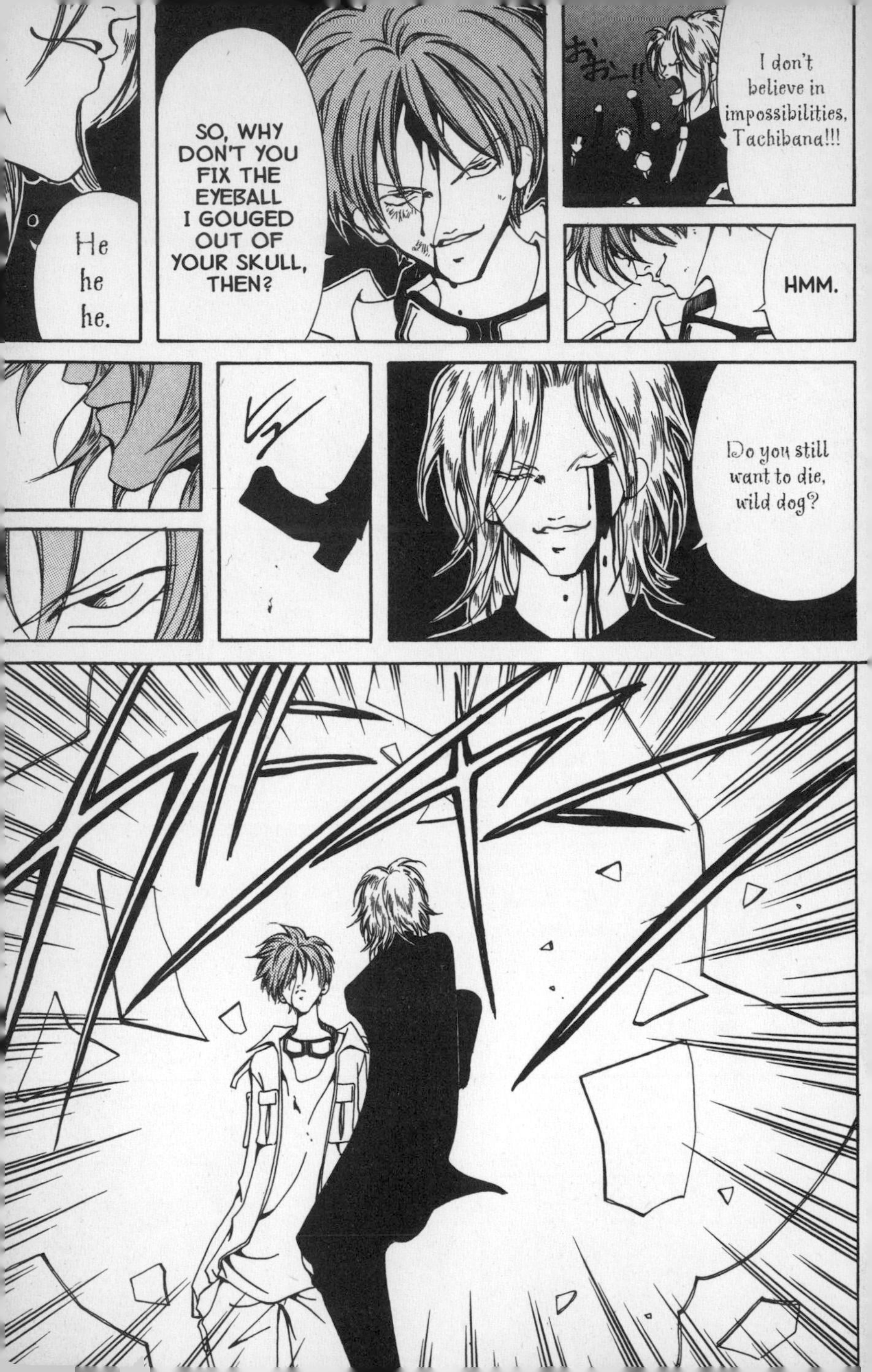
I don't believe in impossibilities, Tachibana!!!
HMM.
SO, WHY DON'T YOU FIX THE EYEBALL I GOUGED OUT OF YOUR SKULL, THEN?
He he he.
Do you still want to die, wild dog?

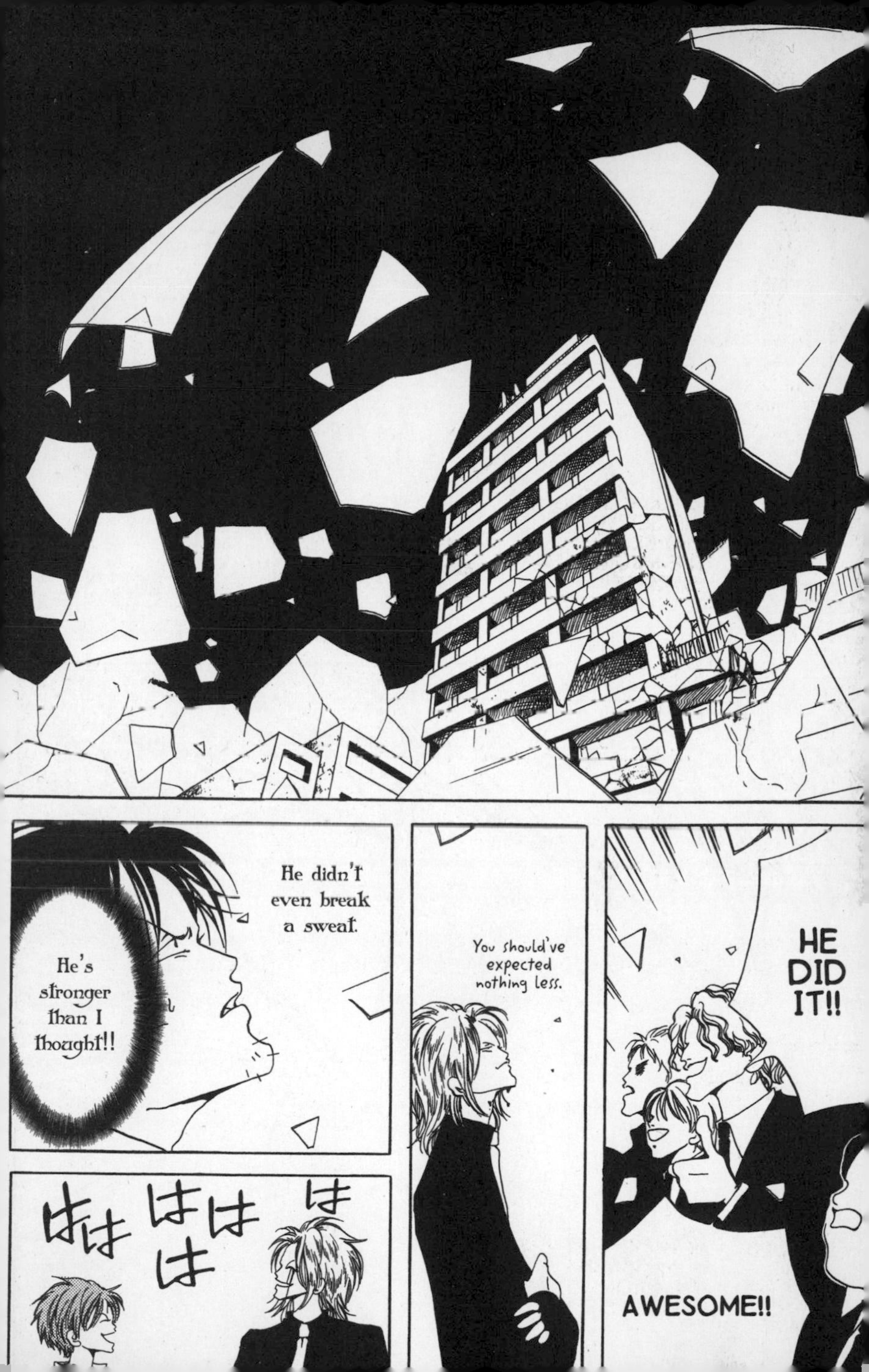
HE DID IT!!
AWESOME!!
You should've expected nothing less.
He didn't even break a sweat.
He's stronger than I thought!!
は
はは
は
はは

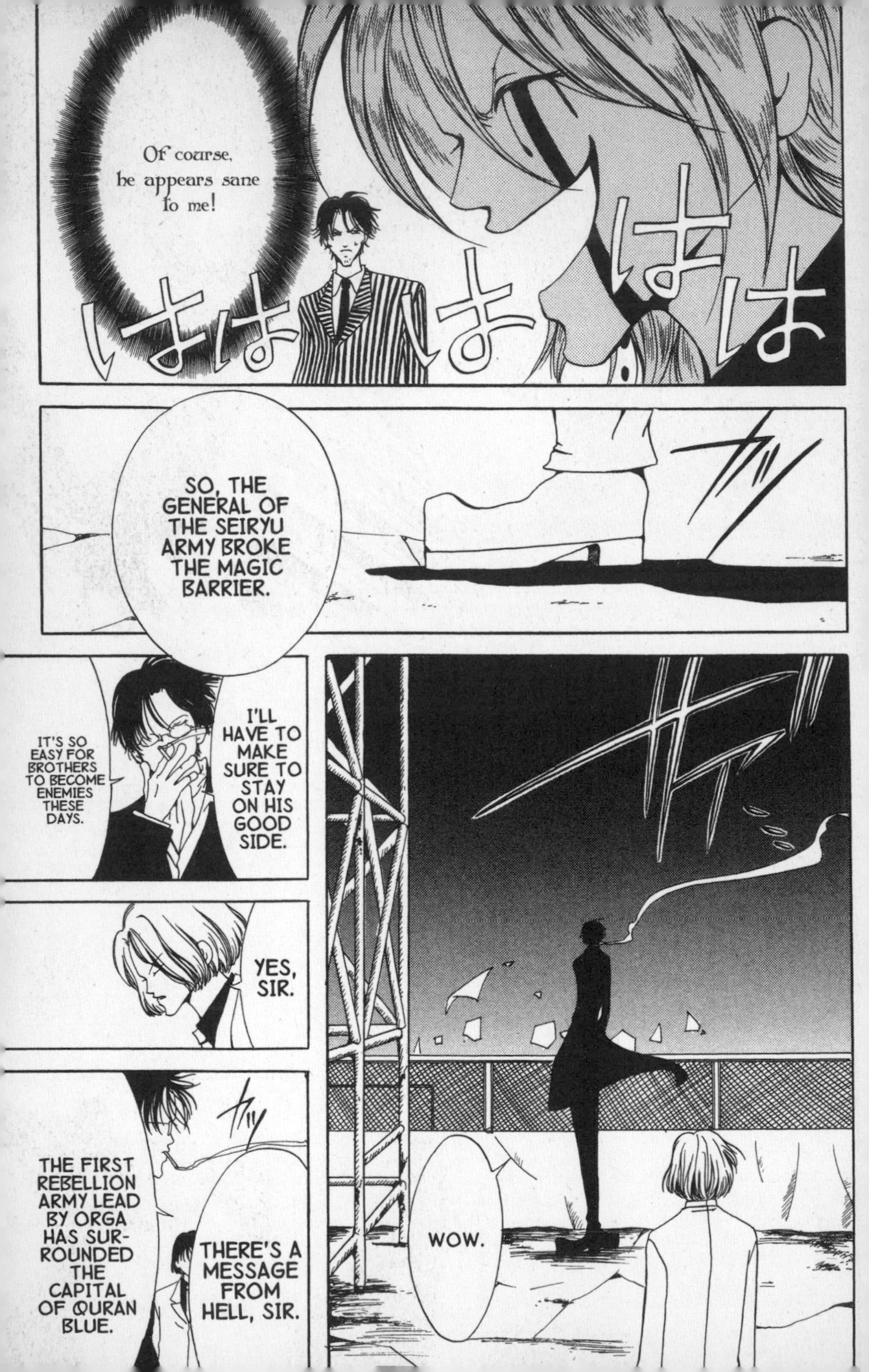
Of course, he appears sane to me!
SO, THE GENERAL OF THE SEIRYU ARMY BROKE THE MAGIC BARRIER.
WOW.
I'LL HAVE TO MAKE SURE TO STAY ON HIS GOOD SIDE.
IT'S SO EASY FOR BROTHERS TO BECOME ENEMIES THESE DAYS.
YES, SIR.
THERE'S A MESSAGE FROM HELL, SIR.
THE FIRST REBELLION ARMY LEAD BY ORGA HAS SUR-ROUNDED THE CAPITAL OF QURAN BLUE.

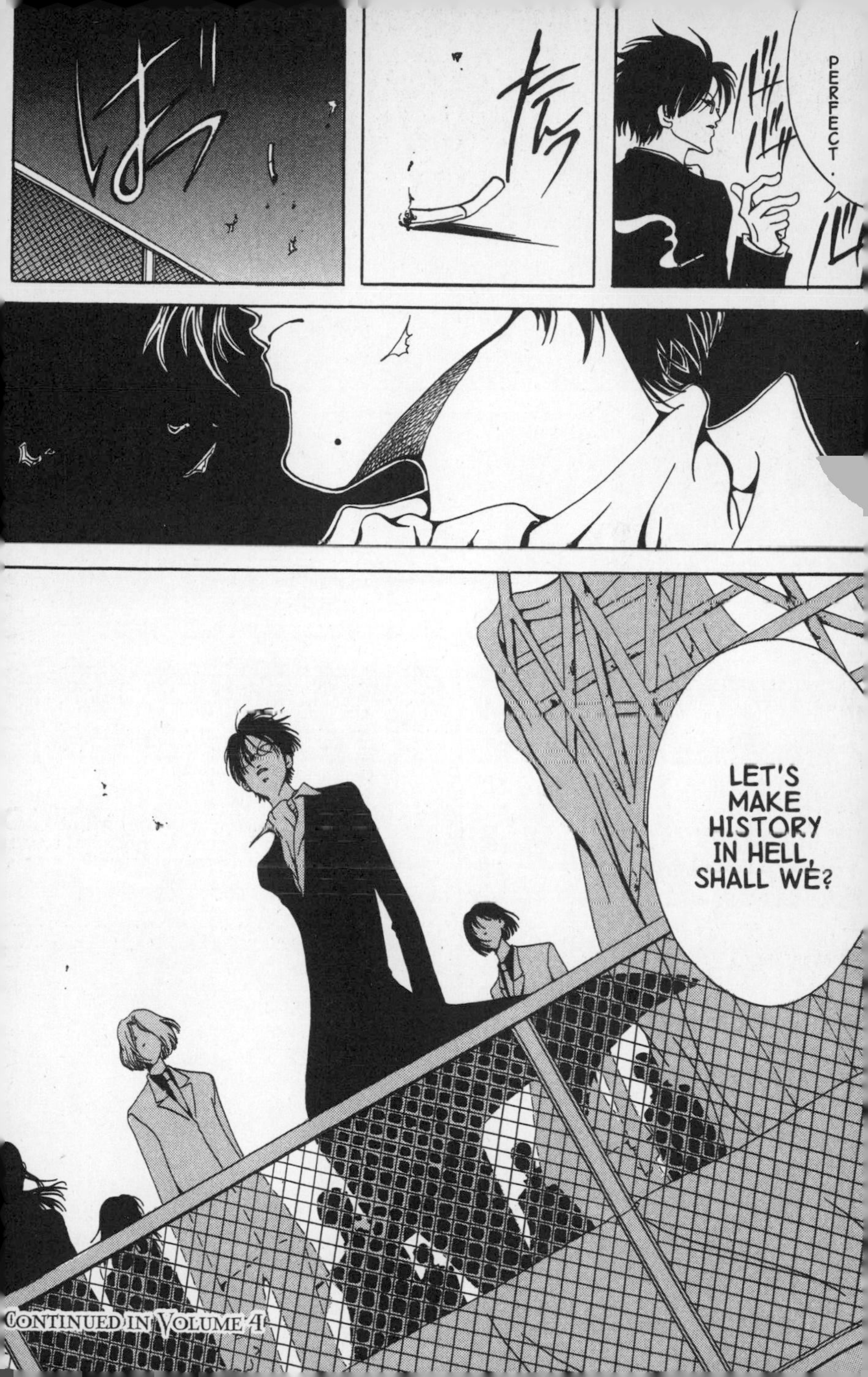
PERFECT.
LET'S MAKE HISTORY IN HELL, SHALL WE?

CONTINUED IN VOLUME 4

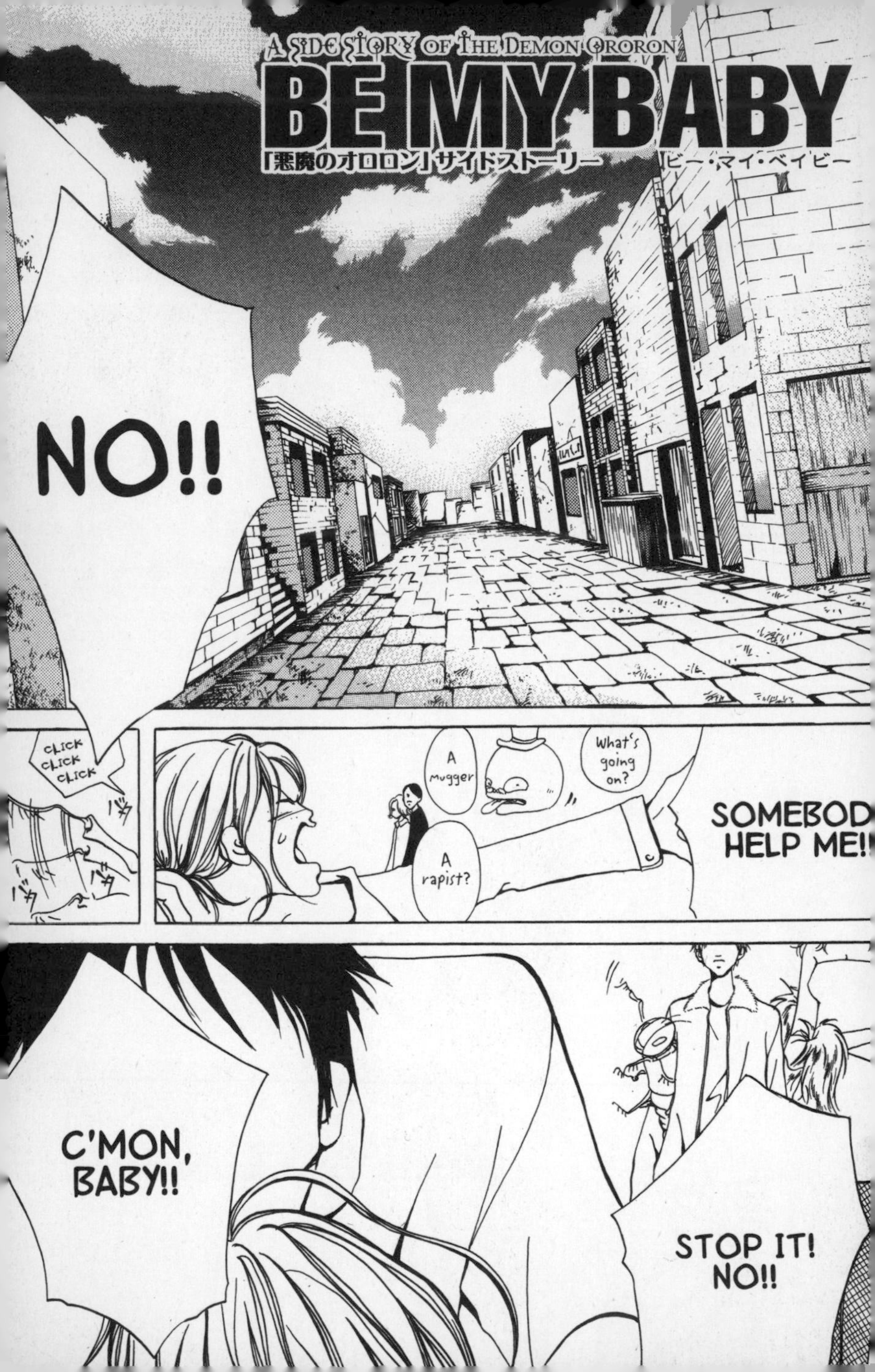
A SIDE STORY OF THE DEMON ORORON
BE MY BABY
「悪魔のオロロン」サイドストーリー
ビー・マイ・ベイビー
NO!!
SOMEBOD HELP ME!!
What's going on?
A mugger
A rapist?
CLICK CLICK CLICK
STOP IT! NO!!
C'MON, BABY!!

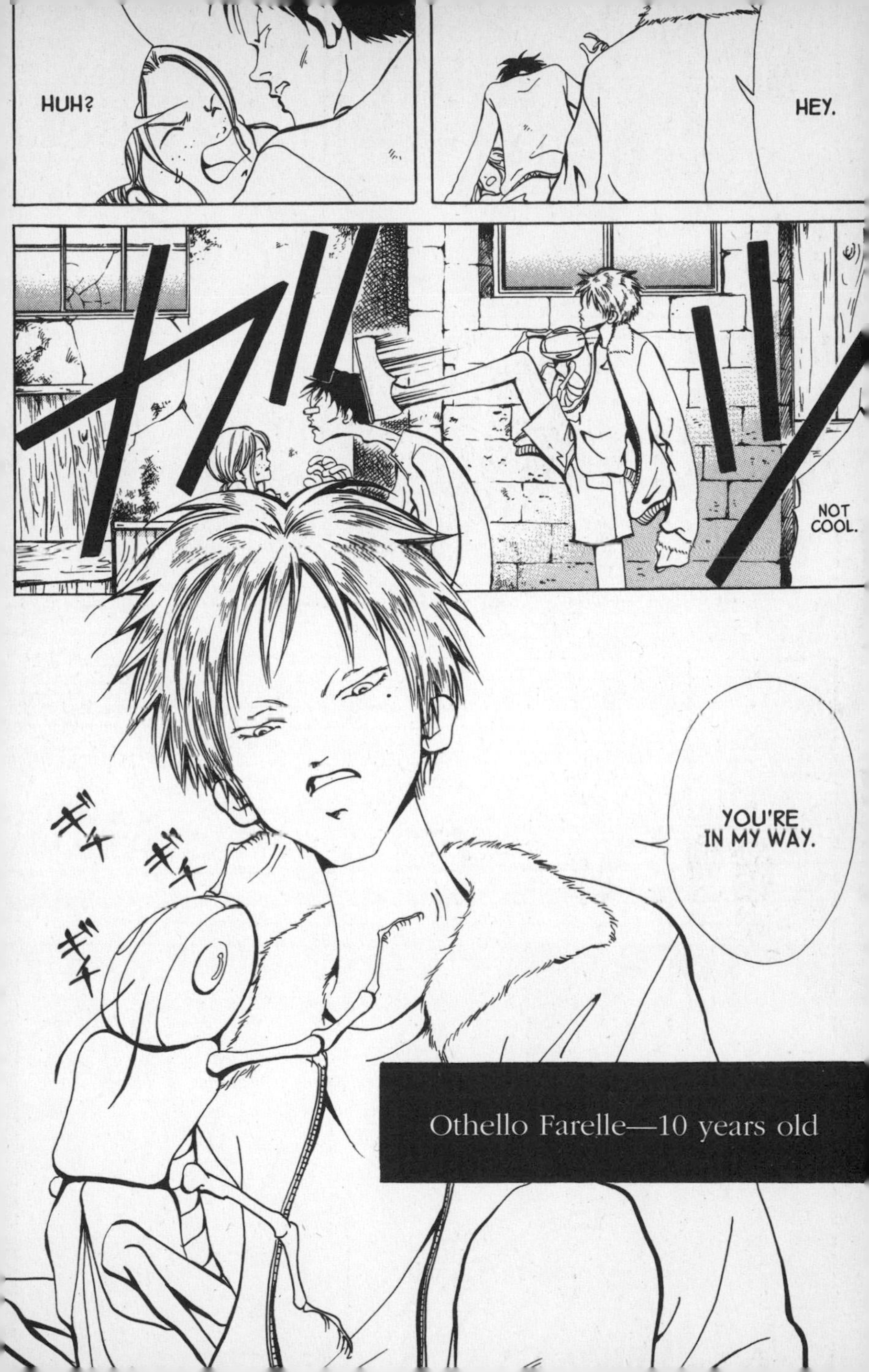
HEY.
HUH?
NOT COOL.
YOU'RE IN MY WAY.
ギチ
ギチ
ギチ
Othello Farelle—10 years old

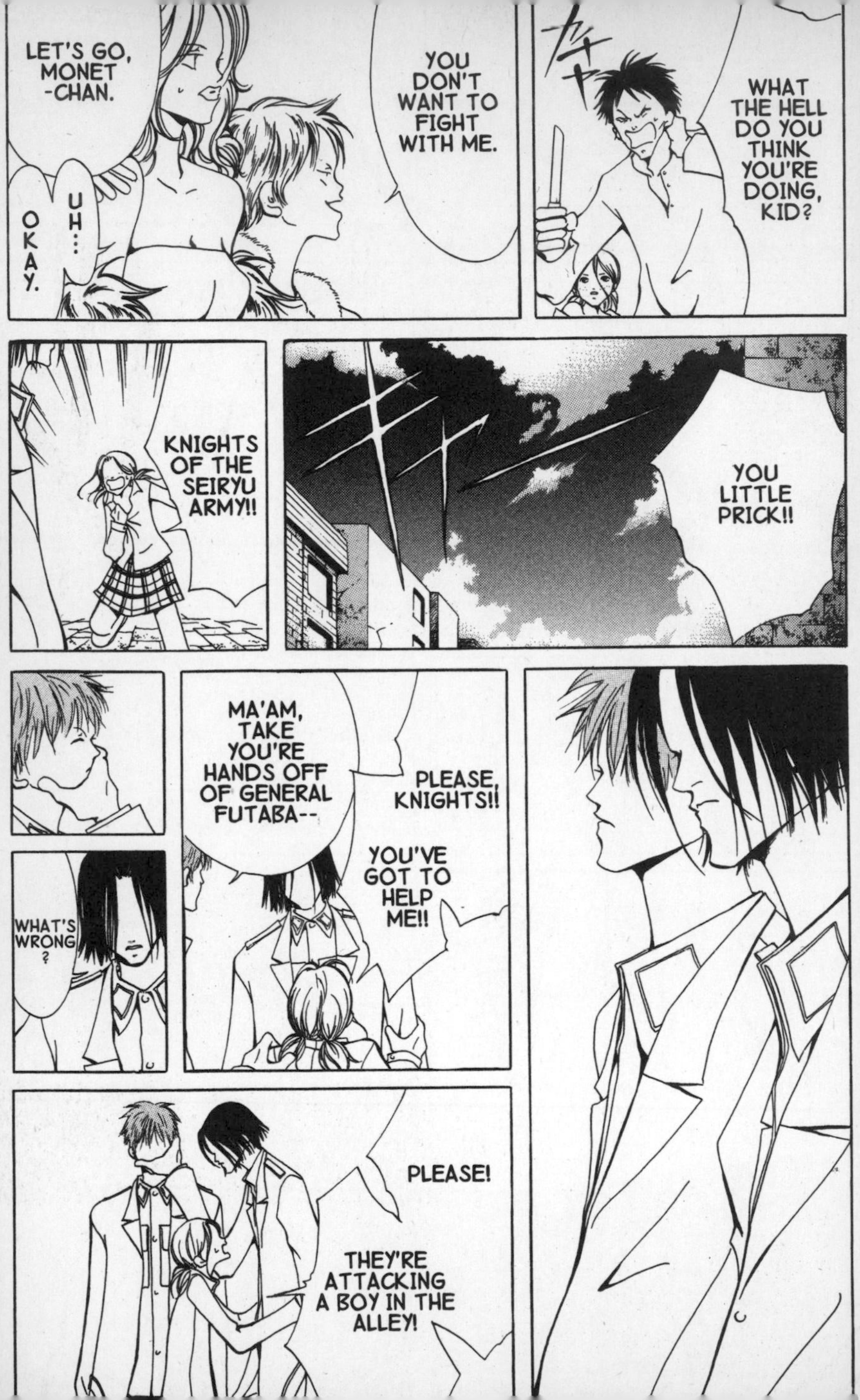
WHAT THE HELL DO YOU THINK YOU'RE DOING, KID?
YOU DON'T WANT TO FIGHT WITH ME.
LET'S GO, MONET -CHAN.
UH... OKAY.
YOU LITTLE PRICK!!
KNIGHTS OF THE SEIRYU ARMY!!
PLEASE, KNIGHTS!!
YOU'VE GOT TO HELP ME!!
MA'AM, TAKE YOU'RE HANDS OFF OF GENERAL FUTABA--
WHAT'S WRONG?
PLEASE!
THEY'RE ATTACKING A BOY IN THE ALLEY!

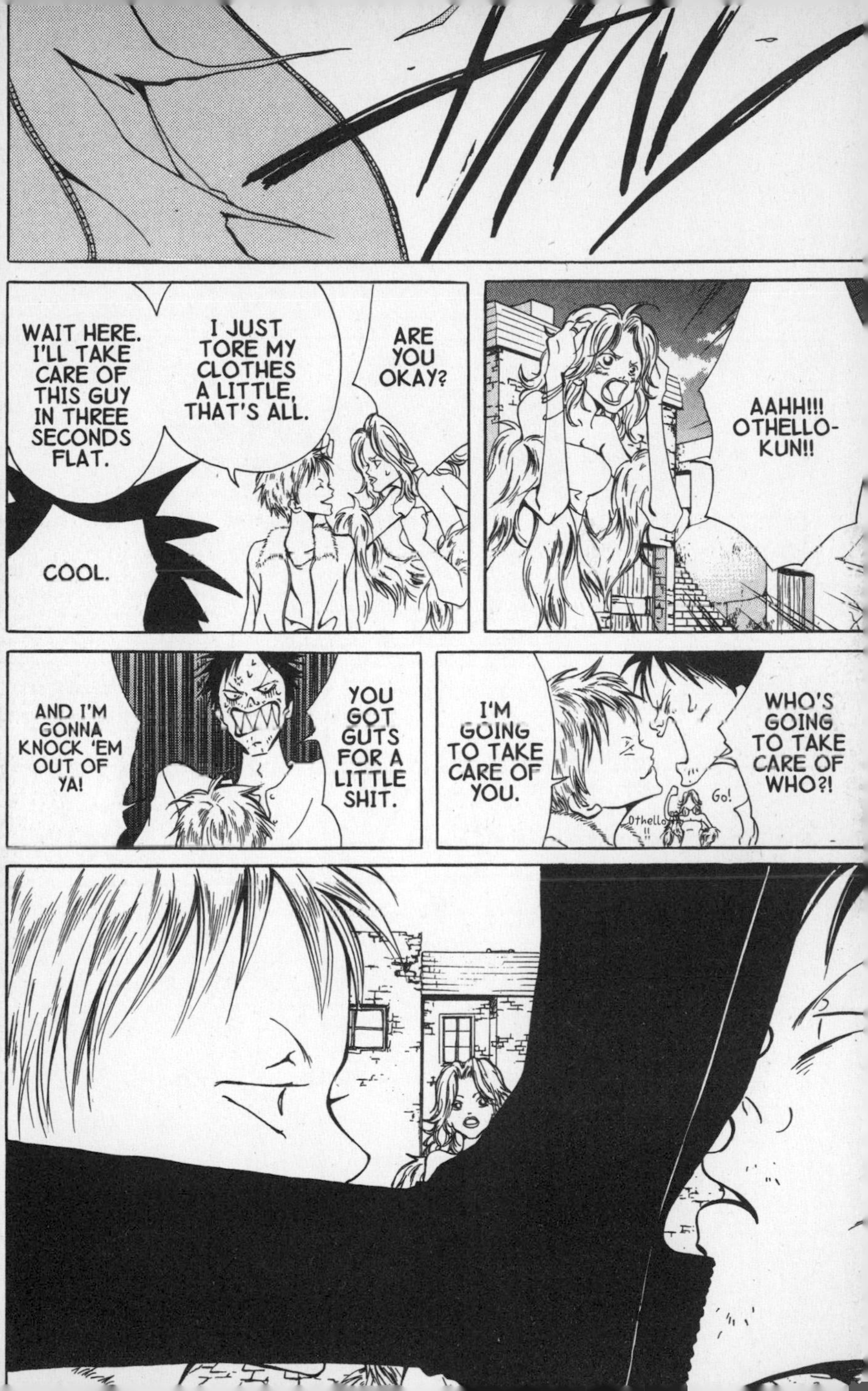

AAHH!!! OTHELLO-KUN!!
ARE YOU OKAY?
I JUST TORE MY CLOTHES A LITTLE, THAT'S ALL.
WAIT HERE. I'LL TAKE CARE OF THIS GUY IN THREE SECONDS FLAT.
COOL.
WHO'S GOING TO TAKE CARE OF WHO?!
Go!
Othello!!
I'M GOING TO TAKE CARE OF YOU.
YOU GOT GUTS FOR A LITTLE SHIT.
AND I'M GONNA KNOCK 'EM OUT OF YA!

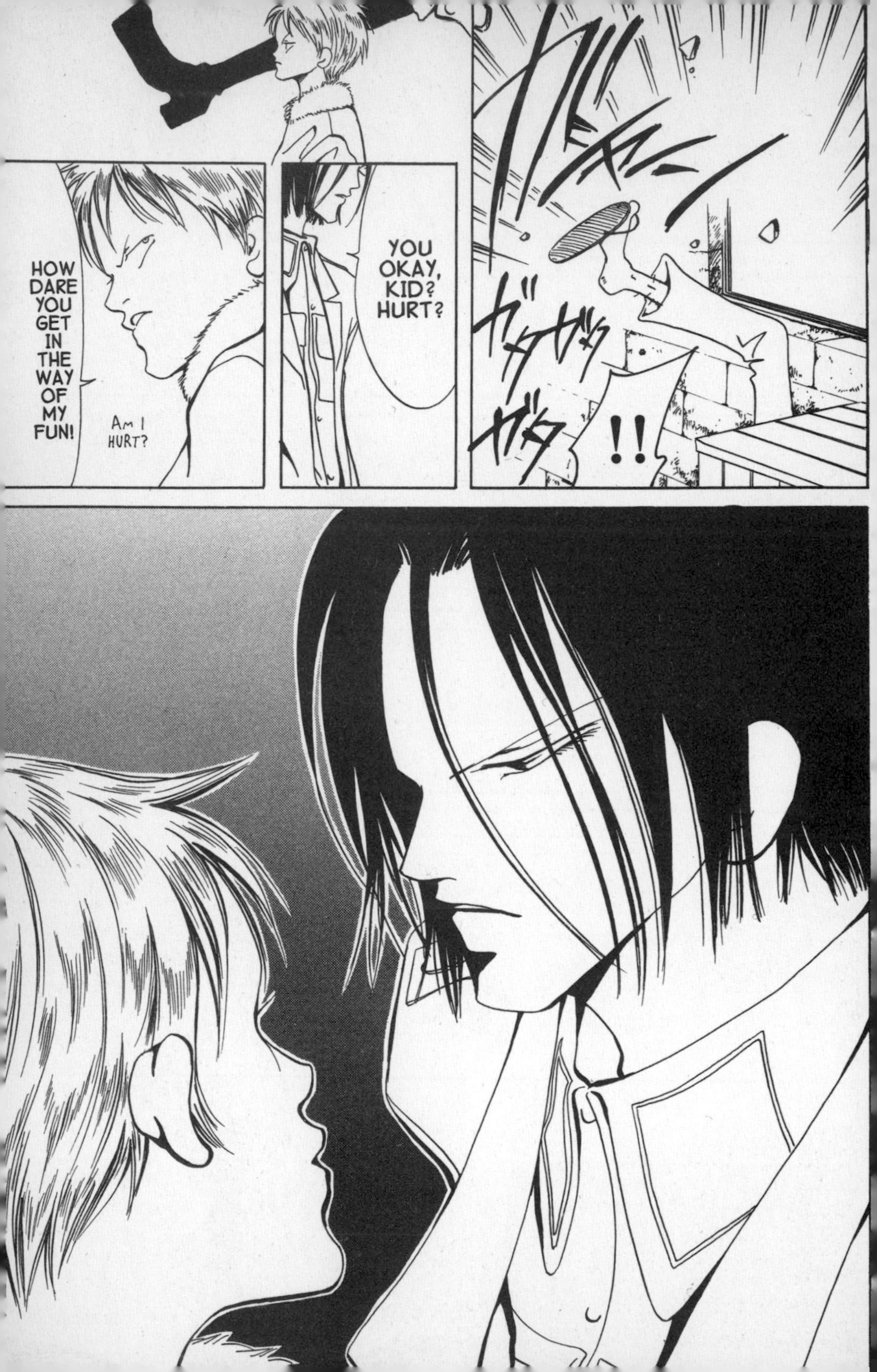
ガタガタ
!!
YOU OKAY, KID? HURT?
Am I HURT?
HOW DARE YOU GET IN THE WAY OF MY FUN!

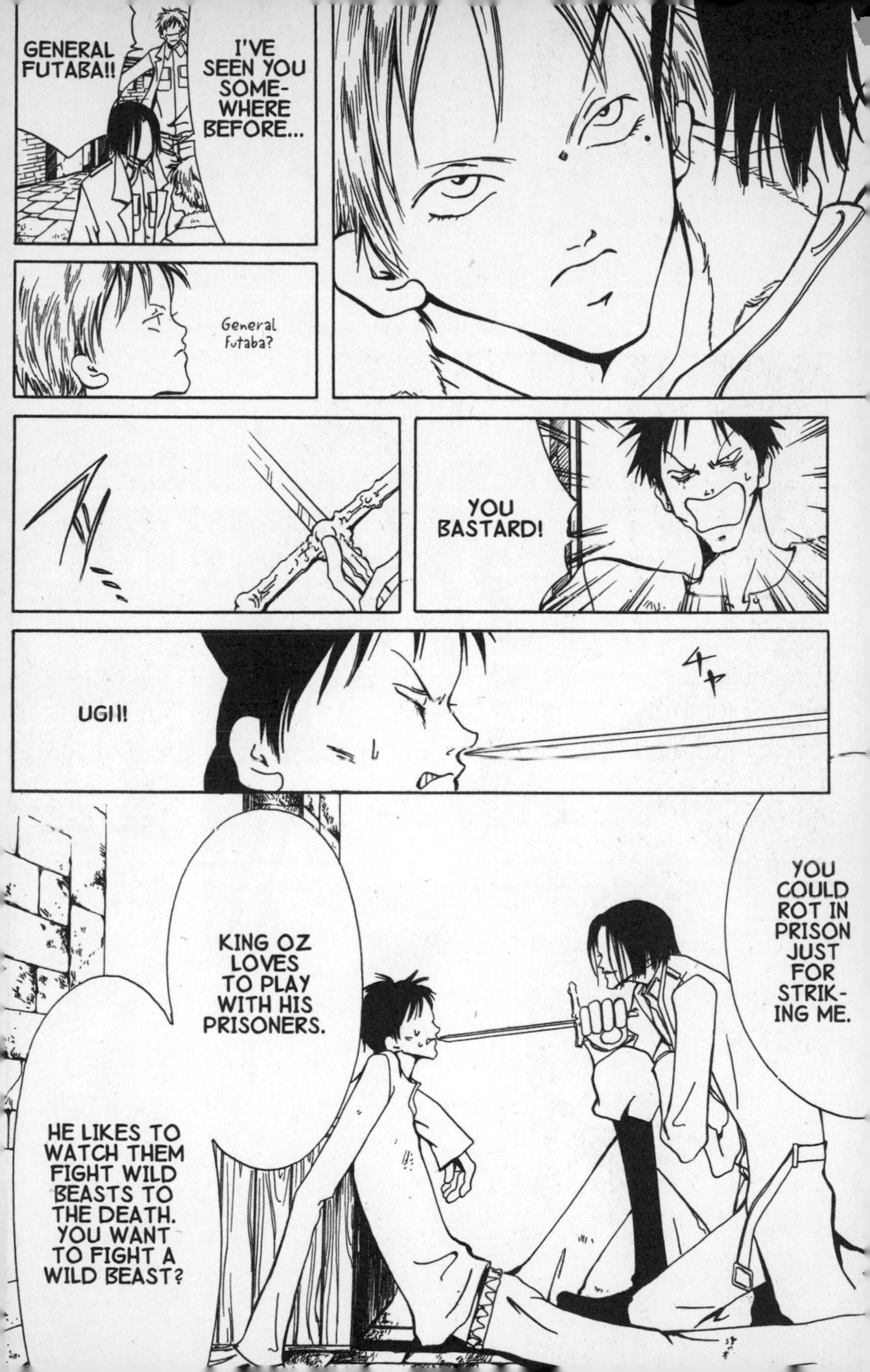

I'VE SEEN YOU SOME-WHERE BEFORE...
GENERAL FUTABA!!
General Futaba?
YOU BASTARD!
UGH!
YOU COULD ROT IN PRISON JUST FOR STRIK-ING ME.
KING OZ LOVES TO PLAY WITH HIS PRISONERS.
HE LIKES TO WATCH THEM FIGHT WILD BEASTS TO THE DEATH. YOU WANT TO FIGHT A WILD BEAST?

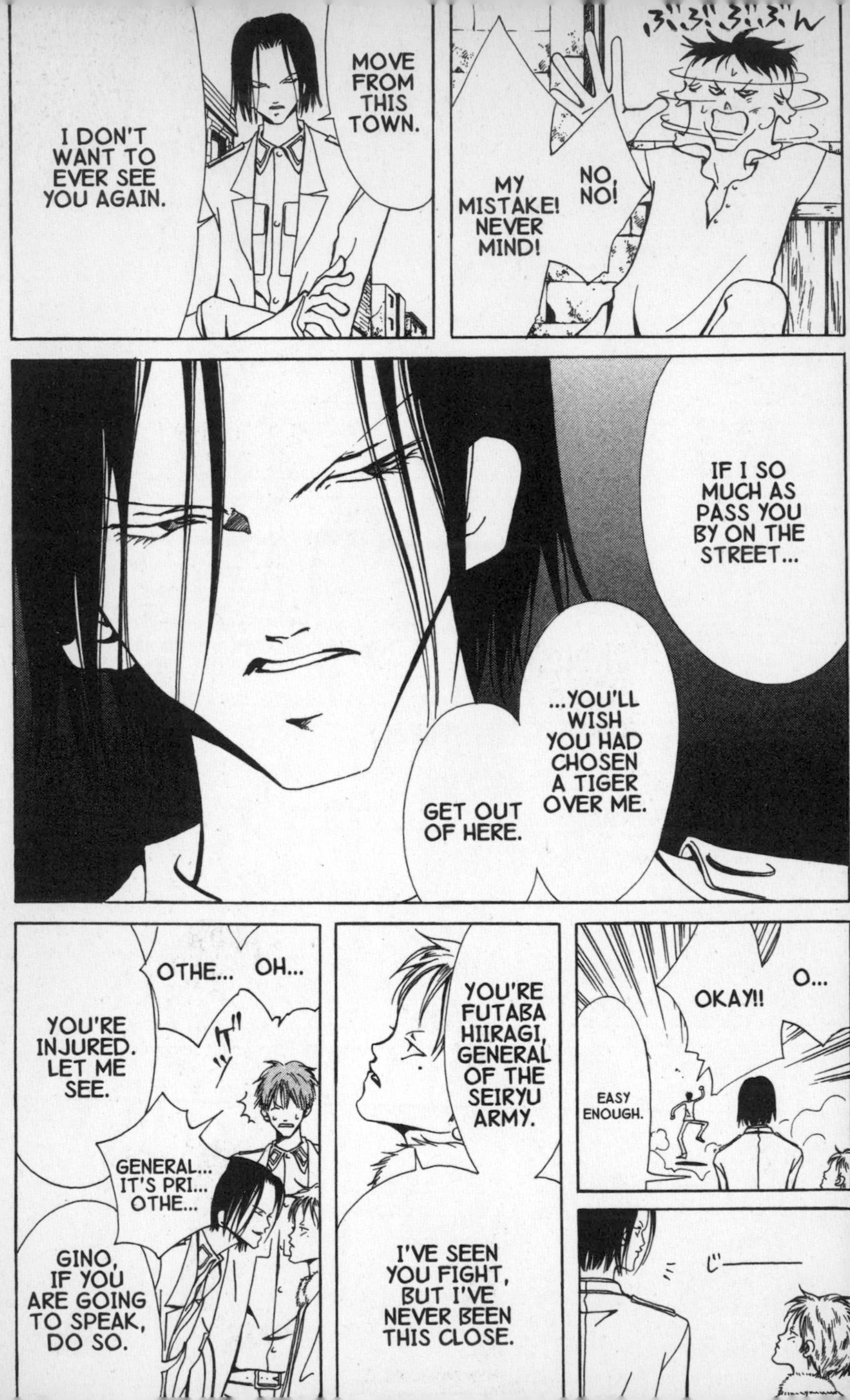
ぶぶぶぶん
NO, NO!
MY MISTAKE! NEVER MIND!
MOVE FROM THIS TOWN.
I DON'T WANT TO EVER SEE YOU AGAIN.
IF I SO MUCH AS PASS YOU BY ON THE STREET...
...YOU'LL WISH YOU HAD CHOSEN A TIGER OVER ME.
GET OUT OF HERE.
O... OKAY!!
EASY ENOUGH.
じーーー
YOU'RE FUTABA HIIRAGI, GENERAL OF THE SEIRYU ARMY.
I'VE SEEN YOU FIGHT, BUT I'VE NEVER BEEN THIS CLOSE.
OTHE... OH...
YOU'RE INJURED. LET ME SEE.
ゲッ
GENERAL... IT'S PRI... OTHE...
GINO, IF YOU ARE GOING TO SPEAK, DO SO.

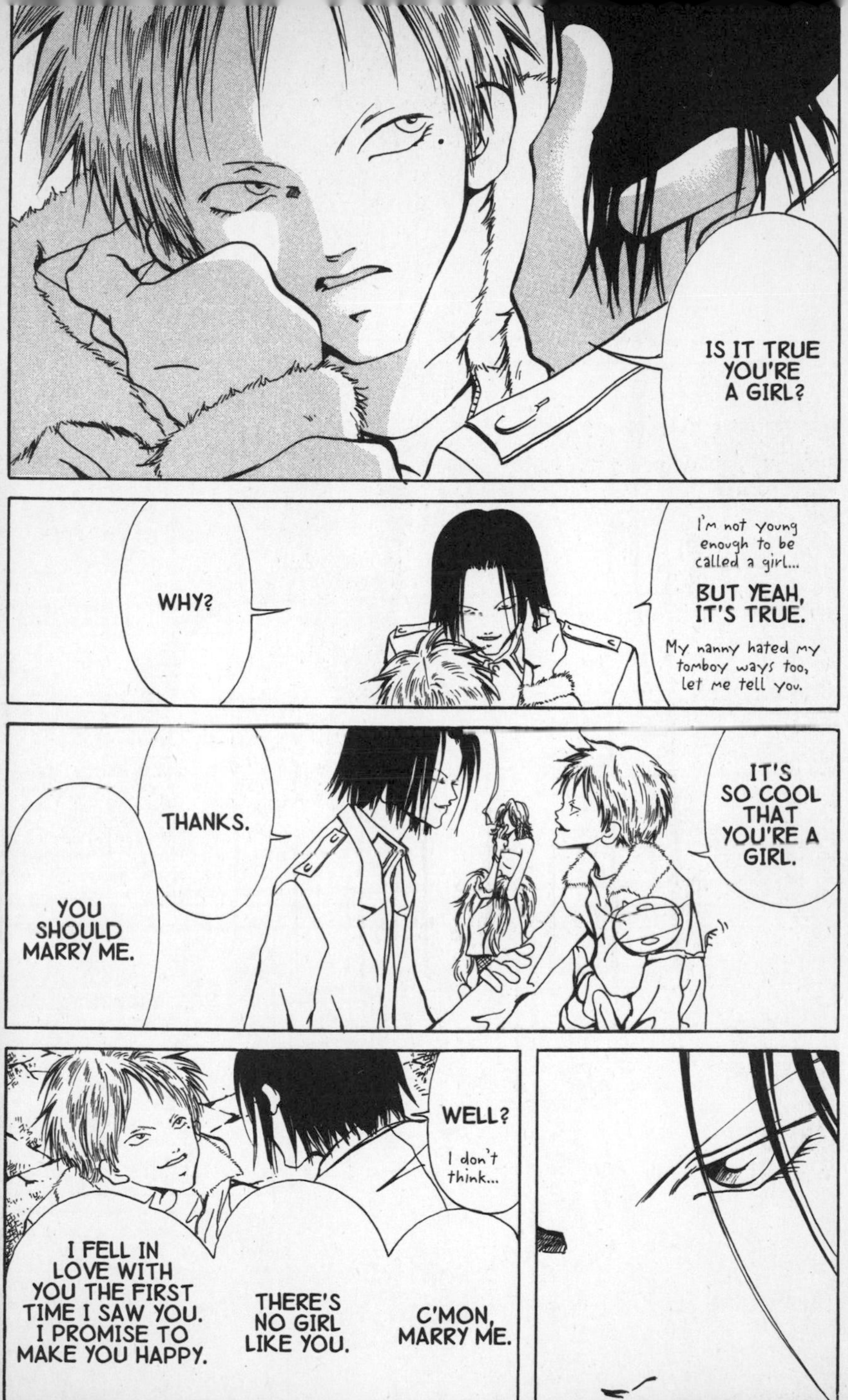
IS IT TRUE YOU'RE A GIRL?
I'm not young enough to be called a girl...
BUT YEAH, IT'S TRUE.
My nanny hated my tomboy ways too, let me tell you.
WHY?
IT'S SO COOL THAT YOU'RE A GIRL.
THANKS.
YOU SHOULD MARRY ME.
WELL?
I don't think...
C'MON, MARRY ME.
THERE'S NO GIRL LIKE YOU.
I FELL IN LOVE WITH YOU THE FIRST TIME I SAW YOU. I PROMISE TO MAKE YOU HAPPY.

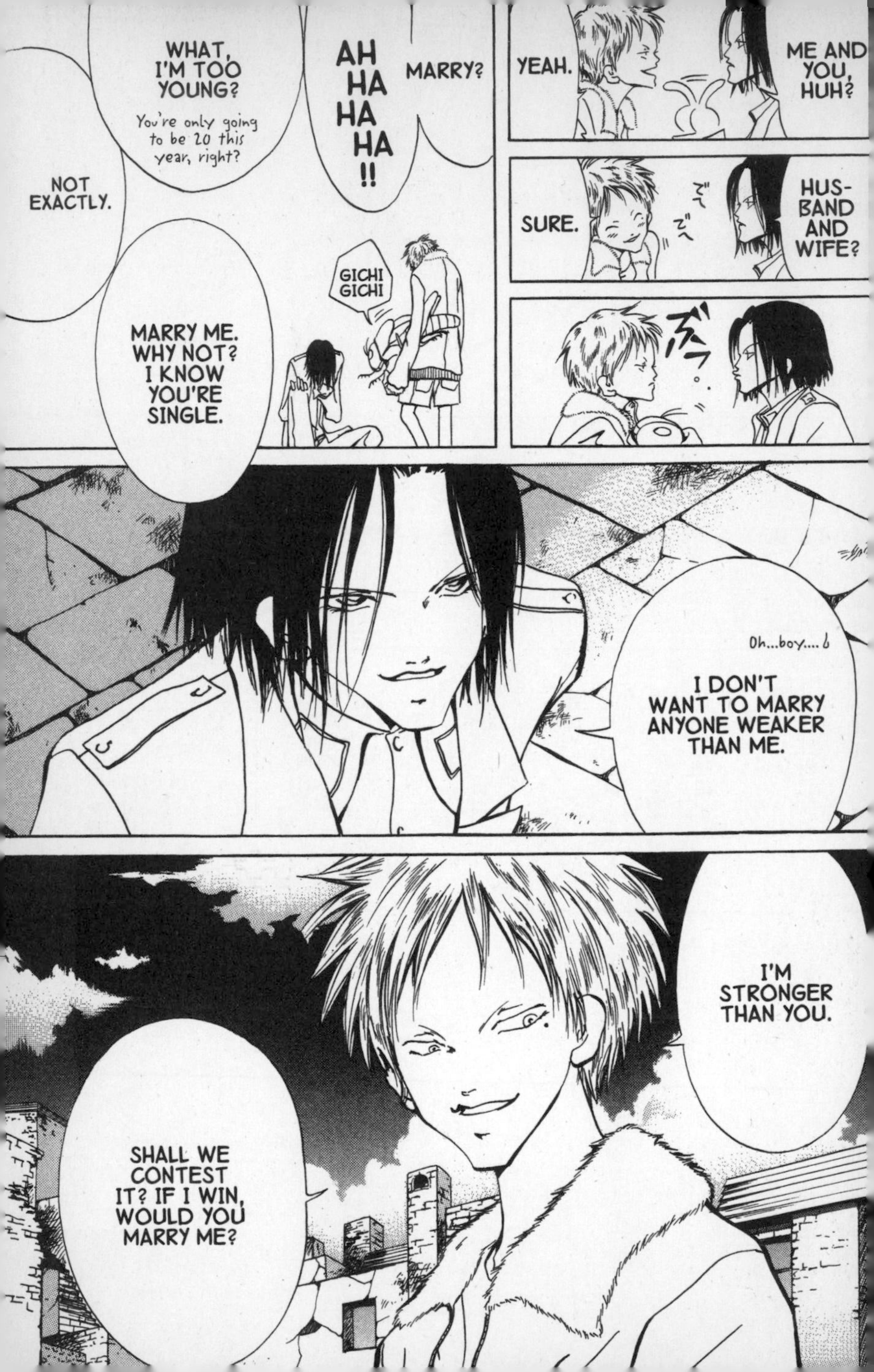
ME AND YOU, HUH?
YEAH.
HUS-BAND AND WIFE?
でへでへ
SURE.
MARRY?
AH HA HA HA!!
WHAT, I'M TOO YOUNG?
You're only going to be 20 this year, right?
NOT EXACTLY.
GICHI GICHI
MARRY ME. WHY NOT? I KNOW YOU'RE SINGLE.
Oh...boy....
I DON'T WANT TO MARRY ANYONE WEAKER THAN ME.
I'M STRONGER THAN YOU.
SHALL WE CONTEST IT? IF I WIN, WOULD YOU MARRY ME?

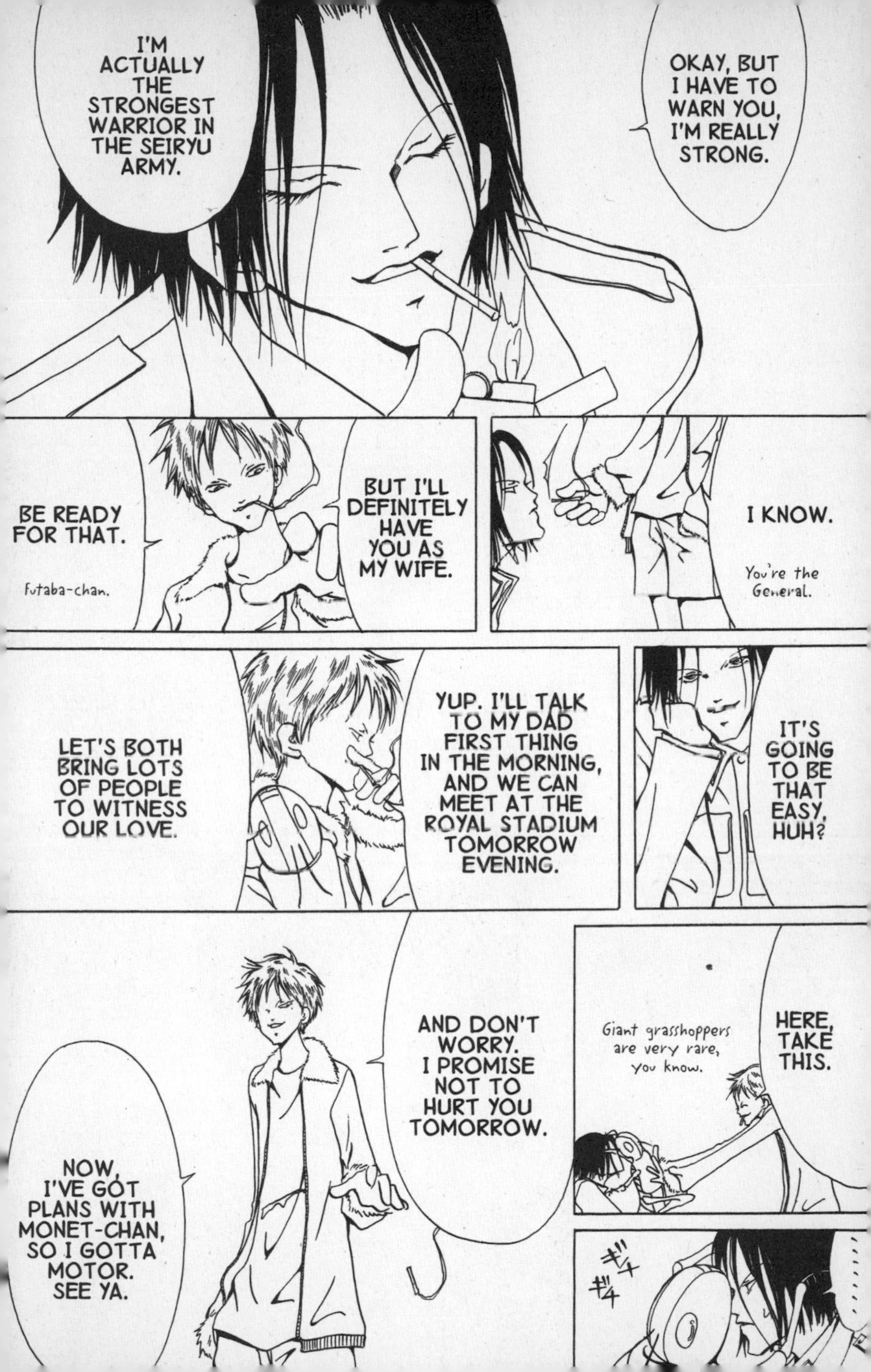
OKAY, BUT I HAVE TO WARN YOU, I'M REALLY STRONG.
I'M ACTUALLY THE STRONGEST WARRIOR IN THE SEIRYU ARMY.
I KNOW.
You're the General.
BUT I'LL DEFINITELY HAVE YOU AS MY WIFE.
BE READY FOR THAT.
Futaba-chan.
IT'S GOING TO BE THAT EASY, HUH?
YUP. I'LL TALK TO MY DAD FIRST THING IN THE MORNING, AND WE CAN MEET AT THE ROYAL STADIUM TOMORROW EVENING.
LET'S BOTH BRING LOTS OF PEOPLE TO WITNESS OUR LOVE.
HERE, TAKE THIS.
Giant grasshoppers are very rare, you know.
ギィ
ギィ
AND DON'T WORRY. I PROMISE NOT TO HURT YOU TOMORROW.
NOW, I'VE GOT PLANS WITH MONET-CHAN, SO I GOTTA MOTOR. SEE YA.

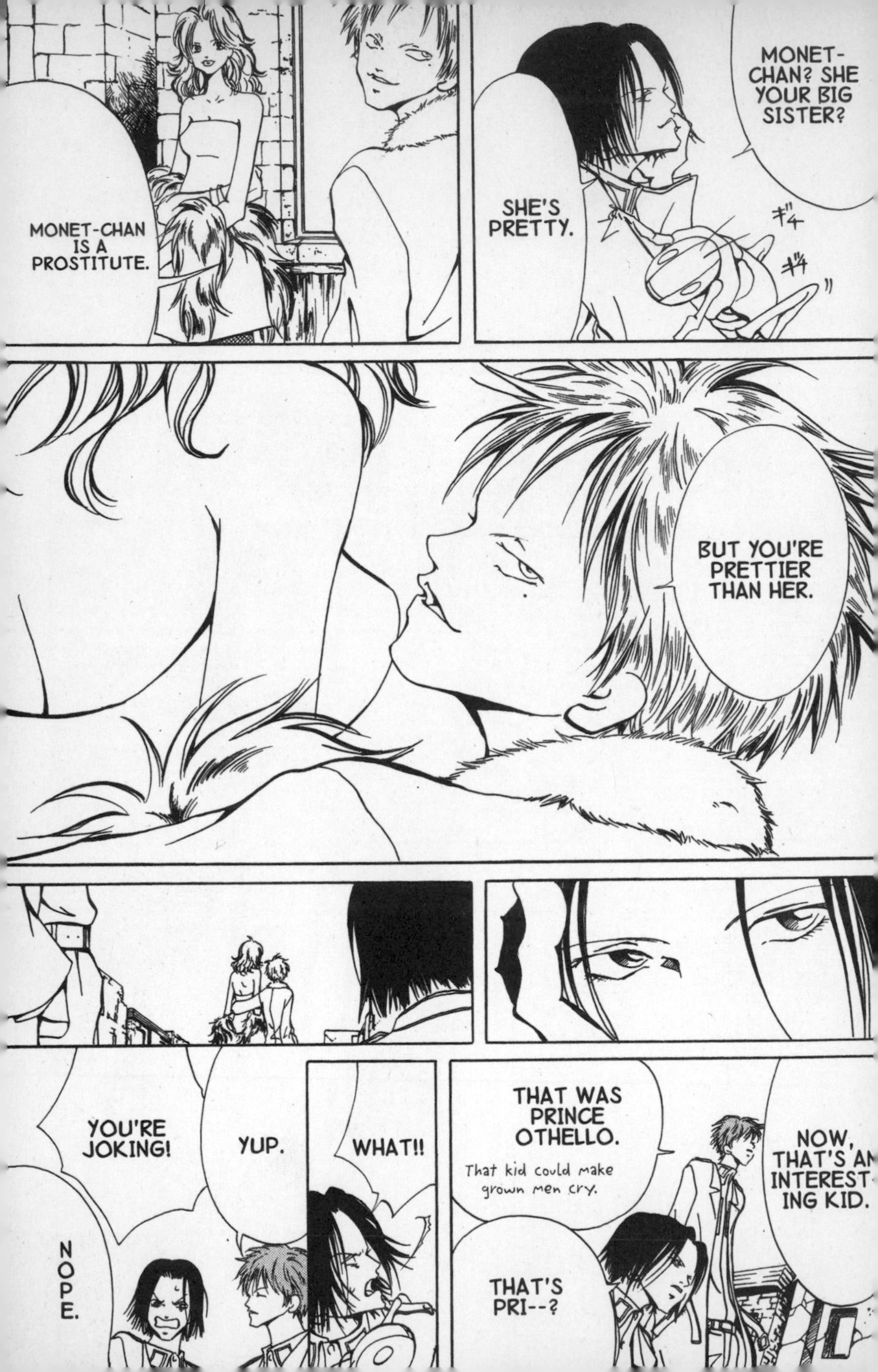

MONET-CHAN? SHE YOUR BIG SISTER?
SHE'S PRETTY.
ギィ
ギィ
MONET-CHAN IS A PROSTITUTE.
BUT YOU'RE PRETTIER THAN HER.
NOW, THAT'S AN INTERESTING KID.
THAT WAS PRINCE OTHELLO.
That kid could make grown men cry.
THAT'S PRI--?
WHAT!!
YUP.
YOU'RE JOKING!
NOPE.

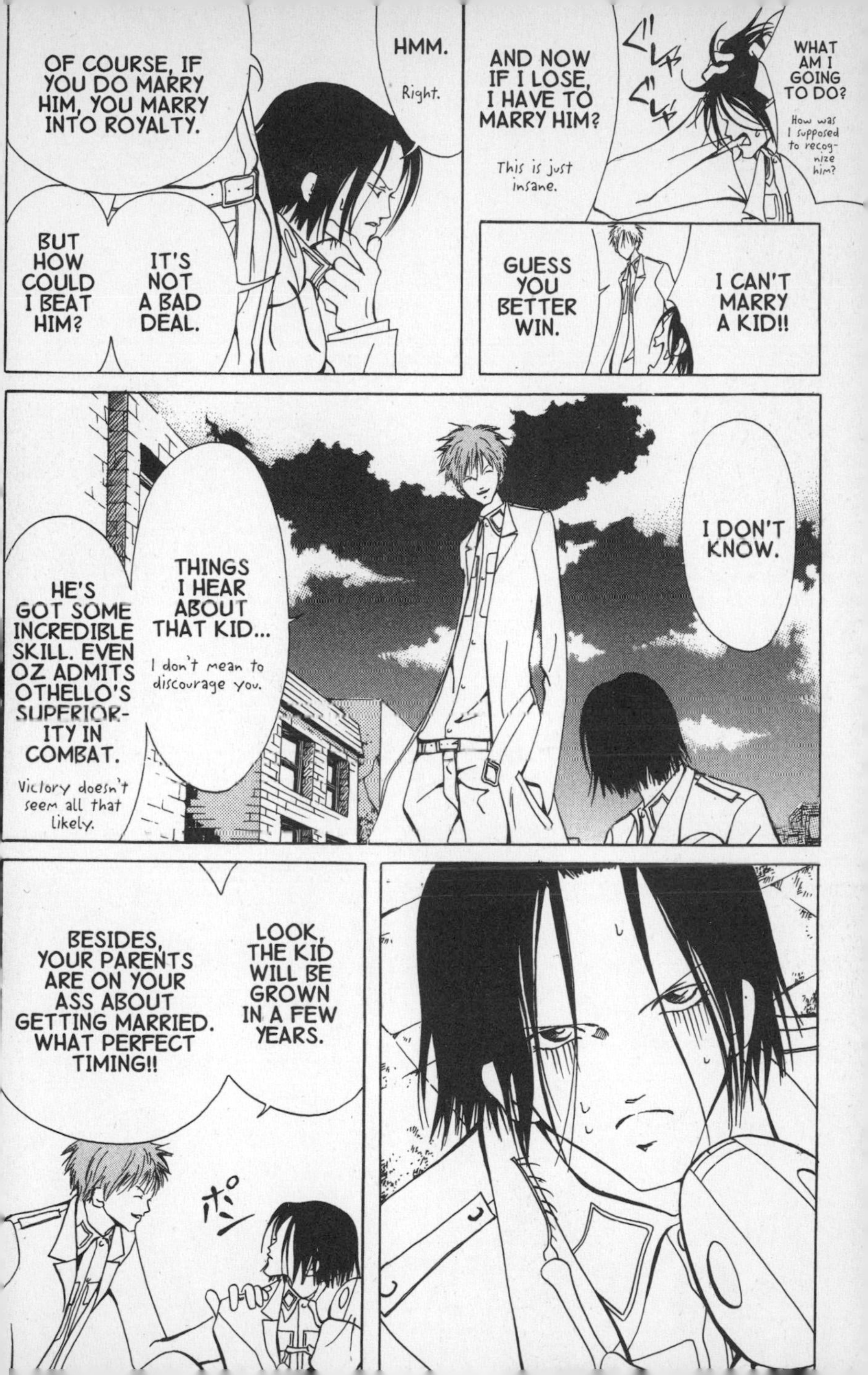
WHAT AM I GOING TO DO?
How was I supposed to recognize him?
AND NOW IF I LOSE, I HAVE TO MARRY HIM?
This is just insane.
I CAN'T MARRY A KID!!
GUESS YOU BETTER WIN.
HMM.
Right.
OF COURSE, IF YOU DO MARRY HIM, YOU MARRY INTO ROYALTY.
IT'S NOT A BAD DEAL.
BUT HOW COULD I BEAT HIM?
I DON'T KNOW.
THINGS I HEAR ABOUT THAT KID...
I don't mean to discourage you.
HE'S GOT SOME INCREDIBLE SKILL. EVEN OZ ADMITS OTHELLO'S SUPERIORITY IN COMBAT.
Victory doesn't seem all that likely.
LOOK, THE KID WILL BE GROWN IN A FEW YEARS.
BESIDES, YOUR PARENTS ARE ON YOUR ASS ABOUT GETTING MARRIED. WHAT PERFECT TIMING!!
ポン

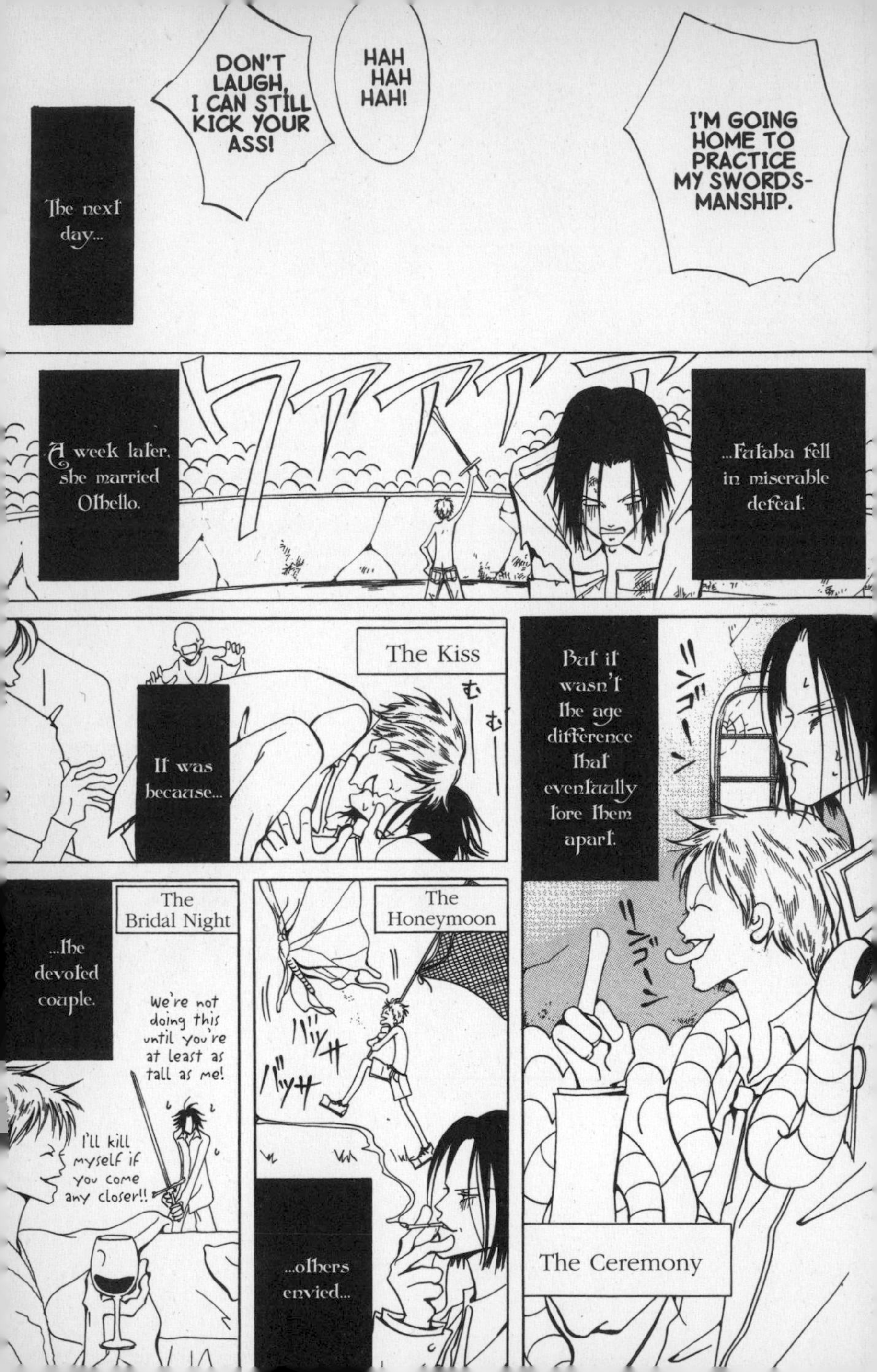
I'M GOING HOME TO PRACTICE MY SWORDS-MANSHIP.
HAH HAH HAH!
DON'T LAUGH, I CAN STILL KICK YOUR ASS!
The next day...
...Futaba fell in miserable defeat.
A week later, she married Othello.
But it wasn't the age difference that eventually tore them apart.
The Ceremony
The Kiss
It was because...
The Honeymoon
...others envied...
The Bridal Night
...the devoted couple.
We're not doing this until you're at least as tall as me!
I'll kill myself if you come any closer!!

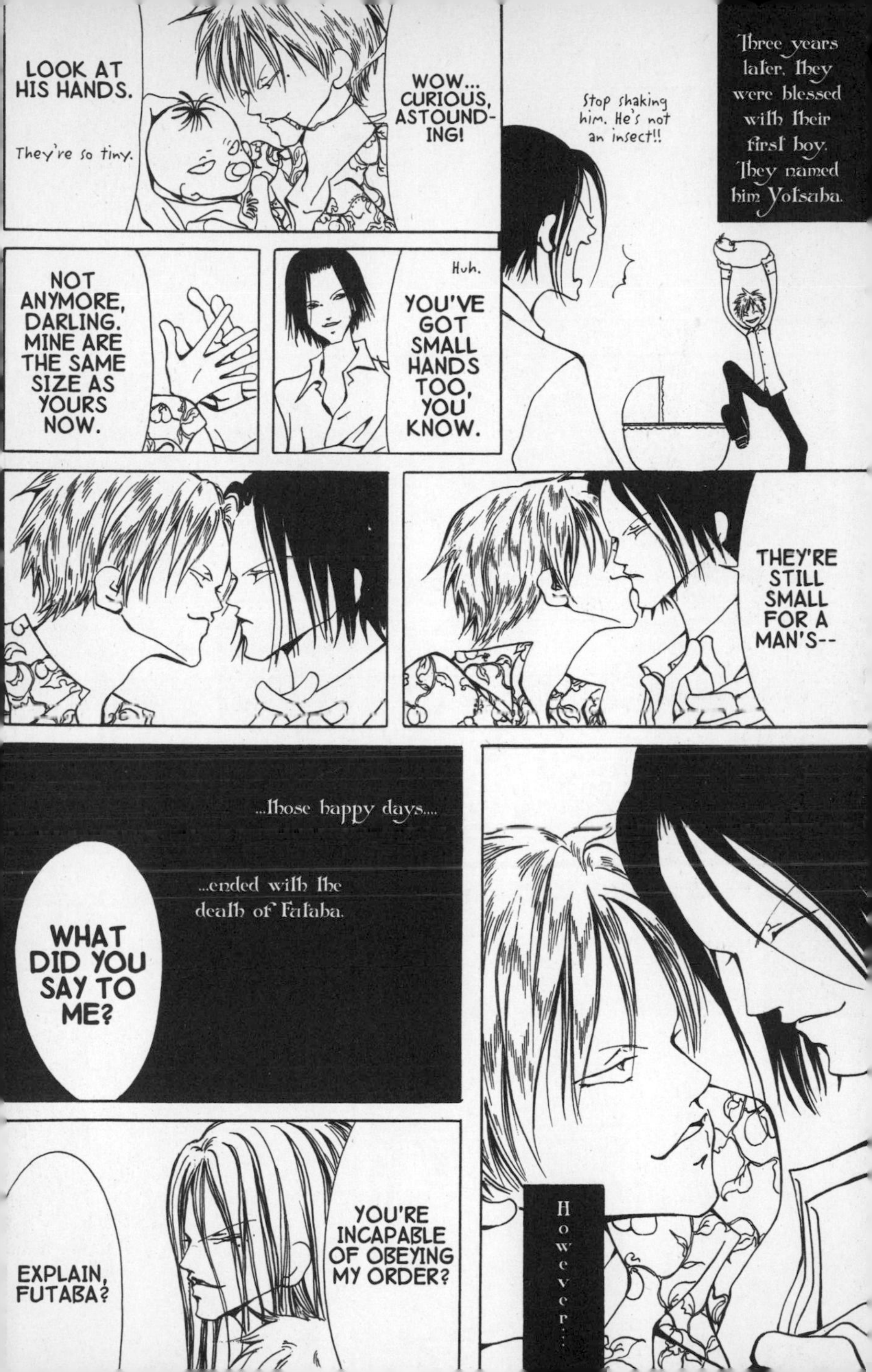
Three years later. They were blessed with their first boy. They named him Yotsuba.
Stop shaking him. He's not an insect!!
WOW... CURIOUS, ASTOUNDING!
LOOK AT HIS HANDS.
They're so tiny.
Huh.
YOU'VE GOT SMALL HANDS TOO, YOU KNOW.
NOT ANYMORE, DARLING. MINE ARE THE SAME SIZE AS YOURS NOW.
THEY'RE STILL SMALL FOR A MAN'S--
However...
...those happy days....
...ended with the death of Futaba.
WHAT DID YOU SAY TO ME?
YOU'RE INCAPABLE OF OBEYING MY ORDER?
EXPLAIN, FUTABA?

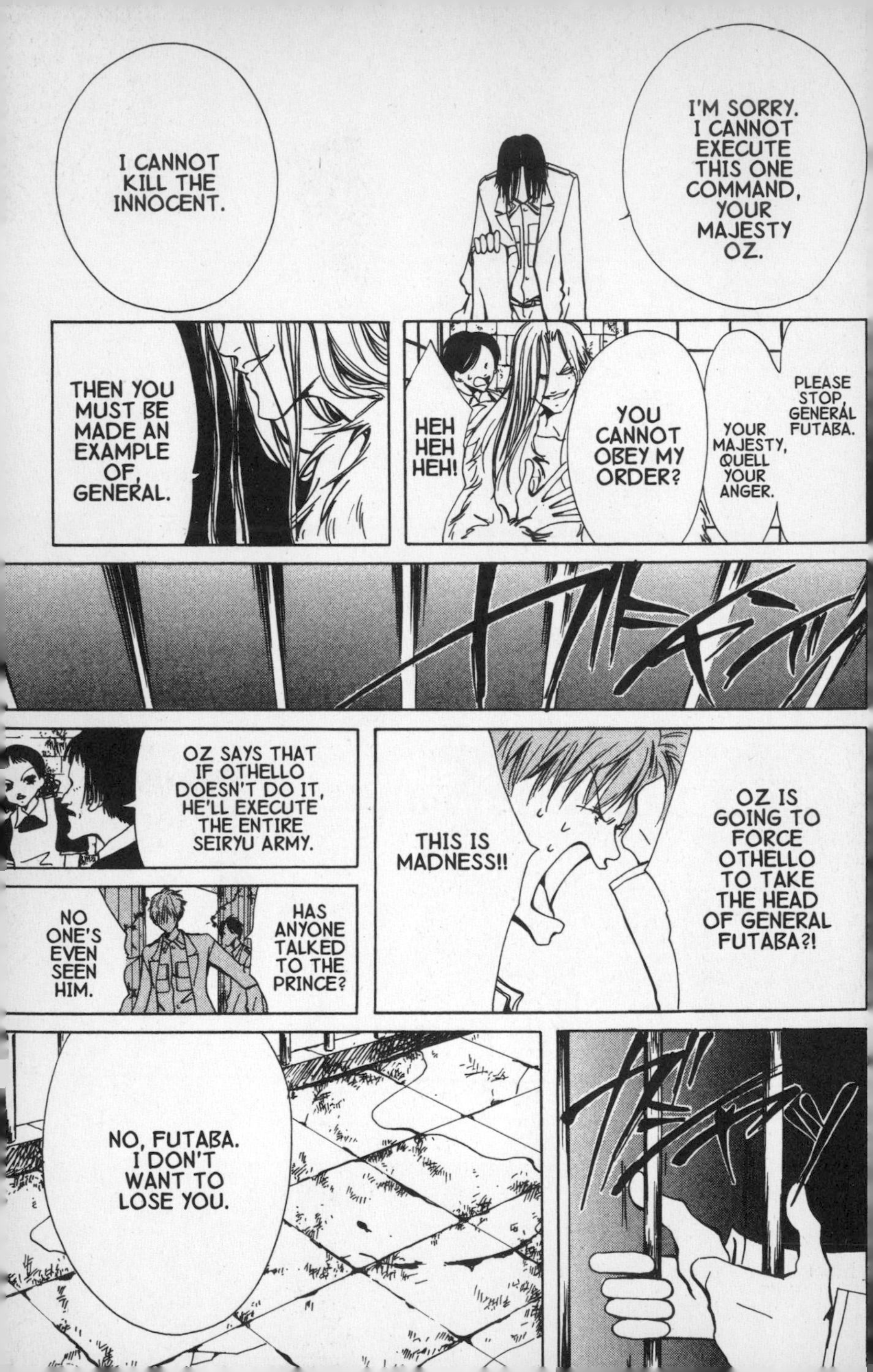
I'M SORRY. I CANNOT EXECUTE THIS ONE COMMAND, YOUR MAJESTY OZ.
I CANNOT KILL THE INNOCENT.
PLEASE STOP, GENERAL FUTABA.
YOUR MAJESTY, QUELL YOUR ANGER.
YOU CANNOT OBEY MY ORDER?
HEH HEH HEH!
THEN YOU MUST BE MADE AN EXAMPLE OF, GENERAL.
OZ IS GOING TO FORCE OTHELLO TO TAKE THE HEAD OF GENERAL FUTABA?!
THIS IS MADNESS!!
OZ SAYS THAT IF OTHELLO DOESN'T DO IT, HE'LL EXECUTE THE ENTIRE SEIRYU ARMY.
HAS ANYONE TALKED TO THE PRINCE?
NO ONE'S EVEN SEEN HIM.
NO, FUTABA. I DON'T WANT TO LOSE YOU.

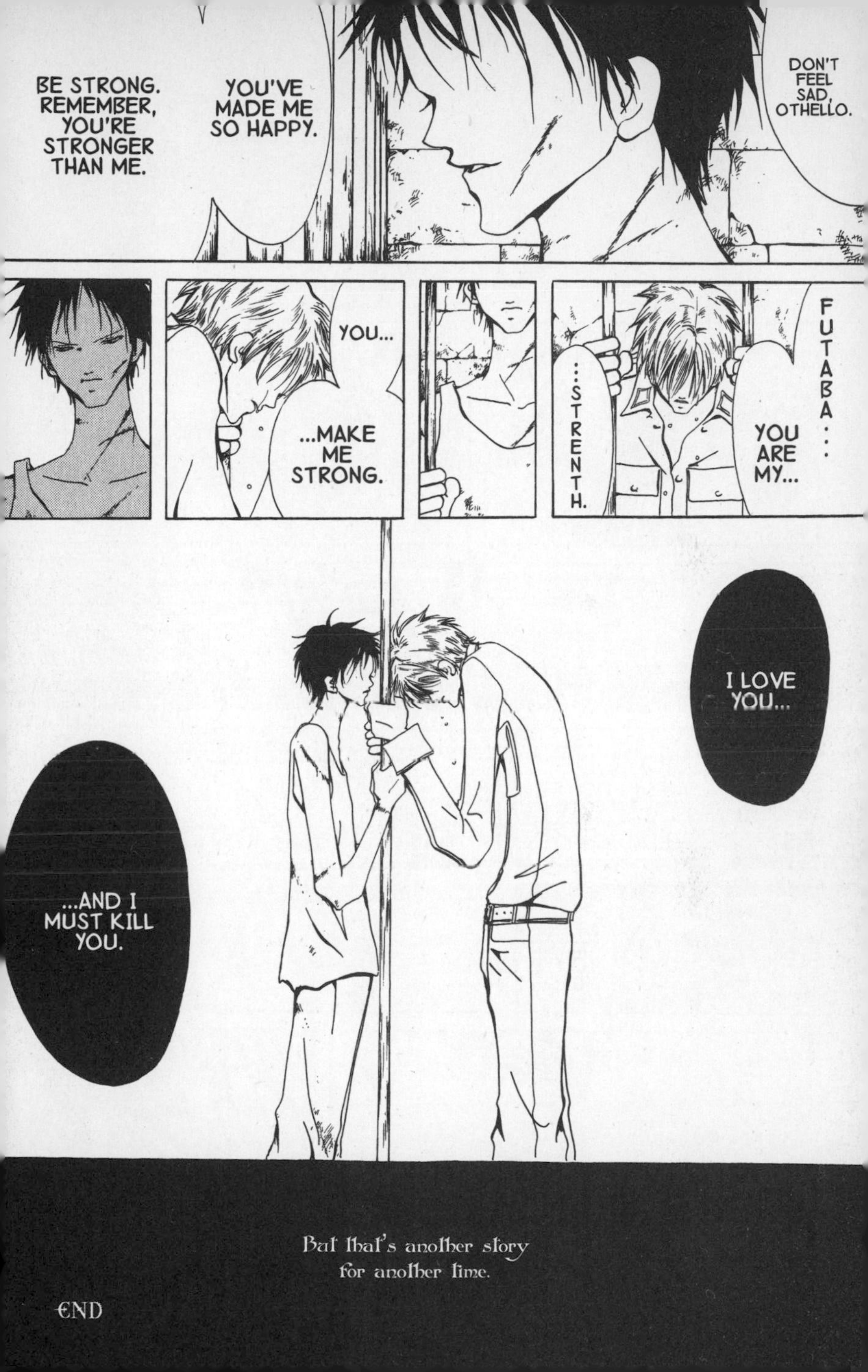
DON'T FEEL SAD, OTHELLO.
YOU'VE MADE ME SO HAPPY.
BE STRONG. REMEMBER, YOU'RE STRONGER THAN ME.
FUTABA...
YOU ARE MY...
...STRENTH.
YOU...
...MAKE ME STRONG.
I LOVE YOU...
...AND I MUST KILL YOU.
But that's another story for another time.
END

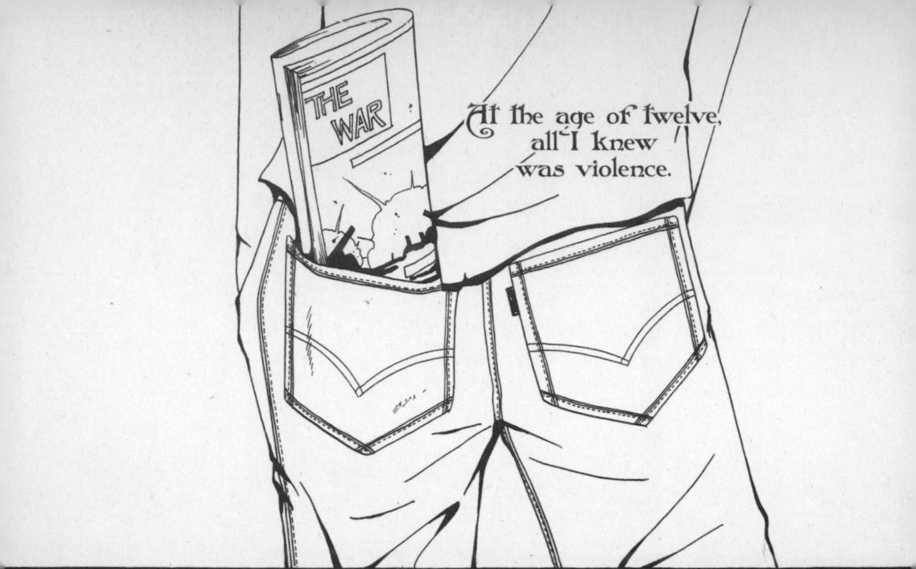
THE WAR
At the age of twelve, all I knew was violence.

raison d'être

「悪魔のオロロン」サイドストーリー レゾン・デートル

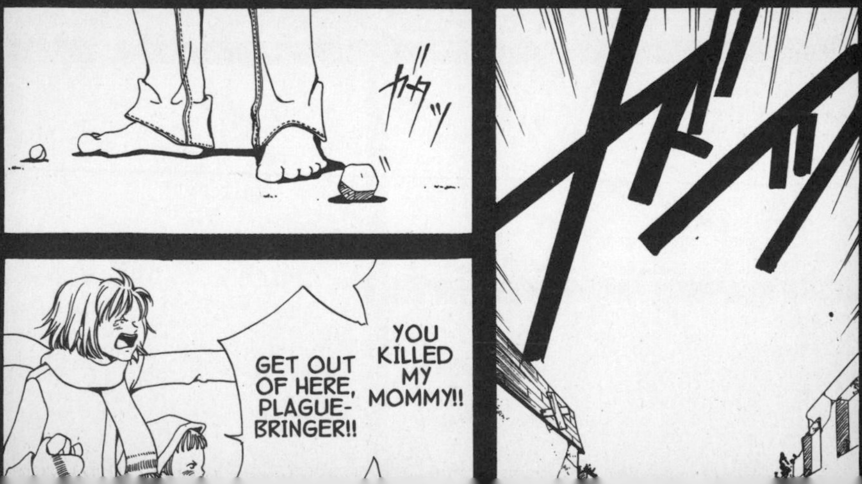
ガタッ
YOU KILLED MY MOMMY!!
GET OUT OF HERE, PLAGUE-BRINGER!!

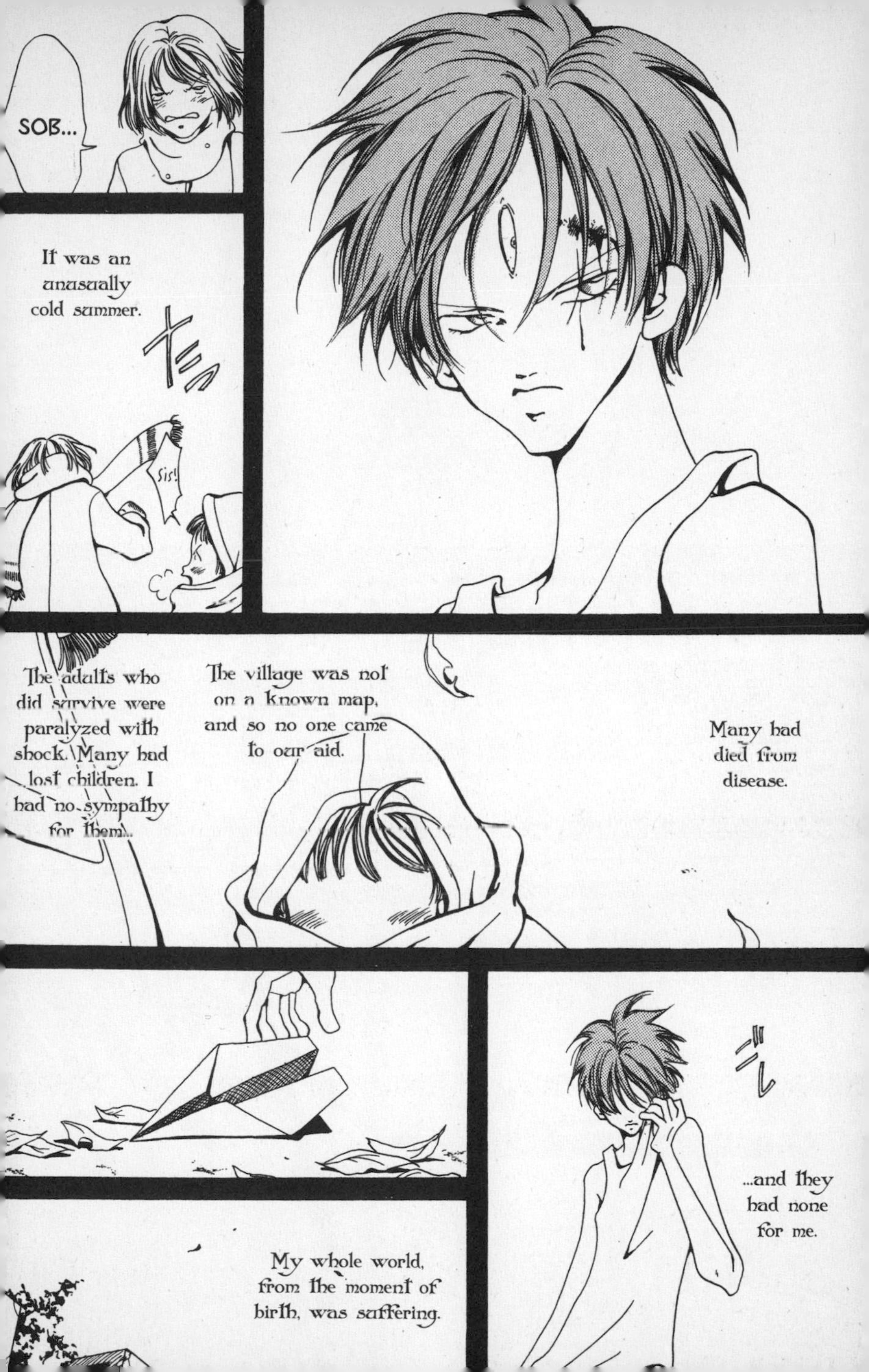
SOB...
It was an unusually cold summer.
Sis!
Many had died from disease.
The village was not on a known map, and so no one came to our aid.
The adults who did survive were paralyzed with shock. Many had lost children. I had no sympathy for them.
...and they had none for me.
My whole world, from the moment of birth, was suffering.

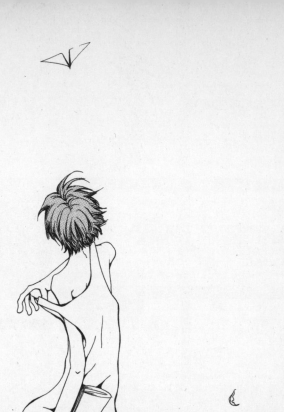

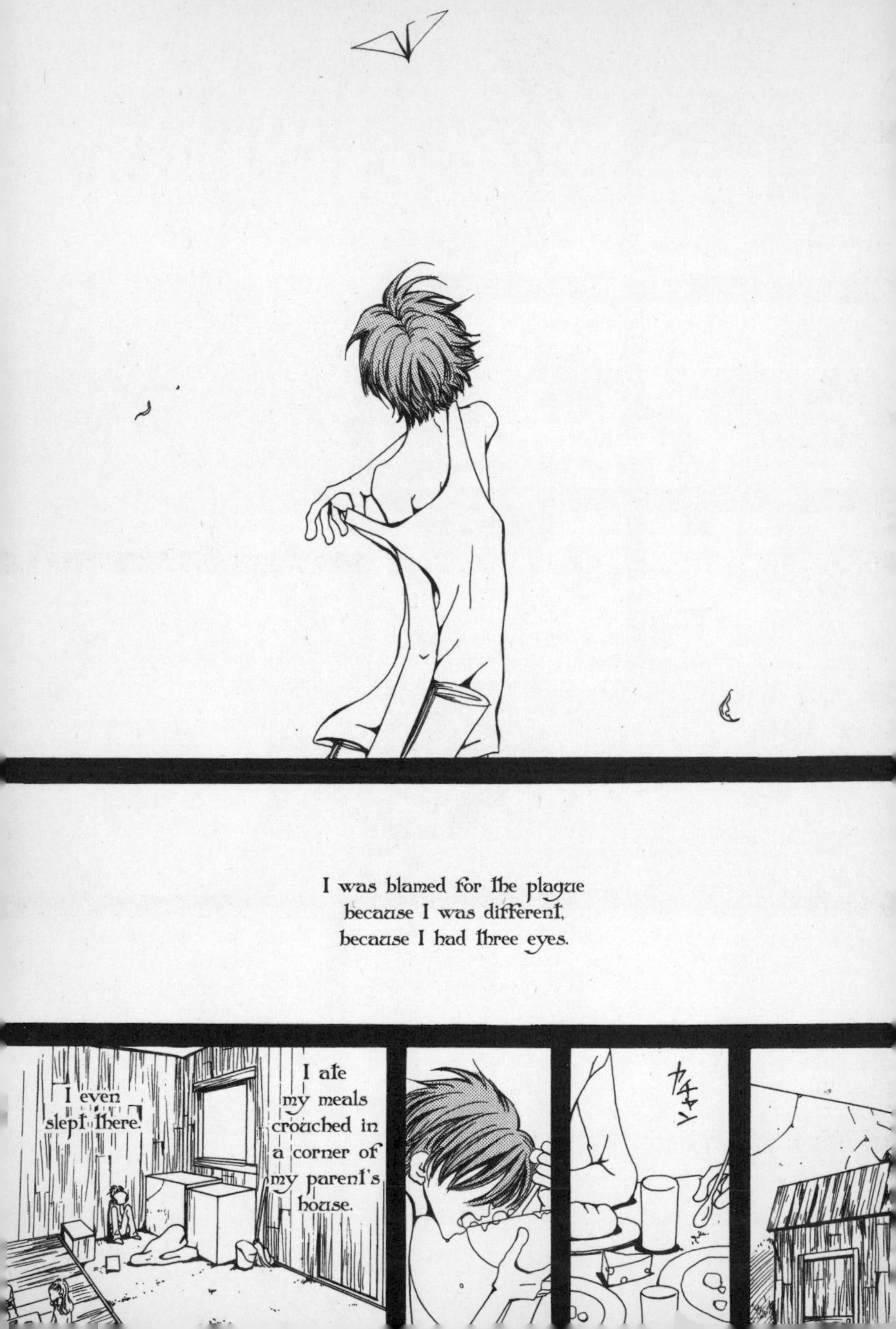
I was blamed for the plague
because I was different,
because I had three eyes.
カチャン
I ate my meals crouched in a corner of my parent's house.
I even slept there.

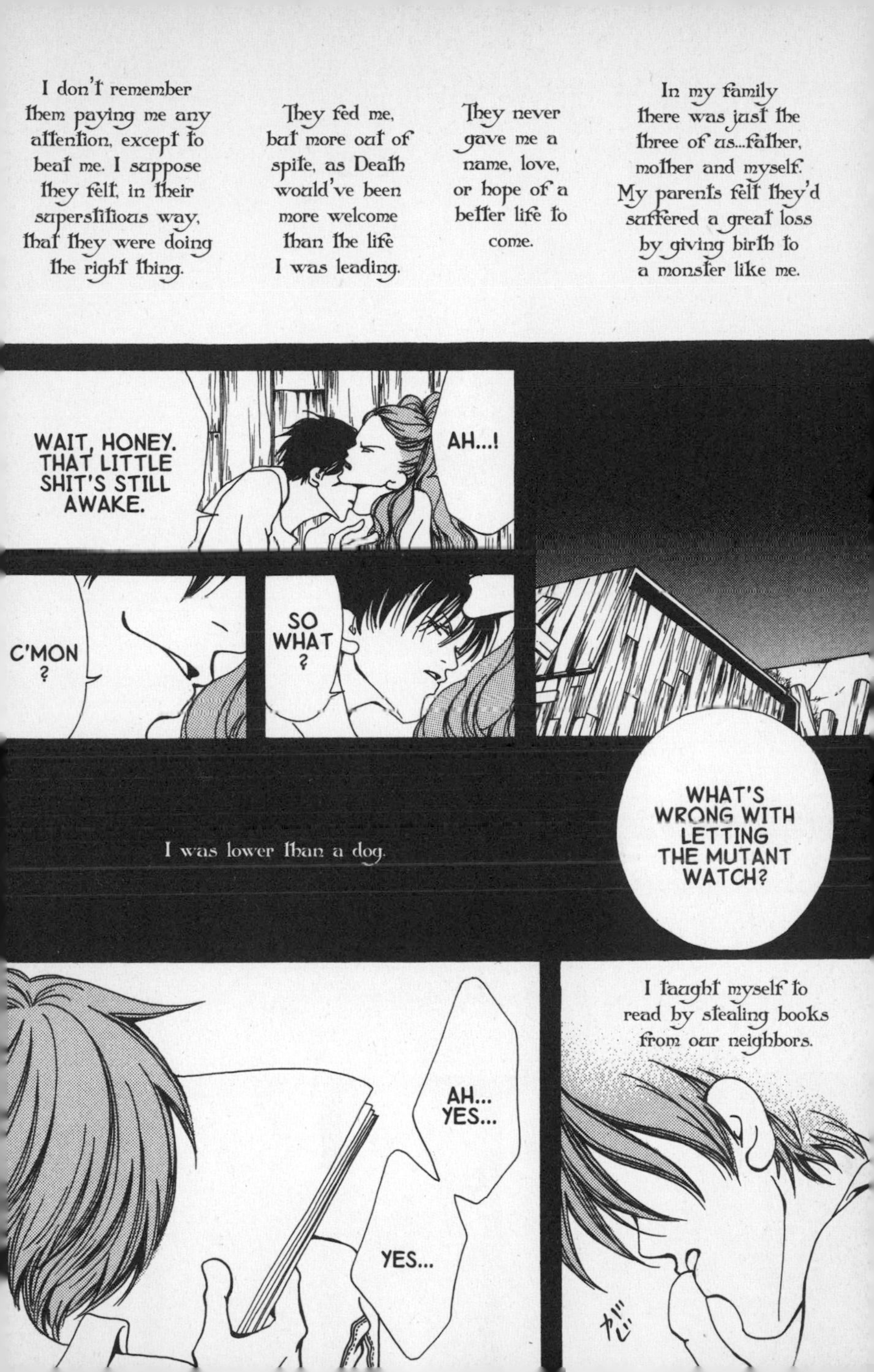
In my family there was just the three of us...father, mother and myself. My parents felt they'd suffered a great loss by giving birth to a monster like me.
They never gave me a name, love, or hope of a better life to come.
They fed me, but more out of spite, as Death would've been more welcome than the life I was leading.
I don't remember them paying me any attention, except to beat me. I suppose they felt, in their superstitious way, that they were doing the right thing.
AH...!
WAIT, HONEY. THAT LITTLE SHIT'S STILL AWAKE.
SO WHAT?
C'MON?
WHAT'S WRONG WITH LETTING THE MUTANT WATCH?
I was lower than a dog.
I taught myself to read by stealing books from our neighbors.
AH... YES...
YES...

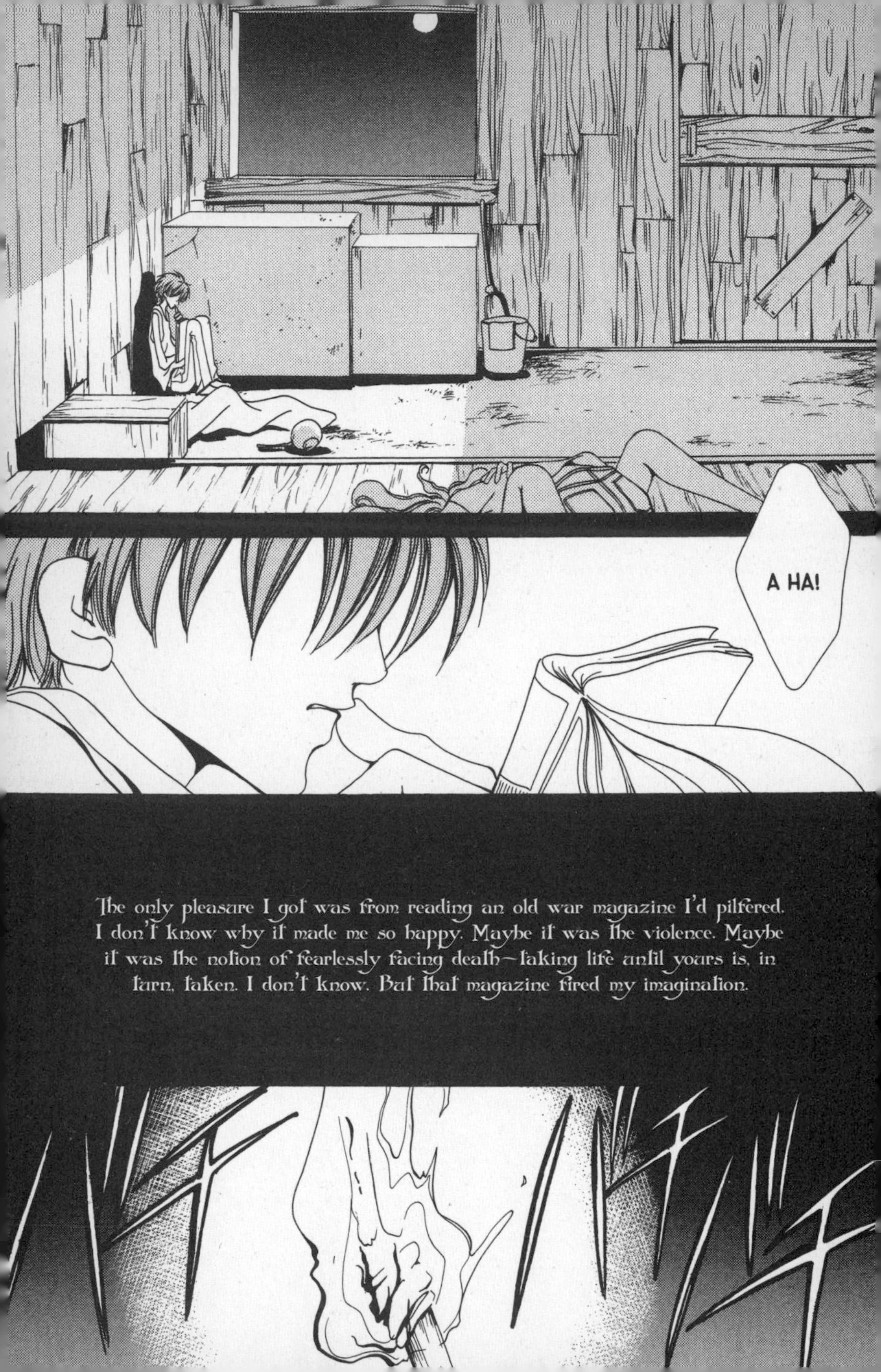
A HA!
The only pleasure I got was from reading an old war magazine I'd pilfered. I don't know why it made me so happy. Maybe it was the violence. Maybe it was the notion of fearlessly facing death—taking life until yours is, in turn, taken. I don't know. But that magazine fired my imagination.

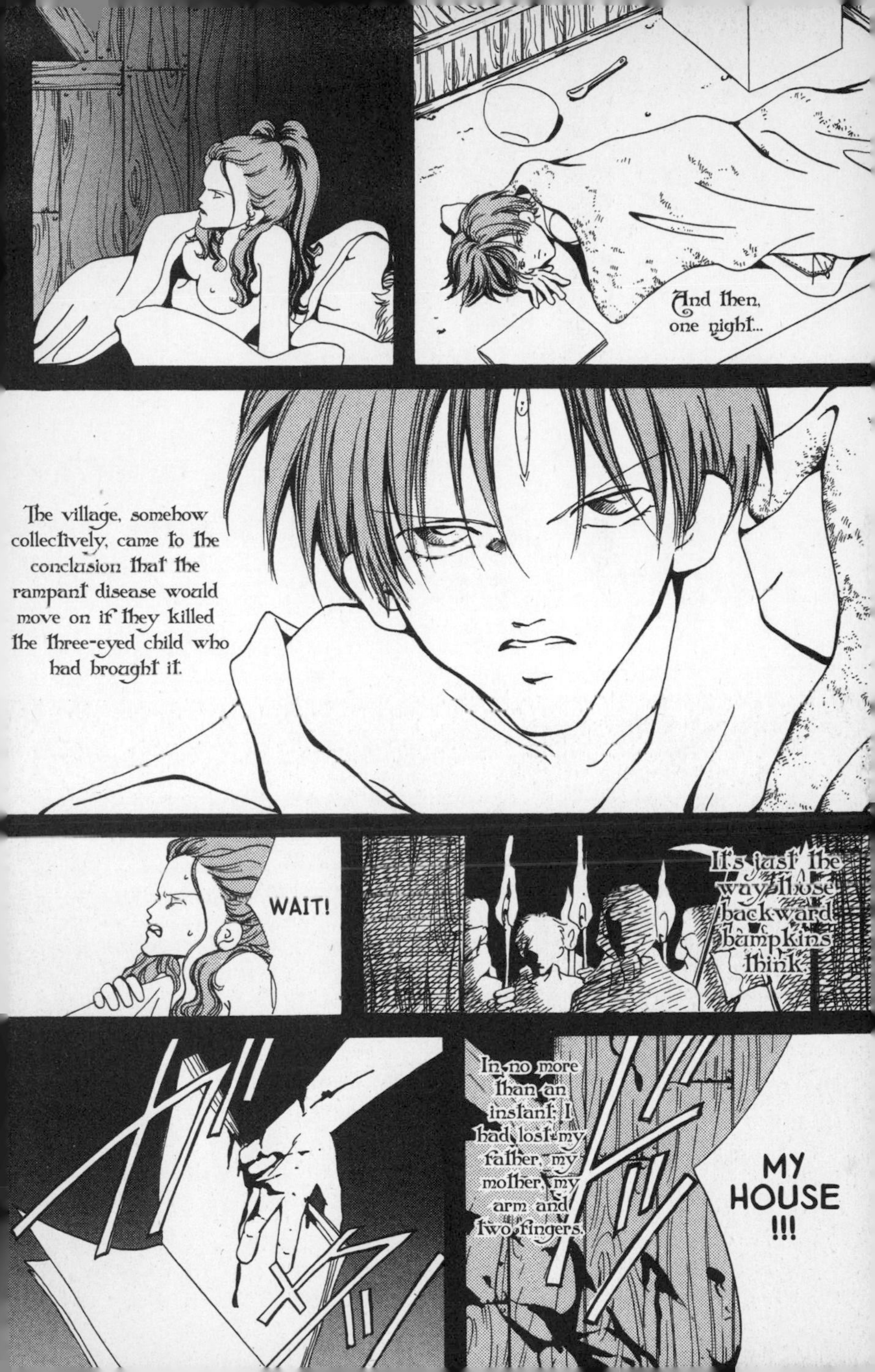
And then, one night...
The village, somehow collectively, came to the conclusion that the rampant disease would move on if they killed the three-eyed child who had brought it.
It's just the way those backward bumpkins think.
WAIT!
In no more than an instant, I had lost my father, my mother, my arm and two fingers.
MY HOUSE !!!

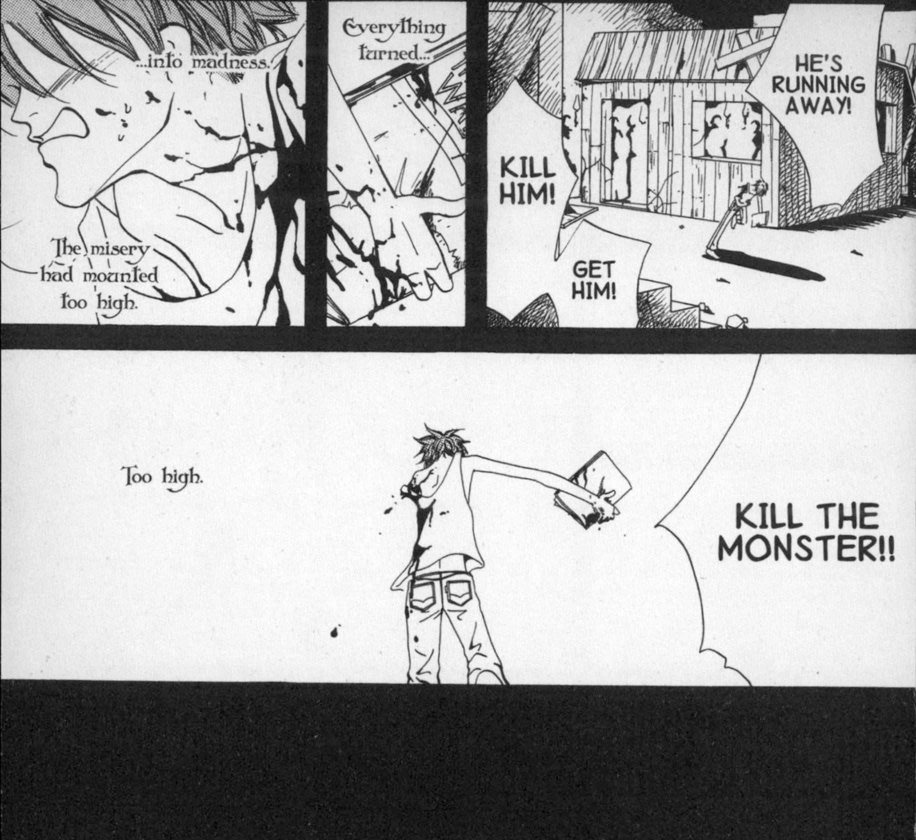
HE'S RUNNING AWAY!
KILL HIM!
GET HIM!
Everything turned...
...into madness.
The misery had mounted too high.
KILL THE MONSTER!!
Too high.

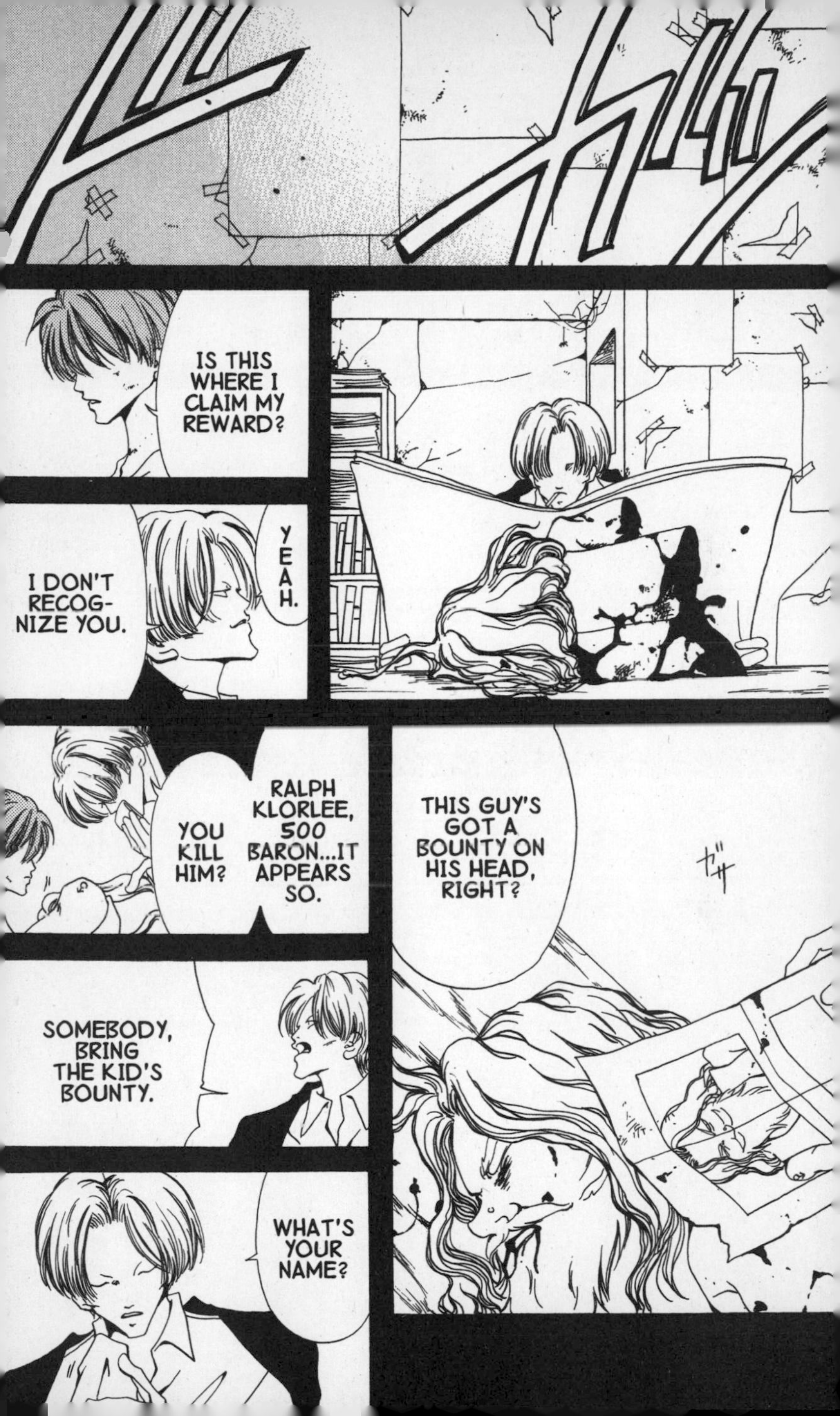
IS THIS WHERE I CLAIM MY REWARD?
YEAH.
I DON'T RECOG-NIZE YOU.
THIS GUY'S GOT A BOUNTY ON HIS HEAD, RIGHT?
RALPH KLORLEE, 500 BARON...IT APPEARS SO.
YOU KILL HIM?
SOMEBODY, BRING THE KID'S BOUNTY.
WHAT'S YOUR NAME?

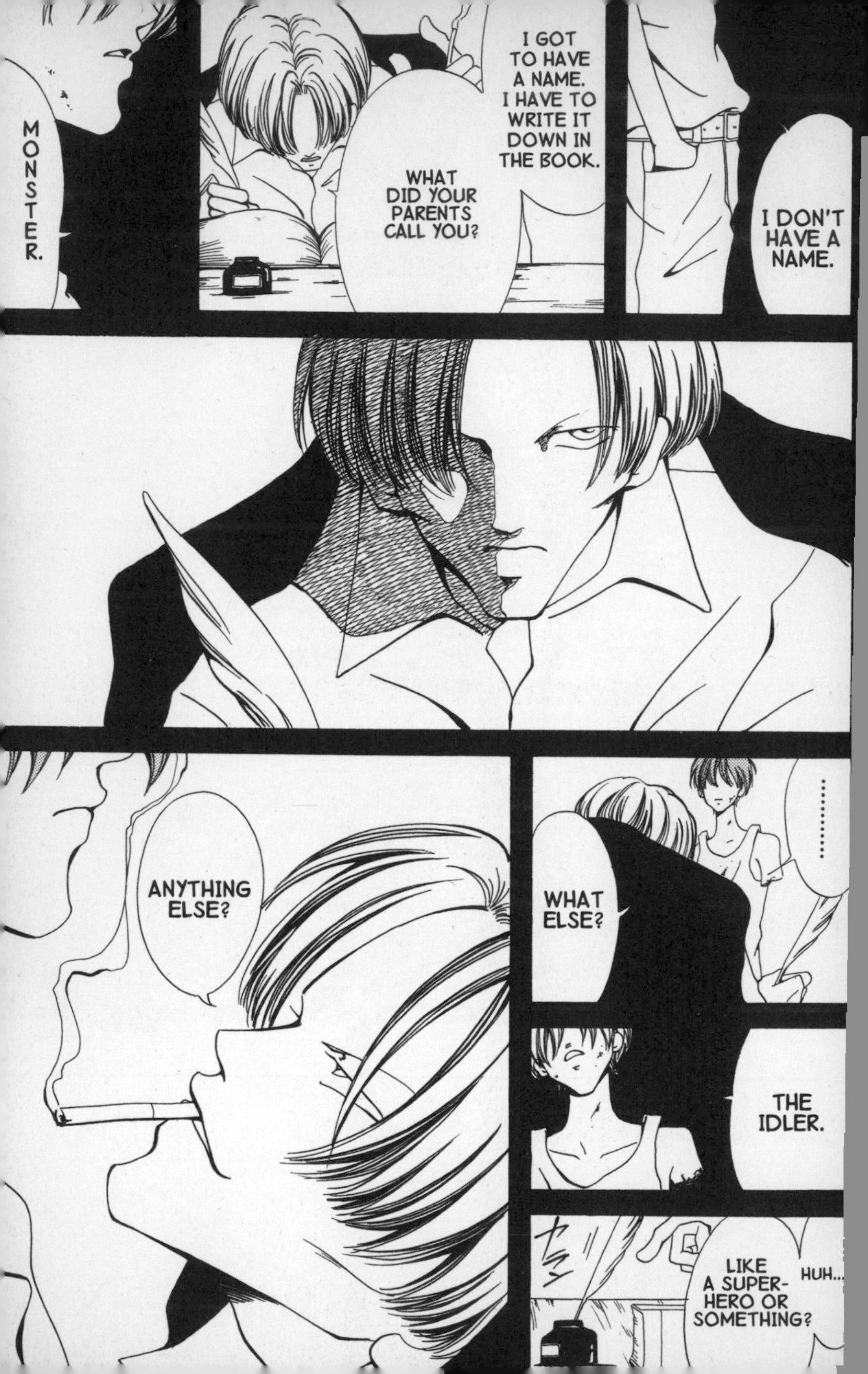
I DON'T HAVE A NAME.
I GOT TO HAVE A NAME. I HAVE TO WRITE IT DOWN IN THE BOOK.
WHAT DID YOUR PARENTS CALL YOU?
MONSTER.
....
WHAT ELSE?
THE IDLER.
HUH...
LIKE A SUPER-HERO OR SOMETHING?
ANYTHING ELSE?

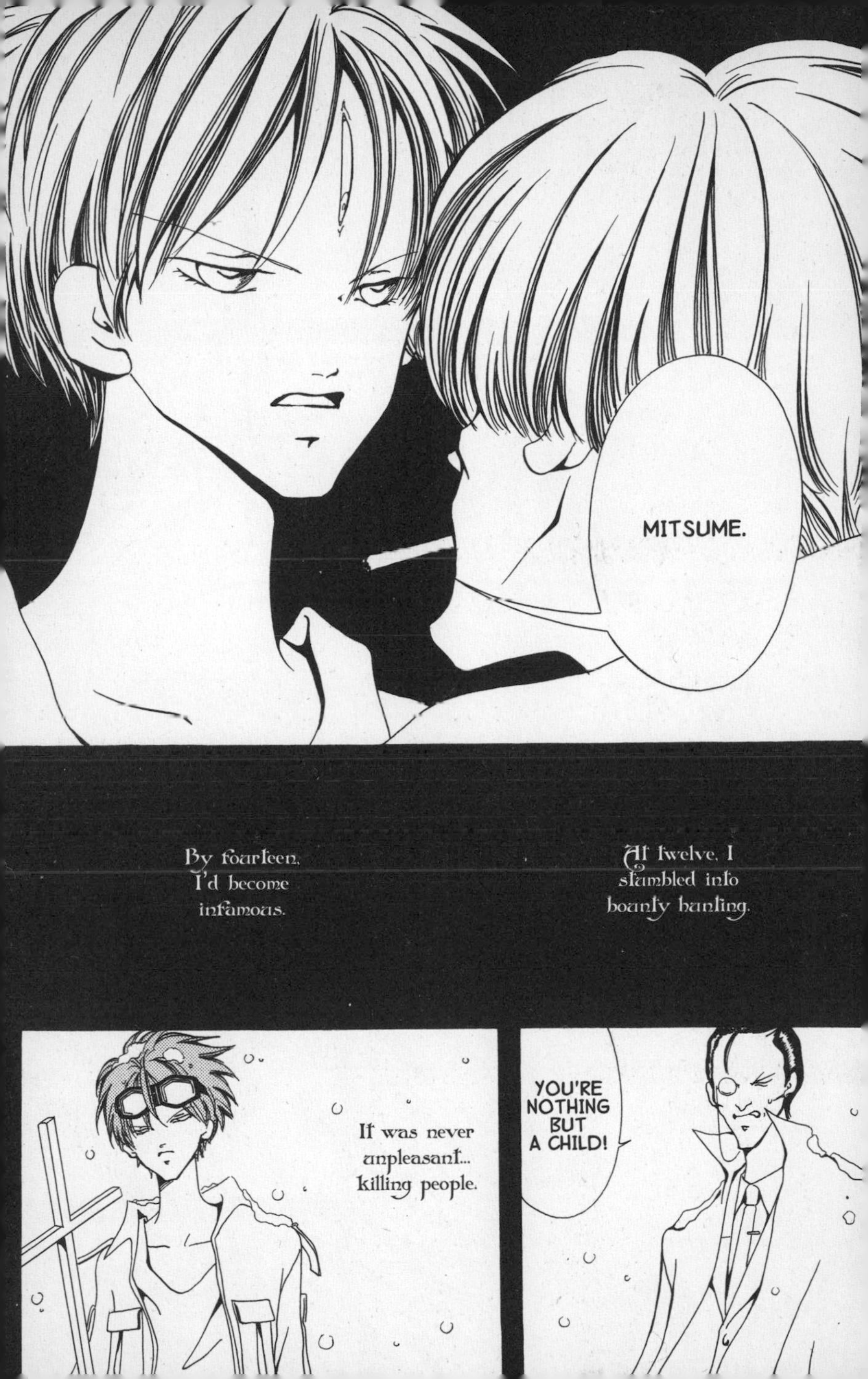
MITSUME.
At twelve, I stumbled into bounty hunting.
By fourteen, I'd become infamous.
YOU'RE NOTHING BUT A CHILD!
It was never unpleasant... killing people.

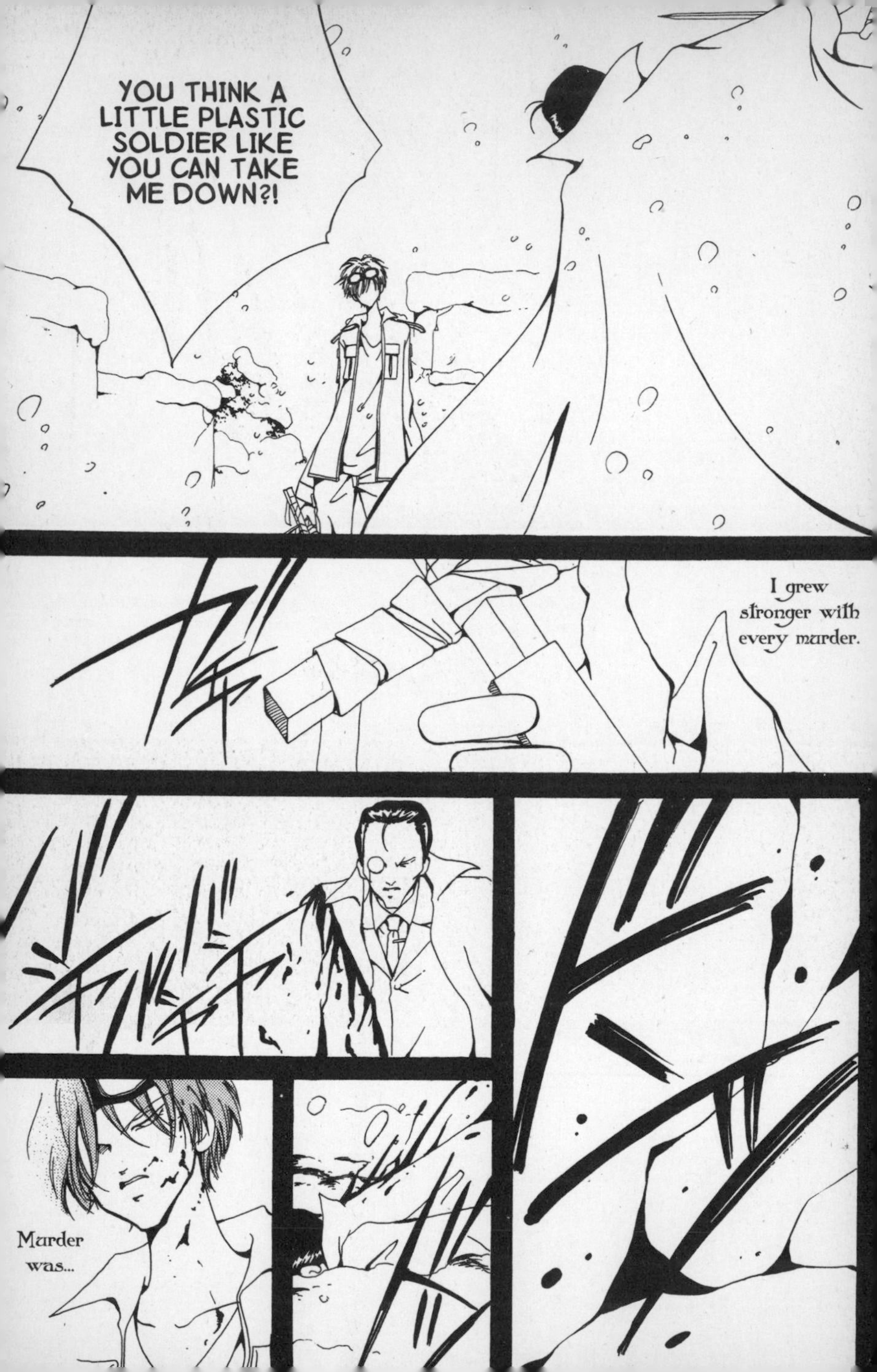
YOU THINK A LITTLE PLASTIC SOLDIER LIKE YOU CAN TAKE ME DOWN?!
I grew stronger with every murder.
Murder was...

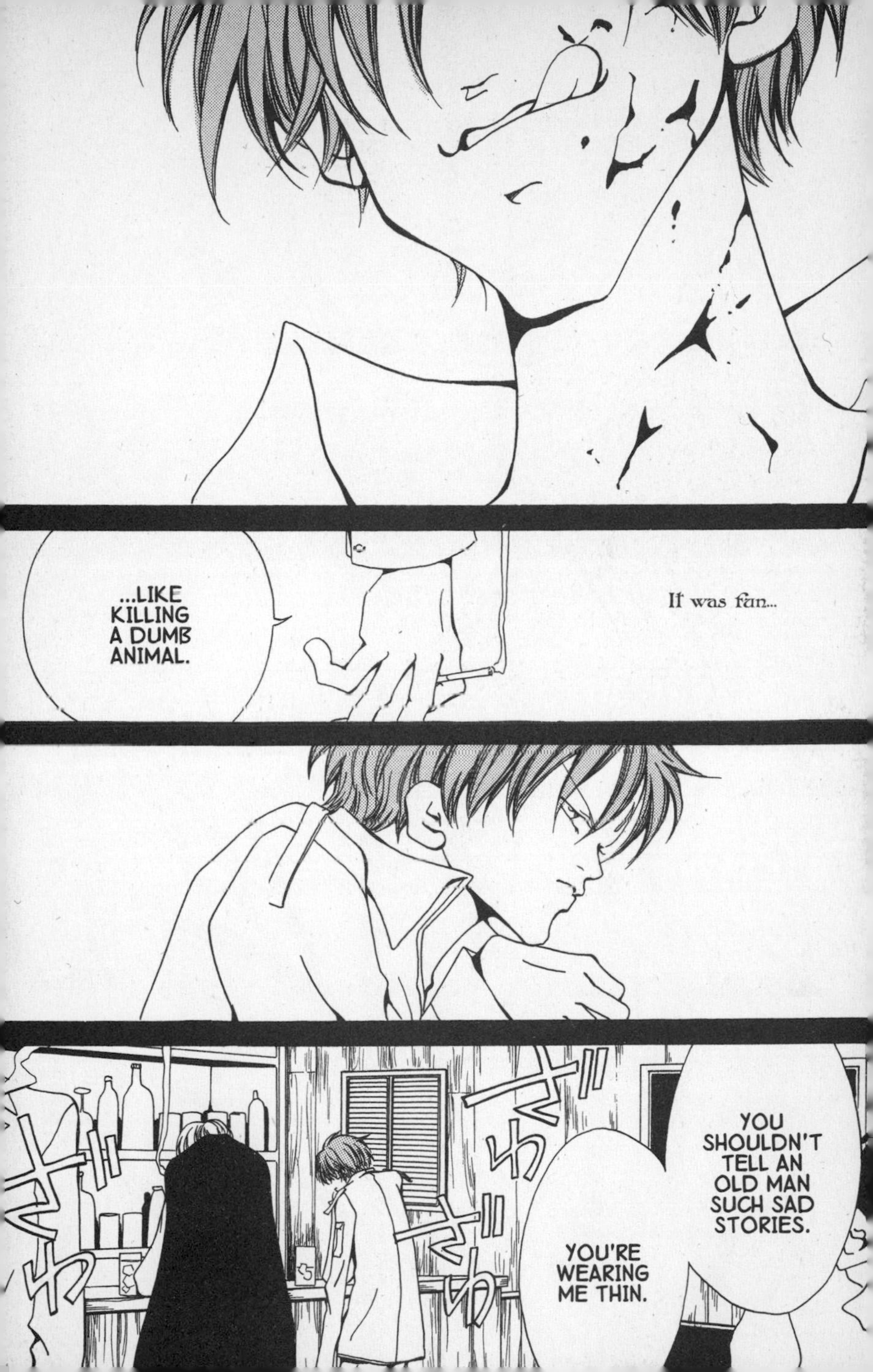
It was fun...
...LIKE KILLING A DUMB ANIMAL.
YOU SHOULDN'T TELL AN OLD MAN SUCH SAD STORIES.
YOU'RE WEARING ME THIN.

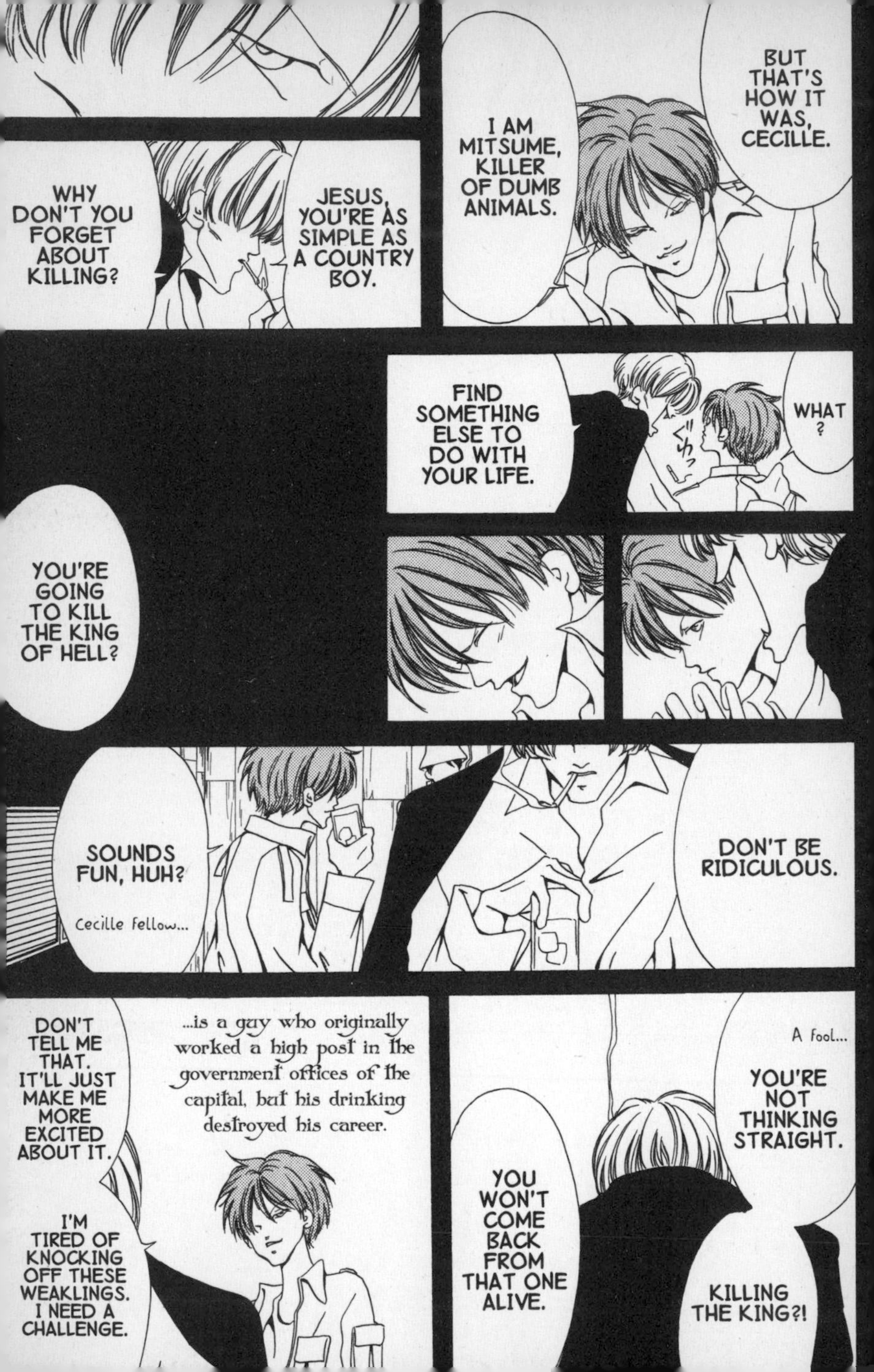
BUT THAT'S HOW IT WAS, CECILLE.
I AM MITSUME, KILLER OF DUMB ANIMALS.
JESUS, YOU'RE AS SIMPLE AS A COUNTRY BOY.
WHY DON'T YOU FORGET ABOUT KILLING?
WHAT?
FIND SOMETHING ELSE TO DO WITH YOUR LIFE.
YOU'RE GOING TO KILL THE KING OF HELL?
DON'T BE RIDICULOUS.
SOUNDS FUN, HUH?
Cecille Fellow...
A Fool...
YOU'RE NOT THINKING STRAIGHT.
KILLING THE KING?!
YOU WON'T COME BACK FROM THAT ONE ALIVE.
...is a guy who originally worked a high post in the government offices of the capital, but his drinking destroyed his career.
DON'T TELL ME THAT. IT'LL JUST MAKE ME MORE EXCITED ABOUT IT.
I'M TIRED OF KNOCKING OFF THESE WEAKLINGS. I NEED A CHALLENGE.

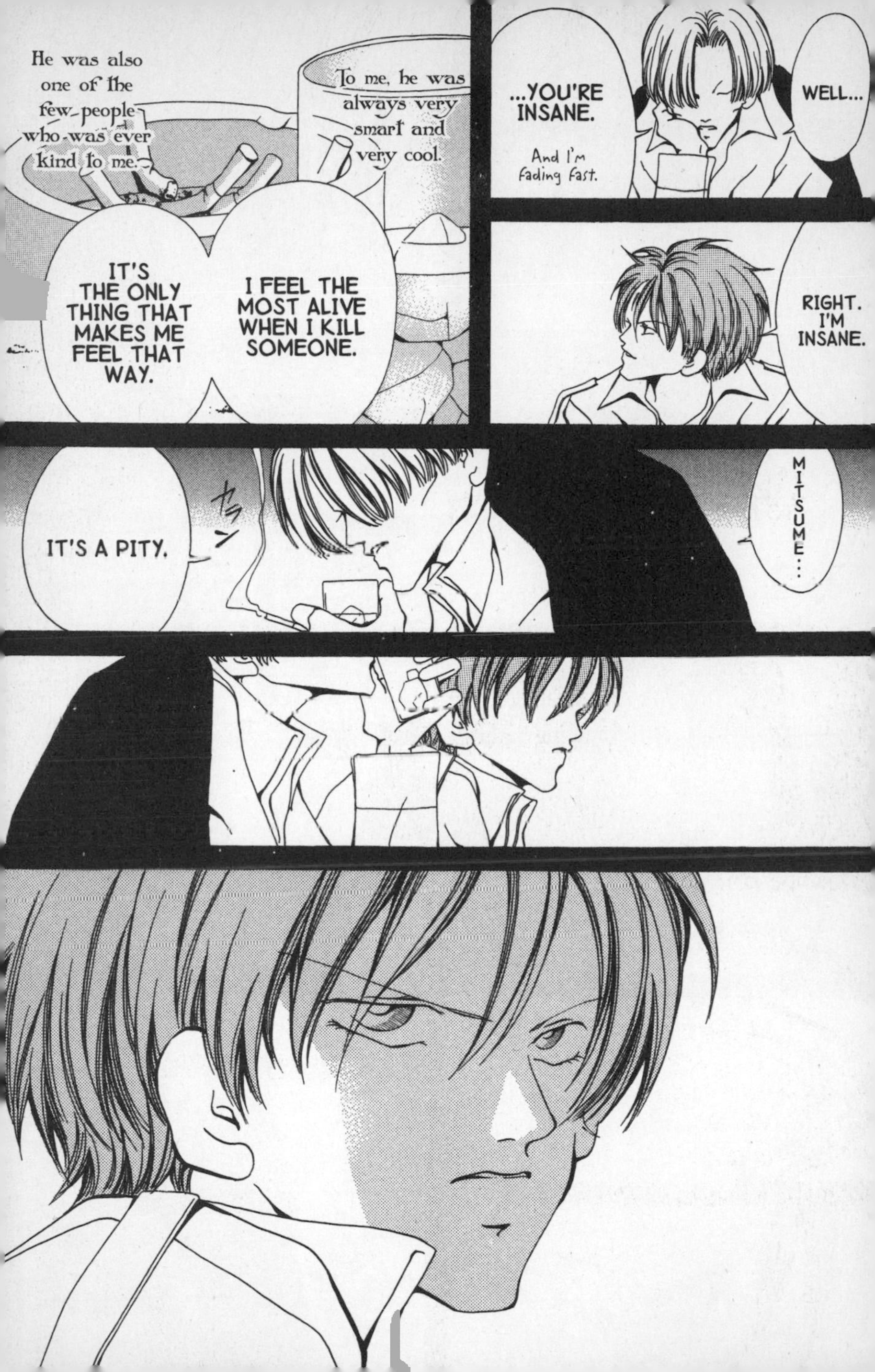
WELL...
...YOU'RE INSANE.
And I'm fading fast.
RIGHT. I'M INSANE.
To me, he was always very smart and very cool.
He was also one of the few people who was ever kind to me.
I FEEL THE MOST ALIVE WHEN I KILL SOMEONE.
IT'S THE ONLY THING THAT MAKES ME FEEL THAT WAY.
MITSUME...
カラン
IT'S A PITY.

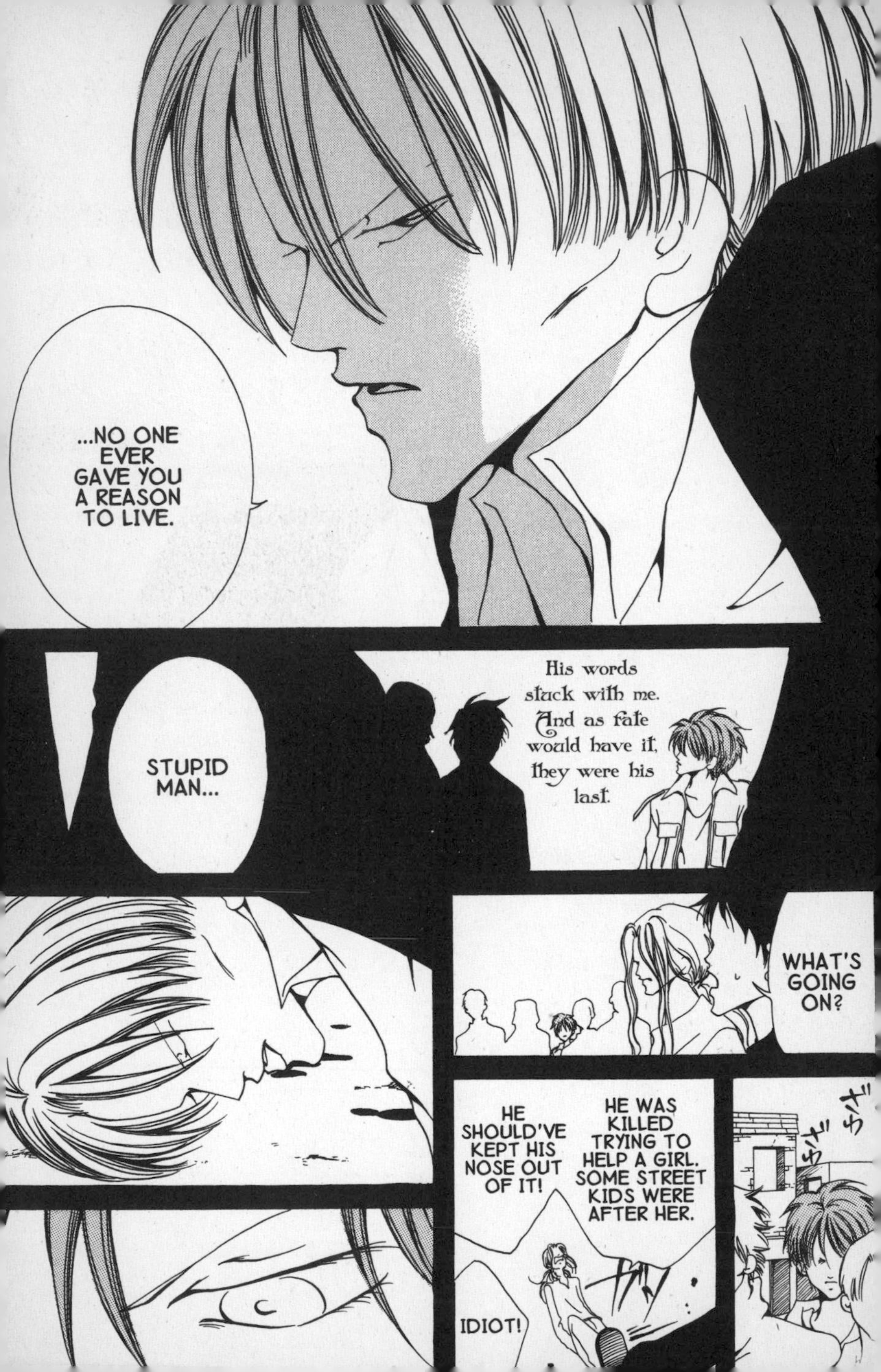
...NO ONE EVER GAVE YOU A REASON TO LIVE.
His words stuck with me. And as fate would have it, they were his last.
STUPID MAN...
WHAT'S GOING ON?
ざわざわ
HE WAS KILLED TRYING TO HELP A GIRL. SOME STREET KIDS WERE AFTER HER.
HE SHOULD'VE KEPT HIS NOSE OUT OF IT!
IDIOT!

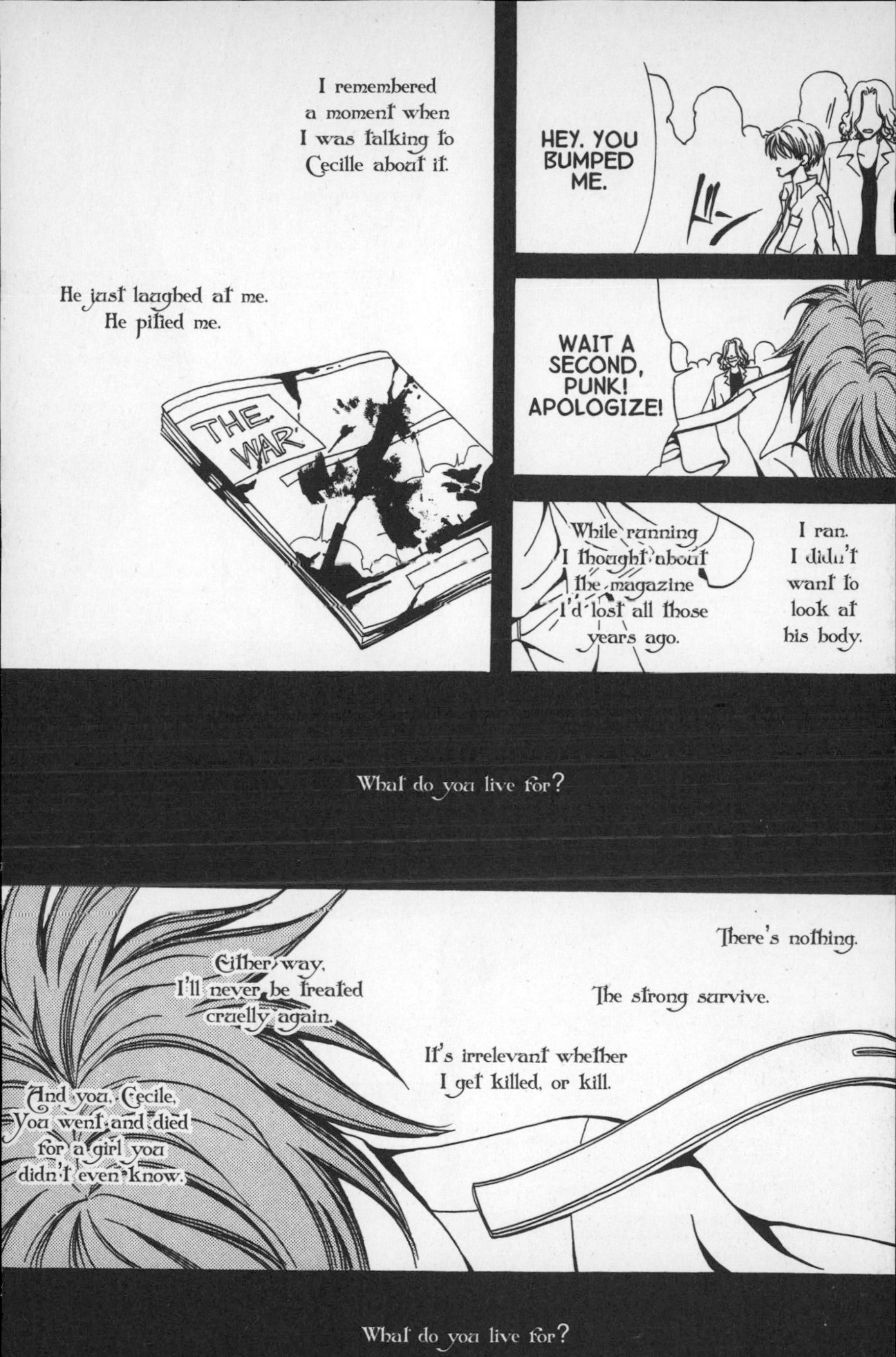
HEY. YOU BUMPED ME.
WAIT A SECOND, PUNK! APOLOGIZE!
I ran. I didn't want to look at his body.
While running I thought about the magazine I'd lost all those years ago.
I remembered a moment when I was talking to Cecille about it.
He just laughed at me. He pitied me.
THE WAR
What do you live for?
There's nothing.
The strong survive.
It's irrelevant whether I get killed, or kill.
Either way, I'll never be treated cruelly again.
And you, Cecile, You went and died for a girl you didn't even know.
What do you live for?

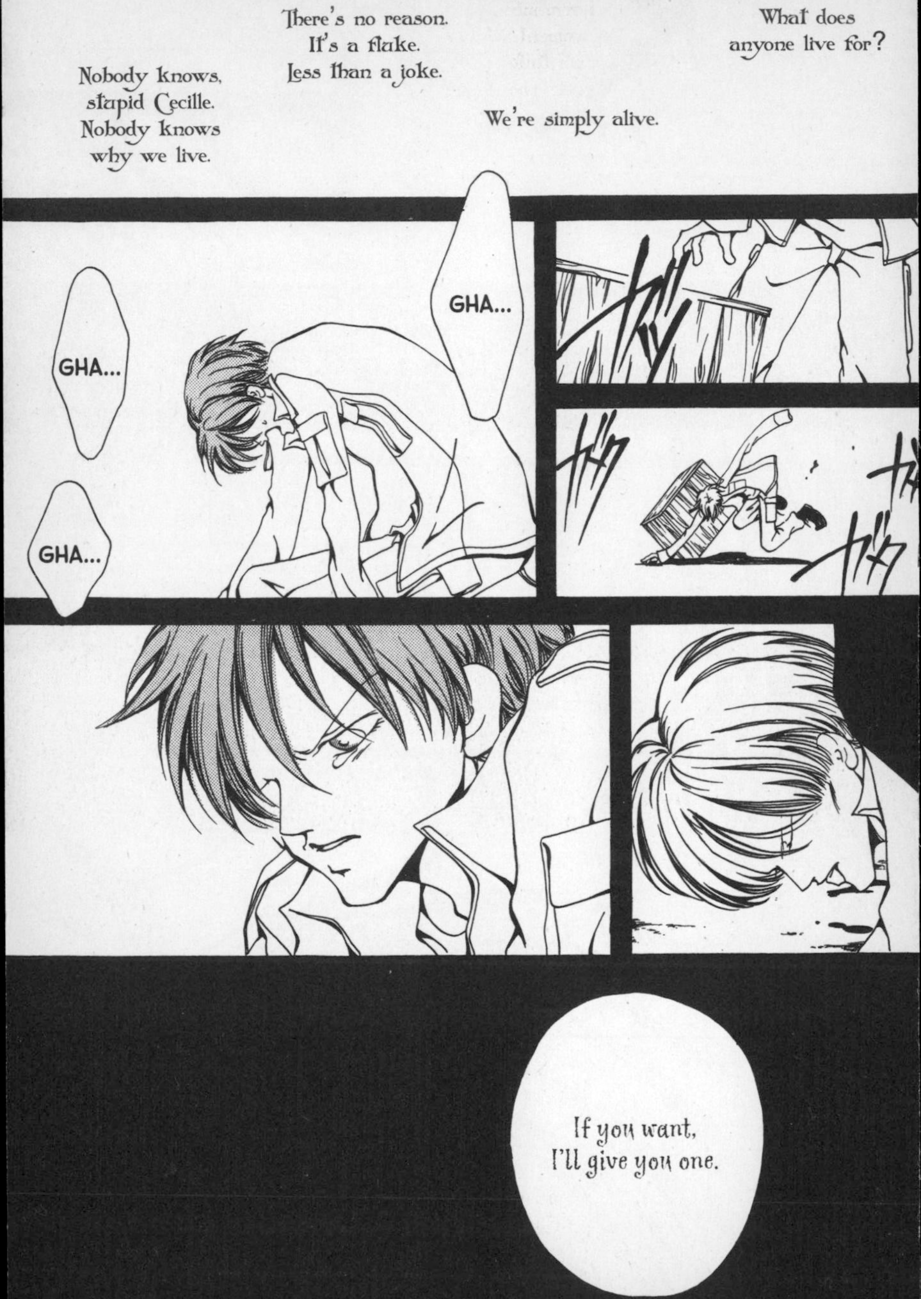
What does anyone live for?
We're simply alive.
There's no reason. It's a fluke. Less than a joke.
Nobody knows, stupid Cecille. Nobody knows why we live.
GHA...
GHA...
GHA...
If you want, I'll give you one.

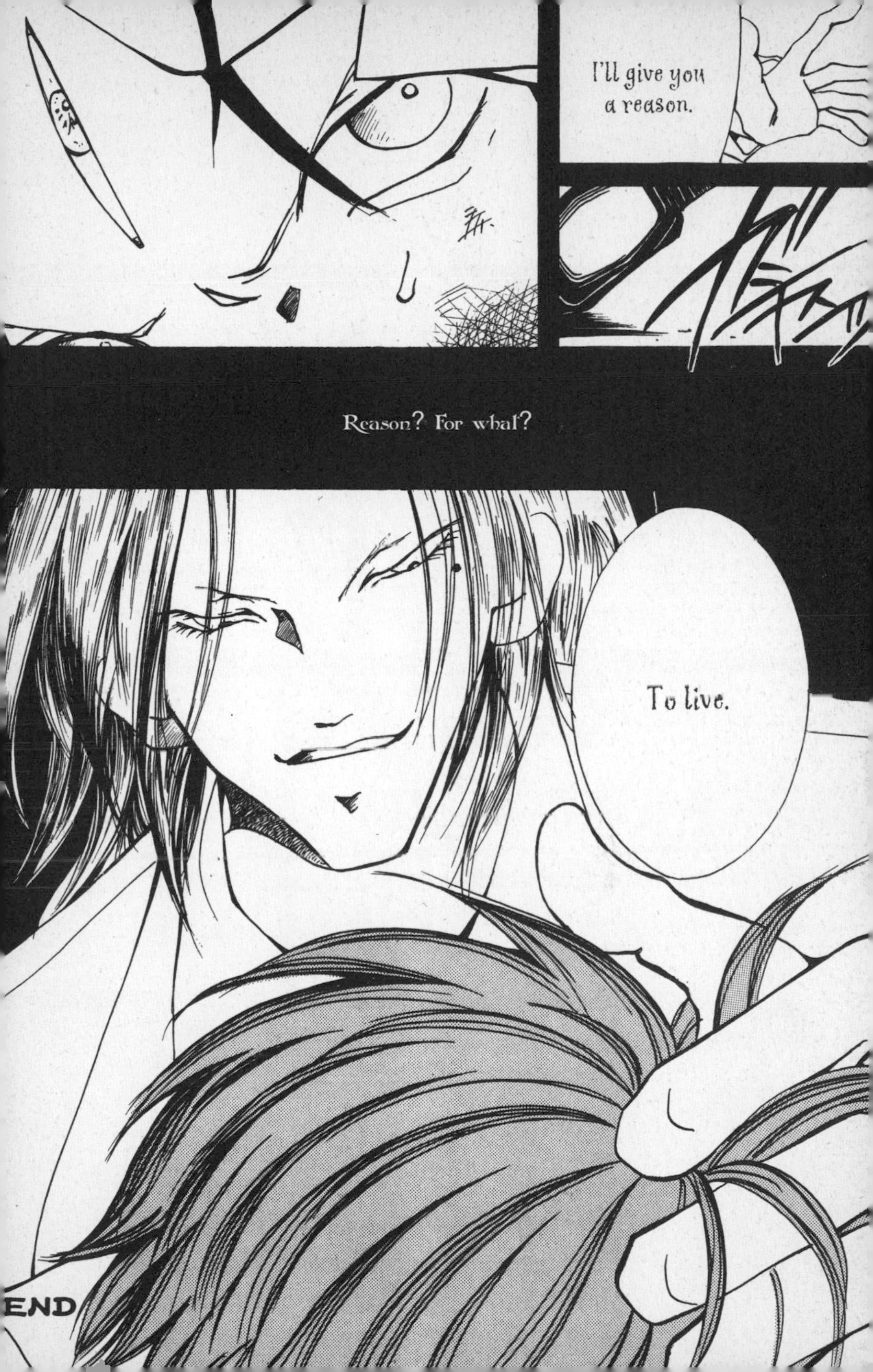
I'll give you a reason.
Reason? For what?
To live.
END

IN THE FINAL INSTALLMENT OF THE DEMON ORORON SAGA...

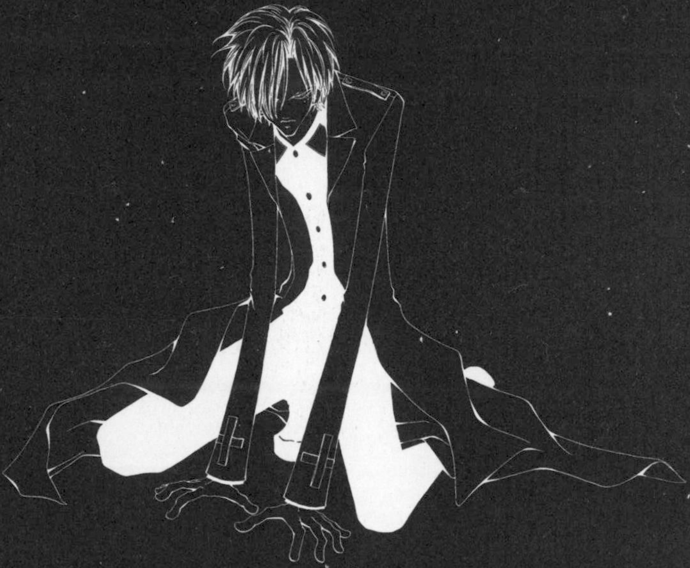

AS CHIAKI AND ORORON FINALLY START TO UNDERSTAND ONE ANOTHER, THEIR PASTS OVERWHELM THEM. ORORON'S BROTHER OSCAR, ALWAYS JEALOUS OF HIS YOUNGER SIBLING'S ASCENSION TO THE THRONE OF HELL, STAGES A COUP, THE CONSEQUENCES OF WHICH COULD ROCK THE VERY FOUNDATION OF THE NETHER WORLDS. OSCAR'S ARMY CLASHES WITH OTHELLO'S ARMY IN A FINAL BATTLE FOR SUPREMACY. AND ORORON AND CHIAKI ARE STUCK IN THE MIDDLE, THE VESSELS OF VAST POWER, BUT BOTH CRIPPLED BY LOVE.

ALSO AVAILABLE FROM TOKYOPOP®

PLANET LADDER
PLANETES
PRIEST
PRINCESS AI
PSYCHIC ACADEMY
QUEEN'S KNIGHT, THE
RAGNAROK
RAVE MASTER
REALITY CHECK
REBIRTH
REBOUND
REMOTE
RISING STARS OF MANGA
SABER MARIONETTE J
SAILOR MOON
SAINT TAIL
SAIYUKI
SAMURAI DEEPER KYO
SAMURAI GIRL REAL BOUT HIGH SCHOOL
SCRYED
SEIKAI TRILOGY, THE
SGT. FROG
SHAOLIN SISTERS
SHIRAHIME-SYO: SNOW GODDESS TALES
SHUTTERBOX
SKULL MAN, THE
SNOW DROP
SORCERER HUNTERS
STONE
SUIKODEN III
SUKI
THREADS OF TIME
TOKYO BABYLON
TOKYO MEW MEW
TOKYO TRIBES
TRAMPS LIKE US
UNDER THE GLASS MOON
VAMPIRE GAME
VISION OF ESCAFLOWNE, THE
WARRIORS OF TAO
WILD ACT
WISH
WORLD OF HARTZ
X-DAY
ZODIAC P.I.

NOVELS

CLAMP SCHOOL PARANORMAL INVESTIGATORS
KARMA CLUB
SAILOR MOON
SLAYERS

ART BOOKS

ART OF CARDCAPTOR SAKURA
ART OF MAGIC KNIGHT RAYEARTH, THE
PEACH: MIWA UEDA ILLUSTRATIONS

ANIME GUIDES

COWBOY BEBOP
GUNDAM TECHNICAL MANUALS
SAILOR MOON SCOUT GUIDES

TOKYOPOP KIDS

STRAY SHEEP

CINE-MANGA™

ALADDIN
CARDCAPTORS
DUEL MASTERS
FAIRLY ODDPARENTS, THE
FAMILY GUY
FINDING NEMO
G.I. JOE SPY TROOPS
GREATEST STARS OF THE NBA
JACKIE CHAN ADVENTURES
JIMMY NEUTRON: BOY GENIUS, THE ADVENTURES OF
KIM POSSIBLE
LILO & STITCH: THE SERIES
LIZZIE MCGUIRE
LIZZIE MCGUIRE MOVIE, THE
MALCOLM IN THE MIDDLE
POWER RANGERS: DINO THUNDER
POWER RANGERS: NINJA STORM
PRINCESS DIARIES 2
RAVE MASTER
SHREK 2
SIMPLE LIFE, THE
SPONGEBOB SQUAREPANTS
SPY KIDS 2
SPY KIDS 3-D: GAME OVER
THAT'S SO RAVEN
TOTALLY SPIES
TRANSFORMERS: ARMADA
TRANSFORMERS: ENERGON

**You want it? We got it!
A full range of TOKYOPOP
products are available now at:
www.TOKYOPOP.com/shop**

05.11.04T

ALSO AVAILABLE FROM 🐢TOKYOPOP®

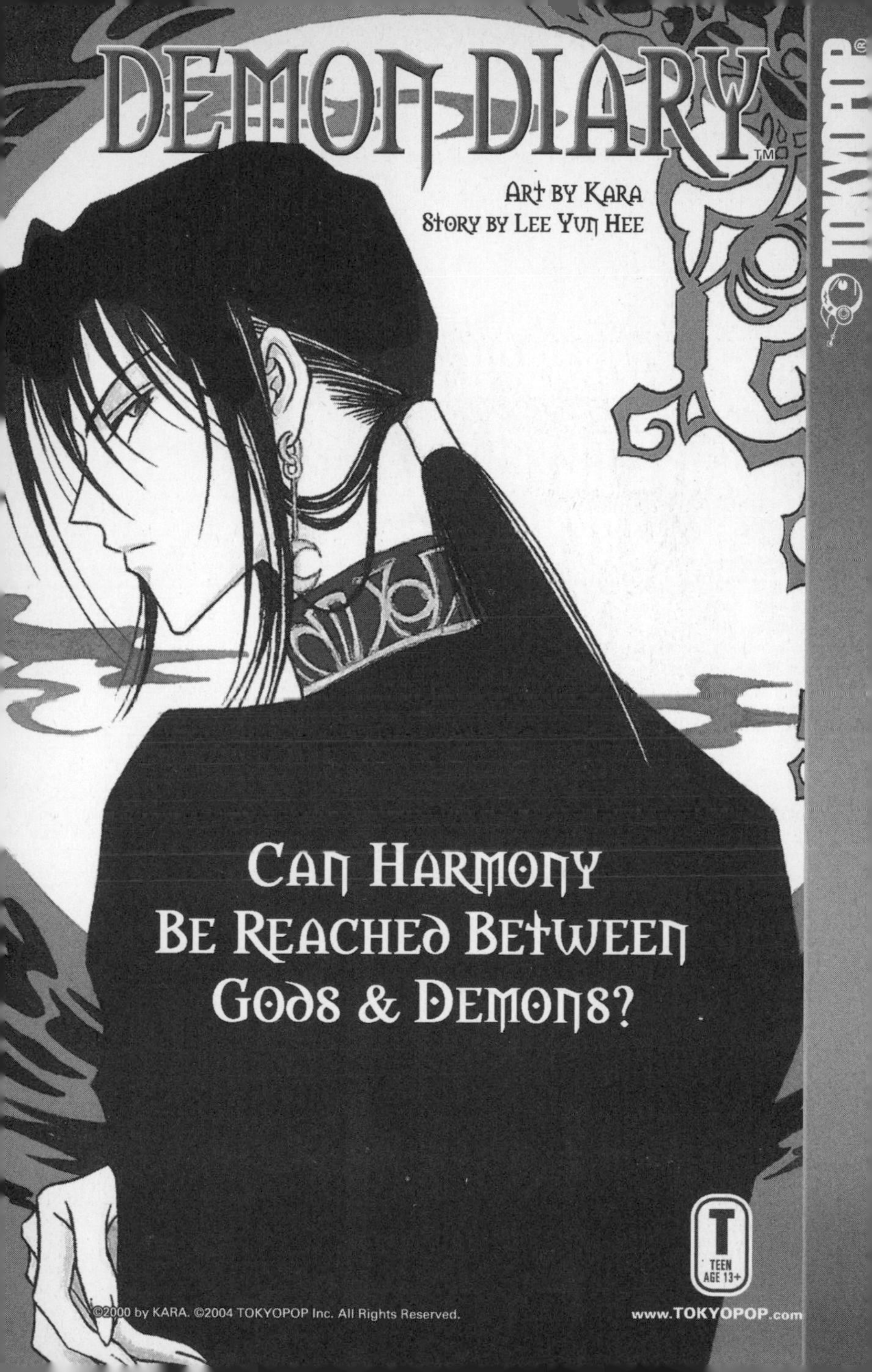
DEMON DIARY™
ART BY KARA
STORY BY LEE YUN HEE
TOKYOPOP®
CAN HARMONY
BE REACHED BETWEEN
GODS & DEMONS?
T
TEEN
AGE 13+
©2000 by KARA. ©2004 TOKYOPOP Inc. All Rights Reserved.
www.TOKYOPOP.com

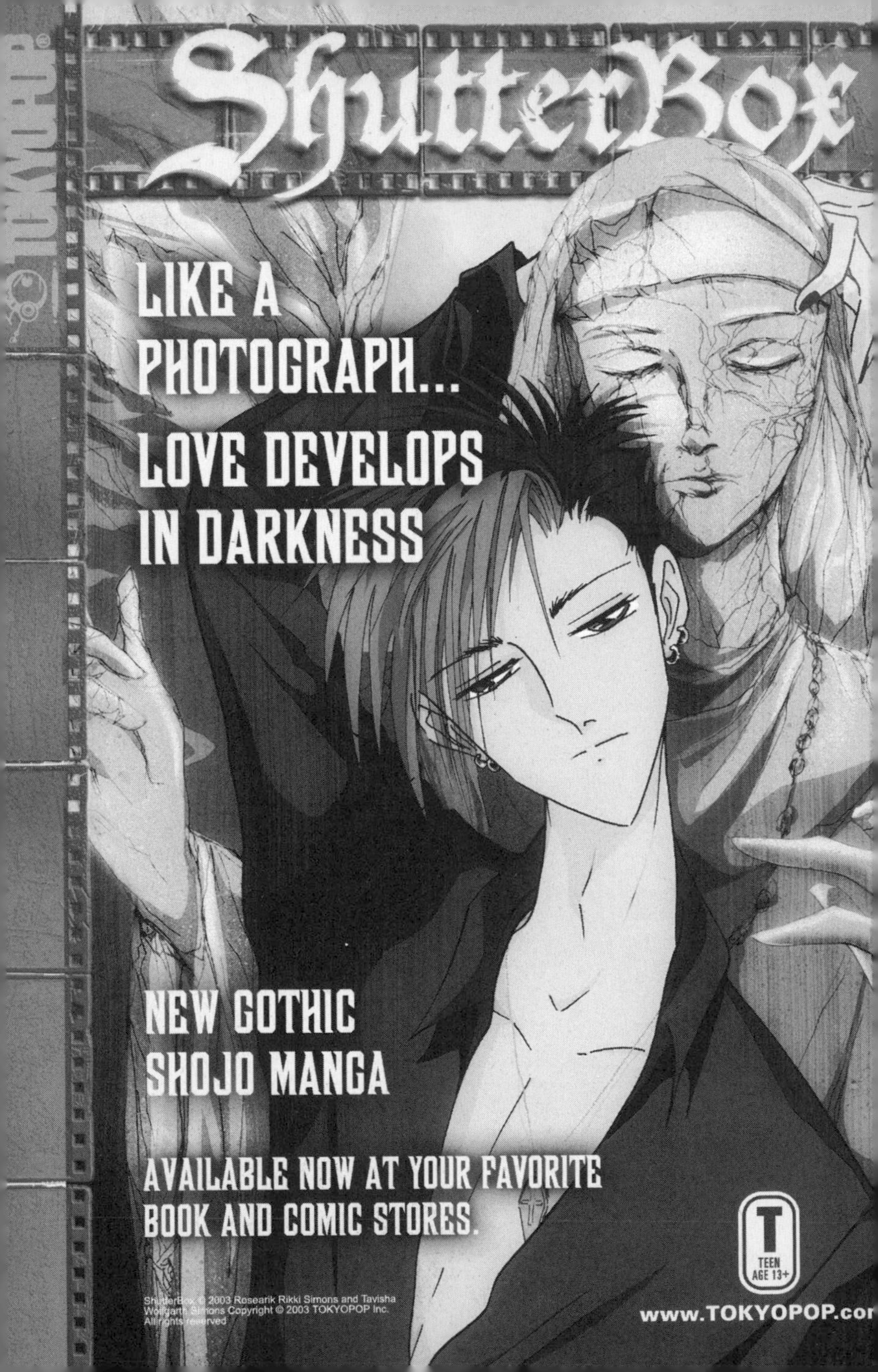
ShutterBox
LIKE A PHOTOGRAPH...
LOVE DEVELOPS IN DARKNESS
NEW GOTHIC SHOJO MANGA
AVAILABLE NOW AT YOUR FAVORITE BOOK AND COMIC STORES.
T TEEN AGE 13+
ShutterBox © 2003 Rosearik Rikki Simons and Tavisha Wolfgarth Simons Copyright © 2003 TOKYOPOP Inc. All rights reserved
www.TOKYOPOP.com

STOP!

This is the back of the book.
You wouldn't want to spoil a great ending!

This book is printed "manga-style," in the authentic Japanese right-to-left format. Since none of the artwork has been flipped or altered, readers get to experience the story just as the creator intended. You've been asking for it, so TOKYOPOP® delivered: authentic, hot-off-the-press, and far more fun!

DIRECTIONS

If this is your first time reading manga-style, here's a quick guide to help you understand how it works.

It's easy... just start in the top right panel and follow the numbers. Have fun, and look for more 100% authentic manga from TOKYOPOP®!

100%
AUTHENTIC
MANGA